Adjudicating New Governance

This book engages with and advances the current debate on new governance by providing a much-needed analysis of its relationship with the courts. New modes of governance have produced a plethora of instruments and actors at various levels that present a challenge to more traditional forms of command-and-control regulation. In this respect, it is commonly maintained that new governance generally – and political experimentation more broadly – weakens the power of the courts, producing a legitimacy problem for new forms of governance and, perhaps more fundamentally, for law itself. Focusing on the European Union, this book offers a new account of the role of the courts in new governance. Connecting new governance with the conception of deliberative democracy, this book demonstrates how the role of courts has been transformed by the legal and political experimentation currently taking place in the European Union. Drawing on a series of case studies, it is argued that, although deliberations in governance frameworks provide little by way of hard, binding law, these collaborative frameworks nevertheless condition judicial decision making. With far-reaching implications for how we understand the justiciability of 'soft law', participation rights, the legitimacy of governance measures, and the role of courts beyond the nation-state, this book argues that, far from undermining the power of the courts, governance regimes assist their functioning. Its analysis will therefore be of considerable interest for lawyers, political scientists and anyone interested in the transformation of the judiciary in the era of new governance.

Emilia Korkea-aho is Visiting Fellow 2014–15 at the European University Institute, Florence, and Academy of Finland Postdoctoral Researcher, University of Helsinki.

Adjudicating New Governance

Deliberative democracy in the European Union

Emilia Korkea-aho

Routledge
Taylor & Francis Group
a GlassHouse Book

First published 2015
by Routledge
2 Park Square, Milton Park, Abingdon, Oxfordshire OX14 4RN

and by Routledge
711 Third Avenue, New York, NY 10017

First issued in paperback 2016

Routledge is an imprint of the Taylor & Francis Group, an informa business

British Library Cataloguing in Publication Data
A catalogue record for this book is available from the British Library

Library of Congress Cataloging-in-Publication Data
Korkea-aho, Emilia, author.
Adjudicating new governance : deliberative democracy in the European Union / Emilia Korkea-aho.
pages cm
"a GlassHouse Book."
Based on author's thesis (doctoral - University of Helsinki, Faculty of Law, 2011) issued under title: New Governance and the EU Courts.
Includes bibliographical references and index.
ISBN 978-1-138-78803-9 (hbk) – ISBN 978-1-315-76572-3 (ebk) 1. Political questions and judicial power–European Union countries. 2. Deliberative democracy–European Union countries. 3. Environmental law–European Union countries. 4. European Union countries–Politics and government. I. Title.
KJE3655.K67 2015
341.242'2–dc23

2014033828

ISBN 13: 978-1-138-24151-0 (pbk)

ISBN 13: 978-1-138-78803-9 (hbk)

Typeset in Baskerville
by RefineCatch Limited, Bungay, Suffolk

Contents

Acknowledgements

This book has been written over the course of five years and in as many cities. Creating an exhaustive list of all of those whose help I would need to acknowledge is impossible – but because I rather like making lists, I don't mind giving it my best shot. As with the book itself, all mistakes and accidental omissions from the list are of my own making.

The book was conceived and completed in Helsinki. It is based on research I originally conducted for a doctoral thesis. I am indebted to my supervisors at the University of Helsinki, Risto Koulu and Kimmo Nuotio, for their support and interest in my work, although it took a turn that they perhaps did not see coming. The Institute of International Economic Law (KATTI) and the Finnish Centre of Excellence in Foundations of European Law and Polity (2008–13) have provided supportive and convivial working environments. The following people deserve particular mention: Kaarlo Tuori, my preliminary examiner, for providing a critical perspective on governance beyond the call of duty; Pia Letto-Vanamo and Thomas Wilhelmsson, for academic leadership; Teemu Juutilainen, for being the best of friends and colleagues; Suvi Sankari, on whose no-nonsense approach and advice in matters of EU law and beyond I have on many occasions relied; Sabine Frerichs; Sakari Hänninen; and Elina Paunio. Julen Etxabe and Mónica López Lerma have enriched my life in many ways, membrillo being but one.

The four other cities have been Florence, London, New York and Amsterdam. I spent a term at the European University Institute (EUI) in Florence, where Neil Walker facilitated my early steps. Joanne Scott supervised my work at University College London (UCL) and carried on doing so after I had left for other cities. She has ploughed through every draft, and has offered intellectual stimulation, support and criticism. The generous help and encouragement that she has continued to provide has been critical in the course of the research project on which this book is based. Charles Sabel mentored me while I was at Columbia Law School. I am truly grateful for his inspiration and the interest that he so generously showed in my work both in New York and, after I returned to Finland, via Skype. William Simon from Columbia Law School acted as my second preliminary examiner and also as my opponent at the public defence in Helsinki. In these tasks, he was encouraging and supportive, offering challenging, yet constructive, criticism of my ideas. When preparing this book for publication, I drew upon his insights and advice on countless occasions.

I have discussed parts of this book with a number of colleagues and friends in addition to those already mentioned. I would especially like to thank Jonathan Zeitlin, to whom I am also grateful for the title of this book, Hans Micklitz, Joxerramon Bengoetxea, Helen Hartnell, Santtu Turunen, Tiina Paloniitty, Sakari Huovinen, Tanja Ehnert and Oana Stefan. Many of the ideas have been further developed in seminars organised by the University of Amsterdam research project on the Architecture of Postnational Rulemaking. Particular thanks go to Deirdre Curtin, Elaine Fahey, Katja Biedenkopf, Chantal Mak, Basje Bender and Tim Staal. Finally, staff at the European Commission have answered my many questions, both in person and by email, quickly and professionally.

My family has never failed to support my every professional and personal move. In particular, my sister Johanna Korkea-aho and brother-in-law Risto Kaartinen have helped and encouraged me more than I can say. Other friends, whose encouragement and hospitality I will never be able to return, include Johanna and Juha Sternberg, the Welsh family, Lisbe Finell, Dewi Hamwijk and Rob Abendroth. Dewi, whom I met at Columbia Law School, worked sometimes literally side-by-side with me and provided companionship in extracurricular research activities that took us to the streets of Lower Manhattan. Upon my return to Europe, she made me feel at home in Amsterdam. Finally, I would like to acknowledge the support of Panu, Mortti and Vikko, to whom I dedicate this book.

The work has been financed by several research bodies, trusts and foundations, which I most gratefully acknowledge. The Academy of Finland financed most of the research work through its graduate school funding, and I am now lucky enough to write these words as Academy of Finland Postdoctoral Researcher. The Finnish Lawyers' Association (*Suomalainen Lakimiesyhdistys*) funded my final year of doctoral studies. Smaller grants were awarded by the Fund for Legal Studies (*Oikeustieteen rahasto*) and the Research Foundation of the Finnish Savings Banks Association (*Säästöpankkien Tutkimussäätiö*). The Centre of Excellence financially supported my research visit to Columbia Law School. In administrative matters, Anna-Maija Ekström has been a great help. In the final critical junctures, I have been able to rely on the help of two research assistants, Inka Vairimaa and Aija Valleala. Finally, I wish to thank Christopher Goddard for editing the language of the book efficiently and diligently, and the editorial staff at Routledge for patience and support in the preparation of the book.

EK
Helsinki, 4 July 2014

List of abbreviations

ACSH	Advisory Committee on Safety and Health at Work
AG	Advocate General
AGS	Annual Growth Survey
ChemSec	International Chemical Secretariat
CIRCABC	Communication and Information Resource Centre for Administrations, Businesses and Citizens
CIS	Common Implementation Strategy
CJEU	Court of Justice of the European Union
CoJ	Court of Justice
CoR	Committee of the Regions
CoRAP	Community Rolling Action Plan
CPMP	Committee for Proprietary Medicinal Products
CPVO	Community Plant Variety Office
DG Environment	Directorate-General for the Environment
EAP	Environmental Action Programme
EASA	European Aviation Safety Agency
EBA	European Banking Authority
EC	European Community
ECHA	European Chemicals Agency
EEB	European Environmental Bureau
EES	European Employment Strategy
EESC	European Economic and Social Committee
EFSA	European Food Safety Agency
EMA	European Medicines Agency (formerly EMEA)
EMU	Economic and Monetary Union
ENISA	European Union Agency for Network and Information Security
ERA	European Railways Agency
ESMA	European Securities and Markets Authority
ETS	European Emissions Trading Scheme
EU	European Union
EU SDS	European Sustainable Development Strategy

FECOAV	Federación de Cooperativas Agrarias de la Communidad Valenciana
GAL	global administrative law
GC	General Court
GDP	gross domestic product
GGP	Good Guidance Practices
GMO	genetically modified organism
IGC	intergovernmental conference
IMF	International Monetary Fund
IPPC	Integrated Pollution Prevention and Control Directive
IR	international relations
ISEAL	International Social and Environmental Accrediting and Labelling Alliance
MSC	(ECHA) Member State Committee
NAFTA	North American Free Trade Agreement
NAP	National Allocation Plan
NGO	non-governmental organisation
NRP	national reform programme
OECD	Organisation for Economic Co-operation and Development
OHIM	Office of Harmonization in the Internal Market
OMC	Open Method of Coordination
PIA	partnership implementation agreement
RAC	(ECHA) Committee for Risk Assessment
REACH	Registration, Evaluation, Authorisation and Restriction of Chemicals
RIPs	REACH Implementation Projects
SCPs	stability and convergence programmes
SEA	Single European Act
SEAC	(ECHA) Committee for Socio-economic Analysis
SCG	Strategic Co-ordination Group
SCP	stability and convergence programme
SGP	Stability and Growth Pact
SIIF	Structured Implementation and Information Framework
SME	small or medium-sized enterprise
SVHCs	substances of very high concern
TEU	Treaty on the European Union
TFEU	Treaty on the Functioning of the European Union
WFD	Water Framework Directive
WTO	World Trade Organization
WWF	Worldwide Fund for Nature

Chapter 1

Out with the courts, in with new governance?

In the comic strip that Kevin Tuma drew for the periodical *Regulation*, a big-eyed, bald man stares, with a kind of exasperated expression on his face, at a piece of paper that reads: 'The Very Big Regulatory Agency of America has issued the following Guidelines: We Recommend that YOU MUST DO THE FOLLOWING . . .' The accompanying text presents a situation that unfortunately does not fall too far short of the illustration. The author charts the explosive growth of regulatory agencies and their activities in the United States since 1946, and particularly the increased use of guidance intended to fill the gaps in laws or regulations. In 2005, the Office of Management and Budget proposed 'Good Guidance Practices', aiming to rein in agencies. By introducing such practices, the Office hoped to protect the public from guidance written as though it were legally binding norms. A specific feature of the GGPs is that they forbid the use of language that 'might imply that a guidance represents a legally binding document'.[1] As is readily apparent, the outcome is simply laughable: the GGPs themselves *require* that regulatory agencies *shall not* use words such as 'shall', 'must', or 'required'!

The reason why I have begun by citing the confused message that the guidances are sending, and the flat and unimaginative attempts to do something to resolve the situation, is that when I first saw the picture, in the early stages of writing this book, I intuitively thought of the man in the picture as an innocent individual. Now, when I look at the picture again, I see a puzzled judge. This does not mean that I would care less now than I did back then about the legal rights of the individual. Quite the contrary: very soon after embarking upon writing, I realised that the most adroit way in which to ensure the legal protection of the individual is to figure out what is happening to lawyers – especially judges. Lawyers – including our bald and baffled friend, the judge – increasingly work with 'processes that employ experimentation, bottom-up deliberation, benchmarking, monitoring, indicators, league tables and the like'.[2] They deal with legally binding

1 Walling, 2006, p 7. The Office of Management and Budget published its *Final Bulletin for Agency Good Guidance Practices* (the 'Final Bulletin') on 25 January 2007.

2 Trubek and Trubek, 2010, p 722.

norms that pretend to be something else, with norms that say very little, or with norms that go on and on, to the utter exasperation of all affected. Are these new developments then threatening the judiciary, and drowning them in the stormy sea of non-traditional process and unconventional norms? Or are judges at risk of being left behind safely on dry land whilst the rest of us set sail for more promising horizons? Some see a little bit of truth in both of these scenarios; some believe one to be the case, but not the other; some doubt both. I believe in neither – and this book is written to explain why.

1.1 Research agenda and design

This book aims to engage in a critical appraisal of the relationship between emerging governance discourses and the courts. In other words, it intends to bring out how a 'whole new ball game' of governance (the emergence of EU governance) manifests itself in the legal sphere (the judiciary). In so doing, the book has two central claims to make: the first argument is simply that legislators still matter; the second, equally simply, is that courts also matter. But both institutions face some serious changes and challenges.

Now, given that the focus of the book is on new approaches to governance in the European Union, the first aim seems counterintuitive, to say the least. Since the first argument requires context, let us begin with the second, in respect of which the research can be contextualised. New approaches to law and governance have raised unprecedented interest in national and international contexts in recent years. This has manifested in a plethora of instruments and actors at various levels, which challenge the more traditional paradigm of legal regulation and the institutions developed over time to administer them. One of these institutions is the judiciary. It is commonly thought that new governance, and political experimentation more broadly, sap the ability of the courts to monitor and review those experiments. Scholars of all stripes are nearly united in the conviction that the courts – more specifically, the Court of Justice of the European Union (CJEU) – have no, or at least a strictly limited, role to play in what has come to be referred to as 'new governance'.[3]

For some, the emergence of new modes of governance has been a deliberate counterstrategy to an 'activist' Court. Comitology, for instance, has been celebrated 'as removing crucial decisions concerning the necessary level of risk-protection away from the Court to non-court-centric, "political", and "self-regulatory" arenas of law-making'.[4] Among others (perhaps the majority of commentators), however, the CJEU is seen as a sympathetic actor that just happens to be out of sync with existing trends in EU law and governance. The marginalised role of the CJEU

3 The few exceptions include: Armstrong, 1998; Gerstenberg and Sabel, 2002; Sabel and Simon, 2004; Sabel and Simon, 2006; Scott, 1998; Scott and Sturm, 2007; and Scott and Trubek, 2002.

4 Gerstenberg, 2002, p 174.

does not result from a deliberate attempt to remove decisions away from the Court, but from a set of unfortunate circumstances. These include, for example, the non-justiciability of social and economic rights, and the fact that new governance does not usually give rise to acts with binding legal effects. Judicial control is also frequently considered inappropriate because the courts cannot adequately respond to the dilemmas of modern life emerging from rapid technological and economic developments.[5] The exclusion of the courts is viewed with concern because it adds to the legitimacy problem of new forms of governance and, perhaps more fundamentally, to the legitimacy problem of legal regulation more generally.

Setting differences aside, the virtual consensus is that judicial control mechanisms are not suitable for monitoring new governance. This seems problematic for several reasons. First, the marginalisation of the courts is an inaccurate description of the present situation. The EU courts are already – and increasingly – dealing with new governance instruments. In the absence of an overarching sense of what is happening, the precedential and practice-guiding value of these rulings is potentially a great deal stronger than is usually acknowledged.

Second, although a plethora of reasons have been presented for the alleged marginalisation of the EU courts, these are often based on anecdotal observations rather than on a systematic attempt to evaluate those reasons in light of the concrete circumstances of EU governance.

Third, even more ambitious and systematic contributions tend to focus on a single governance instrument. Most typically, this instrument is the Open Method of Coordination (OMC). As a consequence, a comparative perspective is missing: for instance, we are largely clueless as to whether the issue of stakeholder involvement and the problems that it engenders in judicial review are specific only to the OMC, or whether framework directives (to mention just one possible example) involve overlapping concerns.

Fourth, consensus in research is open to contestation, on the basis that analyses of the judicial role in new regulatory environments tend to focus overly on governance and to brush aside legislation. Put differently, law still matters, and if we are to assess the role of courts, we need a better account of the 'hybrid' reality in a particular policy sector, involving multiple legislative and non-legislative, binding and non-binding, old and new instruments. For instance, EU employment governance is a prime example of the hybrid regime, recruiting the European Employment Strategy (EES), the European Social Fund and hard law measures all

5 Sabel and Simon, 2006, p 396. Compare this with the argument of Kelemen (2012) for 'Eurolegalism': the completion of the Internal Market, combined with dynamics of political fragmentation (by which Kelemen means the EU's strong judiciary and weak implementation and enforcement capacity), has hardened the law and bolstered the role of courts in the European Union. Although recognising the challenge to Eurolegalism from modes of governance, Kelemen dismisses them as a public relations exercise for legitimacy.

towards achieving broadly defined objectives in common employment policy. This feature ought to be better internalised in assessments of the challenges that the EES or any other governance instrument poses for judicial control.

The fifth and final reason for disputing the consensus is its one-dimensional (and unidirectional) perception of what is currently taking place: existing research on EU new governance has so far placed greater emphasis on what kind of role the courts could and should occupy in new governance, rather than on how the courts themselves are changing as a result of their inescapable engagement with EU governance.

One of the two main claims that this book makes is that the courts have a role, but that it is a changed role. In order to comprehend this change, the book provides an overview of the disincentives that might exist to judicial review of new governance. This involves systematically studying the role of EU courts in selected areas of EU governance in order to discover what lies behind the widely held view that the courts and new governance sit uncomfortably at the same table.[6] The analysis includes both theoretical and empirical dimensions. The empirical part of the work focuses on EU environmental policy and particularly on three case studies of EU environmental governance: the environmental dimension of the EU 2020 Strategy; the European Chemicals Agency (ECHA); and the Common Implementation Strategy for the Water Framework Directive (WFD CIS). The case studies illustrate problems and barriers to judicial review. These include, for example, the role of courts in shaping revisable and flexible governance frameworks, the use of soft law, questions of institutional design, the standing of individuals before the courts and the reviewability of science-based measures. The book analyses the conditions of judicial review in each governance environment and shows how some concerns can be overcome, while improvements are possible in both court practice and governance regimes themselves by taking into account insights from the theoretical framework of deliberative democracy.

As explained in later in this chapter (see section 1.5, 'A democratic theory of deliberation'), deliberative democracy theory is deployed to deepen our understanding of a range of concepts central to the governance discourse, on the one hand, and to suggest an alternative perspective, on the other. This blueprint lends itself to research that is future-oriented. Rather than simply enumerating concerns associated with the judicial review of governance, the book makes a conscious effort to move 'forward' and 'beyond' to resolve (some of) those problems.[7]

Whilst the case studies suggest that the European courts play a role in realising the potential of governance and checking its excesses, they also indicate that

6 This study is limited to EU governance, thus excluding recent interesting developments in international law, studied under the umbrella of 'global administrative law' (GAL). For GAL research, see, eg, Kingsbury, Krisch and Stewart, 2005.

7 Instead of current crisis talk in EU legal and political scholarship, which seems to fetishise crises, it is more 'difficult and far more urgent to try to explain what makes the system keep on going': Eriksen and Fossum, 2000, p 9.

judicial practices are being transformed as a result of governance processes. This takes us back to the first argument that this book wishes to make. Although it seems nonsensical to argue in a book about new approaches to governance that legislators and legislation are still important, this claim is both necessary and essential.[8] It is *necessary* because new approaches to governance do not operate in a vacuum, but as part of complex regulatory environments. Depending on the particular policy context – that is, other instruments already in use – governance instruments involve different institutional ramifications. Some develop along the lines of supporting and supplementing legislation, whereas other instruments may end up dislodging law altogether; in either case, the full picture requires consideration of a broader dynamic between law and new governance. An appreciation of the role of law and legislation is also *essential* if we are to understand how the courts themselves are changing – that is, how changes in governance are reflected in the legal sphere. All three case studies make explicit that the role of courts is *not* transforming and evolving as a reflection of the political and legal experimentation currently taking place in the European Union, but as a result of the *interplay* between new governance and law.

These are the two main, yet highly generalised, objectives of this book. In what follows, more specific research questions and hypotheses are introduced at the beginning of each chapter. The rest of this chapter offers an overview of the key concepts, debates and methods used.

1.2 New governance: A definition on the move

Governance approaches have become immensely popular in the European Union. The most convincing explanation for their political success appears to be the absence of a 'formal state apparatus', which has spurred and supported experimentation in EU policymaking.[9] Admittedly, the historical and empirical context of the 'formal state apparatus' – that is, the nation-state – is in transition, too, so that experimentation with forms of governance can be found in Member States as well as in the Union.[10] Reflecting changes in the external environment (such as globalisation), the nation-state is moving away from hierarchical, top-down steering and forms of 'command-and-control regulation', in the Weberian

8 A complementary claim in political science is to emphasise the continued relevance of governments. See, eg, Peters and Pierre, 2009, p 92.

9 Walker and de Búrca, 2007, p 528. See also Armstrong, 1998, p 168. For other reasons, see Scott and Trubek, 2002, pp 6–8.

10 Pierre, 2000, p 3. For the nation-state level, see, eg, Tuori, 2011, pp 291–6. In German-speaking areas of research, the theory of state was greatly influenced by systems theory as developed by Talcott Parsons and Niklas Luhmann. This German debate had parallel phenomena in other countries. The Anglo-American analysis of the state and its capacity to govern took place within the scholarship of policy co-ordination and administration. This can be explained by reference to developments in the outside policy world, ie major changes initiated by both the Reagan and Thatcher administrations. See Kohler-Koch and Rittberger, 2006, pp 30–1.

sense, towards flexible and inclusive forms of decision making, taking advantage of non-binding, heterarchical instruments. (New) governance, then, appears to provide both a framework and a vocabulary for coming to grips with changes. While the European Union may have been a contributing and accelerating factor to both empirical and theoretical 'reconfigurations' that have taken place at the national level, a great deal of the literature on the 'governance turn' is 'concerned with unpacking the EU as an evolving system of governance in its own right'.[11] The Union is the chosen level of analysis in this book.

No commonly accepted definition exists of the meaning of the term '(new) governance', and the terms '(new) governance', 'governance approaches' and 'experimentation' are used synonymously in this book, which, however, does not attempt a genealogy of the concept of governance. Suffice it to note here that 'governance' is not a legal notion. A commonly held view is that the concept of governance became popular in the form of 'good governance', as advocated by the World Bank and the Organisation for Economic Co-operation and Development (OECD) from the 1980s onwards. Theoretically, the concept has been used and developed both by international relations (IR) and comparative politics scholars, 'and the "governance turn" in EU studies resembles developments in both the field of policy analysis and in IR'.[12] In the European Union, the 1986 Single European Act (SEA) marked the start of research interested in issues of policymaking and governance.[13] My conviction is that heterogeneous inspiration should not be viewed as a paralysing research problem, but as a research imperative: a diversity of concepts and theoretical frameworks calls for a sincere commitment to openness and transparency about underlying assumptions and values. This imperative is particularly acute given the interdisciplinary richness of normative and empirical standpoints present in EU governance studies. Hence extra care and attention to conceptual clarity and openness is required from the outset in order to justify and maintain the relevance of the concept.

Among the multiplicity of definitions available to a researcher of EU governance, that of Scott and Trubek (2002) still seems helpful after more than 10 years after its articulation. They define 'new governance' as having all, or some, of the following characteristics:

- *participation and power-sharing* – non-hierarchical problem-solving by governmental and non-governmental stakeholders at several levels of government;
- *multi-level integration* – co-operation and dialogue between a wide range of actors from different levels of government;

11 Armstrong, 2010, p 8.
12 Kohler-Koch and Rittberger, 2006, p 33.
13 Some legal scholars have traced the origins of governance talk in the European Union to US administrative law. See Shapiro, 2004, p 252.

- *diversity and decentralisation* – leaving final policymaking to the lowest level possible, often in the form of networks;
- *deliberation* – providing support for problem-solving and possibly a new vocabulary for democratic legitimation;
- *flexibility and revisability* – reliance on soft law instruments, and other non-binding and revisable standards, to reflect rapid changes in the regulatory environment; and
- *experimentation and knowledge creation* – an emphasis on creation of new knowledge from deliberative processes and peer review.[14]

Which instruments and what types of method qualify as 'governance'? Growing interest in instruments of new governance has led some scholars to argue that there is 'an apparent lack of differentiation in the sorts of instruments which may be considered as phenomenologically related to this governance turn'.[15] This seems to be a particular concern for research into the OMC.[16] In my view, there is clearly no need to build a wall between EU new governance instruments and the miscellaneous others (whatever they may be at any given time). What is a great deal more important to keep in mind in analysing EU governance is that conclusions drawn with respect to one EU governance instrument may not be generalisable across the range, and that problems and prospects need be identified on the basis of empirical observations that address each instrument individually.[17]

A more acute challenge relates to the form and shape that a decision-making procedure takes in order to promote the characteristics of new governance. Sabel and Zeitlin (2010) have developed and advanced a 'new architecture of democratic experimentalism', which encompasses the abovementioned characteristics, but also offers a concrete decision-making matrix for tasks involving several levels of government and actors. In other words, it is first and foremost an architecture for decision making, entailing the following steps.

1 Establish framework goals.
2 Elaborate plans by 'lower-level' units for implementing them.
3 Monitor, report on and peer review outcomes.
4 Revise goals and procedures in light of the experience gained in peer review.

On the one hand, EU law is framework law: '[F]ramework goals (such as "good water status", safe food, non-discrimination, and a unified energy grid) and measures for gauging their achievement are established by joint action of Member

14 Scott and Trubek, 2002, pp 5–6.
15 Armstrong and Kilpatrick, 2007, p 656.
16 For instance, Armstrong, 2010.
17 See also Österdahl, 2004, p 37.

States and EU institutions.'[18] On the other hand, EU law uses peer review to monitor progress by comparing achievement by one set of actors to that of another set of actors that pursue the same, or relatively similar, aims and ends. The peer review experience is then deployed in revising and improving framework goals and procedures. This feedback loop between applying and revising rules is crucial to democratic experimentalism – for without it there is no basis for its operation. The basic logic and dynamic of this new architecture has been fleshed out in a variety of substantive EU law fields (most importantly, Sabel and Zeitlin's collection in 2010), but less attention has been paid to understanding the new relationship between the EU courts and forms of governance in this emerging architecture. If anything, many are convinced that experiments with the new architecture do indeed 'weaken the capacity' of the EU courts.[19]

Before I address the question of whether, and on what grounds, it is true that governance modes threaten courts, a working definition of 'new governance' used in this book should be introduced. 'New governance' refers to *instruments, institutions or modes of governance* that can be characterised through three dimensions, which, taken together, delineate the particular form and nature of *public* intervention: *process values* (such as participation or openness); *limited specification of substantive norms* (such as good water status or safe chemicals); and association with *democratic experimentalism*.

1.3 New governance as a challenge for the courts

In order to evaluate the challenge to judicial decision making posed by EU governance and its experimentalist traits, we ought first to outline the main functions of judicial decision making. Keeping in mind the colossal literature dedicated to issues of adjudication and judicial review, any attempt at definition surely appears rather daunting. Rising to the challenge, the recent definition of 'judicial decision making' that Shaffer and Pollack (2010) offer manages to be not only courageous, but also informative. It goes directly to the heart of unspoken and perennial assumptions underlying the role of law and adjudication, public unilateral regulation and its enforcement. Their definition begins with hard law; the courts apply binding rules so as to:

18 Sabel and Zeitlin, 2010, p 3.

19 Magnette, 2006, p 31. Armstrong's criticism is more finely tuned. In his view, if democratic experimentalism needs to involve 'exit options' to resolve conflicts through command-and-control institutions (eg through the courts), its claim to be an alternative to traditional constitutionalism becomes weaker: see Armstrong, 2006, p 62, and Armstrong, 2011, p 13. It seems, however, unlikely that democratic experimentalism is sweeping away the whole traditional architecture altogether, or even desires to do so; rather, the argument in this book – and in democratic experimentalism more generally, I believe – is that although the 'exit options' remain very much in their place and continue to function, they are being challenged and transformed. See also Chapter 7.

- lay out and enforce rights and obligations (*obligation*);
- provide doctrinal elaborations and clarifications (*precision*); and
- settle disputes (*delegation to a third-party decision maker*).[20]

The scale of the challenge for courts starts to become clear. First, 'law' in new governance is often non-binding law – that is, soft law.[21] Clearly, the notion of soft law does not sit well with the function of judges to enforce rights and obligations. The non-binding and non-justiciable nature of much of EU governance complicates and interferes with the courts' traditional responsibility to act with a view to enforcing rights and obligations. In this respect, the general view is that the losers are primarily private parties, who lose their legal rights as a result of a crumbling system of legal remedies.[22]

Second, EU governance mechanisms increasingly turn to the local level, or otherwise 'lowest level possible', in the hope of finding experimental procedures and results, and they look for both formal and informal networks in search of new and updated knowledge. In a way, they come to rival the courts, which have traditionally provided meaning for binding norms and clarified the interpretation of doctrinal material. In other words, the final responsibility for interpretation is being relegated to a position outside the courts, to other governmental actors and non-governmental organisations (NGOs). Now, they give answers traditionally obtained from the courts, challenging the idea of judges as having ultimate and autonomous interpretative authority.

The third issue is that new governance bodies encourage non-hierarchical problem-solving within networks and other collaborative sites. A wide range of actors pursue common goals by means of consensual and deliberative co-operation, often in close co-ordination with the Commission. In contrast, hard law delegates dispute settlement to a third party – usually the courts or administrative tribunals. When networks arrive at a common understanding, for example of a complex provision contained in a directive, accordingly less demand exists for the courts to act in their capacity of final arbiter. In this respect, one might recall the argument according to which the shift from negative to positive

20 Shaffer and Pollack, 2010, 748. Those who are familiar with the IR literature will recognise a connection to the well-known article by Abbott and Snidal (2000) in which they encapsulate legalisation in IR using three dimensions: precision, obligation and delegation.

21 'Soft law' has not been authoritatively or consistently defined. In the IR literature, in which the term was first used, it was contrasted with 'hard law': 'hard law' comprises 'treaty rule which States expect will be carried out and complied with', whereas soft law norms 'do not create enforceable rights and duties': Baxter, 1980, p 549. A similar juxtaposition is taken in EU law too, in which hard law is associated with treaties, regulations and directives. See Senden, 2004, p 45, and Trubek, Cottrell and Nance, 2006, p 65. The classic definition of EU soft law is given by Snyder, 1995, p 64: soft law instruments are 'rules of conduct which, in principle, have no legally binding force but which nevertheless may have some practical effects', and as he has later added, also legal effects. For the addition of legal effects, see Stefan, 2008, p 756.

22 Trubek and Trubek, 2007, p 10.

integration has diminished the role of supranational actors, including the CJEU. Positive integration has proved more difficult for supranational actors to influence because of its co-operative and deliberative elements.[23]

By way of conclusion, EU governance differently delivers the functions that we normally associate with judicial decision making. New governance, by deploying peer review mechanisms, elaborates the content of norms (*precision*) and creates a platform to reach a shared decision in situations of policy conflicts (*delegation*) on the basis of 'law', which eschews and escapes legal enforcement (*obligation*). Already this rudimentary account reveals not only that we will face difficulties and resistance in attempting to subject evolving EU governance to traditional legal oversight mechanisms, but also that we will have to account for the change in court practices. But just as different governance bodies canvass the characteristics of new governance to varying degrees and lead to different forms of institutional practice, the role of, and conditions for, judicial decision making varies too. This warrants a case study approach.

1.4 New approaches to governance in EU environmental law: 'The early bird catches the worm'?

The policy area that serves as an empirical context for this book and a common baseline to all three case studies is EU environmental law and policymaking.

The original EC Treaties did not include environmental provisions: the explicit legal basis for common action in environmental matters, Art 174 of the Treaty Establishing the European Community (EC), was established by adoption of the SEA 1986. Since then, environmental policy has belonged to a sphere of shared competences in the European Union. Of course, policy initiatives were adopted, and environmentally relevant EU legislation enacted, from the 1970s onwards. For instance, in 1973, the Commission adopted its first Environmental Action Programme (EAP). This has proved a long-lasting element of EU environmental regulation, with the seventh EAP now in force. It has involved elaborating common environmental principles, identifying areas in need of regulatory action and shaping the general framework for developing a future EU environmental law.[24] Moreover, the EU courts have ruled on environmental matters since the 1970s. But the defining feature of this early stage of EU environmental policies was its economic focus: environmental policies 'could be adopted as long as policy-makers could demonstrate that they were essential for the creation of a common market'.[25] Nowadays, the environment is regarded as a key policy area, and EU-driven environmental policy enjoys widespread political

23 See Scharpf, 1999, p 1; Kohler-Koch and Rittberger, 2006, p 40.

24 See Lenschow, 2007, p 414. Since the Maastricht Treaty changes, action programmes have had the force of a legally binding decision: Art 192(3) TFEU.

25 Lenschow and Sprungk, 2010, p 137.

support from EU citizens as well as from international observers. The Union considers and endorses itself 'an environmental leader' on both European and global levels.[26] A constitutional commitment to 'a high level of protection and improvement of the quality of the environment' is embedded in Art 3(3) of the Treaty on the European Union (TEU). Furthermore, the principle of environmental policy integration, having first been codified in the Amsterdam Treaty, is now anchored in Art 11 of the Treaty on the Functioning of the European Union (TFEU), which requires environmental concerns to be integrated into EU policies and activities, with a view to strengthening commitment to sustainable development. The other relevant Articles can be found in Arts 191–193 TFEU. Finally, changes have not been confined to primary EU legislation; indeed, the number of secondary legal acts has steadily risen, as has the number of areas covered by EU environmental legislation.

Since the turn of the twenty-first century, however, the European Union has been pursuing a different legislative agenda, and the number of legal acts, which had risen without interruption from 1987, plummeted after 2001. It has been suggested that 'the EU environmental governance regimes which strongly rely on legislation . . . have been weakened'.[27] Detailed EU environmental legislation is increasingly being supplanted by open-ended legislation and governance mechanisms.[28] Changes in the governing style include, first, articulating procedures rather than substantive outcomes, allowing Member States to implement EU legislation as they see fit, but in return requiring them to report on their progress. Second, governance tools aim to co-ordinate common policies through learning, information sharing and other flexibility-inducing mechanisms. Finally, environmental problems involve an ostensible socio-political dimension, and the inclusion of a variety of actors, in stages of both policy formulation and implementation, has become common currency.[29] Despite the observable change in governance ideas, some have questioned the rise of governance instruments in empirical terms. In their view, the discrepancy between well-intended declarations and actual practices is particularly glaring in respect of economic instruments, which have not been widely used, unlike the 'context-oriented instruments' that have admittedly increased, but 'relatively little'.[30] The survey, which focused on the period 1967–2000, finds an explanation for this disappointing delivery in the disruptive effect of governance instruments on the legal harmonisation project, which has been at the heart of EU integration. However, the more general

26 Ibid, p 134.
27 von Homeyer, 2009, p 25. See also Lenschow and Sprungk, 2010, p 139. The first signs of the new approach to environmental law were visible in the fifth EAP of 1992. See Fisher, 2001, p 11, and Weale et al, 2000, p 61.
28 See Holzinger, Knill and Schäfer, 2006, p 409; Lenschow, 2002; Lenschow and Sprungk, 2010; von Homeyer, 2009, p 16; Weale et al, 2000.
29 Fisher, 2001, p 6.
30 Holzinger, Knill and Schäfer, 2006, p 404.

implications of its findings can now be challenged on the basis that 2000 may have marked the beginning of an era of governance instruments rather than the apogee of such an era. In addition, some major legislative reforms have now been pushed through and the focus seems currently to be moving from legislation to implementation, which reduces the pressure on governance regimes induced by EU-wide harmonisation efforts.

The impetus to develop and promote procedural and substantive innovations is clear. During the 1990s, it became clear that the problems of EU environmental policymaking could no longer be glossed over. Despite ambitious and wide-reaching legislation, problems of implementation at the national level have persisted.[31] The environmental policy sector is one of the most infringed-upon sectors in the European Union.[32] Another problem relates to weak or non-existent horizontal policy co-ordination, for example between the environmental and agricultural sectors. Influenced by the more general change in governing ideas mentioned earlier and frustrated at the slow progress of the Member States toward reform, the Union decided to move from legally binding, top-down steering to a more heterarchical and non-binding regulation in its approach to environmental policymaking. A particularly apt instance of this can be found in environmental law directives. While these used to be 'highly prescriptive and set out precise minimum standards', so that Member State discretion focused on 'deciding what exactly a directive applies to' rather than on taking up reform,[33] environmental directives now tend to steer clear of prescriptive norms and to rely instead on framework norms, which place their successes and failures within a broader context of Member State discretion in implementation.

Environmental policymaking is a relatively early, and thus established, example of a policy area in which the European Union has moved from legally binding top-down regulation to more reflective and flexible procedural-type regulation. Hence it seems well suited to contribute to a more general discussion about the nature and dynamics of changes in EU regulation. This should not be read to mean that the findings of this book are universal and can be straightforwardly generalised to explain future developments in other areas of EU law; rather, EU environmental governance needs be analysed in light of, say, EU environmental competences, existing legislation, or the strong legitimacy of EU

31 Implementation can mean two things. 'Legal' implementation refers to the transposition of EU legislation (directives) into national law, ensuring that national legislation is formally in line with EU requirements; 'practical' implementation encompasses the 'street level', ie how EU-derived law is applied in practice by domestic actors. See Weale et al, 2000, p 297. For present purposes, I adopt a broad definition of implementation that covers the stages of both formal transposition and practical implementation.

32 European Parliament and Council, *Decision No. 1386/2013/EU of the European Parliament and of the Council of 20 November 2013 on a General Union Environment Action Programme to 2020 'Living Well, within the Limits of Our Planet', 28 December 2013*, OJ L 354/171 ('Seventh EAP'), p 53.

33 Fisher, 2001, p 5.

environmental action in the eyes of EU citizens. But because environmental policymaking has been a forerunner in using new governance strategies, the present findings are broadly useful as likely indicators of future directions in other policy fields. Moreover, environmental policymaking offers multiple discrete governance instruments from which to choose.

The first case study focuses on the environmental dimension of the EU 2020 Strategy. It builds on research on the OMC – or, more accurately, the family of OMCs – which is sometimes considered a 'flagship' model of EU governance, at least if judged on the basis of the academic and political attention that it has elicited over the last decade.

The second case study concerns agency governance: in particular, the ECHA. Agencies are a relatively 'old' phenomenon in the EU legal framework, the first going back to the 1970s. However, while their absolute number has risen in recent years, their scope of activity has expanded and, in many cases, they have acquired quite an influential position in their respective policy fields: '[T]he rise of agencies – and more particularly their rapid proliferation in recent years – has been identified as one of the manifestations of a transformation in European governance.'[34]

Finally, the third case study considers the WFD–CIS. Environmental framework directives first became prevalent during the 1990s. But, as with agencies, their rise has continued steadily during the first decade of the twenty-first century. In addition, these later framework directives are unlike earlier directives in that they are accompanied by informal implementation networks. These networks and their activities can be understood as a way in which to secure correct implementation by Member States without explicitly increasing the powers of the Union to monitor and sanction its Member States in cases of non-compliance,[35] but also – and perhaps more importantly still – as a way in which to support learning and transnational networking.

I decided to select these case studies on the basis that they share sufficient similarities, but at the same time are sufficiently different. As we will see in the case study chapters, they demonstrate varying degrees of intensity and commitment, environmental policy co-ordination being the most modest in both its theoretical potential and actual delivery capacity, whereas the CIS convincingly reveals the seriousness with which more fully fledged governance instruments go about their business. However, together they provide a good overview of the multiplicity of issues and challenges involved with the justiciability of new governance measures. For instance, the problem of expertise or use of soft law cuts across all three examples, but the specific questions that this entails for the courts depend on the context.

34 de Búrca, 2006, p 112. See also Smismans, 2007, p 603.
35 Dehousse, 1997.

1.5 A democratic theory of deliberation

A democratic theory of deliberation (or 'deliberative democracy') provides the theoretical framework for the analysis in this book. Deliberation assumed a particular importance in democratic theory in the early 1990s and the concept has been influential ever since. As with the term 'governance', no single universally accepted idea or definition explains what 'deliberation' means or does not mean; rather, several theories exist. Despite obvious problems resulting from a flux of research, we have good reasons to familiarise ourselves with the theory of deliberative democracy. The reason for deploying the deliberative theory framework is that more traditional forms of representative democracy are increasingly failing to make sense of governance arrangements and frustrate subsequent judicial action.[36] Moreover, although deliberative democracy has often been mentioned in works on new governance, no comprehensive analysis exists of the emergence of the governance paradigm and deliberative democracy. Furthermore, much of the research on deliberative democracy analyses deliberation in the policy formulation and legislative process, but less attention has been given to stages of policy implementation and execution. Since all three case studies focus on stages that occur after policy has been decided, the analysis here sheds new light on conditions of deliberation in law application and administrative implementation.

It should be emphasised that this book will not argue that deliberative democracy offers a democratic justification for new governance – although I suspect that deliberative democracy is more responsive to the features of EU governance than the alternatives, and that a strong resemblance exists between EU governance and the deliberative democracy paradigm. To argue that new governance, as a whole or in terms of more limited case studies, is democratically legitimate from a deliberative democratic perspective would go beyond the reach and capacity of this work, which is legal in its orientation. Crucially, by this I do not mean to imply that the governance arrangements found in the case studies would not be assessed by reference to theories of deliberative democracy; on the contrary, this book aims to do just that. Chapter 3 introduces the theory of democratic deliberation with a view toward identifying a set of benchmarks against which to evaluate concrete examples of EU governance from a deliberative democracy perspective and toward operationalising those standards in the review function of the EU courts. Now, labelling the book as 'legal' is a disclaimer, intended to caution readers with an expert background in political theory that although much time has been spent on researching their discipline, they may still find a work in law that combines both legal research and political theory lacking in the latter. This risk should not stop legal scholars from discussing deliberative

36 For the usefulness of 'supplementary forms of democracy' in democratising executive rule-making, see Curtin, Hofmann and Mendes, 2013, p 5.

democracy, because works that straddle insights from several disciplines are highly necessary in exploring cutting-edge developments such as governance.[37] Moreover, the tendency in EU governance discussion is to invoke the concepts and standards of deliberative democracy, and it is critical not to isolate legal research from this discourse.[38] The value of deliberative democracy to legal governance research is clear on one further ground: there is no denying that any account of judicial review is premised on a number of considerations as to the form and nature of democracy; by envisaging an alternative content of democracy, we can allegedly also envisage a new content of judicial activities. The next section takes up this link between democracy and judicial review, and addresses it at greater length.

1.6 The judicial role: Clarifications and limitations

The role of the judiciary and the nature of judicial decision making are among the most researched theoretical questions in jurisprudence. The most determined debate has taken place with respect to judicial review in the US context of the separation of powers, hence often called 'constitutional review'. Constitutional review is a type of judicial review that involves courts in scrutinising laws to establish whether they contradict some higher law – normally, a constitutional law – and, if necessary, invalidating them. Judicial review can also refer to review of the executive branch, which, in the American context, means monitoring the activities of independent regulatory agencies.[39] EU governance raises many issues that logically fall into this latter tradition. Theories of judicial review of administrative action have, however, traditionally overlooked the problems of governance for judicial review.[40] There also is a risk of conceptual overstretching. Certainly, some arguments in relation to administration may well apply to governance. However, to assume that the arguments are transferable in this way appears to miss something fundamental about governance: that governance arrangements are not simply administrative and executive decisions. In many ways, new governance marks an alternative paradigm to a set of conceptions held about both legislation and administration, and it (in)famously blurs the distinction between the tasks of the legislative and the executive, thus raising new questions never considered in more traditionally grounded theories of judicial review.

37 As is typical of EU governance literature, which conveniently mixes and draws inspiration from political and social sciences, history, law, political theory and sociology, this book also attempts – to the extent possible and whenever advantageous to the research questions – to heed research undertaken in disciplines other than law.

38 For a similar critique of Smismans' work, see Bignami, 2006, p 446. She also argues that (political) theorists have not quite understood the extent to which these ideas can already be found in current decision-making practices in the European Union, and the empirical case study material might in turn give some new content to the (political) theory of deliberation.

39 Cane, 2004, p 16.

40 See ibid.

The seminal question that usually occupies these discussions on judicial review is its relationship to democracy. Among others, Waldron (1999) criticises judicial review on the basis of a conviction that whatever arguments and arrangements are needed to specify what democracy requires in our everyday lives, these should be assessed and decided by citizens or their representatives, rather than by unaccountable judges.[41] The ideal type of democracy, often found in arguments for and against judicial review, is some form of representative democracy in the context of which 'unelected and unaccountable judges' and 'elected legislators' are pitted against each other in a never-ending contest for ultimate democratic authority.[42] Exactly where the ultimate authority lies alternates according to the weight of the arguments on either side of the issue. It is, however, unclear to what extent depiction of a battle can assist in exploring the transformation of judicial review in a situation in which unelected judges and elected legislators may be equally impotent – a situation in which the exercise of political power occurs in highly diverse forms and results in a variety of inconsistently normative practices. Hence attention should focus on discovering and exploring the underlying democratic underpinnings of judicial review. Ultimately, these determine how the judiciary perceives its role and undertakes its activities, both in terms of access and in terms of substantive grounds of review.

Let us touch on a couple of examples that expressly concretise these democratic underpinnings of judicial review. The case law of the EU courts on the standing of non-privileged applicants reflects the view that 'an uphill task'[43] to convince the courts is justified on the basis of the deeply held democratic ideal according to which the people are represented through a parliamentary or other assembly and therefore cannot bring successful judicial claims to be consulted in rule-making.[44] The fact that the courts are wary of treating guidelines as law can be understood as an attempt to avoid certain consequences, 'because to [treat guidelines as law] would recognise that public administration is subject to laws of its own design rather than subordinate to the will of Parliament'.[45] Or, to give one more example, the concept of 'justiciability', which determines what is judicially reviewable and which plays an important role in the previous example, is 'a self-referential criterion. It merely reflects what the Court believes it can review.'[46] These beliefs

41 For discussion, see, eg, Kavanagh, 2003, and Lever, 2009.

42 Mendes, 2009, p 69. He holds that these expressions emanate from a desire to pin down the 'internal sovereign', giving infallible answers to questions that arise in a democratic society.

43 Craig and de Búrca, 2011, p 493.

44 The important case in this respect is Case T-521/93 *Atlanta AG and others v European Community* [1996] ECR II-1707, especially [65]–[78]. See also Mendes, 2011, pp 215–20 and 457, especially at p 217, where she criticises the Court's reasoning in the *Atlanta* case as 'enervated'.

45 Sossin, 2004, p 137.

46 Somek, 2008, p 128. Of course, one should recall Art 263 TFEU, which determines the types of act susceptible to judicial review. Clearly, however, the EU Court itself ultimately interprets what the requirement of an act 'intended to produce legal effects' means and what the relevant standards are in light of which the decision is to be taken.

are anchored in an idea of democracy that the CJEU has accepted. All of these examples, and many similar examples not suggested here, teach us something about what the EU courts understand as democratically legitimate or publicly supported in the polity in which they deliver their judgments. However, this understanding is now profoundly challenged by the rapid decentralisation of normative practices and the evolution of EU law. Just as I have pointed out earlier in this chapter that notions of representative democracy no longer capture governance developments in the European Union and that notions of deliberative democracy may be more helpful, so judicial decision making also encounters problems when attempting to subject EU governance to evaluation according to standards derived from a representative form of democracy. The case studies in Chapters 4, 5 and 6 provide us with 'peepholes', or 'glimpses', into difficulties and problems that have arisen in these governance environments. Having pinned down the problems of judicial review and opened up the logic that might be their cause, the last step then involves revisiting each problem and suggesting how concerns can be mitigated and alleviated by taking into account the benchmarks of deliberative democracy.

Some additional clarifications and definitions are in order. This book focuses on the EU courts, but the study does not address dilemmas such as the role of national courts in reviewing EU governance, or the relationship between EU courts and national courts. The CJEU includes (after entry into force of the Lisbon Treaty) three courts: the Court of Justice (CoJ), the General Court (GC) and the Civil Service Tribunal.[47] For the sake of simplicity, throughout this book I will use the post-Lisbon names of the EU courts. The terms 'CJEU', 'the courts' and 'the EU courts' refer to both the Court of Justice and the General Court. The task of the EU courts is to ensure that, when interpreting and applying EU law, the law is duly observed (Art 19 TEU). More specifically, the EU courts decide on the interpretation of EU law in preliminary rulings at the request of a national court, or on the validity of acts adopted by the institutions, or in actions raised by a Member State, an institution, or a natural or legal person. Finally, for present purposes, the terms 'judicial decision making', 'adjudication' and 'judicial review' are used interchangeably, and understood to encompass all three dimensions mentioned by Abbott and Snidal (2000) – that is, that the courts apply binding rules in order to enforce rights and obligations, provide general doctrinal pronouncements and settle disputes. This description of the elements of judicial decision making corresponds well with a statutory account of the different functions of the EU courts.

1.7 Current research: Whence and whither to proceed?

The question about the relationship between adjudication and new governance is rooted in a more far-reaching understanding about law and governance. The latter

47 Article 19 TEU does not name the Civil Service Tribunal, but speaks of 'specialised courts'. Annex 1 includes provisions on the Civil Service Tribunal.

relationship, unlike the former, has been analysed quite extensively. I will describe the main arguments because they help to explain the underlying assumptions behind the interest in the courts and new governance, and in particular why there has been so little research. The relationship between law and governance has been aligned along three main lines: 'gap'; 'hybridity'; and 'transformation'.[48]

- The *gap* thesis identifies and describes those approaches according to which law and new governance work with palpably different attributes, and with differing purposes and goals. Law is perceived as an instrument to ensure legal certainty, to safeguard legitimate expectations and to organise formal positions predictably, whereas governance provides a shared framework for the virtues of learning, revisability and respect for diversity. Those who adopt this approach see little value in engaging in research such as this book.
- The *hybridity* thesis anticipates a more positive interaction between law and governance, but the scope and degree of this interaction, and the subsequent adjustment potential, differs between authors who adopt hybridity as their starting point.
- The *transformation* group is the most radical and aims high, levelling criticism at what it perceives to be 'an unduly formalistic and positivistic account of law'.[49] This third thesis emphasises how law and governance mutually constitute and shape one another.

Scott and Trubek (2002) have applied this categorisation to analysis of the case law of the EU courts, finding despairingly little evidence of their willingness to engage seriously with legal dilemmas arising from EU governance. The EU courts appear to be gap theorists. In order to nudge the courts in a more progressive direction, Scott and Sturm (2007) later proposed a 'courts as catalysts' approach. In short, courts are to function 'as a catalyst by facilitating the elaboration and implementation of public law norms by other actors, and the productive engagement of normative inquiry among relevant institutional actors, including the judiciary itself'.[50] In this way, judges are prevented from frustrating the good results and outcomes of governance institutions, whilst still being in a position to enhance their 'legitimacy', 'accountability' and 'efficacy'. Scott and Sturm's suggestion is in some ways similar to a related, but broader, theoretical inquiry about institutional reform litigation in the US context: judicial review should be reconceptualised as a practice of 'destabilization', the idea being to provoke and make accountable those public agencies that keep failing to meet their official functions and public obligations. The aim of judicial intervention is to 'destabilize the parties'

48 de Búrca and Scott, 2006, pp 4–10. This cluster overlaps with the 'separation', 'mutual penetration' and 'absorption' theses articulated in Walker and de Búrca, 2007.
49 de Búrca and Scott, 2006, p 9.
50 Scott and Sturm, 2007, p 571.

pre-litigation expectations through political, cognitive, and psychological effects that widen the possibilities of experimentalist collaboration'.[51] By 'experimentalist collaboration', the authors, in essence, mean a pragmatic account of democratic experimentalism that emphasises the capacity of local administrative units to enjoy broad discretion, subjecting the development of local solutions to centralised monitoring according to commonly agreed benchmarks, as briefly explained earlier (see section 1.2, 'New governance: A definition on the move').

The role of courts reviewing governance structures has also been discussed in the contexts of accountability studies and general EU administrative law, or those combining both.[52] In the accountability debate, the crucial question is whether forms of political or semi-political accountability (parliaments, ombudsmen) should be preferred over legal accountability mechanisms such as the courts.[53] Political accountability mechanisms have indisputable merits because they offer perhaps more sensible and less rigid alternatives to judicial review. However, analysis of judicial accountability is inevitable irrespective of whether one wants to promote primarily legal or political means. Assuming that political and legal accountability are not mutually exclusive, but together form a commitment to accountable governing, it makes sense to gain a more elaborate understanding of where precisely it is that judicial review falters and where it succeeds, in order to promote and design political accountability mechanisms.

Despite its name, general EU administrative law is not a generalist topic. It 'consists of a patchwork of scattered EC treaty provisions, general principles of European law shaped by the ECJ and its case-law, and secondary norms within special fields of regulation',[54] and its evolution has not yet been fully worked out. The work of Hofmann and Türk (2006) on integrated administration is important not only in uncovering changes in EU and national administrations, but also in seeking to update the traditional rule-of-law principle in light of these changes. According to them, the courts are central actors in monitoring administrative activity and in ensuring that the principles of good governance are observed in EU administration, but Hofmann and Türk admit that the EU courts encounter problems in trying to do so owing to the evolutionary nature of forms of

51 Sabel and Simon, 2004, p 1020. For such judicial intervention in US child welfare reform, see Noonan, Sabel and Simon, 2009, p 559.

52 New governance has been studied from another possible framework: (EU) constitutional law. See, eg, articles in the edited collection by de Búrca and Scott, 2006. EU constitutional law can be argued to consist of two levels: the 'macro' level, dealing with problems such as competences; and the 'micro' level, analysing decision-making procedures, effectively coming close to administrative law. For the distinction, see Fisher, 2001, p 36. Whilst the question of the relationship between courts and governance has macro-level constitutional implications, the bulk of the book is devoted to discussing questions of institutional design, usually considered to be micro-level issues.

53 For a general overview of accountability issues in multi-level governance, see: Curtin, 2005; Harlow and Rawlings, 2007; and Hofmann and Türk, 2006.

54 Nickel, 2006, p 4. For reviews of EU administrative law and policy, see Craig, 2012, and Hofmann, Rowe and Türk, 2011.

governance.[55] In her book on executive power in the European Union, Curtin (2009) seeks to combine research on both accountability and administrative law by unveiling the genesis of the executive power of the Union, which lurks in dark corners and tries not to draw attention. She approaches the executive power 'in a holistic fashion as a patchwork of legal provisions and institutional practices', revealing the empirical implausibility of the view that the Commission holds very dear – namely, that it is the sole locus of executive power in the European Union.[56] Continuing in the same spirit, she warns against expecting too much of the capacity of the formal constitution to hold the fragmented executive to account; instead, she attempts to unearth the pieces of the 'composite living constitution' still evolving in order to increase the visibility and transparency of the executive power. For Curtin, accountability is an *ex post* act of explaining and justifying one's actions.[57] It bears resemblance to democratic experimentalism in that neither primarily conceptualises accountability in the relationship between principal and agent. But whereas Curtin locates accountability in the so-called 'accountability forums', such as courts and ombudsmen, or parliaments, democratic experimentalism's idea of accountability is dynamic, highlighting the function of peer review, meaning one actor justifying its performance to others doing the same thing. External monitoring and scrutiny then tap into the insights that emerge from peer review. In this book, I strive to empirically substantiate this argument about how peer review is important to subsequent judicial control.

My framework for thinking about courts draws on two of the abovementioned approaches. The first is the work of Scott and Sturm (2007) on catalyst litigation. Whilst those authors provide important insights and robust suggestions for improvement, I wish to develop and elaborate their argument further. More specifically, their proposed approach attempts to empower judges to 'enhance legitimacy, accountability, and efficacy of new governance institutions',[58] yet they are reluctant to explain why these aspects should be highlighted (despite this being a point of criticism commonly put forward about new governance), what each element entails and what each means in various settings, and whether judicial action is appropriate or suitable, and if so, why. Scott and Sturm point out in their article that they do not wish to set out what 'participation' or 'transparency' mean as elements of legitimacy, or to claim that they have an 'enduring value';[59] instead, they refer to the new governance literature to furnish them with a foundation. However, those concepts – although regularly embraced and discussed in EU

55 Hofmann and Türk, 2006, pp 588–9. Theorists of legal interpretation have rarely shown any interest in problems that governance entails for courts. Cf. Maduro, 2007, on 'new forms of power' as a type of internal pluralism affecting adjudication in the European Union.

56 Curtin, 2009, p 21.

57 Ibid, p 248.

58 Scott and Sturm, 2007, p 568.

59 Ibid, p 572. They continue that those principles are enshrined in the 'constitutional and legislative framework of the European Union'.

governance literature – are not axiomatic, either in their value or in their meaning. For Hervey (2006), fundamental values are in a state of limbo. She contends that:

> [U]nder 'old governance', although we may not agree with the precise contours of these backstopping values, at least we know which institutions and mechanisms (largely, courts and litigation, with the possibility of legislation where Community competence allows) are responsible for generating them. [Footnote omitted] Under 'new governance' arrangements, it is less clear whence these values emanate.[60]

Moreover, without an explicit link to democratic theory, the critique and further elaboration of values and concepts is made difficult, if not impossible (assuming, as I do, that the suggestions that Scott and Sturm envisage for judicial review of governance can broadly be associated with a deliberative conception of democracy).

The second approach connects to the democratic experimentalism developed by Sabel and his collaborators,[61] in particular the work that they have done on dynamic accountability structures. Their view, accordingly mirrored by me in this book, is that law and governance do not form closed and insulated universes that operate independently of one another, but mutually influence each other normatively and empirically. Whilst courts necessitate changes from governance, some degree of change and transformation is equally demanded from the system and institutions of law too. It is the latter type of transformation that forms the focal point of interest of this book. Accepting the recommendations made by Scott and Sturm, as well by Sabel and his collaborators, that the courts should be actively involved in exhorting governance bodies to correct and rectify problems themselves, and in encouraging the peer review potential thus emerging, I work towards showing how such peer review activities are influencing the exercise of judicial review.

1.8 Book structure

This book includes seven chapters. In Chapter 2, I give a more detailed account of EU governance – more particularly, of its democratic legitimation. Chapter 3 introduces the theory and practice of democratic deliberation, with the aim of identifying a set of benchmarks to be invoked by the courts in evaluating forms of governance. The next three chapters introduce a series of case studies. First to be analysed is the environmental dimension of the EU 2020 Strategy (Chapter 4), followed by the ECHA (Chapter 5), and finally the WFD CIS

60 Hervey, 2006, pp 208–9.
61 See, eg, Sabel and Zeitlin, 2010.

(Chapter 6). Each case study begins with a brief overview of the governance instrument, before moving on to study barriers and disincentives to its judicial review. Each case study concludes with a discussion of what the deliberative democracy paradigm would mean for judicial practice and how the benchmarks developed in Chapter 3 may help to address problems thus identified.

Chapter 7 deepens and further develops the discussion of matters introduced in the case study chapters by proposing a five-dimensional account of the relationship between the courts and new governance, after which it recapitulates the main findings, going on to offer some general conclusions, caveats and recommendations for future discussion.

Chapter 2

New governance in the European Union

2.1 Introduction: The peril of presumed premises

Since the turn of the twenty-first century, the European Union has been making a sustained attempt to develop more effective and legitimate regulatory instruments. The intricate nature of contemporary problems and challenges such as wide-ranging environmental concerns, the scope of social rights beyond the nation-state, or the new institutional environment with 28 Member States have heightened the sense of the inadequacy of past methods and instruments. In particular, the Commission has expressly talked of new and alternative modes of governance in its numerous policy documents.[1] As a result, a rich scholarly debate emerged in the Union (surfacing in the mid-1990s and maturing soon after the turn of the twenty-first century) about whether new modes of governance exist, and if so, what might be their scope, function, pitfalls or future.[2] These contributions, loosely defined, form the body of EU new governance research. Controversies continue – one of the most persistent squabbles relates to the question of whether 'new' is the right label – while competing classifications abound, which gives EU governance research a unique and precarious flavour of its own. Of course, some classifications are more influential than others and some sort of common ground has been found over the instruments (such as framework directives, the Open Method of Coordination, or OMC, and the Social Dialogue) and attributes (such as participatory, deliberative or 'soft law'-like). Their prevalence, identity and significance give rise to fundamental disagreements among observers – but this is ultimately a question of how to reconcile many competing answers, which is hardly a situation unheard of in research.

This seemingly straightforward, yet fundamental, issue is important to understand, simply because if foundational concepts and ideas are contested and

1 See, most importantly, the *White Paper on European Governance*, the definition of 'governance' of which is extensive, encompassing 'rules, processes and behaviour that affect the way in which powers are exercised at European level': European Commission, July 2001, COM(2001) 428 final, p 8, fn 1.

2 For early EU governance research, see Armstrong, 1998, p 168.

in a state of flux, this requires more of the researcher. Conceptual and theoretical diversity demand a genuine commitment to openness and transparency about underlying assumptions. While reviewing the discussion about the relationship between law and new governance, Walker and de Búrca (2007) do indeed warn about the perils of presumed 'theoretical premises': although the answers can be many, they stress that there can be no 'theoretically innocent or neutral answers', because any preferred answer will bring its own theoretical understanding of the concepts.[3] Their example of the relationship between law and new governance is a good one, because the visible tendency is to treat 'law' as a given (or, to borrow from a political scientist's vocabulary, a constant variable) and to proceed to the analysis. The possibility of democratic legitimation for new governance is another instructive example. Many analyses have appeared in recent years that do not at first seem to share anything other than a massively critical tone. As shown in this chapter, however, many also have something else in common: they tacitly assume particular normative ideals of democracy without fully noting – let alone explaining – what those ideals actually imply. It is upon this desire for greater transparency and clarity that the rest of this chapter builds.

In this chapter, I introduce new governance in the European Union, but rather than cataloguing the relevant literature, I make two claims: first, that the theory of new governance is increasingly based on the concepts of deliberation and participation, and that their rapid proliferation is felt most conspicuously in the area of evolving EU administrative law; and second, that these two foundational concepts are linked only vaguely and ambiguously to a democratic theory of deliberation, which can (in the worst-case scenario) lead to hidden assumptions and indeterminacies. I believe that building the chapter around these two claims has the potential to pin down and illustrate the essentials of the new governance discussion in the European Union, and, most importantly, to strip the concepts of their 'theoretical innocence' and 'neutrality'.

2.2 'It's all about democracy'

The literature on democracy and democratic legitimacy[4] at the EU level is, even by a conservative estimate, large and continuously evolving. Therefore, I survey only briefly how the European Union came to gain democratic credentials, or

3 Walker and de Búrca, 2007, p 523.

4 By 'legitimacy', I do not mean only a sociological legitimacy about how something is believed to be legitimate, but rather a normative account of legitimacy according to which something has justified reasons to be considered legitimate and people generally comply with this something. For the sake of simplicity, I speak of 'democratic legitimacy' throughout the book, although democracy and legitimacy do not necessarily imply one another, and legitimacy can be maintained through other means than democracy. See Føllesdal, 2007, p 324.

perhaps more correctly, a 'democratic deficit', with the aim of offering a better-informed position from which to understand and appreciate the context in which 'deliberation' and 'participation' first struck root in the Union.

2.2.1 Indirect democracy: Nation-states

Democracy was not on the agenda of the Treaty of Rome in 1957. For Monnet and his contemporaries, democracy was 'a secondary consideration, since it was felt that the best way to secure peace and prosperity was by technocratic elite-led guidance'.[5] The idea was that the stability and wealth ensuing from ever-deepening integration resulted in a 'permissive consensus' that cleared the way for bureaucrats to do their jobs.[6] When European integration expanded in terms of Member States and policy areas, the permissive consensus no longer sufficed to convince the larger community to let the bureaucrats continue 'business as usual'. The dominant view on democracy came then to adopt the indirect legitimatisation thesis, which in essence meant that the European Union could legitimise its activities through national popular democracy. This understanding sat rather nicely with the way in which European integration was generally perceived at that time: as national institutions tapping into the dynamics of supranational integration in order to arrive at aims that were otherwise unattainable for them in domestic settings.[7] If integration was prominently understood to work for the benefit and development of the participating Member States, it seemed fitting to legitimise the emerging political system by means of the democratic mechanisms of those nation-states involved.

By today's standards intense debate about democracy within the Union began to grow after the realisation that the indirect legitimatisation thesis was not enough and that if, for some reason, it ever had been, it was no longer working. Acknowledgement of the limits of indirect legitimatisation had two main sources. On the one hand, indirect democracy overlooked the important role of the European Union in reducing and downsizing the regulatory autonomy of Member States. Most acutely, the negative integration programme at which it aimed did not succeed in developing a corresponding supranational 'governance capacity' that was 'both substantial and democratically legitimate'.[8] EU internal market regulations, combined with decisions of the Court of Justice of the European Union (CJEU), eroded and invalidated domestic social regulations, thus overriding democratically expressed preferences at the national level. On the other hand, increasingly pragmatic difficulties hindered the maintenance of a convincing picture of Member States (parliaments) holding EU decision makers to

5 Craig, 2011a, pp 16–17.
6 Ibid.
7 Ibid, p 21.
8 Pollack, 2005, p 41.

account. Scandinavian countries – most prominently, Denmark, and to some extent Finland too – succeeded in securing a degree of electoral accountability of ministers to domestic parliaments, but on the whole problems and limitations were too substantial, and perhaps too systemic, to encourage any attempt at (effective) remedy.[9] From the theoretical point of view, this coincided with the early rise of theories of multi-level governance, trying to come to terms with strong supranational institutions.[10]

2.2.2 *Direct democracy: The European Parliament*

A greater appreciation of the limits of indirect democratic legitimisation led commentators to entertain the idea of establishing democratic values within the European Union itself. Since the 1992 Maastricht Treaty, the democratic character of EU decision making as a normative commitment made in both national and EU constitutional law has been widely accepted. Chronologically, the first and perhaps still the most important institution to sustain democracy in the Union is the European Parliament. It was to be expected that the Parliament would be seen as the main mechanism for proclaiming the commitment to democracy: a directly elected assembly fits the direct legitimacy thesis – namely, that the power-wielding institutions should be authorised by, and made meaningfully accountable to, the people. The role of the European Parliament was first constitutionally acknowledged in the Single European Act (SEA) in 1986, and was then subsequently augmented in the Maastricht, Amsterdam and Lisbon Treaties, especially by reforms in relation to co-decision (now the Ordinary Legislative Procedure).[11] Several inter-institutional agreements have depicted a strong EU parliament as the most promising antidote to a legitimacy crisis precipitated by ever-increasing integration. The CJEU also anticipated and institutionally accommodated the rise in significance of parliamentary democracy by ruling on parliamentary prerogatives.[12]

Efforts to make the European Union democratic by means of the European Parliament were not emphatically successful. More than one reason might plausibly explain why direct democracy by this means disappointed many and was increasingly seen as insufficient: voting is generally less important at the international level than at the national level; the intergovernmental character of law-making and policymaking (which, interestingly, is the claim that new modes of governance revived, at least partially) operates to oust legislatures; and a transnational (European) demos, which is perceived as a necessary condition for

9 For the role of national parliaments, see, more generally, Raunio, 2009.

10 Craig, 2011a, p 26.

11 Craig, 2011b, pp 54 and 56–9.

12 Case 138/79 *Roquette Frères v Council* [1980] ECR 3333 (imposing an obligation on the Council to consult the Parliament); Case C-70/88 *European Parliament v Council* [1990] ECR I-2041 (allowing the Parliament a right to standing to defend its rights before the EU courts).

establishing democracy beyond the nation-state, has remained only wishful thinking. These reasons alone could be considered sufficient for sowing the seeds of the now-influential parlance of 'democratic deficit', but further reasons that are highly specific to the overall institutional architecture within which the Parliament operates might usefully augment these three reasons. First, the European people have a parliament, but they cannot vote out members of the other supranational institutions that have primary control over the legislative agenda.[13] In this respect, the argument has been made that the European Parliament is expected to work much like national legislatures. This is not realistic given the markedly different nature of EU policymaking. These expectations are also based on increasingly unrealistic assumptions as to the nature of national parliaments. Evaluations of the stature of the Parliament are usually based on the idea that national parliaments 'really control national legislation', but which assumption 'no longer comports with reality in many Member States'.[14] Second, despite the fact that the European Parliament has attained some major gains, with the result that it now exerts a real role over legislative drafting, it could not quite repeat this success with respect to executive decision making, which – most outstandingly in the form of comitology – has always been important for the European Union. Neither national nor European legislatures have been meaningfully included in controlling 'executive dominance'.[15]

2.2.3 *'Democracy everywhere': Civil society*

The twenty-first century has seen less optimism and more criticism about strengthening parliamentary democracy in the European Union, and the main interest has turned to the possibility of the revival of civil society. Civil society actors have been ascribed the task of maintaining and redefining the boundaries between themselves and the public power, as well as economic actors. The 'reinvention' of the European Economic and Social Committee (EESC), which was originally established in 1957 to tackle discrepancies that derived from traditional social and political hierarchies, is an illustrative example of the importance that the civil society paradigm has obtained in institutional terms in

13 Note, though, that the role of the European Parliament in choosing the Commission president could be depicted as an increase in direct legitimation. See Art 17 TEU.

14 Craig, 2011a, p 31.

15 Ibid, p 30. It should be noted that Parliament involvement has grown over the years. Its dissatisfaction with the 'original' 1987 comitology peaked in the 1990s, and in 1999 the revised Comitology Decision was adopted. In 2006, this decision was amended to include a new 'regulatory procedure with scrutiny procedure' empowering the European Parliament. A new Regulation 182/2011 was adopted in the aftermath of the Lisbon Treaty. Two comitology procedures now exist: the advisory procedure, which is the same as in the old regime; and the examination procedure, which replaced the management and regulatory procedures. For analysis of the new provisions, see Peers and Costa, 2012, and Schütze, 2011.

recent years.[16] As Bignami (2006), in a review of Smismans' work on functional participation in social regulation, explains the transformation:

> [T[he Economic and Social Committee has set out to re-invent itself. Membership is no longer limited to economic groups – groups defined by their structural position in the market – but extends to 'civil society organizations' throughout Europe. Thus associations promoting the environment, human rights, charity, consumer interests, family life, religion, and all other aspects of social and civic life are to be included, together with the traditional economic groups. If the official documents are any guide, the Economic and Social Committee is to become an assembly of civic associations, not only a forum for economic groups.[17]

The EESC may have begun the discourse on the potential of civil society in the Union, but in recent years it has been the European Commission that has carried its torch.[18] The concrete actions that the Commission has taken range from consultations to forms of self- and co-regulation, and anything in between, although with emphasis on pre-decision consultation. For this reason, its approach to civil society is regarded as 'top-down' and 'corporatist'.[19] The Commission has been remarkably (it might even be said artfully) convoluted when it comes to the democratic potential of civil society. Whilst scholars are not nervous about suggestions that the European Union 'sees itself as a strong promoter of participatory governance, and clearly favours extending the involvement of elements within civil society',[20] they readily admit that the democratic dimension that this might involve is a 'non-issue' for EU institutions.[21] Besides, academic observers are, and appear to remain, largely sceptical about the democratic potential of civil society. In my view, this scepticism results in great measure from the fact that representative accounts of democracy have struggled to provide a theoretically convincing rationale for civil society – that is, how to understand civil society as a representative of the people. In addition, concrete difficulties have arisen in ensuring that civil society involvement is not simply a spectacle for its own sake, but actually delivers some real advantages for those involved.

By way of summary, the vocabulary of representative democracy, although essential to illuminate problems about indirect legitimatisation, has become an impediment. In keeping with the prevailing vocabulary of representative democracy, we have developed little more than an understanding that democracy

16 de Búrca and Walker, 2003, p 389.
17 Bignami, 2006, p 440.
18 Smismans, 2006, p 4. For the Commission understanding of what civil society includes, see European Commission, July 2001, COM(2001) 428 final.
19 Curtin, 2006, p 139. See also Bignami, 2004, pp 75–8.
20 Mair, 2005, p 17.
21 Mörth, 2004, p 198.

without the nation-state paradigm seems unlikely.[22] We appreciate the problems of the current system, but we do not know where to look for feasible or desirable alternatives. Peters (2004), after carefully analysing the then-draft Convention's provisions in light of democratic theories, concluded that the democratic deficit still exists. She moved on to assess possible responses to the deficit and ended up rejecting nearly all of them for various reasons, before saying equivocally that the Union needs more democracy, but not necessarily through the Parliament.[23] A sort of compromise has now been factored into the Lisbon Treaty: Art 10(1) TEU provides that the Union is founded upon representative democracy. Citizens are represented directly in the European Parliament and indirectly through Member State governments in the European Council or in the Council of Ministers. A tension remains, however: the people are not able 'directly to vote out those in power and substitute a different party with different policies, since Member State representatives in the Council and European Council are not chosen in this manner'.[24] The tension is addressed at some level by inclusion of the second democratic principle. A full expression of the right to participation is found in Art 11 TEU, which contains the principle of participatory democracy.[25] These Articles represent a high-level give and take, the precise contours of which remain to be influenced by what is a huge and still growing literature on the possibilities of EU-level democracy. Precisely how the European Union goes about democratically legitimising its day-to-day activities, including the entire 'governance sphere' not included in formal Treaty Articles, is an open question.[26] There simply is no canonical form of democracy that promotes a search for feasible alternatives. Shaw (2000) writes that 'democracy remains both a conceptual problem and a practical challenge, requiring multilevel and multi-actor solutions that are "beyond the state" and, perhaps, also beyond the conventions of Western-style representative liberal democracy'.[27] Another trend, reflecting efforts to come to grips with what awaits beyond those conventions, is a more empirical, or 'hands-on', approach to studying democracy in fragmented normative frameworks of decision making, to which we will turn next.

2.3 Is new governance democratic?

It is difficult to pinpoint when new governance first made its appearance in EU legal studies. Legal scholarship on EU governance was fragmentary at the end of

22 de Búrca, 2008.
23 Peters, 2004, pp 69–70.
24 Craig, 2011a, p 37.
25 For the legislative history of these principles, see Peters, 2004, pp 43–5. For analysis of the meaning of the principles of democratic governance, see Bredt, 2011.
26 See also Curtin, Hofmann and Mendes, 2013.
27 Shaw, 2000, p 291 (emphasis omitted). The first signs of democracy 'fatigue' are to be seen in recent EU literature: see Neyer, 2010.

the 1990s, consisting primarily of individual journal articles, and the concept of (new) governance was not truly known to a more general legal audience until 2002, when Scott and Trubek published their article. Being aware of the avant-garde nature of the task, their work is informed by an unremitting effort to contextualise the concept. Scott and Trubek begin their inquiry by sketching out new governance as 'any major departure' from the Community Method.[28] Two discrete categories can be identified here. The first is called 'new, old governance' in the sense that it has elements of continuity with the Community Method, whilst it also departs from it in one or more major ways. The flexibility principle, framework directives or comitology fit the bill here. For example, the flexibility principle, which in a way recasts the much more familiar subsidiarity and proportionality principles, adds much-needed variation to the Community Method while, broadly speaking, complying with its core requirements. The second category of 'new, new governance' is characterised by the logic of policymaking that is clearly distinct from, or even opposite to, the Community Method. The Social Dialogue and the OMC represent fully fledged alternatives to the Community Method.[29]

More recently, what is essentially the same claim has been formulated in the argument for the 'shift away from hierarchical governance'.[30] To answer the question of what has changed in the European Union, Craig and de Búrca (2011) draw attention to a move away from the hierarchical architecture of governance, referring to three factors. First, policymaking is top-down, which indicates that it derives either from above or from the centre. Second, policies are comparatively conclusive, which means that room for discretion is commensurately limited. Third, policymaking results in binding outcomes that can be legally enforced if needed. Together, these three provide a body of benchmarks for a 'normal' way of regulation against which the move away can be measured. Then again, this kind of assemblage of standards allows different things to be implicated in a more detailed analysis of EU governance, whether it be a change in actors, regulatory instruments or modes of governing.

While these baseline descriptions have now been widely accepted and endorsed, attempts to explain what is at stake in terms of the democratic legitimacy of EU governance have proven a great deal more problematic. Indeed, a certain

28 Commission monopoly of the right of initiative; widespread use of qualified majority voting in the Council; the European Parliament's active role; and uniform interpretation of law by the CJEU: accessed 30 June 2014, http://europa.eu/scadplus/glossary/community_intergovernmental_methods_en.htm. More recent research indicates that the Community Method has also changed: see Dehousse, 2011.

29 Scott and Trubek, 2002, pp 1–5.

30 Craig and de Búrca, 2011, p 159. For Rhodes, 2003, p 65, governance 'signifies a change in the meaning of government, referring to a *new* process of governing; or a *changed* condition of ordered rule; or the *new* method by which society is governed' (emphasis original).

ambivalence exists about the democratic implications of the shift that has taken place. The first group of scholars argue that new modes of governance have nothing to do with democracy, but can be condoned if submitted to effective 'democratic review' (whatever that may mean).[31] Menéndez (2008) is equally straightforward when writing: '[A]s is well-known, there has [*sic*] indeed existed many *non-democratic* procedural conceptions of legitimacy throughout history . . . Concerning the EU, the most articulated conception of this kind is the one associated with the "governance" paradigm.'[32] The core idea is that democracy and governance are mutually exclusive, or, as Allot (2002) has succinctly put the problem, 'as the idea of *democracy* decays, the ideas of *governance* and *civil society* flourish'.[33] These views have been echoed by (good) governance research, which suggests that international and transnational institutions, such as the World Bank, have simply put democracy to work in the service of economic development, efficiency concerns and the competition imperative, sidelining social and environmental concerns. To make matters worse, international institutions are also often expert institutions to which members are appointed or elected because they have themselves been acknowledged as experts in a certain area, resulting in rule-making that is more 'technocratic', more 'depoliticised' and less 'democratic'.[34]

The second group levels its criticisms against a development that could be described as hollowing out the people, and filling up the space with functional and non-representative actors. One of the most common characterisations of EU governance relates to its participatory and inclusive nature. The extent to which this characterisation holds true is frequently disputed.[35] Discussing the Social Dialogue, Betten (1998) argues that:

> [I]t is here that, arguably, a form of participation in law making by 'the people' is created. This, in terms of *democracy*, could in theory enhance the legitimacy of Community decision-making. The question is whether this indeed is the case . . . trade unions, in particular, represent a very small proportion of 'the people'.[36]

Among concrete governance instruments, the OMC has been the most vulnerable to attacks on this particular front, and has prompted pointed and unapologetic criticism. Hatzopoulos (2007) addressed his 'letter' to the European Union,

31 Magnette, 2007, p 252.
32 Menéndez, 2008, pp 2–3 (emphasis added, footnote omitted).
33 Allott, 2002, p 60 (emphasis original).
34 See, eg, Devaux, 2013; Nanz and Steffek, 2004; and the debate between Cooney and Lang, 2007, and Lang and Cooney, 2009, vs García-Salmones, 2009.
35 Smismans, 2008.
36 Betten, 1998, pp 34–5 (emphasis added).

proclaiming that participatory democracy has not been realised through the OMCs, and that:

> [T]he risks of the various OMCs for *democracy*, representativeness and participation have been highlighted. All the empirical evidence available points to the findings that participation in the OMCs has been a) extremely restricted; b) highly uneven between Member States; and c) hardly representative of the stakeholders in each particular OMC.[37]

After cataloguing a number of legal and political correctives, Hatzopoulos concludes that one should 'try to ground these [governance instruments] on generally accepted and valued principles, such as democracy . . .'.[38]

Further complications arise when commentators find a 'normative democratic claim' to be associated with civil society inclusion. Smismans (2008), for instance, finds this link and explains that, 'from a *democratic* normative perspective, new governance would involve novel ways to expand participation by elements of civil society in policy-making and to extend deliberation among stakeholders'.[39] He is not, in his own words, interested in providing 'a normative model' for new governance, and he proceeds, by pitting new and old governance against each other, to show that new forms of governance are not, by definition, more participatory than forms of old governance – although he stops short of arguing that new governance is undemocratic. However, his article adds to the apparently habitual use of the words 'democracy', 'democratic' or 'undemocratic' without any discernible attempt to describe or open up the conception of democracy (what kind of 'democratic normative' perspective?) that one has in mind. Is it the capacity of voters to periodically remove elected legislators from office? Or perhaps it is the capacity of people to raise topics of concern to be included on the public agenda, or to subject them to effective democratic review? Perhaps we should be attempting to increase the direct input of citizens in democratic self-government? Or should we be pursuing more than one of these aims? These conclusions are undeniably sound, but conclusions would be more convincing and persuasive if the authors were to openly articulate their conceptions of democracy, and to explain what standards are being used to measure representation, participation, deliberation and expertise.[40]

As argued earlier in this chapter, the EU debate on democracy has emphasised two institutions, and it is precisely their function, influence and competence that seem ultimately to determine and qualify the democratic credentials of new

37 Hatzopoulos, 2007, pp 340–2 (emphasis added).

38 Ibid.

39 Smismans, 2008, p 877 (emphasis added).

40 See also Bignami, 2006, p 447, in the review of Smismans, 2004. Admittedly, this is a tall order: Lord, 2001, has argued that since we do not have a commonly accepted method for assessing democracy, it is difficult to say what forms a sufficiently democratic institution.

governance in the European Union as well. The first institution writ large is the European Parliament. Its role has, generally speaking, remained weak and unsystematic despite various reforms; clearly, as long as this continues to be the case, the (representative parliamentary) democratic nature of EU governance will, quite naturally, be perceived to be unsatisfactory too. The mirror image of this observation is that the notion of democracy in terms of elections and parliamentary bodies does not capture governance developments in the Union.

The second institution is civil society. This has attracted considerable attention in recent years, but to measure the advances that it has made in terms of democratic progress is a task fraught with difficulty. While the cause of parliaments fits hand in glove with the paradigm of representative democracy, the role of civil society has always been, as noted, a deeply special case in the same paradigm. How does this manifest? When we look at the analyses undertaken of civil society and its role, first to emerge is confusion over what should be the ideal: representative democracy with a strong civil society, or participatory democracy, or possibly something else? But, to a certain extent, incommensurability may be a blessing in disguise:

> [T]he famous 'no demos' problem . . . is also an opportunity. It means that, at the collective level, transnational European civil society, unlike its national counterparts, does not have to struggle for recognition and a distinctive identity within the public sphere alongside more established and institutionalised structures of political representation . . . [41]

A second, and not unrelated, argument is that the standards by which we measure the 'representativeness' or 'deliberativeness' of civil society are either vague, or nowhere to be found. By way of illustration: in the case of the Social Dialogue, trade unions arguably represent a very small proportion of the people – but how do we identify what is an adequate proportion of the people?[42] Again, participatory democracy appears not to be ensured by means of the OMCs – but how do we know when it is ensured? Should we require that all those affected participate in decision making? Or that all relevant interests are reviewed during decision making? Or that those who participate really represent all those who are affected?

To summarise, the emergence and evolution of new governance has come to mark 'the end of the separate treatment of European and national politics'.[43] It also explains why EU governance, from its inception, has been very much occupied with the need to develop processes of legitimation and to acquire some degree of democratic legitimacy. But, as a whole, the debate on democracy and new

41 de Búrca and Walker, 2003, p 400.
42 This was the question underpinning Case T-135/96 *UEAPME v Council* [1998] ECR II-2335.
43 Lenschow, 2006, p 56.

governance makes one wonder whether we are actually attempting to explain the new empirical reality of EU decision making so that it might match our normative vision of democracy and fit our established patterns of critique, when we should in fact perhaps finally venture to see what lies 'beyond the conventions of Western-style representative liberal democracy', to borrow Shaw's expression.[44] This argument should not be dismissed as a claim that our notion of democracy is wrong because it does not fit new governance, so that we need to change the notion of democracy to make it 'blend in'; rather, it is simply an observation that whilst representative democracy still has its place, it no longer occupies *pride* of place. More importantly still, the discussion over the democratic legitimacy of new governance that is solely informed by representative notions of democracy does not enjoy full critical potential, as illustrated by the debates over civil society.

2.4 The 'deliberative turn'[45] in EU studies

Against this backcloth of declining trust in representation, it is natural to note an increasing interest in attempts to salvage the European Union's democratic legitimacy by turning to deliberation as an ideal of political legitimation. We find this in areas as heterogeneous as the debates about EU constitutional theories, the intergovernmental Convention on the Future of Europe, the comitology procedure, and the role played by functional participation in occupational health and safety. I will address each example respectively.

Theories of European constitutionalism began to take new shape in the aftermath of the Maastricht Treaty in 1992, when it finally dawned upon EU political and administrative leaders that the once-sufficient indirect legitimatisation thesis no longer sustained developments in the European Union. This new form of constitutionalism promised to be 'more deliberative, inclusive, contestatory and bottom-up . . . based on the equal dignity and human rights of citizens'.[46] Such promises could easily have been dismissed as idealistic and impractical folly had some novel and promising developments not emerged. The EU Charter on Fundamental Rights and its subsequent adoption as part of the Lisbon Treaty, the appointment of the Convention on the Future of Europe, the debate on European governance, and the concrete and empirical manifestations of that debate, including acknowledgement of the role constructed for civil society, all strengthened the claim over the need for, and possibility of, reform. A place in the European constitutional and political order was thus carved out in which deliberation could operate. However, only a few proposals have been advanced in concrete terms beyond the level of abstract theory. The Convention

44 Shaw, 2000, p 291 (emphasis omitted).
45 Not unexpectedly, interest in deliberation has been characterised as the 'deliberative turn': see Neyer, 2006.
46 de Búrca, 2003, p 820.

on the Future of Europe, which convened to draft a Constitution for the Union, is an instructive, although highly controversial, example. In 2001, the European Council set up a body to prepare a draft Constitution as a response to the request included in the Laeken Declaration. The Convention began its work in February 2002, meeting once or twice a month in plenary sessions. It comprised 102 members from national parliaments, the Member States and the candidate countries, the European Parliament and the Commission, as well as representatives appointed by national governments. Civil society elements were included in the form of observers from the EESC, the Committee of the Regions (CoR) and the social partners, in addition to the consultation process ('the Forum') that took place while the Convention was convened. The Forum – a network of civil society organisations providing feedback on the work of the Convention[47] – was largely organised through a website to which organisations sent their contributions. What made the work of the Convention quite extraordinary and unlike anything that had been attempted before in the European Union was that it conducted its deliberations in public in Brussels. The Convention submitted its draft Treaty establishing a Constitution for Europe to the European Council in July 2003.

But do public deliberations necessarily make the work of the Convention deliberative?[48] Andreas Maurer (2003) argues that the Convention method is a better alternative to intergovernmental conferences (IGCs) for preparing and publicly presenting a blueprint for fundamental reforms of the Union. More specifically, the Convention working methods rely on consensus-building, which makes the Convention superior to the IGC because of its connections to deliberative democracy. Its distinctive characteristics, which are also its deliberative democratic merits, are participative forms of deliberation, the inclusion of minority positions and views, the establishment of an open forum for parliamentary discourse and the incorporation of national parliaments from an early stage of the work. From these elements, Maurer draws the conclusion that the Convention method has great potential to become a future model for a more democratically enhanced set-up in the EU context.[49] A controversial issue, however, is whether the Convention deliberated sincerely or whether it merely negotiated from fixed national positions. Bohman (2006), for instance, sees no genuine indication of deliberative or popular legitimacy in the Convention discussions and argues that the source of the legitimacy of the Convention was purely intergovernmental.[50] The subsequent

47 See Lombardo, 2007, p 158.

48 The Convention method was first tried in the autumn of 1999, when work on the Convention on the Charter of Fundamental Rights commenced. A crucial difference between this earlier Convention and the 2002 Convention was that only the latter included consultation of civil society. See Karolewski, 2011, p 68.

49 Maurer, 2003. See also Eriksen, 2006, pp 22–4, and Fossum and Menéndez, 2005. For a more critical view of the real influence of civil society, see de Búrca and Walker, 2003, p 395, and Lombardo, 2007, pp 154–5.

50 Bohman, 2006, p 218.

failure of the Constitutional Treaty in national referenda has been considered a failure of the Convention method too, and one commentator considers the rejections 'a salutary lesson in the difficulty of designing governance mechanisms that are perceived to be legitimate'.[51] Doubts about the true commitment and sincerity of participants (that is, how to distinguish arguing from bargaining) are an endless source of controversy in deliberative democratic theory,[52] and whilst I do not see reasons to engage with that discussion here, one thing should be noted: generally speaking, as a mode of decision making intergovernmentalism is not incompatible with certain ideals of deliberative democracy, such as the force of the better argument. Intergovernmental co-operation – in particular, EU foreign policy – is sometimes characterised by 'hard' bargaining that results in a compromise between big Member States. However, research suggests that big states sometimes acquire entirely new preferences or modify existing ones 'as a result of "well" argued proposals from smaller states, ie that learning takes place'.[53] The case study on the basis of which the suggestion was made related to the foreign policy initiative called the 'Northern Dimension' proposed by Finland in 1997. That policy initiative was later included as part of the European Union's external relations.

The second group of arguments, which provides my focus here, grows out of an appreciation of the more general limits of the state's regulatory capacity and suggests preliminary, yet concrete, analyses as to how go about a deliberative mode in ordinary law-making outside constitution-building. The first example is given by Joerges and Neyer (1997), whose influential study anatomised what they called 'deliberative supranationalism' in the context of comitology. Employing the Habermasian notion of deliberative democracy and complemented by constructive analysis from political science, they attempted to show how national and supranational officials deliberate with a view to finding a common solution; hence the name 'deliberative supranationalism'.[54] Here, deliberation constitutes a co-ordination mechanism, which contributes to rational problem-solving and, by providing solutions to shared problems, enhances the legitimacy of political integration as a whole.[55] The legitimacy argument that Joerges and Neyer put forward is that the comitology procedure enjoys a special kind of legitimacy that results from the fact that the procedure allows experts and other interest groups to express their views on certain policy matters. For many commentators, however, the evidence of deliberation is neither sufficient nor definitive: they are all deeply

51 Colin Scott, 2009, p 171. Note also that the Lisbon Treaty, which in essence builds on the provisions of the failed Treaty, was prepared and finalised 'in diplomatic negotiations behind closed doors, with little possibility for input by national parliaments or civil society': Curtin, 2009, p 16.

52 Føllesdal, 2007, p 329.

53 Romsloe, 2005, p 23. For deliberative intergovernmentalism in EU foreign and security policies, see Puetter, 2012.

54 Joerges and Neyer, 1997. See also Joerges, 2006.

55 This argument has subsequently come to be associated with Erik Eriksen, who embodies it in his numerous articles. See, eg, Eriksen, 2000, and Eriksen, 2006.

troubled by the fact that committees deliberate in the shadow of Member States, being constrained by the vested interests of their national governments, and thus unable to genuinely discuss with and learn from others. In addition to these institutional constraints, others have expressed concerns about deliberation occurring without any degree of public or popular accountability.[56] Deliberation among 'experts' – meaning scientists, national representatives and Commission officials – does not, as critics emphasise, contribute to realisation of democratic legitimacy in the European Union. Vos (1999) also draws attention to the empirical weakness of deliberative supranationalism: the normative claim is founded on two committees in the field of foodstuffs.[57] Bredt (2011) sums up the critical commentary with some sympathy for the original argument, saying that 'the supranational deliberative theory does not claim to provide genuine democratic legitimacy but a form of supranational legitimacy'.[58]

The second example takes up the advisory bodies in occupational health and safety policy: the EESC, the Advisory Committee on Safety and Health at Work (ACSH),[59] the Social Dialogue, and the European Agency for Safety and Health Protection at Work. In his work, Smismans (2004) set out to demonstrate that functional participation through these bodies can contribute to the legitimacy of European decision making, albeit imperfectly and only as a result of institutional reform. He uses standards of input and output legitimacy, and identifies at least four elements of legitimacy falling into these two categories: representation of socio-economic groups, technical expertise, deliberation and transparency – with 'deliberation' meaning consensual discussion and debate. Each of these four institutions gives a different perspective on the mix of legitimacy elements. For instance, EESC members are appointed to represent socio-economic groups rather than the national interests of their respective countries; accordingly, the mode of working is deliberative – organised with a view to securing consensual outcomes whenever possible. Conversely, ACSH members have a dual mandate: they are both representatives of national trade unions and employer organisations, as well as experts on occupational health and safety. Naturally, ACSH outcomes are derived from an especial mix between science-based consensus and deliberation from representative positions.[60]

These examples of comitology and the advisory bodies in occupational health and safety policy reify the early interest in deliberation by EU legal studies. Against this backdrop, it is understandable that studies have focused on evaluating its chances of survival in the 'squeeze' of the representative model of democracy.

56 Nanz and Steffek, 2004, p 319, fn 13; de la Porte and Nanz, 2004, pp 270–1.

57 Vos, 1999, p 57.

58 Bredt, 2011, p 43.

59 This is a body established in 2003 by Council Decision 2003/C 218/01, comprising members from governments and industrial relations organisations, and advising the Commission on matters in the field of safety and health at work.

60 Smismans, 2004, pp 72–5.

Where, in comitology, a deliberative potential is circumscribed by the interests of the Member States, the EESC instead is admittedly somewhat paradoxically being held to ransom by the sectarian interests of organised civil society. Bignami (2006) asks, in her excellent review of Smismans' work: '[C]an an individual, appointed to a governing body by virtue of his or her membership in a distinct interest organization, both represent a specific socio-economic reality and engage in democratic deliberation?'[61] She continues to assert that the ACSH is something of a special case. In the worst-case scenario, it lives up to the ideals of neither representation nor deliberation. Because its members are expected to find a scientific consensus, they may not be able to represent the interests of their background organisations. Nevertheless, these organisations exert influence upon their members, who cannot then find a common (scientific) understanding on matters of substance.

Now, while governance literature interested in deliberation clearly expands on this nascent work on deliberation, later research differs from earlier research in one important respect: because EU governance is moving away from traditional legal and political institutions, the squeeze of representative institutions (which debilitates the potential of deliberation in the foregoing examples of comitology and occupational health and safety policymaking), although not entirely disappearing, weakens, thus carving out a space for deliberation in new contexts. James Tully (2002) leads the way and his prescription is worth quoting in full:

> [T]he study of practices of democratic deliberation could not be restricted to constitutional essentials and constitutional referenda or to the genres of adversarial reasoning in the traditional legal and political institutions. To test the constitutional and democratic legitimacy of dispersed, overlapping and multi-layered regimes of constitutional democracy it is necessary to study the practices of democratic freedom – the modes of dispute conciliation – in any practice of governance in which those subject to, or affected by it, seek to reignite the members of public autonomy and have an effective say over how their conduct is governed.[62]

2.5 Deliberative new governance?

One of the most common attributes used to describe governance developments is 'deliberative'. Commentators, by and large, agree that new governance reflects a certain deliberative mode.[63] To give a representative example: the Water Framework Directive (WFD) combines 'classic top-down regulatory modes and legally binding requirements with decentralized, bottom-up, participatory and

61 Bignami, 2006, p 445.
62 Tully, 2002, p 219.
63 Scott and Trubek, 2002. See also Sabel and Zeitlin, 2007, and Trubek and Trubek, 2007.

deliberative processes; iterative planning; horizontal networks; stakeholder participation; information pooling; sharing of best practices; and non-binding guidance'.[64] Likewise, 'innovative patterns of deliberation' are found in EU enlargement policy, as well as in the work of the Committee of European Securities Regulators.[65] The latter is a body set up by the Commission as part of 'Level 3' of the so-called 'Lamfalussy Process'. The objective of this Committee is to facilitate co-ordination among securities regulators, to advise the Commission on matters pertaining to its expertise and to assist Member States in implementing EU legislation. Sometimes, deliberative attributes are sought, but are nowhere to be found. The EU regime for genetically modified organisms (GMOs), for instance, is understood to be 'far from reaching any constructive compromise, as well as from the ideals of deliberative decision-making'.[66]

Even this brief recapitulation makes a good case for increasing recognition of deliberation in EU new governance. The OMC, an instrument first envisaged at the Lisbon European Council in March 2000, provides a popular test case. The OMC is a soft policy co-ordination mechanism designed to offer a flexible way in which to address common issues without interfering too much with sensitive areas of national governance capacity and to contribute to learning among, and within, Member States. Learning is encouraged through peer review, which puts practices of deliberation to use. Member States must produce annual national reform programmes (NRPs), and submit them to a process of review by other Member States and EU institutions.[67] The OMC is believed to 'foster convergence on common interest and on some agreed common priorities while respecting national and regional diversities'.[68] Moreover, deliberation can guarantee a form of discipline: what Jacobsson (2004) calls 'the self-discipline following from deliberation, learning and voluntary acceptance of norms'.[69] Nevertheless, the authority and capability of deliberation to bring out a common agenda from a pool of interests and preferences seems highly controversial, at least in empirical terms. Many do indeed claim that Member States are drawn back to, and captured by, their national interests in the event of a sensitive political dilemma. In other words, the force of the better argument falls short of prevailing over national preferences and priorities.[70] Finally, there is inconclusive evidence about the capacity of deliberation to encourage Member States to comply with the policy outcomes of co-ordination processes, and to inflict a sense of guilt and duty on Member States.[71]

64 Trubek and Trubek, 2007, p 12.
65 For enlargement policies, see Tulmets, 2010; for experimentalist securities regulation, see Posner, 2010.
66 Dąbrowska, 2010, p 195 (emphasis omitted).
67 Armstrong and Kilpatrick, 2007, p 664.
68 João Rodrigues, 2001, p 103.
69 Jacobsson, 2004, p 99.
70 Pollack, 2005, pp 42–5.
71 López-Santana, 2006; see also Benz, 2007.

In particular, the OMC's dimensions of transparency, democratic participation, exchange of information and ideas, as well as learning, have given rise to an influential corpus of studies in evaluating it from the perspective of deliberative democracy. Among others, de la Porte and Nanz (2004) analyse the democratic legitimacy of the OMC from normative and empirical perspectives, first introducing the deliberative democratic theory literature, from the review of which they compile a list of normative criteria: transparency, public debate, participation and learning. They then deploy these criteria toward understanding and gauging the democratic quality of the OMC in the areas of employment and pensions. Their empirically robust analysis reveals significant variation in the democratic quality of the OMC between the two policy areas, but, as a whole, they conclude that the OMC does not live up to its own democratic ambitions.[72] Frykman and Mörth (2004), with emphasis also on the institution of the OMC, arrive at a similar conclusion. In their view, EU governance is compatible with the tenets of deliberative democracy, but the promise of democratic legitimacy is not fulfilled.[73] In the summary appended to the edited collection in which their analysis appeared, Mörth writes that:

> [D]emocratic problems in the EU will increase if the gap increases between the formal constitution, based upon a traditional mode of command and control, and the day-to-day activities that are increasingly based on soft law and governance. The former system is democratically legitimate, albeit not without problems, whereas the latter system has a much weaker democratic base, if any.[74]

It is not readily apparent whether she means that the theory of deliberative democracy is weak or that EU governance poorly reflects the ideals of deliberative democracy in practice.

The theory of directly deliberative polyarchy or democratic experimentalism was the first to be serious about the need to develop an approach to deliberation that remains fully aware of both the normative and the empirical realities of forms of EU governance. The theory seeks to construct a model in which local actors are more directly involved in collective problem-solving under some sort of centre that co-ordinates and monitors them, yet resists the desire to determine the detailed content of locally produced solutions. Local (administrative) units are accorded the autonomy to produce their own solutions to problems. In return for that autonomy, lower-level actors then provide higher-level actors with information about their specific aims, as well as about the progress that they are making. Periodic pooling and review of the results provides an opportunity to elaborate standards

72 de la Porte and Nanz, 2004.
73 Frykman and Mörth, 2004, p 160.
74 Mörth, 2004, p 199.

by comparing local achievements, thereby subjecting poor performers to peer review and (re)commending better alternatives.[75]

The theory is 'deliberative' because it employs arguments to 'destabilise' and challenge entrenched practices and received truths, yet at the same time treats its own solutions as provisional. It is 'directly deliberative' because it is interested in actors using tried-and-tested knowledge to produce alternative solutions and strategies. Finally, it is 'polyarchic' because it creates a system in which local actors with similar problems can learn from each other, set standards and monitor their observance. Its ramifications for democratic legitimacy are radical. According to Sabel and Simon (2006), innovations of local-level governance will inevitably precede and result in 'an explosion', after which 'discussion of the democratic legitimacy of new governance can no longer be deferred'; the democratic legitimacy of the peer review process (which represents a baseline governance model in democratic experimentalism) is found 'within the review processes themselves'. Consequently, legitimacy will come to depend on the transparency of review processes and, 'more ambitiously, on their openness to directly deliberative participation by affected stakeholders'.[76] This prophecy is empirically believable, for major regulatory innovations are animated by a concern to increase the extent to which stakeholders can participate or be included. Many governance mechanisms embrace a variety of actors, and participation is one of the attributes most often associated (alongside deliberation) with governance structures.[77] Participation is viewed positively because it adds to a variety of views and thus increases the richness of solutions. Moreover, participation facilitates the idea of locality in terms of solving problems and reviewing them amongst peers.[78] Virtues of participation are endorsed even in the absence of a collective or ethnic community. Modes of governance do not usually limit participation to nationals, and by reaching towards civil society organisations over borders, these new instruments are bound to break the link between common identity and participation.[79] Affected stakeholders are, through the exercise of their common reason, capable of solving significant mutual problems and bringing their local reasoning at large to bear directly on decision making involving contested regulatory issues.

Although well in tune with EU policy directions and priorities, the theory has its critics as well. For instance, Somek (2010a) views deliberative and experimentalist policymaking with suspicion, arguing that it 'represents, paradoxically, a disembodied form of democracy. Rationality matters more than participation.

75 Cohen and Sabel, 1997; also Gerstenberg and Sabel, 2002. Most recently, see Sabel and Zeitlin, 2010, pp 5–6.

76 Sabel and Simon, 2006, pp 402–3.

77 Scott and Trubek, 2002, p 6.

78 Borrás and Jacobsson, 2004, p 200.

79 Smismans, 2007, p 607. See also Flyvbjerg, 1998. In a global governance context, see Nanz and Steffek, 2004.

The latter is desirable only if, and insofar as, it is conducive to the former.'[80] Smismans (2010), on the other hand, rejects democratic experimentalism because its potential rests on a degree of participation that simply 'won't happen' in the European Union. According to Smismans, deliberation does not flow organically and inexorably between stakeholders, but 'tends naturally to evolve among functional actors within subsystems'.[81] His argument seems to miss the mark to a certain extent, though: a 'local' actor in democratic experimentalism does not have to be the tiniest environmental association imaginable – that is, local in a strictly geographical sense – but could be a nation-state, or a neighbourhood association, or anything in between. The term 'local' is determined in reference to the 'new centre', a central unit that co-ordinates and monitors activities by collecting information, ensuring due reflection and learning, formulating benchmarks and organising monitoring in case of problems.[82]

The discussion around the 'new centre' relates to the criticism levelled against democratic experimentalism as having failed to elaborate the link between direct forms of participation and representative democracy.[83] Armstrong (2006) puts the problem in a wider context by contending that 'it is unclear how much of the architecture of "traditional democratic constitutionalism" is presupposed and how much remains once experimental democracy takes hold'.[84] There appears to be confusion as to how 'alternative' democratic experimentalism really is and whether it has actually claimed to be an alternative to 'traditionalism'. In my view, however, this indeterminacy may in practice be what the scholars of experimentalism intended. I think it is a pragmatic choice, on the one hand, but a deliberate preference, on the other. Only by leaving the contours of experimentalism open is it possible to analyse its evolving manifestations in practice and, perhaps most importantly, to understand how traditional and experimental constitutionalism transform each other (the relationship between adjudication and new governance being one of the questions to be implied here).

Unlike in the once-fashionable 'shadow of hierarchy' argument, the centre does not necessarily refer to the Commission or other Brussels-based bureaucrats. The idea of this older centralisation literature was that softer regulatory mechanisms could work in so far as they are supported by the Commission, which was accordingly tasked with developing new managerial skills and capacities.[85] Instead, democratic experimentalism builds on peer review. Practices of peer review do not rely in every instance on the same actor at the centre and may locate the centre at the same time in multiple locations: in EU chemicals regulation, for instance, the

80 Somek, 2010a, p 343.
81 Smismans, 2010, p 182.
82 For the original formulation, see Gerstenberg and Sabel, 2002. See also Karkkainen, 2006, p 315.
83 See Magnette, 2006, and Smismans, 2010.
84 Armstrong, 2006, p 62.
85 Among others, see Héritier, 2002, and Lenschow, 2007, p 422.

new centre would be projected on the European Chemicals Agency (ECHA), whilst in the WFD it is for the Common Implementation Strategy (CIS) to play the role of the new centre. The natural consequence of this fluidity in determining the centre is that a participant is not destined to be eternally local or, conversely, non-local. Further, a participant is understood more generically, and beyond certain social and geographical capacities. This reflects the development in which 'elected and nonelected government officers, nongovernmental organizations, political parties, interest groups, policy entrepreneurs, "epistemic communities", and "networks" are all relevant actors in the decision-making that produce government action'.[86]

Smismans' criticism, however, reveals an interesting and more generally noteworthy difference between the (US-dominated) political theory of deliberation and EU deliberation analyses. Thus far, almost all analyses among the former group, both normative and empirical, have been interested in deliberation among ordinary citizens (so-called 'town hall deliberation') rather than that among politicians or administrators, hence avoiding the problems that relate to deliberations intended to reach a decision.[87] This stands in direct opposition to EU deliberation research, which has acquired a life of its own. As already indicated, EU scholars interested in deliberation have primarily investigated deliberation by politicians and experts in the contexts of comitology and the OMC, which can easily be depicted as being amongst the most elitist and technocratic forms of EU governance.[88] The findings are therefore for the most part foreseeable, and the major body of research could be summarised as follows: EU governance has grown detached from domains of everyday morality and lay politics, and technocratic decision making is seen as faceless and alienating to citizens. The following observation of Möllers (2006) neatly captures the essence of a visceral distrust of deliberation: '[The] identification of deliberation with democracy is not democratic but elitist.'[89]

The turn taken by many scholars of EU deliberation can be explained by the fact that most scholars are indebted to Habermas. The Habermasian type of deliberation envisions disinterested participants; this means that they do not have a special stake (or even a self-serving interest) in the outcome of deliberations. For instance, participants in the discussion over the Union's constitutional future or in the abortion argument can generally (with caveats, of course) be conceived of as having no particular or personal interest in the outcome of deliberations. On the contrary, deliberation in new governance structures is a smaller scale, niche deliberation and assumes participants to have interests that matter, specifically and

86 Shapiro, 2001, p 369. Note, though, that this quotation is meant to criticise governance, not to commend it.

87 Thompson, 2008, p 503.

88 One of the early exceptions is Curtin, 1999. Her later article is another rare examination of the conditions of deliberation in the civil society context: Curtin, 2006.

89 Möllers, 2006, p 321.

individually, to them. This new configuration is particularly troublesome for Habermas, because his theory leaves out from decision making a whole bunch of potential interests. In particular, Habermas' 'theory distinguishes between political institutions (or decision-making bodies) and the broader, decentred public sphere'.[90] This model does not allow stakeholders or civil society organisations to be placed as participants '*within* governance regimes';[91] EU governance instead places participants, who are not indifferent to or unconcerned with the result of deliberations, as part of decision-making structures. With deliberation by interested parties, certain problems disappear or lessen,[92] whilst others emerge afresh or become more pressing. Here, I will mention one issue only briefly: when each governance regime creates its participants and the interests at stake construct a stakeholder, general rules about participation are difficult to devise. When the public cannot generally be defined in contrast to political bodies or decision-making institutions, the issue of participation is an ad hoc problem, requiring case-by-case problem-solving. This means that solutions also become provisional, and the risk arises that civil society and non-organised interests, as well as reviewing judges, may be paralysed and disillusioned by a deluge of complaints aimed at proving an interest.

It was not until democratic experimentalism that a more 'interested' conception of participation became entrenched as part of EU deliberation studies and was widely taken up. However, all of these studies analysed have exhibited some confusion about the role of participation. One indication is the habit of some scholars to speak of 'participatory' and 'deliberative' democracy in the same sentence, virtually conflating the two.[93] Another is that multiple aims are sought after through participation and that possible tensions are frequently downplayed. In this respect, Fisher (2001) makes an essentially similar argument. She submits that 'while the role of private actors may be favoured by some because of deregulatory ideology . . . others, such as those supporting discourse theories, favour it because of the way it transforms and strengthens public authority'.[94] As a result, the role that private actors play is not 'as straightforward as the "new" approach suggests . . .'.[95]

90 Nanz and Steffek, 2004, p 321 (emphasis original). For application of Habermas to EU governance, see also Armstrong, 2006.
91 Nanz and Steffek, 2004, p 321 (emphasis original).
92 For instance, the risk of ideological domination (ie that deliberation makes participants adopt views that are not in their best interests) is reduced, rational apathy (meaning that the voter declines to vote on the grounds that he or she does not think that his or her voice matters) is less of a problem, time constraints may be alleviated (assuming that interests help people to formulate opinions and make decisions more swiftly) and the persistent question of self-interest skewing the deliberative process disappears because each participant is a stakeholder (although the problems of resources and information, and their fair division, still persist).
93 For instance, see Benz, 2007, p 514.
94 Fisher, 2001, pp 22–3.
95 Ibid.

More research is sorely needed – not only because democratic experimentalism seems vulnerable to a host of misunderstandings and representations, at least in so far as participation is concerned, but also because it is in this area that the most difficult questions for the EU courts emerge. It seems credible to expect 'the growth of a European administrative law of rule-making' that encompasses the concepts of participation, governance and deliberation.[96] Because the EU courts are an important – indeed, essential – part of this emerging corpus of EU administrative law, the incorporation of participation and deliberation into EU administrative law involves significant consequences for the EU courts. Developments in EU new governance indeed augur 'practical and normative problems for law in constitutional and administrative law terms'.[97] Wilkinson (2007), for one, asks whether advances in practices of participation inevitably take us back 'to a traditional model of law or judicial review for its enforcement'.[98] How should law approach conflicts deriving from EU new governance? Most importantly of all: who is to decide the standards by which participants are included or kept outside, and what are those standards like? Sabel and Simon (2006) recognise the 'critical' importance of these questions, arguing that they will ultimately 'require us to rethink the very ideas of democracy on which our inveterate ideas of accountability are founded'.[99]

2.6 Conclusion

New governance is a relatively new term, which, in the last 15 years, has provided a home for an impressive volume of studies exploring changes to ways of governing in the European Union. Although short of a commonly accepted definition – or perhaps for that very reason – new governance has successfully continued to explore and speculate upon where the Union is going. Governance research has been an eye-opening exercise (at least if the degree of opposition and scepticism is any guide), in particular for lawyers who have at least had to tolerate and then to account for non-legal processes and non-established actors shaping spaces that the lawyers have traditionally regarded as being shielded from too much external interference and from other nuisances created by political experimentation. From the start, the new governance project has been a normative one, and studies evaluating the democratic legitimacy of forms of new governance are multiple and manifold. EU new governance is sometimes seen as undemocratic, or a threat to

96 Shapiro, 2004, p 257.

97 Armstrong, 1998, p 170. However, he later warns again of crisis-mongering, saying that '[t]he earlier empirical analysis of patterns of governance in the EU . . . hardly gives cause to believe we are witnessing a crisis in how we think and do law': Armstrong, 2011, p 34.

98 Wilkinson, 2007, p 694.

99 Sabel and Simon, 2006, p 403. Held, 2002, p 27, writes: '[I]f people are marginalized or fall outside this framework, they are disadvantaged not primarily because they have less than others in this instance, but because they can participate less in the process and institutions that govern their lives.'

a democratic self-governing people, undermining real commitment to the idea of governing by the people. Despite the fact of considerable theoretical imprecision about democratic ideals, it is convenient to conclude that classical accounts of representative democracy no longer capture developments in EU governance. As a result, deliberation has then appeared as an instructive opportunity to rethink and reimagine the democratic legitimacy of both the European Union and its governance processes. Despite increased interest in deliberation, there is also a noticeable reluctance – clearly related to a genuine uncertainty that surrounds the theory itself – to abandon the vocabulary of representative democracy and to adopt that of deliberative democratic. Whilst that sentiment is fully endorsed in this book, the diminishing ability of the representative model to make sense of EU governance justifies at least a sincere consideration of other interpretative frameworks for alternative and complementary democratic justifications.

In the more limited context of current EU governance theory, it is argued that the whole governance discourse is based on endorsement and validation of the concepts of participation and deliberation. Furthermore, I have quoted observations from several sources that note the concrete and practical problems that this evolution poses for EU constitutional and administrative law, and which places EU governance theory in a privileged position for providing guidance. The general overview of this discussion nevertheless shows that, since it has taken place at some distance from the underlying democratic theory of deliberation, it may have promoted confusion rather than clarification of the standards involved. This is surely a cogent reason to convince those who may be dithering over whether or not it is necessary to analyse deliberative democracy – something to which I intend to turn right now.

Chapter 3

Deliberative democracy in the European Union

3.1 The deliberative democracy paradigm: Mapping out the ground

Deliberative democracy has received more attention than any other form of contemporary democratic theory in recent years.[1] Its form and content are continuously disputed, and no single definition that would be acceptable to all, or which would do justice to the enormous variety of different views, seems feasible or likely.[2] Moreover, it seems apt to observe that different theories of deliberative democracy address substantially different questions of public decision making: some understand deliberative democracy as a way in which to form public opinion through open discussion; others, as a way in which to ensure that elections, parliamentary discussions, or debates within the judiciary or regulatory agencies are characterised by, and imbued with, reasoning; yet others, as a way in which to ensure that citizens' reasoning is genuinely connected to decision making on common concerns. Nevertheless, all scholars of deliberative democracy arguably share the following key objective: to move from bargaining and interest aggregation to mutual reason-giving by equal citizens. Rather than engaging in the politics of self-interest and power games, deliberative democrats favour an ambitious mode of politics in which 'citizens address public problems by reasoning together about how best to solve them'.[3]

Like most political theories, deliberative theory can also best be understood in terms of what it is *not*. Deliberative democracy grew out of dissatisfaction with two anti-populist theories, elitist and economic, which were highly influential up to the 1970s. The *elitist* theory of democracy was based on the findings of the political sociology of its time, which understood citizens in modern democracies to be

1 The term was first used by Joseph Bessette in 1980, when referring to a particular conception of US constitutional democracy. See Bessette, 1980, pp 102–16. For a historical argument that deliberation is a revival not an innovation, see Elster, 1998, pp 1–5.

2 Variations of deliberative democracy are discussed under headings such as 'associative democracy' (see Hirst, 1994), 'post-sovereign global governance' (see Scholte, 2000, pp 256–73), or 'reflexive democracy' (see Barnett, 1996, pp 157–75).

3 Cohen and Fung, 2004, p 24.

apathetic and manipulable. The main theorist of this school, Joseph Schumpeter, famously contended that decision making was best entrusted to the political elite, hence limiting democracy to the ability of citizens to periodically turn decision makers out of office. The *economic* theory of democracy, meanwhile, focused on the institution of voting. As the name readily suggests, it viewed voting as comparable to transactions such as buying and selling. Accordingly, the theory perceived voters as consumers, democracy as a marketplace and voting as a means to aggregate preferences. Both theories shared a view of citizens as passive consumers, who contributed to public decision making primarily through voting, and underlined the nature of the political process as a competition towards some given ends.[4]

With elitist and economic theories going out of fashion, aggregative democracy took their place as a target against which the critique of deliberative democracy has been levelled and against which deliberative democracy has reacted by providing an alternative agenda for political decision making.[5] Aggregative democracy usually denotes a mode of decision making that seeks, first, to articulate preferences and, second, to aggregate them. Preferences are aggregated through voting, which determines what policies are implemented. Aggregative democracy is a theoretical model and cannot be found implemented in any political system. However, it is usually liberalism, or liberal theories more broadly, which are alleged to epitomise many of the worst traits of aggregative democracy. For instance, in the view of Baber and Bartlett (2009), theories of deliberative democracy have been 'spawned by a growing realization that contemporary liberalism has lost something of its democratic character'.[6] Even in those arguments that do not refer explicitly to aggregative democracy, the underlying idea is that liberal democracy is not ambitious enough, because it settles for the conventional practices of aggregative democracy.[7]

This is not to say that deliberation has no role to play in liberal democratic thinking: no variant of democratic theory seems to do without discussion and reasoning. For instance, liberal social contract theory, which embodies much of contemporary European liberal thinking, takes deliberation as a means of enhancing the acceptability of decision making by pooling information, and testing arguments and opinions.[8] Likewise, for republican theory, the public interest that ultimately guides decision making is constituted and articulated in those arguments that are best supported by public reasoning. Proposals evolve through discussion and reflection into a constituency's common decision. When criticising interest group bargaining, Pettit (1998) writes that if society 'is to hold out any

4 Bohman and Rehg, 1997, pp x–xiii, and Dowding, Goodin and Pateman, 2004, p 2.

5 Bohman, 1998, p 400; Thompson, 2008, p 498; Weale, 2004, p 80.

6 Baber and Bartlett, 2009, p 11. See also Dryzek, 2000.

7 Admittedly, controversies persist as to whether 'liberal' is defined in a particularly narrow, or even misleading, way to fit the role given to it by deliberative democracy: see Dryzek and List, 2003.

8 Bellamy and Attucci, 2009; Bredt, 2011.

chance of avoiding domination, the political system must come to represent a rule of reasons, and the democracy come to display a deliberative rather than a bargaining character'.[9]

Despite the influential role that deliberation has come to play in recent years in shaping and altering preferences in search of a political compromise across the whole spectrum of modern political thought, deliberation as part of contemporary liberal democratic thinking seems nonetheless to face serious problems and challenges. These involve the urgent task of updating existing decision-making bodies to incorporate pragmatic benefits and new actors of deliberation. Dryzek (2000), for one, has criticised those who understand representative institutions and the legal system of a liberal democratic state to be the home of political deliberation. Whilst there is 'nothing intrinsically wrong' in establishing deliberation in those arenas, the risk is that deliberation may become increasingly tied to a thin conception of democracy, 'growing ever thinner in light of the constraints that the capitalist market economy imposes upon effective state democracy'.[10] Another problem with the concept that so many normative theories deploy and which has become part of everyday political vocabulary, with few really articulating what it actually denotes, is that it can be defined and operationalised in multiple, and yet mutually conflicting, ways. With this, however, we begin to understand what makes deliberative democracy so strong: deliberation, in deliberative democracy, is not associated with a particular organisation, such as a legislative assembly, but understood as a legitimating principle.[11] Because of its focus on legitimacy, deliberation does not limit itself to certain types of institution or forms of political action. Deliberation does not rule out bargaining, voting or advocacy, nor does it promote only inclusive forms of governance. Nino (1996) explains that no particular institution is more democratic than any other, but that their epistemic reliability differs. The epistemic value of democracy arises out of the process of discussion and debate in general, not from any specific institution or decision.[12] In a situation in which making and implementing public decisions is increasingly complex, theories of deliberative democracy are capable of acknowledging and sustaining institutional arrangements, 'involving a variety of decision rules and the dispersal of sovereign power between different bodies and diverse locations' that appear elusive to traditional political institutions of representative government.[13]

In this chapter, I aim to establish an understanding of deliberation that resonates with the need to account for a multiplicity of institutional arrangements and for new realities of decision making. It is suggested that three key themes of deliberative

9 See Pettit, 1998, p 95.

10 Dryzek, 2000, p 3. His solution is to reinforce the critical theory roots of deliberative democracy. In this way, deliberative democracy could maintain its distance from (liberal) state construction and the public sphere could be re-emphasised as a main source of democratic critique.

11 Curtin, 2006, p 135; Eriksen, 2000, p 48; Eriksen and Fossum, 2000, p 19.

12 Nino, 1996, pp 128–9.

13 Bellamy and Castiglione, 2000, p 65.

democracy may be identified: reason-giving, the problem-solving orientation and responsive participation. Several deliberative democrats recognise these themes (broadly conceived) as necessary and relevant to generate outcomes typically associated with deliberative forms of democracy. Once these core themes have been identified, an attempt is made at operationalising those concepts. This involves describing the elements that make up each core theme, identifying the objections to which they give rise, and finally relating them to pragmatic conditions. Discussion paves the way for the second aim: identifying benchmarks for the courts when reviewing EU new governance. My suggestion for a set of benchmarks is grouped under the term 'iterated deliberation', which, as my argument goes, opens up new opportunities to hold a variety of actors to account for progress towards more transparent, inclusive and effective forms of governance in the European Union.

3.2 Three constitutive elements of deliberation: A functional conception of deliberation?

Deliberation is not a well-defined concept despite the massive amounts of conceptualisations and elucidations available. Indeed, a wealth of definitions has led one scholar to observe that 'there are as many definitions of deliberation as there are theorists',[14] albeit that numerous similarities are observable among these definitions. However, this fact of 'deliberative pluralism' should not lead us to conclude that the concept is unworkable.

Any normative theory assumes moral and ethical commitments from a researcher: some attitudes and actions need to be preferred or prioritised over other behaviours and outcomes. This means that deliberative democracy is normatively attractive because it is perceived as instrumental to the recognition and protection of certain values and outcomes in democratic societies.[15] For instance, deliberation is espoused on at least four grounds. First, it imparts information: no single individual can envisage and foresee the range of issues, or possess all of the information relevant to making a decision affecting several people. Second, those who favour deliberative democracy argue for decision making that aims to 'get factual beliefs right',[16] to pool diverse opinions, and to amass information for reflection and comparison. The third advantage is found in

14 Mutz, 2008, p 525. Baber and Bartlett, 2009, p 14, offer one categorisation of approaches to deliberative democracy: public reason was identified by Rawls, Habermasian ideal discourse theory and 'full liberalism', as discussed and developed by Bohman, Gutmann and Thompson; building a bridge between Rawls and Habermas, full liberalists approach deliberation from a standpoint that renders deliberation 'feasible in a complex and normatively fragmented society'. For a similar argument, see Everson and Eisner, 2007, p 28. Although I discuss approaches to deliberative democracy with an open mind, it is the full liberalism variant of deliberative democracy that provides deliberative arguments for this book.

15 Mutz, 2008, p 523.

16 Elster, 1998, p 9.

the way in which deliberation assists in controlling 'the emotional factors', and fourth, deliberation reduces the possibility of manipulation of information and abuse of the political agenda.[17] For at least these reasons, deliberation is considered the best way in which to solve common problems because these features increase the likelihood of arriving at a better outcome. Deliberative democracy theorists also value certain kinds of outcomes and attitudes. These involve, for example, more public-spirited views, a more enlightened citizenry, a deeper appreciation of the reasons for public disagreements, more reason-based decisions, a greater inclination to reach a compromise, or some sort of consensual outcome, and a stronger commitment to political decision making.[18]

Accordingly, three fundamental elements appear to offer preliminary conceptual criteria identifying what is indispensable for a practice to generate the desired outcomes and thus to qualify as deliberation.[19]

1 The *reason-giving requirement* ensures that arguments are weighed on their merits, the result being more reason-based decisions and a greater understanding of the reasons for public disagreements.
2 A *problem-solving orientation* contributes to more public-spirited attitudes and to willingness to compromise.
3 *Responsive participation* guarantees more informed citizens, as well as more informed decisions and a stronger interest in political decision making.

Together, these elements render political decision making deliberative, and enhance the overall quality and legitimacy of decision making. Admittedly, one or more of these elements, and to what values they contribute, can be contested. Others may surely be added to the list. But, above all, these three elements are the baseline 'normative assumptions' that constitute the process of deliberation: a process in which people give and consider reasons in order to come up with collective and legitimate answers to economic and social problems.[20] However, once we depart from the world of pure concepts, things become more complicated. Although deliberative theorists may well all adhere to reason-giving and participation as normative propositions, they hold different conceptions of the individual and the state, or have diverging views concerning conflicts over moral principles. As a result, they 'differ to some extent on what counts as an adequate reason, how extensive the reason-giving forum should be, whether procedural norms are sufficient, and the desirability of consensus as a goal'.[21]

Let me offer an example: deliberative democrats can be divided into two groups, depending on whether deliberation is favoured because of its propensity to result

17 Martí, 2006, pp 42–3. See also Bohman, 1998, p 411; Elster, 1998, p 11.
18 Mutz, 2008, p 523.
19 For analytical elements in the study of deliberation, see Thompson, 2008, p 501.
20 Bohman, 1996, p 15.
21 Thompson, 2008, p 498.

in more reliable and 'better' outcomes (the *epistemic* justification for deliberation), or because of its reliance on impartial procedures (the *intrinsic* justification for democracy). For intrinsic justification, the significance of deliberation is not based, in the first instance, on its capacity to produce better quality decisions, but on its ability to emulate as closely as possible the intrinsic standard of political equality.[22] Even as factitious, the epistemic/intrinsic distinction helps to demonstrate that there exists no single clear understanding of the idea of deliberation and why it is that scholars seem, at times, to be speaking past each other. For others, deliberative democracy is about reflecting the (expert) debates that take place at a distance from the people who are eventually affected by the consequences of policymaking. Deliberation is, even at its best, restrictive and elitist; hence it is strongly misguided or inappropriate to associate deliberation with democratic justifications.[23] Mirroring this 'elitist' argument is the 'idealistic' argument. Efforts to include people, so the critics argue, are not enough. If anything, it is romantic and naive to think that people would be willing to gauge democratic decision making solely by reference to inclusiveness. Although inclusiveness provides a measure against which procedures can be compared, it does not 'fully exploit the critical idea of doing better'.[24]

This and many other similar differences in conceptions and value judgements are real and cannot (or should not) be eliminated. But it also means that I see little use – at least for present purposes – in debating these issues as abstract conceptions in general. Discussion about the epistemic and intrinsic virtues of deliberation is 'a particular case of the more general tension between procedure and substance in their role as values relevant to characterize [*sic*] legitimacy'.[25] And it is a question for which no definite solution exists; instead, concrete problems need to be addressed – 'the ultimate test of the fully developed conception of deliberative democracy' being 'practical'.[26] Hence my immediate aim is to move from a theoretical discussion about the elements of deliberation to a more operational account of what they command in the particular institutional setting of EU decision making.[27] Placing the three key elements of deliberation in a more operational setting exposes a great deal of conceptual confusion over what deliberation is and what it is expected to be, and how 'the conditions that promote some values of deliberative democracy may undermine other values, including some that deliberative democrats favor'.[28] This is what Thompson (2008) calls 'the

22 Eriksen, 2006, p 6; Martí, 2006, p 35.

23 Möllers, 2006, p 321; Weiler, 1999, pp 339 and 347.

24 Schmalz-Bruns, 2007, p 285.

25 Martí, 2006, p 37.

26 Bohman and Rehg, 1997, p xxvii.

27 This should also give the lie to persistent accusations that deliberative democracy is unrealistic and impractical, and 'more appropriate to university seminars and scientific communities than to the general public': Bohman, 1996, p 3. He observes elsewhere that these accusations seem to 'confuse deliberative democracy with rule by face-to-face assemblies . . .': Bohman, 1998, p 418.

28 See Thompson, 2008, p 500.

internal conflicts problem'. Studying elements of deliberation in actual decision-making conditions should respond to his call to stay close to the fundamental problem that deliberative democracy addresses: how citizens can collectively reach a decision that is legitimate despite reasonable agreement.[29] Although the above core elements can be disputed on a general level, their appropriateness is strengthened by their relevance to EU governance and the revisable framework that they provide for concrete deliberations.[30] Finally, this context-based approach to deliberation has the benefit of pointing tentatively in the direction of a set of benchmarks for the courts to use while reviewing forms of EU governance from a deliberative democracy perspective.

3.2.1 The reason-giving requirement

The most important characteristic of deliberation is the 'reason-giving requirement'. I use the term to describe and highlight the importance of presenting and responding to reasons intended to justify a political outcome. To deliberate is to give reasons that (one thinks) others will accept and, respectively, to interrogate and test one another's judgements and reasoning. Deliberative democrats believe that any decision that citizens or officials take must be based on reasons that can be justified to the people upon whom that decision will be imposed.[31] Reasons must be given 'not only about procedures and principles, but also about the concrete application of principles to particular cases'.[32] This process of offering reasons and interrogating them has an epistemic power, as intimated in the section above. This means that decisions are more likely to be right and correct if people are required to articulate and provide reasons for the arguments that they hold.

But what does it mean to offer a reason for something? Should some kinds of reasons be ruled out in advance and not be allowed in public discussion? Rather than determining *a priori* what reason stipulates, most theorists acknowledge that prejudices and biases will not simply disappear when prevented from playing a part in the discussion; instead, such theorists argue that 'we should rely as far as possible on mechanisms endogenous to deliberation itself' as a way in which to inculcate civility and reciprocity.[33] Elster (1998) speaks of the 'civilising force of hypocrisy', by which he means that participation in discussions makes participants present their selfish claims as having something to do with merit or legitimacy.[34] Despite the hypocritical nature of these arguments, they 'may lead to making

29 Ibid.
30 So far, the best application of deliberative ideals to the European Union is by Cohen and Sabel, 1997.
31 Gutmann and Thompson, 2004, p 3.
32 Cheneval, 2006, p 168.
33 Ibid, p 169.
34 Elster, 1998, p 12.

concessions to the general interest or to the interests of other groups'.[35] But, in reality, the scope of reason-based argument is somewhat narrower. Deliberative democrats specify a set of commitments to be in place in deliberation, and those commitments (in)directly qualify an act of offering reason. For instance, Gutmann and Thompson (2004) have outlined two broader principles that rule out biased, racist or otherwise prejudiced arguments. They argue that reasons have to be generally accessible and mutually acceptable.[36] For a reason to be *accessible*, it must be given in a public place, and its substantive content must be understandable to all and thus available to criticism from anyone's point of view; for a reason to be *mutually acceptable*, it should appeal to 'principles that individuals who are trying to find fair terms of cooperation cannot reasonably reject'.[37] The latter now means that the requirement of reason-giving is not only about firing off reasons to others, even though they are likely to accept them; reason must also constitute a *justification*.[38] Consequently, the aim of deliberation is not to identify the epistemically best decisions, but rather the best among those that can obtain the free and reasoned assent of the parties to deliberation – that is, rather than pursuing epistemically correct reasons, we should opt for reasons justifiable to others.[39] In order not to raise the bar too high, it is nevertheless important to remember that a reason that someone puts forward does not have to be acceptable to other people in particular, but only in general. In other words, acceptability is not a matter of empirically ascertaining whether people do, in fact, accept something.[40] But if we are to accept that reason is not an empirically contingent matter and that we should be satisfied with a kind of generic acceptability, how can we ever be sure that what we present as a reason could be generally held acceptable to others?

The solution to this dilemma is neither easy nor obvious. Indeed, one of the most common arguments against deliberative democracy is precisely that people often do not find one another's arguments persuasive and acceptable. Moreover, some arguments remind us of situations in which civility and reciprocity break down. These are all valid arguments and warnings, but heeding them does not mean that mutual acceptability of reason-giving becomes a redundant concept. Assuming that biased, racist or otherwise prejudiced arguments are debarred, theories of deliberative democracy suggest that the general acceptability of arguments arises from the process of providing and responding to the reasons presented by us and to us. Rather than being straightforwardly a mode of decision making, mutual justifiability implies the role of reflection and critical appraisal.

35 Gambetta, 1998, p 23.
36 Gutmann and Thompson, 2004, p 7.
37 Ibid, p 3.
38 Ibid, p 4; Thompson, 2008, p 498.
39 Lafont, 2006, p 8, with references to Cohen, 1997a, p 73.
40 Besson and Martí, 2006, p xvi.

The value of democracy is discharged in discussion and arguing, not in any particular decision.[41] This surely does not solve the problem of having many reasonable, but conflicting, proposals that cannot all be accommodated at the same time – but it does help us to recognise that the proposals we make and the reasons we give for them are mediated by subjective interests and values. Those interests and values that we all hold will be drawn out (however imperfectly and incompletely) by discussion and reflection. In that way, we gain a more elaborate understanding of how people understand and interpret the different reasons and justifications that they may have in policymaking and decision-making processes. As a result, it may be easier for a minority to accept the outcome if they know what reasons and justifications supported the winning proposition, and if they can be sure that they will have a chance to start the process again – that is, to argue their case again in the future.[42]

3.2.1.1 The 'race to the reasonable bottom'?

In light of these considerations, we will now take up the claim according to which insistence on the mutual acceptability of reason-giving tends to focus on reasons that are not 'demanding enough', for example in terms of equal distribution, hence undermining the 'doing better' power of democracy. Deliberation may better serve the status quo than the cause of thinking more expansively, for insistence on finding mutually acceptable reasons runs the risk of focusing on reasons that are substandard from the point of view of those treated unjustly. So how to determine 'reasonable' or 'mutually acceptable' so as not to favour or privilege 'a minimum conception of political morality'?[43] This dilemma appears to lie at the very heart of the problems of EU governance, particularly so in the Open Method of Coordination (OMC). The OMC, at the same time as it seeks to find common ground and attend to different national concerns, seems to be a forthright instance of bias towards a conception of social justice or environmental fairness that is premised on minimum standards at a very basic level. How might this sort of tendency toward a 'race to the reasonable bottom' in terms of social and environmental protection be rectified? The same issue can be asked in a different way: to what extent is deliberative democracy predicated upon a prevailing framework of rights guarantees or stable political cultures?[44]

41 Nino, 1996, p 129.

42 See also Bohman, 1998, p 407. Note that there is a legal duty to give reasons: Art 296(2) TFEU provides that '[l]egal acts shall state the reasons on which they are based and shall refer to any proposals, initiatives, recommendations, requests or opinions required by the Treaties'. For the duty, see Türk, 2013, p 134. However, the reason-giving requirement advocated here has a potentially wider scope, because it does not apply only to legal acts.

43 Weale, 2004, p 94.

44 For values and their relationship to deliberative democracy, see Bohman, 1998, pp 411–12, and Weale, 2004, p 94. Some argue that, at least in so far as the European Union is concerned, the

Deliberative democracy theories are united in their contention that there is something special about social and economic rights – in particular, about how they are connected to rights of participation. To be fully able to exercise the rights enshrined in the ideal of political participation, they agree, is to have social and economic rights.[45] Yet a relevant distinction should be observed here: social and economic rights are the liberties of the moderns, in contrast to the liberties of the ancients, such as the right to political participation. Modern liberties have no direct or self-evident connection to the conditions of democratic self-government; rather, they are appreciated as a way in which to express certain minimum conditions, so that the political involvement of the most disadvantaged is not hindered in the absence of some fundamental goods. In contrast, the liberties of the ancients are understood as directly contributing to, and safeguarding, the democratic process.[46] As one might expect, this distinction comes with very real consequences. Whenever social rights or environmental protection have distributive implications, conflicts relating to material and other interests are going to arise. In these situations, it may prove difficult to include anything more than fundamental goods with social and economic rights corresponding to the most minimum spending of the national gross domestic product (GDP).

Although we may argue that social rights are necessary to guarantee the moral autonomy of citizens, and subsequently the principle of reason-giving, it is precisely this very practice of reason-giving that may be fatal for thinking expansively about social and economic rights. This would not matter so much if we were able to agree on some sort of substantive standards to guide decision making. Now, the social OMC literature has proposed a role for fundamental rights that comes close to such agreement. The entry into force of the Lisbon Treaty has marked a radical improvement in the legal status of EU fundamental rights by making them legally binding. There is no single correct pattern of how fundamental rights apply in each individual situation, yet a strong case exists for considering fundamental rights as some kind of epistemic standard to guide and monitor policymaking. Fundamental rights would set standards below which a Member State could not fall, and which would trigger review and revision.[47] For instance, de Schutter (2004) maintains that 'a fundamental rights policy led by the Union will serve to avoid a "race to the bottom" '.[48] Fundamental rights may be helpful in determining a minimum requirement (in the abstract), but they do not address the problem of how to ensure that governance makers are not satisfied with insufficiently demanding reasons. De Schutter puts the problem in concrete

commitment to get things done (which is the problem-solving orientation to be discussed later in this chapter) is more crucial than a set of collectively owned values of participants: see, in this respect, Steele, 2001, p 435.

45 Sunstein, 2004, p 228.

46 Cohen, 1997b, p 410.

47 Armstrong, 2008, p 423; de Búrca, 2003, p 834; Smismans, 2005, p 237.

48 de Schutter, 2004, p 26.

terms: '[S]tates are neither encouraged, nor do they have incentives to, *develop* human rights beyond the minimal obligation to respect them.'[49] Fundamental rights are, in addition, vague and ambiguous, and their application in the European Union – where different Member States hold highly divergent views of the appropriate organisation of social and environmental matters – aggravates the situation. Finally, fundamental rights assume 'a significant role for courts in enforcing the content of the legal commitment, while in the new governance . . . the role of courts is at best a residual one'.[50]

In terms of deliberative democracy, we seem to be struggling with the mere impracticality and blind optimism of mutually acceptable reasons: the likelihood that good reasons convince others of their superiority is fairly insubstantial,[51] so it seems that we are destined to accept that bargaining and self-interested politics (the lowest possible standards) win in the end. Whilst it is true that not even long and tedious discussions always convince people to find one another's arguments persuasive and mutually acceptable, this does not mean that the reason-giving requirement is good in theory, but weak in practice. The focus of mutual justifiability on reason-giving and reason-testing creates a suitable and conducive environment in which peer review can take place. Peer review is a strategic element of all governance examples in this book. Now, assuming that peer review, broadly speaking, means the mutual monitoring of one another's performance by all those actors with the same concerns and interests, the commitment to provide reasons and to test those of others (that is, long and tedious discussions) draws out, and contributes to, what we perceive as the 'best argument(s)' of the peer review process.

The EU-level peer review of policymaking seeks to highlight the best approaches and solutions to problems that most Member States share in one form or another. Mutual justifiability generates those best arguments or best approaches that peer review deploys in its scrutiny, monitoring and benchmarking. Assessment by the European Commission of the social OMC – although in spirit perhaps too buoyant – is illustrative of this logic:

> It is recognized as a tool to promote progress in the social sphere and as an innovative instrument in European governance. It has furthered reform, fostered a willingness to cooperate and learn from each other in the search for the best solutions to achieve social progress, without the obligation to define a 'minimum common denominator'.[52]

But surely we can argue that peers can together decide to disregard the 'best approach' that emerges from a reason-giving process and to set the bar as low as

49 Ibid, p 4 (emphasis original).
50 de Búrca, 2005, p 31. See also Armstrong, 2010, p 258.
51 See Neyer, 2010, p 911.
52 European Commission, July 2008, COM(2008) 418, p 3.

possible. Whilst such a concerted effort to disregard the results of reason-giving is less likely to actualise, another problem is more likely and acute. Suppose that some Member States would like to adopt the 'best approach', as has emerged from mutual discussions, but that their initiative is blocked by other Member States with whom a common understanding (a common denominator) must be reached: are we going to observe adoption of a common understanding as promoted by more scrupulous Member States? I return to the issue in Chapter 6, but suffice to say now that reason-giving among peers creates new opportunities and mechanisms for the Member States themselves, the Commission, civil society and possibly also for the EU courts to reverse this kind of 'race to the reasonable bottom'.

3.2.2 The problem-solving character

Deliberation is an intentional activity, and if a decision is to be made deliberatively, this means that reasons are given to other speakers with a view to addressing a certain problem, and that these reasons will then regulate, and have a bearing on, subsequent action. So far, the best formulation of the problem-solving orientation to deliberation is offered by Cohen and Sabel (1997), whose 'directly deliberative polyarchy' is meant to capture a mode of policymaking 'distinguished by the presence of a substantial degree of directly-deliberative problem-solving'.[53] More recently, Rosenberg (2007) has described deliberation as a process in which citizens consider and reconsider 'common conceptions and values in the course of defining specific problems and determining how they should be addressed'.[54]

Problem-solving implies that we need to arrive at a common decision, either by defining the problem or determining how it should be dealt with, or both. This immediately gives rise to an objection associated with deliberative conceptions of democracy more generally: that the problem-solving aspect of deliberation can be trivialised by 'criticising the assumptions about consensus on which it depends'.[55] Translated to the particular context of governance, information generated during deliberation presents a risk: '[T]here is some tendency to assume that comprehensive and widespread information on an issue will eventually lead people to converge on the same positions.'[56] This line of criticism seems, however, to be based on a common (mis)perception about deliberative democracy – namely, that 'there is no consensus among deliberative democrats themselves that consensus should be a goal of deliberation'.[57] To be fair, at least in everyday images of deliberation, it comes across as being associated with

53 Cohen and Sabel, 1997, p 318. The problem-solving character of deliberative democracy has been disputed by Somek, who argues that 'it is a type of democracy where nobody decides . . .': see Somek, 2010a, pp 327 and again at 342–3.

54 Rosenberg, 2007, p 8.

55 Cohen and Sabel, 1997, p 323.

56 Lobel, 2004, p 376.

57 Thompson, 2008, p 508.

consensual forms of decision making. This view of deliberation is underpinned by its explicit rejection of aggregative institutions and interest bargaining. By insisting upon deliberation, which takes sustained reflection on arguments and their mutual justification as its focal point, deliberative democracy arguably orientates towards consensus as the aim of political decision making.[58]

It should be noted that consensus does not follow logically out of a kind of conceptual, much less empirical, necessity from mutually justifiable reason-giving. Certainly, individuals may change their minds and concede to new arguments where they are sufficiently convinced by the superiority of those other arguments. It is important to realise, however, that while this may occur, we should not take it for granted. That participants change their minds if persuaded by others' argumentation means that the *potential* of democracy lies in transformation of preferences rather than in their mere aggregation. But it is quite unrealistic to think that deliberation *normally* culminates in amicable agreement in normatively fragmented societies; indeed, 'few deliberative democrats now think of deliberation independently from voting or bargaining'.[59] Why, then, should we bother to deliberate if electoral interests dictate over considerations of what we see as good and legitimate reasons for a political action?[60] Because this argument is too narrowly focused: a debate may not give rise to modification of the opinions and beliefs of those participating in deliberation, but it can provide them with an opportunity to explicate arguments and to question the justifications provided by others. Sometimes, the aim of deliberative politics is to 'have as much deliberation as possible in the public sphere and then have citizens vote'.[61] Public reasoning and arguing prior to voting may result in fewer divergent views than would otherwise be the case. Moreover, it is sometimes assumed that the outcome of voting by those who are committed to appealing to reasons is likely to be different from the result of voting amongst those who do not share a similar commitment to mutual justification.[62]

Let us now return to the problem-solving orientation of deliberation: the dilemma is not that it assumes consensus, but that it assumes that 'people come to the table with opinions and that they are willing to justify those views publicly in a way that brings people's views closer together rather than increases conflict'.[63] Whilst we have tackled the normative problem about consensus, we seem to be grappling with an empirical problem once again: the empirical outcome of reason-giving (which is the first element of deliberation) appears to be a heightened state of conflict and stagnant diversity. Yet it is precisely the latter that sets

58 Whether the right term would then be 'consensus', 'compromise' or 'co-operation' is open to interpretation: see Bohman and Rehg, 1997, pp xvii–xviii.

59 Bohman, 1998, p 415.

60 For an illustration of the problem, see Cohen and Sabel, 1997, p 321.

61 Bohman, 1998, p 416. See also Cohen, 1998, p 199.

62 See Cohen, 1997a, p 75.

63 Mutz, 2008, p 534.

problem-solving in motion: diversity and conflict are indispensable to deliberation, which integrates the problem-solving character, and 'deliberative decision making is driven at least as much by the discussion and elaboration of difference'.[64] Those interested in concrete and decision-driven experiments of deliberation tend to underline uncertainty too. They note that people have a propensity to resolve differences in opinion when they have a problem to which they need to find an answer (a state of uncertainty exists), rather than when they are merely gathered together to air their views and opinions.[65]

From the empirical point of view, the problem-solving orientation of deliberation (whether arising from disagreement or uncertainty) closely relates to the current evolutionary phase of EU law: the adoption of EU legislation is not an end, but the 'beginning of a long and slow process involving successively lower levels of governance'.[66] Several years of what Baber and Bartlett (2009) call 'entrepreneurial activity' is required from network participants and other actors to fill in the gaps and to make legislation susceptible to implementation.[67] This elaboration of the time frame points to one additional condition on which the problem-solving orientation is predicated: whilst uncertainty and disagreement may encourage participants to enter into deliberation, long-standing commitment to years of work and experimentation can be most reliably explained by taking into account the interests and stakes that the participants hold in decisions.

3.2.2.1 How to represent competing and differing views in consensual decision making?

The problem-solving character should be seen as a key constituent of deliberation because of its potential to take advantage of the conflict and diversity that arise as part of mutual reason-giving. Its argumentative logic may be attractive, but its implications for institutional design are not clear, as is now argued.

Consensual decision making runs the risk of making competing and differing opinions more difficult to represent. Just think of Member States attempting to reach a common and binding understanding on a matter of substance, such as nanomaterials. Agreement will most likely require intense and prolonged discussions, during which Member States will find a solution that is somehow acceptable to all of them. But it seems obvious to us that the more Member States there are, the less likely will be a consensus, or any kind of provisional agreement conventionally expected of deliberation. The first institutional lesson to draw from this hypothetical example is the following: to facilitate a deliberative mode of decision making, it appears helpful to narrow down the number of Member States that are allowed to be participants in deliberations. To take another example that

64 Sabel and Zeitlin, 2007, p 7.
65 Simon, 2006, p 46; Steele, 2001, p 428.
66 Baber and Bartlett, 2009, p 98.
67 Ibid.

is not merely hypothetical: under Arts 154 and 155 TFEU, the European Commission is required to consult management and labour on certain issues relating to social policies that, in the European Union, go by the name of the 'Social Dialogue'. The social partners inform the Commission about their wish to start negotiating an agreement between them, setting in motion a period of nine months during which the social partners are to seek a consensual outcome. Christodoulidis and Dukes (2008) criticise the Social Dialogue for 'the absence of any guarantees of effective bargaining power or representativity', which particularly weakens the position of labour in the process.[68] However, what really informs their critique is the naive assumption of 'constructive', 'undistorted' or 'communicative' dialogue or deliberation leading to consensus as a 'natural end'.[69] On their reading, if participants fail to reach consensus, that failure is prominently attributed to the bad faith of participants or some incidental (as opposed to structural) limitations and restraints.

Since the Social Dialogue is an insulated decision-making process to which access is difficult to obtain – as is well known from the *UEAPME* case[70] – it could be argued to be advantageous for both insiders and outsiders (prospective insiders) to adopt non-confrontational policies and attitudes, and a tone of responsibility, which may then 'legitimate' efforts to retain insider status.[71] The possibility of contestation is not necessarily realised at the national level either. Agreements reached by the social partners can be implemented either via a Council directive, or by the social partners themselves using soft law instruments. Since 2000, the social partners have rather implemented agreements themselves, 'with the instruments of industrial relations available to them at the national level'.[72] On the whole, the Social Dialogue does not seem to be a fitting institutional arrangement with which to deliver a vision of confrontation and contest in EU social policies.

From these examples, what we can infer is that the tendency towards consensus seems to come at much too high a price. The desire to reach a consensus in practical instances of EU governance appears to lead to a logic, intended or unintended, which favours limitations to the number of participants, and which renders non-confrontation as a condition for gaining and keeping insider status. Of course, these are only hypotheses and isolated examples, but I believe that a lesson of a general kind is to be learnt from these particular situations: we can also derive from these examples a recommendation to adopt the idea of consensus as an absence of sustained opposition.

Understanding consensus as an absence of sustained opposition is rooted in the governance of the World Trade Organization (WTO). Its Agreement on Technical

68 Christodoulidis and Dukes, 2008, p 417.
69 Ibid.
70 Case T-135/96 *UEAPME v Council* [1998] ECR II-2335.
71 Lowe and Wilkinson, 2009, p 78, in the context of pressure group strategies.
72 Smismans, 2007, p 612.

Barriers to Trade involves the provision that participating states can take advantage of a rebuttable presumption of WTO compatibility where their own technical restrictions on imports follow international standards. A specialised standardisation body, the International Social and Environmental Accrediting and Labelling Alliance (ISEAL), is an umbrella organisation for eight standard-setting organisations. ISEAL, which operates on a consensual basis, as do most expert bodies, has adopted a code of practice requiring, among other things, two cycles of consultation on the content of suggested standards and a public written reply to each substantive issue that has been touched upon by commentators. Interestingly, it has defined consensus as 'general agreement, characterized by *the absence of sustained opposition* to substantial issues by any important part of the concerned interests and by a process seeking to take into account the views of interested parties'.[73] Certainly, such a definition is open to contestation. Is there any threshold for 'sustained opposition'? What is meant by 'substantial issues'? How are disputes on these issues to be decided? And by whom? Without discussing these issues at length, it should nevertheless be clear that, above all, these are questions that have a more institutional flavour – that is, what is feasible, practical or operational, rather than some fundamental restrictions that derive their strength from some normative theory rejecting the idea of consensus.

This reinterpretation of consensus as an absence of sustained opposition appears highly promising and is actually already available in the European Union. In the context of EU food regulation, a company wishing to place a novel food product on the market must submit a request and a technical dossier to the competent national authority in the Member State in which the novel food is to be introduced.[74] A copy of this request must be submitted to the European Food Safety Authority (EFSA) and the European Commission too. Within three months of receipt of the request, the competent national authority needs to undertake a preliminary scientific assessment, then forward it to other Member States and the Commission. Each Member State and the EFSA then have 60 days in which to give comments or 'reasoned opinions' on the preliminary assessment. In the *absence* of comments or reasoned objections, and if no need appears for additional scientific assessment, the competent national authority must inform the applicant that the product can be placed on the market.[75]

In proposing adoption of a reinterpretation of consensus, the underlying idea is simply to make conflicts visible and hence render them among the factors relevant to problem-solving. Disagreements will not be considered to imply 'bad faith' on the part of participants or be perceived as critical malfunctions of the process, but as precisely what they are: contradictory views to be evaluated, negotiated and managed through jointly agreed rules of procedure. Food regulation in the European Union is but one among many examples that might be given here.

73 Kingsbury, 2009, p 37 (emphasis added).

74 Article 4 of Regulation (EC) No 258/97 concerning novel foods and novel food ingredients.

75 Article 6. For a similar procedure in REACH, see Scott, 2009b, p 70.

In the case study chapters that follow (Chapters 4, 5 and 6), I will consider other examples, which are all highly instructive, demonstrating that consensual decision making can lead to effective problem-solving, even with the involvement of all concerned. A common denominator among these cases is the availability of a basic institutional framework, or some rules of evaluation by means of which confrontation and conflicts are managed and changes implemented. It is important that this basic framework is, or rules of evaluation are, laid down explicitly (formalised) or publicly accessible (the basic framework rules concerning food experts affiliated with the EFSA is a commendable example here). Formalisation not only enhances a governance regime's operational performance, but also helps external (judicial) monitoring.[76] Confrontation and conflict can also be encouraged and made visible by deliberation attempting to take into account the views of interested parties – and not only taking them into account, but also ensuring a written reply to issues mentioned in the comments, as exemplified by the practices of ISEAL. The potential benefits here include fewer tendencies to constrain participation and advances in the epistemic quality of democracy by encouraging the opposition to actively present alternatives to, and criticism of, proposals on the table and to demand that others respond to them.

Finally, focus on conflict staves off the most quixotic expectations placed on information, and the way in which it naturally leads people to gain a shared view of the matter as soon as the situation has been fully unfolded and elucidated. Although increased information may certainly reduce disagreements, it can be used strategically by different participants to deliberation with the result of entrenching the status quo. This leads us to consider the final element of deliberation: participation.

3.2.3 *Responsive participation*

A strong tendency exists to assume that deliberative democracy virtually comes with a participatory approach to politics. True, in a historical perspective, deliberative democracy has emerged from leftist political activism, which rose in opposition to the political climate prevalent in the United States in the 1960s and 70s.[77] In particular, the idea of politics as struggle was increasingly seen to favour bargaining as the main form of political decision making, and the view of citizens as passive consumers was claimed to reduce democracy to periodic voting. And, at least until the end of the 1980s, deliberative democracy was commonly discussed in relation to the paradigm of participatory democracy.

Despite the shared historical development between participatory and deliberative democracy, it is incorrect to assume that the latter is tied up with a participatory

76 Simon, 2006, p 48.

77 These ideas started to dissipate after the Vietnam War. A new politically active individual emerged into the political realm, which in turn gave rise to gradual and incremental developments in the theory of popular participation. See Bohman and Rehg, 1997, pp xii–xiii.

or directly democratic ideal.[78] That decisions are made deliberatively does not guarantee – either politically or conceptually – that rights of participation are an essential quality of collective choice and hence automatically safeguarded. The mistake is natural, given the close affinity between the two schools of thought, but it is a mistake nonetheless: participation and deliberation are two different concepts that make up different strands of theoretical literature and empirical research, and they are intended to rectify different shortcomings of representation.[79] The literature on participatory democracy that blossomed in the 1970s tended to focus on participation through politically active groups and to construe participation as a means of emancipation from the hegemony of dominant classes in societies of that time.[80] A more modern variant of participatory democracy has been influential in the area of environmental governance, because a balancing act between environmental and economic aims is highly dependent on generating a basis for continued dialogue with a multiplicity of stakeholders.

Contemporary deliberative democracy is quite ambiguous in terms of the issue of participation. Certainly, deliberative democracy is ideally committed to public participation in decision-making processes by all those concerned or affected. Yet considerable variation exists between specifying whether participation should be limited to representative institutions, or whether a broad and active citizenship (also in the form of a more direct and radical democracy) is pivotal to a coherent and legitimate defence of deliberative policy-making. Theories of deliberative democracy appear to support and encourage forms of 'popular participation that increase the quality of deliberation and the fairness of representation', yet they do not insist that 'ordinary citizens regularly take part in public deliberations, and most favour some form of representative democracy'.[81] Most typically, deliberative democrats privilege representative democracy, together with a strong civil society: combining multiple forms of associations and networks with existing institutions of representative democracy ensures a public sphere.[82]

Whilst recognition of deliberation and participation as distinct ideas rooted in different intellectual traditions of thought and action is certainly welcomed by the terms of the theory itself, it is also important to acknowledge and interrogate the significant practical consequences that follow from this recognition. Does a tension exist between deliberation and participation, and if so, how and where does it manifest itself? Thompson (2008) continues:

78 Besson and Martí, 2006, p xix; Cohen, 1997a, p 85; Cohen, 1997b, p 422; Gutmann and Thompson, 2004, p 30; Renn, 2009, p 232; Thompson, 2008, pp 511–12.

79 Cohen and Fung, 2004, p 24. See also Dowding, Goodin and Pateman, 2004, p 4.

80 Barber, 1984; Mansbridge, 1983; Pateman, 1970. By the late 1970s, themes of participatory democracy 'seemed to have run their course': see Dowding, Goodin and Pateman, 2004, p 3.

81 Gutmann and Thompson, 2004, p 30. See also Bohman, 1998, p 416.

82 Benhabib, 1996, pp 73–4.

> [I]s it more likely in discussions about certain kinds of issues? Is it more common in discussions among ordinary citizens than among political leaders? Is it more frequent in informal interactions than in formal institutions? Can forums for deliberation be structured in ways to avoid or mitigate the conflict?[83]

Despite the subtlety of these questions, the basic logic seems fairly straightforward: the effort to enhance the quality of deliberation may serve to subvert participation, whereas the attempt to broaden the scope of participation – either the number of people, or the range of issues subject to public discussion – discourages reasoned discussion and decreases the quality of deliberation.[84]

The first strategy and its undesirable consequences are amply manifest in the European Union. Sometimes, the inclusion of all affected is irrelevant and ineffectual because most individuals lack substantive knowledge and interest in the matters under discussion. Furthermore, in many areas of governance, the number of qualified individuals is never going to be large. Even openness may be antithetical to deliberation. Sometimes, success requires strict confidentiality of deliberations, which isolates participants from less primed and less knowledgeable public opinion.[85] With the second strategy of maximally inclusive decision making, on the other hand, come harmful effects on effectiveness and coherency. Nor is all deliberation pretty and valuable. In May 2003, the Commission published a draft proposal for the Registration, Evaluation, Authorisation and Restriction of Chemicals (REACH) and requested that interested actors comment on the internet. The Commission received some 6,400 comments. The majority were from workers 'mobilised by their respective companies and trade-unions in order to complain about potential job-losses'.[86] Of course, deliberation may enhance the knowledge of participants, so that over time the number of people with sufficient knowledge and interest might then increase; yet it is hard to disagree that 'time and resource constraints make it undesirable for any particular area of public governance to be both fully deliberative and inclusively participatory'.[87] In addition, a growing body of empirical research is sounding a cautionary note: aiming at full participation and deliberation is not only impractical, but also undesirable, because each may operate to exclude the other. The research of Mutz (2006) suggests that whilst participating in politics brings (modest) increases in terms of tolerance of diverse views, continued exposure to a diversity of views decreases participation in politics. The logic of her argument is certainly persuasive: the more people participate, the less they deliberate. She then concludes that the two contemporary ideals of

83 Thompson, 2008, p 512.
84 Cohen and Fung, 2004, p 27.
85 In the context of comitology, see Vos, 1999, p 183.
86 Hey, Jacob and Volkery, 2007, p 1869. See also Fisher, 2008, p 547.
87 Cohen and Fung, 2004, p 27.

democratic politics, deliberative and participatory democracy, conflict with rather than complement one another.[88]

Of course, the extent to which deliberation and participation can be integrated turns on the particular institutional structure in which they operate.[89] What I would like to emphasise here is that participation needs to be given content in light of the expectations we have developed from deliberative decision making. It is difficult to establish criteria about who should be participating, at what point and to what degree without some kind of generalised idea as to what kind of outcome is advantageous or preferable.[90] Put simply, participation is an element of deliberation, not the other way around, and thus the question in any given decision-making situation is whether we want to promote democratic participation because of its implications for the citizen as a moral agent, or because it enhances the quality of discussion and decisions. Although the question may be of a general nature, answers are sought in the particular environment of governance, in which the stakes and interests of participants play an important role. Viewed in this way, the dilemma of participation begins to take concrete shape. The criteria for participation lose their universal character, which they have traditionally enjoyed in representative democracy. When each governance regime has a fresh take on whom it accepts as a participant (to be judged in light of a whole deliberative setting), then general rules about participation are difficult to devise. The lack of similar default rules is particularly problematic for the courts; as argued in Chapter 7, the courts' role in shaping governance frameworks in light of popular participation may never be crucial.

3.2.3.1 'The (Commission) computer says ... nothing': Reconciling participation and deliberation

Participation has become a key concept in the theory and practice of modern democracy. As a result, political systems are everywhere overburdened with what have been described as 'insatiable demands' to participate and to be included.[91] One of the key criticisms routinely levelled against new modes of governance in the European Union is also that they have adopted the genuinely empathetic, yet vague, language of participation in reliance upon others' assurances, not enforceable obligations. Admittedly, the Union does not on every occasion live up to the expectations to which it has committed itself, and it sometimes leaves

88 See also Thompson, 2008, p 512.

89 Cohen and Fung, 2004, pp 28–31, suggest two grand schemes for serving both ends. The first strategy aims to increase popular participation, but, in view of the potential harm to which it gives rise, leaves it with fewer points of access to the exercise of power. The second strategy attempts to ensure a better quality of deliberative participation, with a more influential and decisive impact on the exercise of power, but confines participation to fewer people.

90 Also Bellamy, 1999, p 125.

91 Nino, 1996, p 154.

observers nonplussed and disappointed. Yet to be fair, the number of opportunities to participate has increased in recent years, even in deliberately modest evaluations. For instance, the existence of networks 'renders the policy-making process of the Union more inclusive than [that of] many of its member-states',[92] but this development does not seem to have any power whatsoever to change the general perception of EU (governance) as elitist or technocratic, or maintaining the 'participatory myth'.[93] In my view, this indicates that public participation in the EU context has largely become an empty exercise, with no implications either for the image of the citizen as a moral agent or for a contribution to better outcomes. Much less are there tangible benefits. The European Union seems to 'gather all interested parties around a table and merely hope for the catharsis effect to show up'.[94] This wishful thinking again proves (at least) one thing: that no conceptual link exists between participation and deliberation. But it also proves something else important for institutional design: that participation does not reap the benefits that it is intended to – that is, to lead deliberation – unless devised and structured appropriately.

I am suggesting not simply that we should participate more often, but that we should participate *better*. The strength and virtue of public participation and involvement does not rely only on the *quantity*, but also on the *quality* of the participation process.[95] We should not design participatory-inclusive processes as such, but structure these processes so that participation plays a role that is both relevant and meaningful. One way in which we might do so is to increase the responsiveness of governance, which would then improve both the epistemic and moral value of participation.[96] In the best-case scenario, these can both be obtained, and without requiring too much from familiar decision-making bodies. For instance, responsiveness would not assume a decision-making body that meekly acts on comments from civil society, but rather one that actively demonstrates that it has taken the views of civil society on board. Civil society would benefit too: on seeing how its views have been understood, it would not only be inspired, but also be better equipped to comment in the next round. Moreover, the account of responsiveness is a general value that can be judicially mandated quite irrespective of a governance design.[97]

92 Sbragia, 2000, p 234.

93 Smismans, 2008. See also Möllers, 2006, p 321, and Somek, 2010a, pp 342–3.

94 Renn, 2009, p 243.

95 Ibid.

96 For the importance of responsiveness, see, eg, von Homeyer, 2006; Lombardo, 2007; Usui, 2007. Galligan, 2007, p 343, has also insisted on a more ambitious 'right to consideration', not only a right to take part and to have one's opinions and interests represented.

97 'Much consultation is a sham; easily manipulated consultation exercises are not taken seriously, degenerating into a way to buy legitimacy without sacrificing control. By forcing administration into "synoptic dialogue" . . . courts can rectify this situation': this account of 'synoptic dialogue' is borrowed from Shapiro, cited in Harlow, 2006, p 135.

This might, in fact, not be far from the direction in which the European Union is heading. Concrete manifestations of responsiveness are slowly emerging in different areas of substantive EU policymaking. Ten years ago, the Commission published a document laying out general principles and minimum standards for consulting interested parties, promising (among other things) that 'the Commission will provide adequate feedback to responding parties and to the public at large'.[98] Whilst the Commission has increased the use of explanatory memoranda accompanying its legislative proposals to comment on contributions submitted to it, still the establishment of rules on feedback as a better administration strategy generally seems as remote as ever.[99] Inclusion of civil society in the Convention formed to prepare a draft Constitution is a salutary reminder of the difficulties involved in implementing good causes. Lombardo (2007) quotes a member of the non-governmental organisation (NGO) that took part in the work of the Convention: '[I]nteraction with the Convention is proof positive of the existence of black holes. You send something but nothing ever comes out. No answer to any letters. No acknowledgment of receipt. Nothing.'[100]

In less high-flying contexts, the value of responsiveness is being tried again. Dąbrowska (2010) analyses the conditions of deliberative decision making in policymaking relating to genetically modified organisms (GMOs), and notes that 'EFSA opinions now include a new annex explaining how each comment provided by the Member States was considered'.[101] Also, interestingly enough, in the Commission proposal for a new Comitology Regulation, the Commission was required, in the advisory procedure, to take 'the utmost account' of the conclusions and opinion of the committee and to 'inform the committee of the manner in which the opinion has been taken into account'.[102] However, this second requirement, included in Art 4, was omitted from the final text of the Regulation.[103] Whilst, in these empirical examples, a responsive interaction seems mainly to be taking place between the EU level and that of the Member States, the case studies at which we look in later chapters involve experiments with a more ambitious mandate and a sincere interest in increasing responsiveness to civil society.

Another way in which to ensure that participation matters is the rejection of dichotomisation between politics and expertise. Whilst democratic theorists generally remain suspicious of experts, recognising the undemocratic tendencies

98 European Commission, December 2002, COM(2002) 704 final, pp 21–2.
99 European Commission, March 2007, COM(2007) 127 final.
100 Lombardo, 2007, p 155.
101 Dąbrowska, 2010, p 210.
102 European Commission, March 2010, COM(2010) 83 final, Art 4(2).
103 Note, though, that now Art 3, 'Common provisions', includes a similar obligation, providing that the chair of the committee 'shall inform the committee of the manner in which the discussions and suggestions for amendments have been taken into account, in particular as regards those suggestions which have been largely supported within the committee'. See Arts 3(4)2 and 6(2)3 of Regulation 182/2011.

in recourse to technocratic and expert-driven politics serves that suspicion little in identifying potential modifications to existing institutional structures to ensure fair regard to each and every one. One way forward is to realise that the exercise of political power will always, to a certain extent, be moderated by experts and their approaches to construing the world and its affairs, with obvious consequences and problems.[104] This more ambitious step acknowledges that the relevant choice is not, in fact, between expertise and politics, not 'between forms of global governance based on knowledge and those that are more "politicized"'.[105] This is because the language of expertise and knowledge has pervaded ever more fields, with the result that attempts to pinpoint politics exclusively on parliamentary assemblies and civil society, and expertise on 'lab coats', no longer succeed. Politicians can also be conceived of as experts, in possession of political knowledge and expertise that has accumulated over their years as professional politicians. Similarly, particularly large NGOs should not be mistaken as operating on the political side of the boundary, for their uses of expert knowledge are professional and serious. Rather than policing the boundary between expertise and politics, any evaluations of participation must encompass many simultaneously applicable elements: when a Member State official travels to Helsinki to attend a meeting of a Member State committee at the European Chemicals Agency (ECHA), his or her role yokes together expertise and politics – that is, the expertise that the attending official invokes is technocratic knowledge grounded by a spatial sense of representation. Similarly, a representative of Swedish NGO the International Chemicals Secretariat (ChemSec) is probably just as knowledgeable as an average expert in the field of chemicals and is likely to be driven by an overwhelming feeling of representation of the public interest. Who, if any, then represents civic interests better? Just as much as expertise and politics have been dissociated from their archetypical context of performance, the criteria for participation lose their universal character and become manipulable depending on the particular context of decision making.

3.3 Towards benchmarks: Introducing iterated deliberation

In looking for a possible way in which to define the concept of deliberation that acknowledges its relevance both in normative political theory and in the real life of the European Union, we have come across several, often contradictory, ideas and approaches. Although considerable obscurity and vagueness remain, we seem to have succeeded in developing – admittedly still limited and in many respects unfinished – criteria for a practice to be termed 'deliberative'. By providing an

104 Bohman, 1996, p 168. For how expertise has changed in comitology post-Lisbon, see Peers and Costa, 2012, p 454; on expertise in the elaboration of the Cape Town Convention, see Devaux, 2013.

105 Lang and Cooney, 2009, p 188.

account of the key elements of deliberation – 'reason-giving', a 'problem-solving character' and 'responsive participation' – I have not attempted to offer yet another concept of deliberation; rather, I have sought (in anticipation of the case study chapters) to provide preliminary and tentative criteria for a set of benchmarks that courts might use when evaluating EU governance.

My suggestion for these benchmarks is grouped under the term 'iterated deliberation'. The term was first used by Dennis Thompson (2008), who opens up the concept by giving the following generalised example. A political body (deliberative or not) suggests a policy to a deliberative body, which, after consideration, returns a revised version of the policy to the first body. The political body then reconsiders the revised policy and resubmits the final draft to the deliberative body for further evaluation before its final adoption. This 'loop' can involve more phases, and may be widened to include other actors and bodies. The specific example that Thompson then gives concerns the organisation of health services in the US state of Oregon. Oregon's Health Services Commission drafted a priority list determining the conditions of treatments, in which order they should receive treatment and of what kind. The list came in for criticism from several civic and other such associations, and the Commission decided to consult those associations and other interested actors. The consultation resulted in a number of substantive changes to the list, which was resubmitted to the Commission as well as to the legislature. Thompson notes that while the outcome could have been better, 'it was better than the earlier proposals'.[106]

But certainly there is nothing new in requesting comments from interested parties on a policy proposal; the key element lies not in the practice of requesting input from other actors, but in the *repetition and iteration of deliberation*. Unfortunately, the example that Thompson gives is not one that corresponds to the strength of his theoretical argument, and my belief is that EU governance, to which we will soon turn, offers better and more convincing examples of iterated deliberation of this kind. With that in mind, I have reworked his approach and articulated a set of benchmarks for iterated deliberation. Governance is both a deliberative and an iterative process. It has a deliberative nature, because a wide variety of actors are encouraged to come forward to present reasons and interrogate those of others, with a view to solving problems and providing norm guidance after an exchange of opinions and views. How different institutions respond to this descriptive imperative changes, but the three general characteristics introduced earlier in this chapter guide the organisation of deliberation – that is:

1 reason-based decision making;
2 a problem-solving character; and
3 participation of all those affected (or their representatives).

106 Thompson, 2008, p 515. See also Gutmann and Thompson, 2004, pp 17–18.

It also has an iterative nature because of the importance assigned to response and consideration. It is precisely the iterative character (which again can take many different institutional forms) that corrects the problems and shortcomings to which deliberative decision making as an organisational form may be vulnerable.

1 There is a rather small (empirical) possibility of good reasons convincing others of their superiority, which appears – as a highly generalised argument – to trivialise the importance of providing reasons. The iteration of reason-giving, although not guaranteeing the triumph of good reasons, puts reasons and arguments to good use. In other words, mutual reason-giving generates those best arguments or best approaches that peer review deploys in its scrutiny, monitoring and benchmarking.
2 The problem-solving orientation may turn (too vigorously) towards compromise and consensus as an aim of decision making, or take certain actors or working assumptions for granted or to be unproblematised. The iteration of arguments and reasons attempts to highlight diversity and conflict. It also seeks to ensure that should there be a consensual mode of making a decision, that conflicting voices are heard and that no sustained opposition remains.
3 Ever more frequent opportunities to participate risk creating an empty exercise or machinery serving (one hopes) self-fulfilling prophecies without any obligation on the part of policymakers to give regard to what comes out of discussions and consultations. Iteration underlines the importance of enhancing the responsiveness of policymakers.

As a whole, the iterative character of deliberations involves not only anticipation of a singular response, but also anticipation about a system of 'responsiveness and accountability to others'.[107] This general orientation fits with the context and focus of the book.

What does iterated deliberation look like in the European Union? What are its merits and demerits? First, it is well suited to a context such as the Union, in which deliberative and non-deliberative elements are in existence. It means that the 'different capacities' of institutions are taken into account and that decision making does not have to be fully deliberative if a decision is made in the context of distributed deliberation.[108]

Second, it also adopts a more realistic view of the use of expertise and the role of experts. Whilst being aware that 'knowledge and information are scarce resources in complex societies' and that 'citizens surrender their autonomy to experts, delegates, and other forms of the division of labor',[109] iterated deliberation

107 Bohman, 2004, p 136.
108 Thompson, 2008, p 515.
109 Bohman, 1996, p 168.

attempts to destabilise the received boundary between politics and expertise, and to make expert decision making as accessible as possible to outside control and influence.

Third, it makes sense of circumstances under which EU law has to be made applicable to diverse environments. Deliberative problem-solving is needed to bring people together to clarify, elaborate and revise norms in order to solve specific problems, and to make law applicable and enforceable in concrete cases. With the case studies focusing on administrative implementation and law application, the analysis in this book gives insight into uses of deliberation in these less-studied environments. For instance, specific mention has been made earlier in this chapter of the tendency to assume that information is 'a cure to all ills', which leads people to converge in terms of the conclusions that they draw and the decisions that they make. When assessing the role of information in implementation and application, information is appreciated for its capability to enhance *ex post* monitoring, rather than to facilitate decision making. Indeed, and fourth, it is helpful for those wanting to rethink the organisation and function of judicial review – but what do I mean by that?

Iterated deliberation is built on peer review in the sense that deliberators have come to identify a common problem, which they attempt to solve by exchanging reasons, then subjecting those reasons to the scrutiny of those who are also dealing with the same problem and who have stakes in the outcome. This element of peer scrutiny not only makes speakers accountable to one another, but also facilitates the task of outside monitoring and makes judicial control more straightforward. In other words, peer review provides material on the basis of which judicial control takes place. Standards of iterated deliberation then guide the judiciary to place emphasis upon the inclusion and treatment of reasoned justifications (*reason-giving*), opportunities for contestation and conflict (*problem-solving*), and the openness and responsiveness of decision making (*participation*). This 'checklist' of standards assists the judiciary in determining the intensity of judicial review: for instance, sustained opposition (or, for that matter, a complete lack of conflicting voices), or the absence of parliamentary or civil society input, justifies a more invasive form of judicial control, whereas a well-functioning peer review might compensate for, or entirely substitute, full-scale review. In the case studies that follow in Chapters 4, 5 and 6, I engage in closer scrutiny of the potential or limits of judicial intervention with respect to enhancing iterated deliberation along these lines.

It should finally be noted that focus on the intensity of judicial review serves the same purpose – but in a new context – that the dichotomy between substance and procedure has traditionally performed. To put it very roughly, it means that judiciaries should be occupied with how things have been done, not with what action has been decided upon. In presenting my account of deliberative democracy, I have intentionally neglected and avoided this debate, because it seems clear that a sharp separation between substance and procedure is not sustainable for both pragmatic and theoretical reasons. This view is widely shared. Gutmann and Thompson (2004), for instance, argue that a deliberative perspective, which insists on mutual justification, is 'both procedural and substantive because mutual justification cannot proceed without appealing to reasons that refer to both procedures of government and substance of laws, often at the same time'.[110] Of course, the fact that democracy cannot proceed without appealing to both substantive and procedural reasons does not mean that this is universally true of judicial review too, especially given that the courts treat the dichotomy as a matter of institutional competence: knowing what they do best and sticking to it. It should nevertheless be noted that the perspective from which we assess institutional competence changes as the EU governance context changes. The argument of Cohen and Sabel (1997) is worth quoting at length:

> Suppose that deliberative decision-makers are required to arrive at decisions with explicit attention to constitutional values and comparable experience. Still, they may make decisions that conflict with the democratic constitution, and courts may be required to review their decisions in this light. But when they are, they will have a record of fact and reasoning to draw on in making their decisions. Because they have imposed requirements of due consideration on problem-solvers themselves, courts will have the information they need to decide whether means are suitably tailored to ends, and whether ends are specified in ways that satisfy constitutional constraints. Judgements about whether or not to defer to problem-solvers will be backed by fact, and not simply by *a priori* estimates of institutional competence.[111]

It is ultimately this 'record of fact', generated by mutual reason-giving, which makes redundant these *a priori* institutional competence assumptions (including the separation of substance and procedure) in the judicial review of EU governance.[112] However, as I will discuss in the case study chapters, the complexity of the 'facts' requires the courts to continue to exercise particular caution. In my view, the intensity of judicial review is a promising, but also prudent, tool for doing so. Focus on the aspect of intensity also respects and reflects the contours of democratic deliberation better than exclusion of issues (substantive or other) from the debate before it has even begun.

To conclude, the benchmarks for iterated deliberation integrate the key elements of deliberative democracy and are quite practical in terms of its concrete ramifications for judicial review. However, the benchmarks should not be articulated in isolation from the practice in which they operate, and the benchmarks are here introduced tentatively in anticipation of the case studies.

110 Gutmann and Thompson, 2004, p 103.

111 Cohen and Sabel, 1997, p 337. See also Simon, 2006, p 57.

112 See also Scott and Sturm, 2007, p 586, but cf. Azoulay, 2001, p 441.

Chapter 4

The environmental dimension of the Lisbon and EU 2020 Strategies

4.1 Introduction

The Open Method of Coordination (OMC) is a soft policy co-ordination mechanism, brought to the general public as the key mechanism for delivering the objectives adopted at the Lisbon European Council in 2000. The new strategic goal of becoming 'the most competitive and dynamic knowledge-based economy in the world', now a classic refrain, required a new strategic instrument.[1] This instrument was to be found in the OMC, which has considerable variation in reach, compliance mechanisms, decision-making rules, involvement of actors, and in the preciseness of targets and objectives. Yet the institutional skeleton was described in Lisbon as involving the following elements: EU-level guidelines; quantitative and qualitative indicators and benchmarks; the tailoring of EU guidelines to national and regional settings; and, finally, EU-level monitoring, evaluation and peer review.[2]

As an instrument, the OMC is a celebrity, having long basked at the centre of both academic and policy attention. Not surprisingly, then, its fall has been as dramatic as its rise: after nearly 15 years since its inception, scholars argue that it has been the classic 'ado about nothing'[3] – and very much for nothing. Whilst the European Commission has sniffed the political wind and ceased referring to the OMC in the EU 2020 Strategy as successor to the Lisbon Strategy, academics have also found more worthwhile subjects to which to devote their attention. Yet continued study of the OMC – or, more broadly, the Lisbon and EU 2020 policy instruments – may be worthwhile for several reasons. First, policy co-ordination remains as an important instrument with which to make policy in the European Union. Although the names of policy instruments may change, the

1 European Council, 2000. Informally, however, the Lisbon Summit introduced something that was already in existence – namely, the OMC can be described as a 'collection of mechanisms previously developed under the broad "soft law" tradition in the EU': Borrás and Jacobsson, 2004, p 188. See also Hatzopoulos, 2007, p 311, and Szyszczak, 2006, p 486.

2 European Council, 2000, para 37.

3 de la Porte and Pochet, 2012, p 336.

need for co-ordination does not disappear, and after the Lisbon Treaty the EU constitutional set-up contains a stronger legal basis for policy co-ordination. The OMC, as a policy instrument, is not defined in the Lisbon Treaty, although suggestions were pointedly made to this effect in the Constitutional Convention. However, new Art 5 TFEU includes co-ordination as a distinct category of EU competences, and refers to guidelines in economic and employment policies.

Second, the governance framework of EU 2020, the new European Semester, comes close to the OMC. Although its main context of application is in economic co-ordination, it has also, as argued in section 4.2, 'A brief history of policy co-ordination instruments in the European Union', emerged as the principal governance tool for other areas of policy co-ordination such as social policy and environmental governance.

Third, individual elements of the OMC have come to stay, quite irrespective of what happens to the overarching governance framework. Features such as scoreboards, peer review processes and public tracking, which the OMC introduced at the EU level, have recently been recommended for a host of different policy sectors. For instance, the use of peer review between competent authorities is a legal requirement enshrined in the founding regulations of three new European-level supervisory authorities.[4] Similarly, scoreboards and public tracking have been introduced in employment policies, and are given serious consideration by environmental policymakers too.[5]

Finally, the first decade of OMC research has concluded that: '[A] standalone OMC process may prove to be a relatively weak institutional design. Yet, when yoked to other instruments that establish framework norms in particular thematic areas, some of the experimental strengths of policy coordination may be unleashed.'[6] This unleashing potential can be particularly well tested in the area of environmental policymaking, comprising legally binding framework norms and policy co-ordination processes. Although not often addressed in the existing academic literature, the area of environmental policy also includes a policy co-ordination instrument. This mechanism, the European Sustainable Development Strategy (EU SDS),[7] was created to provide an overarching framework for environmental policymaking. With the adoption of the

4 For example, Art 30 of Regulation No 1093/2010 on the European Banking Agency (EBA).

5 European Commission, November 2012, COM(2012) 673 final, p 21; European Commission, June 2014, COM(2014) 400 final, p 13; European Parliament and Council, *Decision No. 1386/2013/EU of the European Parliament and of the Council of 20 November 2013 on a General Union Environment Action Programme to 2020 'Living Well, within the Limits of Our Planet', 28 December 2013*, OJ L 354/171 ('Seventh EAP'), p 54.

6 Armstrong, 2011, p 22.

7 While the EU SDS was not widely acknowledged in the existing academic literature, those who did so usually examined it as the emergence and evolution of an OMC, albeit an immature one: see Berger and Steurer, 2007; Berger and Zwirner, 2008; Kraemer, Klasing and von Homeyer, 2003; Szyszczak, 2006, pp 492–3; Usui, 2007.

EU 2020 Strategy, which replaced the Lisbon Strategy, the EU SDS was subsumed by EU 2020.

The environmental dimension of EU 2020 and its manifestation in the European Semester form the main focus of this chapter. In particular, the chapter offers insights into the risks and possibilities of introducing or promoting a soft policy co-ordination mechanism in an area characterised by extensive legislation, legally binding standards and established case law – that is, EU environmental law. When analysing the policy co-ordination mechanisms employed during the Lisbon Strategy (2000–10), the term 'OMC' is used. When the analysis moves to the EU 2020 Strategy, I use the term 'European Semester' to mean the general governance framework of EU 2020.

4.2 A brief history of policy co-ordination instruments in the European Union: 'The future ain't what it used to be'?

Since its formal inception in 2000, the OMC proliferated to an impressive extent both within and outside areas of EU competences. In its heyday, well over 10 different OMCs or other such policy co-ordination processes were in place in the European Union, ranging from immigration policies, through research and development, to employment policies.[8]

Despite the fact that each OMC was different, carefully tailored to meet the needs and requirements of a particular policy area, certain common characteristics of origin were present. At the EU level, the OMC was first put to use as part of the European Economic and Monetary Union (EMU), in the hope that it would make better sense of a policy area characterised by functional interdependencies emerging between national and EU levels of action. A legal framework for common economic policy co-ordination is provided in Arts 120–126 TFEU, requiring Member States to view their economic policies as a matter of common concern and to co-ordinate them within the Council. Economic policy co-ordination is an aberration among policy co-ordination instruments, because it involves opportunities to impose sanctions. The Commission may address a warning to an errant Member State if its economic policies fail to observe the guidelines, or if they risk jeopardising the proper functioning of the EMU. If the Member State does not address the problems, the Council can – pursuant to some procedural rules – address a recommendation to the Member State and make it public.[9] The whole area of

8 The list put together by Laffan and Shaw, 2005, pp 13–14, contains 16 OMC and OMC-type instruments, including the EU SDS.

9 Article 121(2)–(4) TFEU. Warning, as an instrument, has rarely been used. For the history of EU economic policy co-ordination, see Hodson and Maher, 2004. For economic policy assessments in transnational organisations such as the OECD or World Bank, see Schäfer, 2006.

economic co-ordination has been thoroughly reformed since the beginning of the financial crisis.[10]

The OMC was also considered suitable in those policy areas in which common EU action may have previously been attempted, but had never actually succeeded as a result of national sensitivities to EU involvement (for example employment). Following the Amsterdam Treaty establishing a new legal basis for co-ordinating employment policies, the 1997 Employment Summit in Luxembourg marked the start of annually co-ordinated co-operation in employment matters (now known as the 'European Employment Strategy', or EES).[11] Whilst national competences are still preserved, employment is now mooted as 'a matter of common concern' under Art 145 TFEU, so that Member States are asked to work together to produce a co-ordinated approach and strategy. The 2000 Lisbon European Council linked employment co-ordination to the then-new instrument of the OMC. Economic policy co-ordination and the EES form the hard core of policy co-ordination 'in action'. They have both been formally recognised by the treaties. In addition, they can be said to carry extra weight because they 'coincide with the Spring Economic Council and are viewed as the basic economic constitutional documents of the EU and as new forms of economic governance'.[12] Although originally two separate processes, the EES and economic policy co-ordination were brought closer in the mid-term review of the Lisbon Strategy in 2005. The EU 2020 Strategy has now taken determinate steps in the same direction. In so doing, it has relied on the governance framework of the European Semester. One of the rejigs implemented under the European Semester was the merging of matters reported under the Europe 2020 Strategy (including, among others, employment matters) and those reported under the Stability and Growth Pact (economic and budgetary), further strengthening the link created by the mid-term review of the Lisbon Strategy.[13]

The third situation in which the OMC was envisaged to be useful was when national public authorities were faced with intractable problems that would go beyond regulatory resources and capacities available at the Member State level. In this case, national actors could be convinced to try the OMC in order to learn from and to experiment with the alternative approaches of other Member States. Social policy co-ordination is an instructive example and contains a third main context for the OMC. It comprises three strands: social inclusion, pensions, and health

10 For an overview of reforms, see European Commission, 2014, COM(2014) 130 final. From the point of view of soft law, see Senden and van den Brink, 2012, p 52, and Terpan, 2014. For a constitutional law approach, see Tuori and Tuori, 2014.

11 Note, though, that the 1994 Essen European Council had already experimented with forms of soft law co-ordination in employment policies. This 'proto' OMC involved a number of relatively indeterminate and amorphous objectives, and (therefore) the process failed to make progress.

12 Szyszczak, 2006, p 494.

13 For recent developments, especially from the point of view of economic surveillance, see Terpan, 2014.

care and care for the elderly. Unlike the two other instances of policy co-ordination, the social OMC is not governed by formal treaties. It has been inspired by treaty-based policy co-ordination, in particular by the EES, but some notable differences exist.[14] The most important differences relate to the controversial status of social policy targets (the first, concerning the reduction of the number of people at risk of poverty, was not adopted until EU 2020), to ongoing difficulties in agreeing on social policy indicators and to the use of recommendations. However, as argued in section 4.3.3, 'The environmental dimension of the EU 2020 Strategy and "Greening the European Semester" ', implementation of EU 2020 by means of the European Semester may mean that the boundary between treaty-based and non-treaty-mandated co-ordination processes becomes less relevant, and that (for example) recommendations might well then be included in the toolbox of social policymakers.

Fourth, and finally, OMC-type instruments were also used to complement existing competences and to 'revitalise old styles of governance'.[15] This seemed to be precisely the primary function of the environmental OMC-type mechanism: the EU SDS. Traditional EU environmental policymaking had addressed the 'most visible and pressing' environmental problems, and the role of policy co-ordination was then to 'extend and "reprogramme" ' future environmental law-making and policymaking in the European Union.[16]

It should now be clear that the OMC is loaded with a broad range of expectations, but the key that cuts across all of these expectations is that the OMC is 'at once near and far away': it is an appropriate tool for 'placing issues high on the EU agenda whilst preserving national autonomy', thus making progress at the EU level, but retaining Member State control.[17] The core principle of the EU 2020 Strategy too is 'a clear EU value added', which bears resemblance to the standard formulation of the subsidiarity principle in the Treaties.[18] A range of policy tools is available to an OMC policymaker to meet diverging aims. The basic model of the OMC includes guidelines, indicators, national reform programmes and evaluation reports, whereas use of peer review and recommendations depends on which of the various OMCs is being addressed. For instance, prior to the European Semester, there was no peer review in economic policy co-ordination.[19] It should also be noted that deployment of league tables and scoreboards to rank Member States in terms of their national policies

14 For the social OMC, see Armstrong, 2010.
15 Szyszczak, 2006, p 492. See also Sabel and Zeitlin, 2007, p 23.
16 von Homeyer, 2010, p 127. See also Kraemer, Klasing and von Homeyer, 2003, p 22.
17 Borrás and Jacobsson, 2004, p 190.
18 European Commission, March 2010, COM(2010) 2020 final, p 28. For similarities between the principle of subsidiarity and policy co-ordination processes, see de Búrca, 1999.
19 The absence of peer review did not mean that peer pressure would have been similarly lacking. For the mechanism of peer pressure in earlier economic policy co-ordination, see Hodson and Maher, 2004.

has been limited in all sectoral OMCs, but is now becoming more frequent under the European Semester.[20]

If this is the history, what is the present situation like? As has been intimated, the effectiveness and legitimacy of the OMC managed to convince neither public nor academic opinion. In early 2010, the Commission published its evaluation of the Lisbon Strategy. The unequivocal message was that the core targets of the Lisbon Strategy – that is, a 70 per cent employment rate, and 3 per cent of gross domestic product (GDP) to be spent on research and development – would not be achieved.[21] The two failures were certainly interrelated: the Lisbon Strategy deployed the OMC as its main instrument for achieving its objectives. To jump-start the progress, in 2010 the Commission adopted, and the European Council approved, the new EU 2020 Strategy for 'jobs and smart, sustainable and inclusive growth', to replace the Lisbon Strategy.[22] Because of the strongly felt repercussions of the financial crisis, the emphasis of the new strategy was on strengthening economic governance.[23] What is important for present purposes is that the OMC was hardly referred to in official documents and that the Commission called for 'a strong governance framework' to support the aims of EU 2020. This new framework is, as already mentioned, the European Semester.

The main rationale of the European Semester is to reinforce contacts between EU and national levels, as well as between Member States. It does so by means of the following steps.

1 A policy co-ordination cycle opens up, with publication of the Annual Growth Survey (AGS) in the late autumn. Prepared by the Commission, the AGS sets out EU priorities for the next 12–18 months.
2 EU actors, including the European Parliament and the Spring European Council, debate priorities and provide orientations for further action by Member States.
3 Member States prepare and submit to the Commission their plans for public finances (known as 'stability and convergence programmes') and national reform programmes (NRPs) in employment policies.
4 The Commission assesses these plans and provides feedback in the form of country-specific recommendations, officially endorsed by the European Council.[24] The recommendations, in their EU 2020 form, are meant to be precise and set a time frame for action.

20 European Commission, March 2014, COM(2014) 130 final.
21 European Commission, February 2010, SEC(2010) 114 final.
22 European Commission, March 2010, COM(2010) 2020 final.
23 European Council, 2010.
24 Recommendations can be adopted within or outside economic policy co-ordination. Recommendations adopted within economic policy co-ordination take the form of opinions on stability/convergence programmes under Council Regulation (EC) No 1466/97/EC (Art 121(2) TFEU). These recommendations concern significant macro-economic and public finance matters.

5 Member States are required to identify what action they will take in order to implement the recommendations.

In the context of economic policy co-ordination, the Commission can issue a policy warning if a Member State has not taken adequate action within the time frame set or if it has contravened the recommendations (Art 121(4) TFEU).[25] The EU treaties contain no legal basis empowering the Commission to issue warnings in the context of employment co-ordination.

6 Finally, peer reviews are undertaken in the autumn, close to the opening of a new cycle by the Commission, adopting now a new AGS.

Against this backdrop, characterised by much restrained enthusiasm and deficiencies in the operation of EU-level policy co-ordination mechanisms, I now turn to analyse, first, the environmental dimension of the Lisbon Strategy (the EU SDS), and then the environmental dimension of EU 2020.

4.3 The European Sustainable Development Strategy

4.3.1 The emergence of the sustainability paradigm in the European Union

The influential Brundtland Report (1987) defined sustainable development as 'a process of change in which the exploitation of resources, the direction of investment, the orientation of technological development, and institutional change are made consistent with future as well as present needs'.[26] The powerful idea inherent in this definition points to intergenerational justice and the future: one should cater not only for present needs, but also for those of future generations. However, this early definition of sustainable development as a concern for future generations has been more recently replaced by a tripartite account of sustainable development, involving three important, but discrete, pillars: social, economic and environmental.[27] Policymaking is steered by the

Outside economic co-ordination, recommendations include employment recommendations (Art 148 TFEU) and other country-specific recommendations on a set of selected issues, of which the Commission gives as examples the business environment, innovation, the functioning of the single market, and energy and climate change: see European Commission, 2010, COM(2010) 2020, pp 27–8.

25 Since the adoption of six-pack and two-pack legislation, as well as the new Macroeconomic Imbalances Procedure, the European Union has strong and legally binding tools with which to address wayward Member States in the context of economic policy co-ordination.

26 WCED, 1987, pp 8–9.

27 The earliest and most clearly articulated account can be found in the 2002 UN Johannesburg Declaration. See Lee, 2005, pp 26 and 28.

crucial imperative that economic growth, environmental protection, and socially just development go hand in hand, and that these objectives can be achieved together.[28] The concept of sustainable development promises a comprehensive, accommodating and future-oriented approach to political action:

> [It] represents an idea able to facilitate political consensus; it offers a story that is attractive to many actors because it provides a conceptual foundation for the pursuit of widely accepted ethical values (intergenerational equity, alleviation of poverty, environmental protection) at seemingly low financial and political costs.[29]

Early steps towards sustainable development at the EU level materialised in the concept of, and action towards, environmental policy integration. The primary goal was to locate environmental concerns within the nucleus of decision making in non-environmental policy sectors (such as transport or energy). In the course of the 1990s, the principle of environmental policy integration, which was now expressed as a concern for sustainable development, was formulated as a formal treaty obligation, first in the Maastricht Treaty and then in Art 6 of the Amsterdam Treaty. Currently, it is Art 11 TFEU, which embodies an EU-level commitment to both environmental policy integration and sustainable development. Furthermore, the cause of sustainable development is mentioned in both the Preamble to the EU Treaties and in Art 3(3) TEU.

The 1998 Cardiff European Council initiated a policy co-ordination process to give effect to a new Article 6. The outcome, also known as the 'Cardiff Process', involved some elements later to be enshrined in the EU SDS. In essence, it required councils of ministers to develop strategies about how to integrate environmental concerns into their respective fields. In addition, sectoral councils were required to exchange information on best practices.[30] The Cardiff Process never really got off the ground for reasons of a narrow focus: it addressed only high-level EU policymakers – particularly the Council.[31] Some have also noted that despite 'strong conceptual links' between sustainable development and environmental policy integration, EU actors regarded them as separate challenges in policymaking.[32] Towards the end of the twentieth century, the Cardiff Process no longer seemed worth the effort – and one might say that it was formally 'alive but politically speaking . . . dead in the water'.[33] Hence the need arose for a new approach to sustainable development. The search culminated a few years later in Göteborg.

28 European Commission, July 2009, COM(2009) 400 final, p 2.
29 Lenschow, 2002, p 21.
30 Ibid, p 27.
31 von Homeyer, 2010, p 129.
32 See Jordan, Schout and Unfried, 2008, p 164.
33 Ibid, p 169.

In 2001, the Göteborg European Council adopted Conclusions on the EU SDS, which was announced as adding 'a third, environmental dimension to the Lisbon Strategy' and as establishing 'a new approach to policy making'.[34] Despite the intertwined nature of all three elements involved in the sustainability paradigm, one component in the EU SDS prevailed over the other two: '[T]he EU sustainable development regime is most directly concerned with environmental issues.'[35] In light of the Lisbon Strategy, adopted only a year before the Göteborg summit, the emphasis came across as being a rather pragmatic choice. The Lisbon Strategy focused primarily on competitiveness and employment, but had neither an environmental dimension nor a social one; these were added in 2001 by the Göteborg and Nice European Councils, respectively.[36] The Lisbon Strategy, however, reinforced its comprehensive commitment to all three elements of sustainability on several occasions. This double commitment to sustainable development and environmental considerations by both the EU SDS and the Lisbon Strategy gave rise to considerable confusion about how the relationship between them should be understood, as is seen next.

4.3.2 The institutional design of the EU SDS: Fall and rise

The key objective of the EU SDS was, then, to give substance to Treaty-level Articles on sustainable development (now Art 11 TFEU), whilst also contributing to increased flexibility and experimentalism in EU environmental policymaking. The EU SDS could thus be said to have a solid normative basis, yet it was clearly an example of non-treaty-based policy co-ordination processes with no institutional framework provided for in the EU Treaties.[37]

Upon its creation in 2001, the EU SDS lacked much independent content. The original EU SDS worked with objectives borrowed from other environmental policymaking contexts, so that its visionary input became quite indistinguishable from what had already taken place. In other words, the EU SDS picked up existing ideas of sustainable development and continued the race. As far as the design is concerned, it did not include provisions on national plans, which Member States were merely invited to adopt. Reporting was undertaken in the context of the overall Lisbon Strategy: the Commission adopted the annual synthesis report

34 European Council, 2001, para 2.

35 von Homeyer, 2009, p 18. Compare Lee, 2005, p 35, whose concern was that the social development strand of sustainable development would 'squeeze out environmental protection'. This worry was not entirely without merit, for EU actors did emphasise the social dimension. For instance, the Ferreira Report on sustainable development, adopted by the European Parliament in 2005, demanded 'strengthening of the European social model': ibid, p 11, para 60.

36 Armstrong, 2008, p 413.

37 Szyszczak, 2006, p 492, points out that EU legislative competences are weak in sustainable development. On the other hand, a Common Fisheries Policy is broadly understood to be within the sustainable development paradigm. This is an area of policymaking in which Member States have delegated their powers to the European Union. See Herman, 2010, p 397.

addressed to the Spring European Council. On the basis of the synthesis report, the Council then reviewed the EU SDS and adopted headline indicators in order to evaluate and analyse the progress made by the EU SDS. However, and as one might expect, the Spring European Council focused on economic and employment matters, largely leaving aside environmental priorities identified by the EU SDS.[38] Following the relaunch of the Lisbon Strategy in 2005, the EU SDS was next to be reformed.[39] The renewed strategy included more prescriptive provisions on governance and implementation issues, manoeuvring it towards a more fully fledged policy co-ordination mechanism. A total of four key objectives, including climate change and clean energy, were accompanied by more detailed commitments. These usually comprised the quantified or qualified targets and time frames that had already been adopted in other policymaking contexts. In practice, the overhauled EU SDS also usurped political commitments already made in other contexts of policymaking and brought them together under the new wide-ranging policy frame of sustainable development. In order to implement these objectives, Member States were required to adopt national sustainable development strategies (SDSs). Additionally, monitoring and reporting structures underwent changes. The governance cycle was fixed biennially, with the Commission submitting a progress report on implementation of the SDS.[40] On the basis of the report and possible contributions from the Council, the December European Council reviewed progress and priorities every two years, and provided general orientation on policies, strategies and instruments for sustainable development.[41]

The EU SDS had two functions: on the one hand, it operated as a policy imperative for the EU institutions to take sustainability concerns into account in non-environmental policy contexts; on the other, the EU SDS served as a reference point for national strategies. Review of national strategies was undertaken with a view to ensuring mutual supportiveness, as well as learning between EU and Member State levels.[42] The renewed EU SDS also introduced voluntary peer review – absent from the original EU SDS. However, by the end of 2008, only two Member States had engaged in a peer review process of their national SDSs.[43] Nevertheless, the fact that the Commission biennial progress report was based on experiences obtained from peer review made the mechanisms of peer review more influential. In conclusion, however, during its existence, the EU SDS time and time again gave rise to serious doubts about effectiveness and

38 von Homeyer, 2010, pp 132–5.
39 European Council, 2006.
40 For the institutional framework, see European Commission, December 2005, COM(2005) 658 final, p 13; European Council, 2006, pp 26–9. The first report was published in 2007 and the second (and final) one in 2009: European Commission, October 2007, COM(2007) 642 final; European Commission, July 2009, COM(2009) 400 final.
41 European Council, 2007, p 17; European Council, 2009, pp 8–9.
42 European Council, 2006, p 28.
43 Berger and Zwirner, 2008, p 11.

one might say that its potential remained untapped. The EU SDS was at its most viable in the period just after the 2006 reform, but since then its 'political salience' has decreased and problems of implementation have mounted.[44]

4.3.3 The environmental dimension of the EU 2020 Strategy and 'Greening the European Semester'

Now, as noted, towards the end of the first decade of the 2000s, the EU SDS had become 'wraithlike'.[45] To understand the next steps that the Commission took, it is useful to record the critique that was routinely levelled against the EU SDS. One issue in particular seemed to be fuelling most of the criticism: the relationship between the Lisbon Strategy and the EU SDS, which was regarded as ambiguous and confusing.[46] In the 2009 review, the Commission admitted that various stakeholders had been nonplussed by several cross-cutting strategies at the EU level and continued that further clarification of the EU SDS in relation to the Lisbon Strategy was necessary in the future. The reform that the Commission had in mind was radical. With the adoption of the EU 2020 Strategy, the EU SDS was integrated into this larger policy co-ordination framework, and the EU SDS as an independent policy instrument was slain.[47] As an unfortunate reminder of the chaotic and confused state of EU-level policy co-ordination, the decision to integrate the EU SDS with EU 2020 was neither explicitly taken nor publicly announced. The EU 2020 Strategy adopted in June 2010 did not refer to the EU SDS to communicate to a wider audience that EU 2020 would, in the future, cover the sustainability paradigm. The EU SDS disappeared from environmental policy documents too. In the new Seventh Environmental Action Programme (EAP), adopted in autumn 2013, the EU SDS was mentioned only once, not contributing much other than to confuse the status of the EU SDS.[48] Confusion reigned until 2013 when the Commission, still somewhat enigmatically, announced in one of its policy documents that the European Union's commitment to sustainable development takes place 'through a range of overarching policies, in particular through its overarching strategy for smart, inclusive and sustainable growth – Europe 2020'.[49] This is, in fact, a reversal of roles: as intimated earlier, the EU SDS got under way by subsuming the existing (environmentally relevant)

44 Steurer and Berger, 2010, p 6.

45 Derruine and Tiedemann, 2011, p 43.

46 Armstrong, 2010, p 106; von Homeyer, 2010, p 139. In addition, the relationship of the EU SDS to other long-term environmental strategies, such as the EAPs, was perceived as a constant source of confusion and frustration.

47 See personal communication with the Commission, email dated on 3 February 2014 (on file with author).

48 Seventh EAP, p 4.

49 European Commission, February 2013, COM(2013) 92 final, p 6.

policy objectives of the Lisbon Strategy; now, these objectives were reclaimed by EU 2020.

As a result of this incorporation, the European Semester, as a general governance framework of EU 2020, has now emerged as a main policy-making tool in environmental policy co-ordination too.[50] As is clear from the foregoing, the European Semester, although introduced as a yearly cycle of *economic* policy co-ordination, is not confined to economic and fiscal aspects of policy co-ordination. The reason for this is the broad scope of the EU 2020 Strategy, containing, among other things, objectives related to climate change, energy and resource efficiency. Reflecting this broad palette of objectives in EU 2020, the reach of the European Semester has correspondingly been widened to govern a range of reform programmes covering areas such as employment, research, innovation, sustainability and social inclusion. The European Semester has come to provide the Commission with a new tool through which to monitor Member States' progress on various issues, including environmental ones.

Moreover, several environmental policy documents have made an explicit link to the European Semester. In a recent water policy communication, for example, the Commission said that it would use the European Semester to issue water resources recommendations to Member States.[51] The Commission has also sought to explicitly underline the environmental arm of the European Semester under the heading 'Greening the European Semester'. For the Commission, the European Semester is a showcase for demonstrating that environmental and financial matters are not inimical to each other, and can be pursued in mutual support. Following a workshop organised in autumn 2013, the 'Greening the European Semester' expert group was established. This provides a platform from which national and European administrations might exchange experiences on 'greening' the economy in the context of the European Semester. The group, the members of which are appointed by Member States, meets twice yearly, with the first meeting in early 2014. The focus of the first meeting included environmental fiscal reforms, the cost of floods and support for the resource efficiency of small and medium-sized enterprises (SMEs).[52]

In some analyses, the EU 2020 Strategy has been argued to rekindle the original Lisbon Strategy spirit as the latter existed just after the 2001 Göteborg Summit. Scholars observe that, at that time, the Lisbon Strategy attempted to strike a genuine balance between economic, social and environmental concerns.[53]

50 For example, the latest Working Programme for the Common Implementation Strategy (CIS) referred to the European Semester with a view to exploring possible links between the CIS and the European Semester: see Water Directors of EU Member States, 2013, pp 5 and 16.

51 European Commission, November 2012, COM(2012) 673 final. In addition, the Seventh EAP is monitored together with the Europe 2020 Strategy: see Seventh EAP, p 14.

52 Accessed 30 June 2014, http://ec.europa.eu/environment/integration/green_semester/expert_group_en.htm.

53 Armstrong, 2010, p 272.

The same aim can now readily be inferred from the catchphrase of EU 2020: 'smart, sustainable and inclusive'. However, closer scrutiny reveals this to be less than credible. The document persistently refers to largely economically driven aims, even when discussing sustainability issues: a sustainable future involves 'promoting a more resource efficient, greener and more competitive economy'.[54] The preponderance of economic considerations is also clearly visible in the reform of institutional design, such as the merging of reporting and evaluation of Europe 2020 and the Stability and Growth Pact (SGP) within the European Semester, suggesting the upper hand of the latter.

Analysis of the Annual Growth Survey (AGS) highlights that the European Semester process has so far paid little attention to any objectives other than economic, while environmental concerns are approached from the point of view of efficiency concerns. For instance, the 2014 AGSs and country-specific recommendations published in June 2014 focused on resource efficiency by means of improving waste and water management, recycling and energy efficiency.[55] Given the scale of economic problems that have harried Europe, it is natural that the focus of EU 2020 has been on economic recovery and growth, and job creation, but less on environmental objectives. In this respect, it is telling that Member States with few or no recommendations in the area of environmental policy include not only those Member States with environmental credentials (Austria, Sweden), but also countries such as Ireland and Portugal, currently in the midst of budgetary consolidation.[56] However, it is important to note that this sidelining of environmental concerns is not merely a result of the financial crisis, but follows from the institutional logic intrinsic to the European Semester. Its focus is confined to a narrow set of environmental issues with a direct bearing on the overall objectives of Europe 2020.[57] In other words, as long as EU 2020 is interpreted by policymakers as being dominated by economic growth imperatives, wider environmental objectives are bound to be sidetracked in the yearly policy co-ordination process of the European Semester.

4.4 The courts and EU-level policy co-ordination processes

According to a widely held view, the courts have no role in the OMC or other similar policy co-ordination instruments. The OMC displaces the EU courts

54 European Commission, March 2010, COM(2010) 2020 final, p 10.

55 See European Commission, November 2013, COM(2013) 800 final; European Commission, June 2014, COM(2014) 400 final, p 12.

56 Withana, Kretschmer and Farmer, 2013, p 16.

57 Ibid, p 7.

because 'there are no formal sanctions for non-performance and since the operation of the OMC does not give rise to a "legal act" '.[58] This displacement may not be a pure coincidence. The role of the Court of Justice of the European Union (CJEU) in identifying the boundaries of legal integration has not always been met with enthusiasm or even accepted with equanimity in Member States. Some explain the strong role of the CJEU as a 'regulatory shortcoming' that has provoked certain forms of EU governance, including the OMC.[59] It is, however, beyond the scope of this chapter to affirm or reject whether a causal relationship exists between 'inappropriate' judicial activism and the emergence of EU-level policy co-ordination mechanisms.

Instead, the analysis that comprises the rest of this chapter approaches the question of the courts in policy co-ordination from a different perspective altogether. It begins by considering the risks and possibilities of deploying policy co-ordination instruments in an area characterised by extensive legislation. In the early 2000s, a group of legal scholars raised this question about the adverse impact of an environmental OMC on the *acquis communautaire*.[60] The role of the courts is inherent in their analysis, although the courts were not expressly mentioned. The scholars' cautiously optimistic view was that the OMC and traditional legislation can be expected to reinforce each other.[61] Adverse effects on the *acquis* might arise only if existing legislation were to be repealed and if an OMC or OMC-type measure that replaced that legislation were not strong enough to give effect to environmental standards. But the scholars cannot give examples here; instead, they demonstrate a hypothetical risk with reference to an OMC-*type* measure – namely, the Water Framework Directive (WFD), which replaced much of the existing water-related legislation. Yet the replacement of legislation took place through another piece of legislation (albeit framework legislation), not through the OMC.

Despite problems in finding evidence of the practice of replacing legislation with the OMC, discussion of the role of the courts in the OMC and soft policy-making in the European Union more generally has favoured this scenario of replacement over reinforcement. Recall the following quote: 'If the EES is exclusively pursued by means of OMC – and if OMC is indeed successful – in some years' time most of the Member States' regulation in the field of employment will be corresponding to "soft" guidelines and recommendations.'[62] This and many similar observations, animated by the perceived negative consequences of soft

58 Trubek and Trubek, 2007, p 13. See also Armstrong, 2010, p 286; Armstrong and Kilpatrick, 2007, p 672; Borrás and Jacobsson, 2004, p 199; de Búrca, 2003, p 828; Dawson, 2009, p 67; Jacobsson, 2004, p 86; Joerges, 2007, p 13; López-Santana, 2006, p 482; Smismans, 2011, p 518; Szyszczak, 2006, p 495; Terpan, 2014, p 14.

59 Szyszczak, 2006, p 487. See also Gerstenberg and Sabel, 2002, p 330, in relation to comitology.

60 Kraemer, Klasing and von Homeyer, 2003, pp 16–19.

61 Ibid, p 17.

62 Hatzopoulos, 2007, p 335.

policy co-ordination for the role of courts, tend to neglect and overlook – either deliberately or not – the fact that policy co-ordination does not usually constitute a governance instrument that is utilised instead of other possible governance instruments, but rather often forms part of a larger regulatory framework.[63] For instance, for Kilpatrick (2006), EU employment governance is an 'integrated regime' allowing the OMC (the EES), the European Social Fund and hard law measures all to contribute to achieving broadly defined objectives in employment policies.[64] The EES and other EU policy co-ordination instruments are good examples of a hybrid approach to governing: they aim at a systematic and conscious linking of different policies that are worth pursuing simultaneously. I use the term 'hybridity' here so as to envisage a kind of development in which different governance instruments – those of soft law and hard law – are combined and integrated in the governance of a specific policy area.[65] Many of the analyses and gloomy projections as to the role of the courts, however, endorse soft policy co-ordination as the *only* instrument to be used in policymaking – not as one of many possible ways in which to make law and policy. In her study of the EES, Kilpatrick notes an unfortunate tendency 'to present the OMC as a separate governance tool which will therefore be used instead of other possible EU governance tools, most particularly, the hard law of EU employment legislation'.[66] Rather than speculating on what will happen if soft policy instruments replace and substitute hard law, it might be more useful to analyse the role of the EU courts in the perhaps less dramatic, but certainly more accurate, light of hybridity.

Against this background, I shall now proceed to analyse three more specific questions in this section. First, I consider whether instruments to which EU soft policy co-ordination gives rise are susceptible to judicial review. Second, I examine the possible role of the courts in enforcing those instruments against Member States. Finally, I discuss the role of civil society in EU policy co-ordination and whether stakeholders can pursue their 'rights' through the EU courts. Certainly, each of these issues pinpoints the limitations of the EU courts for shaping the contours of EU-level policy co-ordination, but, taken together, I believe that they will also illustrate how analysis that resists the temptation to see the OMC or its successors as an exclusive governance instrument can offer a new perspective on the highly controversial relationship between policy co-ordination processes and the courts. In the next section, I start with an overview of what instruments are involved in EU soft policy co-ordination, before proceeding with the analysis.

63 For rare exceptions, see Terpan, 2014, and Zeitlin, 2011, p 137. This, of course, does not mean that parts of this framework are always harmonious and complementary; rather, tension between parts is likely. See Smismans, 2011, p 513.

64 Kilpatrick, 2006, p 130. See also Zeitlin, 2011, p 138.

65 For different ways in which to determine the term, see Armstrong, 2010, p 47; Armstrong, 2011, p 32; Trubek, Cottrell and Nance, 2006, p 93. Compare Héritier, 2002, p 202, who uses the term to connote soft law regulation, which is framed and supported by 'hierarchy'.

66 Kilpatrick, 2006, pp 130–1.

4.4.1 *Soft law in policy co-ordination processes: Country-specific recommendations*

Some variation exists between sectoral policy co-ordination processes in terms of the prevalence, scope and normative force of recommendations. In the context of economic and employment policy co-ordination, a country-specific recommendation is a Treaty-based instrument. Despite this formal validation, the legal status of recommendations (binding/non-binding, legal/political) has remained unclear, and the Commission has articulated very generally that they are 'politically (if not legally) binding guidelines'.[67]

No comparable legal basis can be found in the Treaties to issue recommendations under the social OMC, and recommendations were not part of the original institutional package.[68] However, in 2008, the Commission proposed a radical reorganisation of the social OMC, including adoption of recommendations. Owing to the lack of a legal basis, the Commission came up with a rather ingenious idea: it announced that it would use the competences vested in it by (ex) Art 211 EC to set out common principles in the form of recommendations.[69] In due course – and ignoring the fact that this Article had been mainly used in internal market matters – the Commission adopted its recommendation on 'active inclusion' in October 2008.[70] However, with the entry into force of the Lisbon Treaty, Art 211 EC was replaced by Art 17 TFEU, providing ambiguously that the Commission 'shall promote the general interest of the Union and take appropriate initiatives to that end'. It is unclear whether the Commission can adopt recommendations on the basis of this Article, despite its not being expressly prohibited in the text.[71] From one perspective, it could be argued that the Lisbon Treaty rendered adoption of Commission recommendations easier than had previously been the case, because adoption of recommendations is no longer linked to the task of ensuring the proper functioning and further development of the Common Market.

Clearly, there is both a temptation and a template to introduce recommendations in the social OMC too, particularly because of the need to strengthen the overall framework. But it is precisely in this context that Armstrong (2010) warns against making overly simplified comparisons between use of recommendations in

67 European Commission, February 2010, SEC(2010) 114 final, p 21.

68 Note, though, that Member States were 'subject to country-specific recommendations on the reform of their social protection systems under the Integrated Guidelines insofar as these may be deemed necessary for public financial sustainability and/or employment promotion': Zeitlin, 2008, p 444.

69 Contrary to common presumption, the European Union does not enjoy unlimited competence to adopt soft law acts and the choice of instruments needs to be appropriate with regard to the means aimed at: see Senden and van den Brink, 2012, pp 21 and 25.

70 Commission Recommendation 2008/867/EC of 3 October 2008 on the active inclusion of people excluded from the labour market.

71 See also Armstrong, 2010, p 282. As for EU legal instruments, Art 292 TFEU simply requires the Commission to adopt recommendations.

the social OMC, on the one hand, and economic and employment co-ordination, on the other. He believes that the top-down approach (in the form of EU-level targets and formal recommendations) would debilitate rather than increase the capacity of social policy co-ordination to affect national policymaking.[72] In contrast, as far as it concerns the old EU SDS or the environmental dimension of the EU 2020 Strategy, no possibility exists to adopt country-specific recommendations. When interviewed, one Commission official said, of the recommendations as part of the earlier EU SDS, that it is a 'very sensitive topic'.[73] It should nevertheless be remembered that the Commission already issues country-specific recommendations in 'selected thematic issues', including energy and climate change, and water-related issues. Hence environmentally relevant recommendations might then have been brought in through the back door in the European Semester.[74]

To summarise, the EU trend has been towards 'hardening', with EU economic co-ordination leading the way with legally binding instruments and hard sanctions.[75] Moreover, EU institutions are, to an increasing extent, highlighting issues of monitoring and implementation, and in particular are promoting the use of recommendations with a view to fortifying monitoring. This will inevitably shift the focus from the Council to the Commission, albeit that the Council retains its formal power to adopt recommendations. Use of recommendations in practice moves EU policy co-ordination closer to similar policy co-ordination models at the international level – that is, those of the World Bank, International Monetary Fund (IMF) and Organisation for Economic Co-operation and Development (OECD). In international contexts, monitoring of policy co-ordination processes is usually entrusted to the administrative level rather than to the political level.[76] In the European Union, it is the political level (the Council) that formally issues recommendations in economic and employment co-ordination, although on the proposal of the Commission and after endorsement by the EU Council.[77] Council recommendations naturally enjoy high-level political visibility, unlike social policy recommendations adopted by the Commission. The authorship of recommendations is, however, only formally attributed to the Council or the Commission. Although officially adopted by different EU institutions depending on the policy area in question, informally recommendations are authored by committees working at the administrative level: the Employment Committee, the

72 Armstrong, 2010, p 282.

73 Berger and Steurer, 2007, interview with Alexander Italianer.

74 European Commission, March 2010, COM(2010) 2020 final, p 28. See also European Commission, November 2012, COM(2012) 673 final, p 16.

75 Senden and van den Brink, 2012, p 53.

76 Jacobsson, 2004, p 86.

77 Article 292 TFEU sets the conditions that the Council must observe when adopting recommendations. Recommendations by both the Council and Commission are published in the L series of the Official Journal.

Economic Policy Committee and the Social Protection Committee. The committees include representatives from both the Member States and the Commission.[78] The Commission perceives OMC recommendations as embodying consensus. Validation of recommendations as the embodiment of consensus undoubtedly increases the visibility and 'normative bite' of those common principles involved in recommendations.[79]

Adoption of country-specific recommendations may also attend to the foundational problem of the OMC and its successors, which is the absence of a legal act as a precondition for judicial review.[80] The procedures and results of the OMC have not been hierarchically structured or clearly delineated to be seen as giving rise to a discernible legal act. With the European Semester now laying emphasis on the country-specific recommendation, this problem may be rectified. It is highly interesting that the Commission used the term 'soft law' for the first time in its EU 2020 stocktaking document.[81]

One consequence of these developments may be an increased possibility to subject recommendations to EU-level judicial review, to which I now turn.

4.4.2 *Judicial review of country-specific recommendations*

The most direct link between the courts and EU-level policy co-ordination is found in recommendations. Although the binary distinction of soft law/hard law is largely renounced in OMC research, it persists when discussing the issue of justiciability.[82]

If policy co-ordination processes result in country-specific recommendations, they may be reviewable by the EU courts. Hatzopoulos (2007) notes that:

> [These acts] may, under specific circumstances, be brought before the [CJEU] with annulment proceedings. In all such atypical acts, the intent of the issuing Institution to create legal effects has been determinative for the court's extending its control. In the OMC framework, however, such intent is, by definition, absent.[83]

78 In addition to preparing recommendations, the committees occupy a central role in determining the indicators and preparing reporting documents formally adopted by the Commission and the Council, but they also draw up reports and opinions at the request of either the Council or the Commission, or on their own initiative: see Borrás and Jacobsson, 2004, p 198. For accountability frameworks in the committees, see Dawson, 2009, p 69.

79 European Commission, July 2008, COM(2008) 418 final, p 5.

80 In this respect, the issue is a familiar one from an old case: Case T-461/93 *An Taisce and WWF UK v Commission* [1994] ECR II-733; appealed as Case C-325/94 P *An Taisce and WWF UK v Commission* [1996] ECR I-3727.

81 See European Commission, March 2014, COM(2014) 130 final, p 16.

82 Especially Armstrong and Kilpatrick, 2007. See also de la Porte and Pochet, 2012, p 339, and Chapter 7 in this book.

83 Hatzopoulos, 2007, p 334.

Are recommendations susceptible to EU-level judicial review? Article 263 TFEU explicitly excludes recommendations and opinions from the list of acts susceptible to judicial review, but again it is the exception that proves the rule. The EU courts are not likely to be deterred from reviewing instruments just because of the political nature of the underlying decision-making process or because the policy co-ordination process is, 'by definition', free of the intention to create legal effects.[84] Detailed case law manifests the willingness of the EU courts to review recommendations, albeit under narrowly defined circumstances. I will not analyse and recapitulate the whole breadth of the relevant case law here, but instead focus on some particularities that are crucial for discussion of recommendations adopted in the context of EU-level policy co-ordination.

Soft law has to meet two main requirements in order to be judicially challengeable.[85] The first concerns authorship and the second, the existence of legal effects. The authorship requirement means that the soft law instrument must be an act adopted by an EU institution. The first precondition is easily met by a country-specific recommendation because it is typically adopted by the Council, or, in the case of social policy co-ordination, by the Commission. Are the authors treated equally in review? The EU courts have fewer preoccupations about reviewing recommendations issued by the Commission than those issued by the Council. The reason is that the Council's activities are regarded as being 'political', which activities cannot usually be subjected to judicial review.[86] Nevertheless, some scholars point out that the CJEU has not fully grasped the administrative nature of EU rule-making and that it therefore 'tends to treat the Council as a normal legislature, enjoying a very wide margin of discretion'.[87]

The other requirement for EU-level judicial review is more complex. The competence of the EU courts to review recommendations is often disputed on this very ground. For a soft law act to be challengeable, a discernible intent must be present on the part of the EU institution to produce legal effects. Article 263 TFEU states explicitly that the CJEU reviews the legality of acts intended to produce legal effects vis-à-vis third parties. However, the EU courts review the existence of legal effects in the actual context, thereby often contradicting the institutions' own perceptions. This means that the CJEU emphasises substance over form: an instrument that is not found in the EU Treaties, or an instrument that is announced to be non-binding, does not prevent the EU court from reviewing

84 For example, Case C-27/04 *Commission v Council* [2004] ECR I-6649.

85 I will build the analysis of legal effects on the categorisation developed in Scott, 2011, especially pp 337–43.

86 Remember that ex Art 230 EC did not refer to the European Council and that its acts were precluded from judicial review. See also Case C-253/94 P *Roujansky v Council* [1995] ECR I-7. Article 263 TFEU now expressly mentions the European Council, the acts of which are reviewable if intended to produce legal effects vis-à-vis third parties.

87 Joerges and Neyer, 1997, p 286.

it.[88] In the *Pension Funds* case, the Court of Justice set the test as follows: '[A]n action for annulment is available in the case of all measures adopted by the institutions, whatever their nature or form, which are intended to have legal effects.'[89] A string of judgments (mostly argued between France and the Commission), in which the Court of Justice has reviewed a Commission communication,[90] the Commission's internal instructions,[91] or a Commission code of conduct,[92] attests to the flexibility of the EU courts in this respect.

Whether country-specific recommendations are challengeable therefore turns on the highly contextualised assessment of the circumstances under which the act has been adopted. The CJEU is particularly prone to find legal effects in three situations. First, a recommendation can be reviewed if it introduces a new obligation or if it goes beyond what is provided by legislation. In other words, this means that where the instrument can be thought to add something to primary or secondary legislation, it is reviewable.[93] In order for the CJEU to arrive at this conclusion, the wording of the recommendation is important: it must be 'imperative'.[94] If the recommendation is taken to be 'fleshing out' existing obligations,[95] or making obligations 'more explicit',[96] it is not deemed to have legal effects.

Second, the recommendation can also have legal effects if its purpose is to give more information about the ways in which an EU institution – usually the Commission – will exercise its discretionary powers. Here, the Court has also required that these rules of conduct have been published and that the EU institution has announced itself bound by them when applying the guidelines to relevant cases. For instance, in *Germany v Commission*,[97] the Court held that the

88 Scott, 2011, p 339.

89 Case C-57/95 *France v Commission* [1997] ECR I-1627, [7]. See also Case 22/70 *Commission v Council (ERTA)* [1971] ECR 263, [42]. In an opinion, AG Jacobs rephrased this test as a question of whether soft law measures 'by themselves and as they stand, have altered the legal situation – understood as the collection of rights and obligations at a given moment in time – of any third party': Opinion on C-301/03 *Italy v Commission* [2005] ECR I-10217, [53].

90 Case C-325/91 *France v Commission* [1993] ECR I-3283.

91 Case C-366/88 *France v Commission* [1990] ECR I-3571.

92 Case C-303/90 *France v Commission* [1991] ECR I-5315.

93 Ibid. [24]. See also the opinion of AG Jacobs in Case C-301/03 *Italy v Commission* [2005] ECR I-10217, [64], in which one of the problems was whether the contested notes, as part of the Structural Funds partnership, 'go beyond what the Structural Funds Regulation requires'. In his assessment, AG Jacobs regarded the possibility that national authorities 'may be led to alter their internal rules and procedures' on the basis of soft law measures as a factor that needs to be taken into account in analysing whether a soft law measure adds to legislation: ibid, [62]. However, he also said that Member States and their authorities are 'familiar' with the procedures, and can therefore be expected to be able to evaluate the legal nature of soft law measures better than, eg, individuals: ibid, [71]. His conclusion was that the measure in question could not be challenged.

94 Scott, 2011, p 340.

95 Case C-325/91 *France v Commission* [1993] ECR I-3283, [14].

96 Case C-366/88 *France v Commission* [1990] ECR I-3571, [23].

97 Case T-374/04 *Germany v Commission* [2007] ECR II-4431. The case concerned the way in which the Commission assessed draft national allocation plans (NAPs) as part of the European Emissions

Commission guidelines, which go beyond the criteria laid down in the directive and which set out the manner in which the Commission will use its review powers, are binding upon the Commission; therefore it cannot then depart from them without giving reasons compatible with the principle of equal treatment. The second category is particularly important in competition law, in which the case law of the EU courts on soft law shapes the bilateral relationship between economic operators and the Commission.

Third, certain soft law measures can generate legal effects even in non-binding form. These are highly exceptional cases, and the normative basis is either found or implied in EU legislation. Some instructive cases exist in state aid policy. For instance, if Member States are tied by legislation to co-operate with the Commission and if a soft law measure has been adopted as part of this statutory co-operation, the soft law measure has legal effects once a Member State has accepted it.[98]

This categorisation of legal effects does not sit well with the overall regulatory architecture of EU-level policy co-ordination. Out of the three ways of recognising legal effects in soft law instruments, the second scenario is most likely. The Commission has announced that it will use country-specific recommendations in its assessment of national programmes under the European Structural and Investment Funds, which not only circumscribes its own discretion, but also makes recommendations legally relevant in the eyes of Member States.[99] The third is so negligible that it can quickly be discounted. The first scenario is technically conceivable, although rather improbable in policy co-ordination, since difficulties are to be expected in applying the 'adding to existing legislation' requirement. The inference from what has been recounted so far is that it is rather unlikely that the EU courts would arrive at the conclusion that a country-specific recommendation adds to existing legislation. Country-specific recommendations are not prescriptive, rather relying on words such as 'improve' and 'encourage', and they often simply specify areas in need of improvement and further action. Accordingly, country-specific recommendations can be construed as encompassing measures that repeat and further specify previous commitments given by Member States in the pronouncedly political context of policy co-ordination, and therefore do not qualify for EU-wide judicial review.

Spurred by recent developments in the EU 2020 Strategy, it could, however, be argued that recommendations are increasingly implementation instruments, written in a country-specific form and addressed to an individual Member State or to a group of them. They do not simply render commonly agreed objectives more explicit and flesh them out, but in fact help in monitoring the national

Trading System (ETS). Article 9(3) of the Emissions Trading Directive (2003/87/EC) mandates adoption of guidelines on the basis of the criteria enshrined in Annex III.

98 Case C-311/94 *IJssel-Vliet Combinatie BV v Minister van Economische Zaken* [1996] ECR I-5023, [37] and [44].

99 European Commission, March 2014, COM(2014) 130 final, p 17. See also Withana, Kretschmer and Farmer, 2013, p 8.

implementation process.[100] In this case, more prescriptive and intrusive language cannot entirely be ruled out. Further, it seems that the Commission may be willing to entertain the idea of recommendations having legal effects (its formulation of recommendations having 'political (if not legal) effects' is telling in this respect) in order to step up implementation in Member States. However, by doing so, the Commission may risk opening up an avenue to the legal challenge of recommendations. It is precisely the danger of legally binding obligations arising from non-binding instruments that has encouraged the EU courts to accept the challengeability of soft law acts.[101] Whether the same danger materialises in situations in which the Commission pushes for the legal effects of country-specific recommendations to speed up the implementation progress is a question to be addressed in years to come.

4.4.3 Monitoring Member States' implementation of policy co-ordination processes

Analysis of the conditions for judicial review of policy co-ordination instruments illustrates it to be a rather remote possibility that country-specific recommendations will be susceptible to EU-level judicial review. Although problems exist with the categorisation itself, which is not suited to the policy co-ordination context, recommendations usually lack the prescriptive language necessary to trigger judicial review. However, the firm tone of the new EU 2020 Strategy suggests that the Commission is determined to bridge the 'delivery gap' by emphasising use of recommendations. Given this recently adopted emphasis, we need to consider the implications that this will have for monitoring implementation of policy co-ordination.

Bernard (2003) recognises that recommendations may be non-binding, yet produce legal effects, thus creating an obligation on Member States to take them into account. He continues to point out that Member States have to give regard to recommendations adopted in economic and employment policies. He nonetheless argues that 'the existence of a specific (political) process to evaluate compliance with the guidelines clearly excludes the existence of a concurrent judicial process of enforcement'.[102] Could the CJEU enforce country-specific recommendations against Member States? Member States enjoy a broad and (at least legally) unbridled discretion in implementation of policy co-ordination processes. The general view is that the Commission (and thus also the CJEU) lacks material resources with which, or indeed a legal basis on which, to effectively monitor

100 Interestingly, in its recent stocktaking document, the Commission avoids talking of recommendations as a means of monitoring; instead, it emphasises the importance of targets in assisting in monitoring Member States. See European Commission, March 2014, COM(2014) 130 final, p 16.

101 See Scott, 2011, p 344.

102 Bernard, 2003, p 256.

Member States in implementing sectoral processes, thereby making policy co-ordination 'not good' for the European Union.[103] Two main problems arise. The first difficulty in monitoring has been to establish sufficient connection between the EU and the national levels. As Armstrong (2010) has argued, 'there are significant problems of causation in tracing domestic change to OMC processes'.[104] Whilst the task of 'tracing domestic change' may become easier as the use of country-specific recommendations becomes more frequent, it is nevertheless not easy. The second problematic issue is uncertainty over whether 'action taken by Member States within the framework of an OMC process would constitute action in implementation of EU law'.[105] For the sake of argument, I assume here that it does.

We can envision three possible scenarios. The first scenario might consist of a Member State adopting national legislation that aims to put in place objectives enshrined in a country-specific recommendation, but whilst doing so manages to run counter to EU legislation and to general principles of law. A case often referred to in this context is *Mangold*,[106] involving a framework agreement between the social partners. It is an important ruling in the sense that it has often been considered a forewarning of the problems that loom ahead if one decides to move forward with the soft policy co-ordination approach. In this preliminary ruling procedure from Germany, the Court of Justice was asked to answer questions concerning interpretation of the Framework Agreement on fixed-term contracts put into effect by Council Directive 1999/70/EC.[107] The aim of this Framework Agreement was to promote the integration of older employees, and the national legislation (implementing the clauses of the Framework Agreement) contained provisions that lowered the age above which fixed-term contracts of employment may be concluded without restrictions. The problem that ensued was whether a national provision that permitted employers to conclude fixed-term contracts with workers over the age of 52 without restrictions was compatible with EU law. The Court's answer was in the negative: it held that such provision allowed a difference of treatment on the grounds of age, and conflicted with secondary legislation – especially the Employment Equality Framework Directive (Directive 2000/78/EC) – and the general principle of non-discrimination in respect of age.

In the second scenario, we have a Member State adopting national measures contrary to the objectives of a country-specific recommendation. For instance, in *Impact*,[108] the Irish Labour Court asked the Court of Justice how to interpret the Framework Agreement on fixed-term work concluded by the social partners and

103 Hatzopoulos, 2007.

104 Armstrong, 2010, p 258, fn 24.

105 Ibid.

106 Case C-144/04 *Werner Mangold v Rüdiger Helm* [2005] ECR I-9981.

107 Remember that a Council directive is here a blank directive, giving effect to an agreement negotiated between the social partners.

108 Case C-268/06 *Impact v Minister for Agriculture and Food and others* [2008] ECR I-2483.

annexed to Council Directive 1999/70/EC. The Framework Agreement sought to constrain abusive use of fixed-term contracts, which means renewal of those contracts for an extraordinarily long time. The Court held that Ireland, in the capacity of a public employer, could not adopt measures contrary to the objective pursued by the Framework Agreement in the period between the deadline for transposing the Directive and the date on which the transposing legislation entered into force.[109]

The *Impact* case was less controversial than *Mangold* because, in the first, the deadline for transposing the Directive had already expired, although national legislation had not yet come into force. However, and to strengthen its conclusions, the Court referred to Art 4(3) TEU and the third paragraph of Art 288(3) TFEU. In light of these Articles, it concluded that Member States must refrain from acting in a way that goes against the objectives of the Directive *and* the Framework Agreement in the period before entry into force of national legislation, but after the deadline for transposition has expired.[110] The arguments that the Court of Justice deployed have a familiar ring. For Senden (2004), in the case of soft law, the co-operation principle in Art 4(3) TEU cannot be considered to impose an obligation on Member States to comply with it without further hard law provisions. Although in careful words, she articulates that a negative obligation may have a wider scope of application and that, in any event, the Member State should, where observable common interests exist, 'refrain from taking measures that go against the few Community rules', even if those rules are merely soft law provisions.[111] Accordingly, a country-specific recommendation could be deemed to impose a *negative* obligation on Member States: not to adopt national measures that go against the objectives pursued by that recommendation. I will return to the scope of the positive obligation shortly.

In *Mangold*, things were certainly more complex. The period prescribed for transposing Directive 2000/78/EC had not expired, which required the Court to find support for its reasoning in the principle of non-discrimination on the grounds of age as a general principle of EU law. The problem that emerged, however, was that the principle of non-discrimination on the grounds of age was not recognised as a general principle of EU law so far, and the Court of Justice had to locate the 'source' of the principle 'in various international instruments and in the constitutional traditions common to the Member States'.[112] The *Mangold* case came in for criticism that challenged the justification of the EU courts in 'finding' general principles of law. With a more specific focus on EU governance, *Mangold*

109 Ibid, [91].
110 Ibid, [92].
111 Senden, 2004, p 356.
112 Case C-144/04 *Werner Mangold v Rüdiger Helm* [2005] ECR I-9981, [74]. However, as noted, 'explicit bans of age discrimination can only be found in the Finnish constitution. International instruments explicitly prohibiting discrimination in respect of age do not exist' (footnote omitted). See Schmidt, 2006, p 519.

animated a plethora of opinions that EU governance arrangements can seriously undermine the democratic commitment to fundamental (social) rights and that they should be kept away from 'any policy field which directly affects enforceable fundamental rights altogether'.[113]

Partially, the criticism levelled against *Mangold* is contingent on the circumstances of the case and is not therefore relevant for other situations in which soft co-ordination processes could possibly result in normative outcomes that are perceived to run counter to legally binding (Treaty or other) obligations. But there is a more general conclusion that can be drawn. One of the crucial questions in *Mangold* was whether lowering the age threshold in German implementing law breached certain clauses of the Framework Agreement, rather than EU legislation. The CJEU could not but hold that the Framework Agreement had in fact *not* been violated by German legislation, and it proceeded (reluctantly) to argue for incompatibility of the German law with primary and secondary EU law. Why? Because the German legislature had not referred to the Framework Agreement when amending domestic legislation, but had justified the amendment 'by the need to encourage the employment of older persons in Germany'.[114] From the point of view of legitimate governance and – for present purposes, in particular – of judicial review, the major problem is that the successive chain of public rule-making had broken down and the links between different levels of norm-elaborating activities were nowhere mentioned or readily seen.

In my view, it is indeed the absence of interlinking (for example from Framework Agreement, through implementing directive, to national legislation) in policymaking that creates problems. This conclusion echoes the findings of Smismans (2011). He completed a key word search on *CURIA* to look for references to Lisbon Council conclusions, guidelines and recommendations issued in relation to macro-economic and employment policy co-ordination. On finding that these did not return matches in the *CURIA* database, he suggested that the reason for this might be that soft policy co-ordination instruments are not explicitly linked to hard law provisions.[115]

113 Hatzopoulos, 2007, p 341.The role of fundamental rights in soft policy co-ordination has given rise to much analysis. Some think that they would be helpful in marking a minimum basis of acceptability that EU governance processes should observe: see also Chapter 3, section 'The "race to the reasonable bottom" '. The necessary pressure for keeping up with these standards would flow from political peer review mechanisms. De Búrca, 2008, p 334, for one, envisioned – although prior to the *Mangold* judgment – that abstract fundamental rights could be used as 'ideal norms' to evaluate policy co-ordination processes and their outcomes. Others draw attention to the soft nature of policy co-ordination and observe that non-bindingness makes judicial review of policy co-ordination instruments inconceivable in light of fundamental rights. Moreover, political peer review is regarded as a better option than judicial review because respect for fundamental (social) rights often depends on material resources that remain to be decided at the political level. See Armstrong, 2010, p 258, Bernard, 2003, and especially for the last argument Smismans, 2005.

114 Schmidt, 2006, p 513.

115 Smismans, 2011.

But at least some critics of the courts seem to overlook one essential fact: in *Mangold*, it was not until the Court's involvement that the policy process was prised open. The Social Dialogue, which was the governance instrument in question and the outcomes of which were implemented through national legislation, is notoriously closed to outsiders. The content of a framework agreement is negotiated by a few insiders to the process of the Social Dialogue. The general public has no role to play there and the documents produced during the negotiation process are neither published nor publicly accessible. Now, although the European Semester, as a governance instrument of the EU 2020 Strategy, may not be any more inclusive than the Social Dialogue, the former does, however, produce more deliberations, which are documented and publicly available. These include, among others:

- the Annual Growth Survey (AGS);
- national reform programmes (NRPs) identifying the actions that Member States intend to take;
- EU-wide monitoring reports;
- country-specific recommendations; and
- (possibly) policy warnings.

Put together, these documents make the process more transparent and easier to follow, and might render subsequent review by the courts more transparent and understandable too. Policy documentation provides an arsenal of comparable experience and mutually acceptable justifications of which the courts can take advantage in their decision making. Should the EU courts deploy this kind of material in order to support the conclusion that national legislation giving effect to a country-specific recommendation is contrary to common European constitutional values, or that it falls short of giving regard to general principles of EU law, their activities might not seem quite so arbitrary or based on unforeseeable findings.[116] Critics may be quick to point out that, despite good intentions, the outcome is still deplorable: the EU courts' interpretation of what is fundamentally involved in soft policy co-ordination is more valid and justifiable than that of a participant in the process. My contention, however, is that it is precisely the absence of 'record of fact and reasoning'[117] that makes the EU courts vulnerable to claims about finding law and forcing their superior interpretation on other actors, both accusations that could be successfully diminished by giving regard to deliberations and debates by the decision-making bodies themselves.

Problems with implementation do not stop here. The third and final scenario relates to the consequences of inaction and delay. Experience suggests that the risk

116 Note, though, that this requires the national legislature to make note of EU soft policy co-ordination, eg a country-specific recommendation.

117 Cohen and Sabel, 1997, p 337.

is pronounced within the context of the environmental dimension of EU 2020. Environmental legislation has always suffered from deficits in implementation, and it is precisely this problem that has encouraged environmental law and governance to be testing grounds for new instruments and approaches. Could country-specific recommendations be of use in forcing Member States to move ahead with implementation? In other words, do they have a positive obligation? No definitive evidence is available about their impact on Member State policies, and the impact of recommendations on national policy reforms before EU 2020 has generated mixed reviews.[118] Perceiving them as a 'success story of the Lisbon Strategy', the Commission reports that:

> [T]hey have helped to address poor performance and focus on main reform priorities, while also playing a key role in policy making in several Member States by increasing political pressure at home. However, in a number of Member States they remained low profile policy advice, and their impact on the reform pace has been less evident.[119]

The precise format and content of recommendations range from detailed micro-level guidance, to general orientations and vague aspirations. Particularly in the latter case, which is perhaps the most common situation, envisaging an act of enforcement is difficult. Consider, for example, the first Commission Recommendation on 'active inclusion'.[120] When addressing the question of adequate income support, it reads that Member States are required to 'recognise the individual's basic right to resources and social assistance sufficient to lead a life that is compatible with human dignity as part of a comprehensive, consistent drive to combat social exclusion'.[121] The recommendation is more aspirational than prescriptive, and it 'certainly avoids any attempt to define or impose common minimum income guarantees'.[122] It is therefore quite implausible that recommendations could be enforced against Member States.

Has the European Semester changed anything? The Commission relates recommendations more strongly to implementation and monitoring, and as a result they have a stronger enforcement capability. Even where its provisions were sufficiently precise and unconditional, however, it would seem highly unlikely that the CJEU would enforce them against Member States in cases of inaction, if for no other reason than because it is unclear how this kind of case would actually end up before the EU courts – that is, who would be a litigant.

118 Jacobsson, 2004, pp 99–100.

119 European Commission, February 2010, SEC(2010) 114 final, p 21.

120 Commission Recommendation 2008/867/EC of 3 October 2008 on the active inclusion of people excluded from the labour market, OJ L 307/11, 18 November 2008.

121 Ibid, Art. 4(a).

122 Armstrong, 2010, p 282.

4.4.4 The involvement of civil society in policy co-ordination processes

The way in which involvement of civil society is organised in EU-level policy co-ordination processes again varies between different policy areas.[123] In general, the role of public participation has remained limited, with some exceptions. No particular processes for stakeholder involvement are in place in the area of economic policy co-ordination. The EES enjoys functional representation by the social partners, but their opportunities to exert a real influence over strategies and projects are generally considered meagre. It is difficult to say whether the EU 2020 Strategy has made any positive difference in this respect, despite previous and continuing efforts by the Commission to implement good causes.[124] The role of public participation in the context of social policy co-ordination is more controversial. Some are sceptical, and refer to the fact that discussions and deliberations take place 'at the formal level between civil servants and an institutionalised Social Protection Committee'.[125] Whilst the Committee has deployed the services of outside experts to a greater degree than is usually the case with EU-level committees,[126] it has no institutionalised links with civil society actors more broadly. Still, in the first book-length analysis of governance of social inclusion in the European Union, Armstrong (2010) concludes that it is 'one of the apparent strengths of the social OMC' that it has included a multiplicity of actors at many levels.[127]

Originally, the EU SDS had no participatory dimension, which can be partly explained by the ad hoc nature of the policy process. The renewed EU SDS engaged in more talk about stakeholders, but in less action. The little influence from environmental non-governmental organisations (NGOs) seemed to revolve around the biennial review of the EU SDS. In 2009, for the first time in the history of the EU SDS, two environmental NGOs – the European Environmental Bureau (EEB) and the Spring Alliance – were mentioned as contributors to the review process.[128] This, although in itself hardly sufficient, attested to the increased visibility of stakeholders within the EU SDS. Nevertheless, the slight progress made in terms of involvement of environmental NGOs occurred at the cost of the European Parliament. This had a very limited role in the EU SDS from the very beginning: it had merely been 'invited to contribute views in the context of future progress reviews and engage in close co-operation with the Council and the

123 I focus on the role of public participation at the EU level, although Member States also have responsibility to incorporate stakeholders into national activities. Very little information exists about the domestic involvement of stakeholders, eg in preparation of NRPs, but a safe bet would be to assume that there is not much involvement. See also European Commission, March 2014, COM(2014) 130 final, p 20.

124 European Commission, October 2013, COM(2013) 690 final.

125 Szyszczak, 2006, p 499.

126 Armstrong, 2010, p 137.

127 Ibid, p 297.

128 European Council, 2009, p 6.

Commission to ensure that the EU SDS enjoys the broadest possible support'.[129] Lack of involvement of both the European Parliament and national parliaments is a concern relating to EU-level policy co-ordination processes more generally,[130] but it was rather bizarre in the case of the EU SDS (as well as in the earlier Cardiff Process) because the Parliament is one of the most vociferous advocates of the 'green Europe' idea and it certainly has some green policy credentials.[131]

Procedure-wise, the European Semester seems to embody learning from mistakes made in respect of the OMC. First, the role of the Parliament has been substantially improved – at least on paper. After publication of the AGS by the Commission, the Parliament debates its priorities ('the parliamentary week') and publishes a report discussing its findings. This report has a dual function: in addition to including the parliamentary commentary, it also encompasses contributions from national parliaments. Around the same time, the European Parliament adopts a resolution on how the AGS addresses social and employment matters. In late autumn, it prepares its opinion on the progress of the policy cycle, also covering country-specific recommendations, again after having consulted national parliaments.[132] With respect to national civil societies, two main improvements are implemented. First, the Commission views country-specific recommendations and their publication in early summer as a means by which to open up policy co-ordination to a wider public.[133] Furthermore, the Commission takes to national streets by engaging in what it calls 'fact-finding missions' in January–February each year. These missions are designed to enable the Commission to get feedback from stakeholders at the national level, as well as to enable stakeholders to express their views and offer input.[134] Concerning specifically the environmental dimension of the European Semester, the inclusion of civil society has unfortunately been left half-finished. The initiative 'Greening the European Semester', mentioned in section 4.3.3, 'The environmental dimension of the EU 2020 Strategy and "Greening the European Semester"', has its origins in a workshop organised between Member States, Norway, NGOs and the Commission. Despite the wide representation in the workshop, the members of the expert group set up after the workshop seemingly come exclusively from European and national

129 European Council, 2006, p 28, as well as European Council, 2009, p 9.

130 Note, though, that consultation with the Parliament is required in the EES by Art 148(2) TFEU.

131 Jordan, Schout and Unfried, 2008, p 165. Further to democratic legitimacy problems, there are also other reasons to worry about the invisibility of national parliaments. It is normally a national parliament that decides about allocation of resources in implementation of policy co-ordination processes. Marginalisation of national parliaments may therefore result in lack of commitment and poor funding. See Jacobsson, 2004, p 88.

132 European Parliament, December 2013. See also de Ruiter, 2013.

133 European Commission, June 2014, COM(2014) 400 final, p 3.

134 Withana, Kretschmer and Farmer, 2013, p 8.

administrations. I say 'seemingly' because the lists of participants both for the first expert meeting and for the workshop have not been made available, despite the link created to this end on the Commission website.[135]

In conclusion, policy co-ordination processes have been difficult for civil society to enter. One possible explanation relates to the fact that EU-level policy co-ordination instruments are not easy to grasp or to work with. They have gradually evolved into a complex structure, with a multiplicity of goals and instruments, accompanied by an unclear division of responsibilities and tasks – particularly between the EU and national levels. Especially in environmental policymaking, it was the cross-cutting nature of the 'big' strategies that made it difficult for stakeholders to know how to divide attention and allocate resources between them in order to maximise input and also to ensure some output. Since the integration of the EU SDS into the EU 2020 Strategy, environmental NGOs have focused their resources on defending the environmental dimension of EU 2020 against the growth imperatives inherent in broad strategic orientations. Moreover, environmental stakeholders in particular grapple to understand to what extent EU 2020 or the European Semester can be harnessed to pursue environmental aims. The fact that even large organised environmental NGOs find it difficult to understand how EU 2020 integrates the environmental dimension implies deficits of transparency and, perhaps more deleteriously, that whatever information might be available is not effectively put to use.

4.4.5 The EU courts and participation in EU-level policy co-ordination

It is commonly held that the EU courts can do very little to uphold procedural standards and good administration principles in relation to policy co-ordination processes.[136] Applying, for example, the minimum consultation requirements adopted by the Commission to policy co-ordination is a task fraught with difficulty, since policy co-ordination processes involve the implementation not exactly of new policies, but of existing ones.[137] For the courts in particular, two specific hurdles await: on the one hand, the fact that the basic outline of the OMC was not included in the Lisbon Treaty has deterred EU judges from getting too close to the OMC;[138] on the other, no clearly defined norm is identified as a challengeable legal act – effectively barring judicial review, both in

135 Accessed 30 June 2014, http://ec.europa.eu/environment/integration/green_semester/expert_group_en.htm.

136 Smismans, 2011, pp 517–19.

137 European Commission, December 2002, COM(2002) 713 final. For legal argumentation, see Senden and van den Brink, 2012, p 30.

138 de Búrca, 2003, p 836. But even then there would have been 'difficult and complex questions to resolve about who the relevant actors and participants should be in any given policy process': ibid, p 837.

terms of access and in terms of substantive grounds of review.[139] For this reason, the effect of the EU courts' rigid reading of standing rules on potential applicants is much less significant in the OMC context.

Although the role of the EU courts is marginal in policy co-ordination and they will not be helpful in enforcing procedural rights such as consultation requirements, a wider perspective is needed on the involvement of civil society actors. As we may remember from earlier in this chapter, policy co-ordination creates – and operates as part of – a hybrid governance architecture. One concrete consequence of this is that the involvement of stakeholders must also be viewed in this wider context of hybridity. Environmental NGOs and other institutionalised stakeholders feed their views into the development of policies and simultaneously monitor policy progress in many different governance contexts (such as environmental framework directives, EU 2020, EU agency decision making). In other words, large EU-level NGOs operate with a broad palette, and stakeholders in EU 2020 are often stakeholders in the implementation of environmental framework directives or in EU chemicals decision making as well. By having such multiple roles, environmental NGOs enhance the transfer of experience and knowledge. They, rather than judges, have a good understanding of 'how each part fits into the whole' in the law and governance of environmental protection.[140] For instance, if environmental NGOs are content with particular innovative practices to improve inclusiveness, they may attempt to transfer them to other contexts; conversely, if an approach tried in one context has failed, they then know to avoid it in another. Also identifying this kind of logic, Curtin (2009) predicts that the EU agencies in particular serve as 'breeding grounds and learning sites' in respect of participation practices that may then spread more broadly.[141]

What does this recognition of fluidity mean for judicial review? When the EU courts interpret and enforce the right to access to documents or access to justice, for example in agency decision making, the effects of these decisions are not necessarily limited to the particular governance arrangement that forms the factual context to the ruling. When enforcing provisions that enable civil society to participate more effectively in one governance context, the EU courts increase the legal and administrative capabilities of civil society actors and stakeholders more generally. In this respect, recent opinions of Advocate General Sharpston in *Djurgården-Lilla*[142] and in *Bund für Umwelt*[143] are noteworthy.[144]

139 See also Case T-461/93 *An Taisce and WWF UK v Commission* [1994] ECR II-733; appealed as Case C-325/94 P *An Taisce and WWF UK v Commission* [1996] ECR I-3727.

140 Simon, 2006, p 51.

141 Curtin, 2009, p 290.

142 Case C-263/08 *Djurgården-Lilla Värtans Miljöskyddsförening v Stockholms kommun genom dess marknämnd* [2009] ECR I-9967.

143 Case C-461/13 *Bund für Umwelt und Naturschutz Deutschland*, pending at time of writing.

144 I will discuss these in more depth in Chapter 6.

The earlier *Turco* judgment[145] also makes for interesting reading. The Court of Justice overruled the General Court, which upheld a Council decision to refuse access to a document from the Council's Legal Service containing legal advice. With respect to the Council's claim that disclosure would create uncertainty concerning the legality of the measure adopted, the Court of Justice held the opposite to be true: increased openness of decision making improves citizens' opportunities to participate, and ensures that the administration enjoys greater legitimacy and effectiveness, and is therefore, as a whole, more accountable to citizens in a democratic system. Certainly, the ruling directly benefited the particular individual who requested that the EU court appreciate and enforce his right to information, yet the ruling could be interpreted more broadly as strengthening the principle of open and transparent government. Shapiro (2005) puts the argument irresistibly: '[The] junk yard dog of judicial review, once unleashed, will likely have a much larger bite than anticipated.'[146]

From this perspective, the emphasis is on changing administrative perceptions. To translate the argument to the context of EU 2020: environmental NGOs have very limited opportunities to enforce their rights through the courts. Although environmental NGOs are therefore hindered by the absence of a legally enforceable act, their marginalisation might be at least partially prevented as a result of the informational and administrative resources that they have acquired, and will acquire, in other contexts (whether or not by virtue of judicial enforcement). Despite the fact that the EU courts cannot help stakeholders in contexts in which no express legal basis exists, their case law may work in favour of a wider range of stakeholders by creating an institutional environment in which EU institutions are increasingly subjected to demands for consultation and provision of information, and where national administrations are prevented from interpreting participation provisions narrowly.

4.5 Iterated deliberation in the EU 2020 Strategy and the European Semester

EU-level policy co-ordination resembles mutual justifiability in deliberative democratic theory: in both, the key idea is to facilitate the emergence of a common understanding among actors and to initiate co-ordinated policy change. This understanding is widely shared, in one form or another, in the literature. Szyszack (2006) writes that the OMC 'can contribute to a common discourse, a common language and a common identification of a particular problem and the diffusion of shared beliefs, the acceptance of common problems and shared beliefs as to what is "good policy" and what is

145 Joined Cases C-39/05 P and C-52/05 P *Sweden and Maurizio Turco v Council of the European Union* [2008] ECR I-4723, overruling the judgment given by the General Court in Case T-84/03 *Turco v Council* [2004] ECR II-4061.

146 Shapiro, 2005, p 356.

"bad policy" '.[147] Likewise, von Homeyer (2009) argues that large-scale environmental strategies reflect attempts to provide an EU-level normative framework, which is deployed to justify measures associated with environmental protection.[148] Member States may disregard country-specific recommendations or perform reporting obligations half-heartedly, but even half-heartedly performed tasks may, in the long run, affect and shape national reforms,[149] giving EU-level strategies the benefit of the 'civilising force of hypocrisy', to borrow the famous expression of Elster (1998). Even the courts are among those affected by a common understanding. Smismans (2011) claims that the ideational repertoire of the Lisbon Strategy – notions such as competitiveness and sustainability – became common purchase in CJEU case law after 2000.

While the OMC as a policymaking instrument might be generalised to be premised on the virtues of deliberation and discussion, it is by no means clear how well it promotes those values in practice. In order to obtain a more accurate picture, it is necessary to analyse the European Semester in light of the elements of iterated deliberation. First is *reason-giving*. After common objectives have been identified and debated at the EU level, Member States adopt their own national programmes and link them to EU-level strategic orientations. Then the Commission reviews national progress and informs the Council/EU Council, which is responsible for reviewing overall progress, considering whether a need arises to modify policy priorities and endorsing recommendations, if available. The policy cycle indeed gives political actors an opportunity to revisit general objectives, but there is little concrete evidence of learning stemming from the further development of arguments and considerations in a discursive process. Peer reviews could have contributed to this end, but they have remained a diffuse phenomenon in both the Lisbon and EU 202 Strategies. In its Lisbon Strategy evaluation report, the Commission recognised the problem, pointing out that 'the European Council was often over-prepared by intensive work in different Council formations, leaving little room for substantive discussions and decisions by Heads of State and Government themselves'.[150] Moreover, preliminary analyses undertaken during the first years of the European Semester have shown that country-specific recommendations have largely repackaged and repeated the findings of the AGS, leaving little space for reflection and catch-up with policy developments.[151] In this respect, EU-level policy co-ordination is deliberative, but not iterative.

147 Szyszczak, 2006, p 489.
148 von Homeyer, 2009, p 22.
149 Begg, 2008, p 435. In the particular context of environmental policy co-ordination, Lee, 2007, p 44, defended the EU SDS against charges of ungrounded optimism, saying that 'this optimism is in a sense the whole point of sustainable development as interpreted by the EU; it enables small managerial steps to be taken without challenging the status quo too profoundly'.
150 European Commission, February 2010, SEC(2010) 114 final, p 6.
151 Withana, Kretschmer and Farmer, 2013, p 14.

Second is the *problem-solving orientation*. Agenda-setting is firmly in the hands of the Commission, which adopts the AGS. Providing a basic understanding of policy orientations, it rarely gives any indication of dissenting opinions, or considers debates or experiences from previous cycles in a more methodical manner. The same applied to the earlier EU SDS process. In a cursory reading of the relevant policy documents of the EU SDS, one could find only a single documented instance in which Member States had allegedly disagreed: the European Council noted that 'a majority of Member States' thought that the EU SDS should have continued as a separate strategy, as opposed to being integrated with the Lisbon Strategy.[152] No additional information was available about the composition of the Member States in the minority, or about the grounds on which they based their positions. Again, it could be concluded that the policy co-ordination mode is deliberative, but not iterative.

The third element is *participation*. The important roles of the European Parliament and national parliaments, as well as stakeholders, have continuously been emphasised in policy documents, but concrete actions have remained few. Lately, the European Semester has taken steps towards institutionalising the role of the Parliament and national parliaments. In addition, the Commission has attempted to regularise consultations of (national) NGOs and stakeholders in the form of fact-finding missions. As yet, their effectiveness remains to be proven. One observer argues that 'executive interaction' between the Commission, Council and the European Council is too close-knit for the Parliament and civil society to enter, despite a 'few deliberative moments'.[153] This observation although made in the context of earlier environmental policy co-ordination, appears to apply broadly to all EU-level policy co-ordination processes. In the third and final respect, then, policy co-ordination appears to be weakly deliberative, but, again, not iterative.

It is precisely the absence of iterative elements in the policymaking process that offers at least a partial explanation as to why EU-level policy co-ordination seems to be failing on account of a legitimate and effective mode of governing. With the halfway point toward the EU 2020 Strategy approaching, it is, however, necessary to observe that the Commission is currently addressing many of these weaknesses. For instance, interest is growing in revitalising peer reviews and strengthening the role of civil society actors.[154] Realising the potential of iterated deliberation in the European Semester nevertheless requires that these be more than cosmetic changes to the institutional architecture. Because the role of recommendations has been central to this chapter, I consider whether the use of recommendations might improve the problems identified, and what both the potential and limitations of judicial action might then be.

152 European Council, 2009, p 7.

153 Usui, 2007, p 631.

154 For reform contemplations, see European Commission, March 2014, COM(2014) 130 final, pp 19–20.

4.5.1 Recommendations: More accountability and transparency?

One of the key problems with EU-level policy co-ordination appears to be that although it is built on deliberation and discussion, the contents of those deliberations are not opened up or communicated to a wider audience. Furthermore, although information may at times be available to stakeholders, as well as to the general public, from which they can find out more about general trends in EU-level policymaking, the trouble often is that this information is in an unclear and confusing format, and is difficult to find. In terms of iterated deliberation, the most important function of recommendations would then be to generate information and to make it publicly available. Recommendations might have some extra-legal potential in that they might help civil society to hold Member States to account on the progress of implementation. How could this happen? Recommendations pin down in a more easily accessible manner what kinds of action are recommended to, and deemed necessary in, each Member State. The reorganised structure of the Joint Reports in the social OMC well serves aspirations to increase accountability through civil society. The Joint Reports have now been helpfully divided into three distinct parts: the 'key messages' report, 'technical statistical analysis', and 'country fiche' reports. Stakeholders can use these analyses 'either as a basis for learning from experience or as means of holding Member States to account for their policy performance'.[155] Stakeholders could also be encouraged to report to the Commission perceived flaws or inaction in the implementation of policy co-ordination instruments. Although the Commission lacks both a legal basis on which and material resources with which to effectively monitor Member States in implementing policy co-ordination instruments, it does exert influence and pressure, which makes it a powerful player in the latter's eyes. Certainly, the effectiveness of this kind of informal arrangement depends on the extent to which civil society actors are embedded in domestic administrations, and on the extent to which the values of transparency and openness are respected in national settings.

From this perspective, country-specific recommendations are therefore a step in the right direction for disclosing information that might otherwise have remained exclusive to national and EU administrations. It is unlikely that the role of the courts would ever be central here. Admittedly, the case law that vigorously enforces the right to access to documents may have indirect implications for data collection and management in policy co-ordination processes as well. However – and given that often the problem is not about accessing information, but rather about gathering and storing information, on the one hand, and locating and finding information, on the other – the appropriate body to address the situation and take action would seem to be outside the judicial branch.

155 Armstrong, 2010, p 134.

4.5.2 *Recommendations: More action?*

The greatest challenge of soft policy co-ordination is to initiate political action and responses in the Member States. Whilst EU-level strategies may have succeeded in setting out the agenda, they have been less successful in delivering concrete results: the 'delivery gap', as the Commission calls it, persists.

It was hoped that country-specific recommendations would step up progress and make monitoring more effective. However, country-specific recommendations adopted prior to the EU 2020 Strategy appear to have failed in this respect; clearly, lessons remain to be learned. When engaging in soul-searching in 2010 to find out what went wrong with the OMC, the Commission noted that, in some Member States, recommendations produced a real impact. Member States used recommendations to build up pressure for domestic reforms, particularly taking advantage of the opportunity to convince the national audience that other countries were dealing better with the same issues and policy imperatives. However, in other cases, recommendations have not led to visible effects, either in terms of political debate or other follow-up action.[156] Drawing inevitable conclusions, the Commission then pointed out that recommendations might have 'gained more acceptance from Member States had they been underpinned by a transparent and robust evaluation framework'.[157] Post-Lisbon recommendations now are precise and, more importantly, accompanied with a follow-up of Member State action.[158] The European Semester dispensed such a framework for evaluation. This new framework involves a discursive dimension too: an opportunity for a Member State to explain why it thinks that the policy advice of the recommendation may not be feasible or desirable to implement. If a Member State ignores a policy recommendation entirely, fails to act within the time frame, or develops policies that go against the recommendation, the Commission can, in the context of economic co-operation, issue a policy warning. In other policymaking contexts, the Commission lacks formal instruments to act against Member States for not giving sufficient regard to recommendations, but at least a policy document exists that bolsters the Commission by identifying dissenting Member States and pinning down issues in need of attention. Nevertheless, it is too early to say whether this makes any positive difference in bridging the delivery gap.

In light of the case law of the EU courts and the nature of existing country-specific recommendations, it seems rather implausible that the EU courts could enforce recommendations against Member States, yet the firmer tone adopted in the EU 2020 Strategy and the European Semester suggests that this might be subject to reconsideration in the future.

156 European Commission, February 2010, SEC(2010) 114 final, p 6.
157 Ibid, p 21.
158 See also Withana, Kretschmer and Farmer, 2013, p 7.

Actually, it might not be so important whether we will see recommendations or some other dimension of follow-up as long as we keep moving in the direction of comparison and evaluation of Member State activities. Emphasis on the deliberative dimension of policy co-ordination seems to have displaced the essential element inherent in democratic experimentalism – that is, that policy learning and discourse are always followed by, and therefore conditioned on, 'periodic pooling of results'.[159] Policy co-ordination in the European Union would arguably benefit from explicit evaluative processes, such as scoreboards and competitive benchmarking, since it is precisely at the reporting and evaluation stage that the deliberative process seems to break down. Within the European Semester, the Commission has now begun preparing thematic documents intended to compare progress across Member States.[160] Recommendations can also serve to help to introduce embryonic elements of pooling and a comparison of outcomes. This positive view is not unequivocally shared by all scholars. It has been argued that, since the 2005 streamlining of the Lisbon Strategy, the Commission has attempted to establish 'bilateral' relationships with individual Member States instead of deploying a more experimental 'multilateral' approach to governing.[161] Armstrong (2010) challenges this change of direction, contending that the original 'iterative' and experimentalist character was substituted for a policymaking mode that 'sought continuity and simplicity in its normative features with a greater emphasis on the accountability of Member States for their policy choices'.[162] Whilst it is less important to determine here whether or not the deliberative character was lost in the reform, it should be realised that experimentalism (at least, democratic experimentalism) is not hostile to structured evaluations and formalised comparison of results, but in fact thrives on them.[163]

4.5.3 Recommendations: More active stakeholders?

As demonstrated in this chapter, EU-level policy co-ordination seems fuzzy and incomprehensible to stakeholders and to the general public, and is not easy to work with. The Commission proposal for the EU 2020 Strategy attempted to address the problem by saying that the European Parliament was to be a driving force to mobilise citizens.[164] The fundamental fact that the Commission nicely manages to overlook is that the role of the Parliament in soft policy co-ordination mechanisms

159 Gerstenberg and Sabel, 2002, p 334. See also Benz, 2007, p 517.

160 Withana, Kretschmer and Farmer, 2013, p 16. The Commission itself highlights the important function of targets allowing for a 'transparent cross comparison': see European Commission, March 2014, COM(2014) 130 final, p 16.

161 Zeitlin, 2008, p 437.

162 Armstrong, 2010, p 117.

163 This comes through particularly strongly in Noonan and others, 2009.

164 European Commission, March 2010, COM(2010) 2020 final, p 6.

is marginalised too. Merging two marginalised groups rarely results in one big powerful group. Strengthening the impact of civil society by means of the Parliament seems rather a wretched hope unless the status of the Parliament is first substantially improved – something that is now on the agenda of the mid-term review of EU 2020. In terms of iterated deliberation, the crucial challenge is not, however, simply to consult or include civil society actors as broadly as possible, but to ensure that practices of participation elicit an answer and contribute to learning. It has already been explained how recommendations could result in more active and effective stakeholders by providing an informational context for stakeholder activities. Country-specific recommendations may strengthen the role of civil society stakeholders against both EU and Member State institutions, in that civil society will understand where the more specific focuses of the policy co-ordination process lie at any given time, and can accordingly challenge and contest such a choice.

The role of the EU courts remains subtle, to say the least. Stakeholders are virtually deprived of opportunities to demand broader participation rights before the EU courts. Although the courts cannot directly rule on the conditions of participation in policy co-ordination processes, their rulings may affect the broad contours of participation as a result of EU-level stakeholders often participating in more than one governance context. Acknowledgement of the manner in which both stakeholders and experience travel between governance regimes is a pragmatic depiction of the account of distributed deliberation. This means – as we remember from Chapter 3 – that it is not practical to require every institution to be deliberative, and that institutions (both deliberative and non-deliberative) can be brought together to create a distributed system of deliberation in which deliberative elements compensate for non-deliberative elements. In this way, non-deliberative institutions may also be encouraged to begin learning from more deliberative institutions. Most importantly, it contributes to seeing the role of the courts in a more elaborate manner. My argument is that slowly evolving judicial practice in response to forms of EU governance gives rise to far-reaching, unanticipated and potentially long-lasting consequences that serve to bridge the gap between deliberative and less deliberative institutions more broadly. Its precise contours remain open to further discussion and testing, but it should be noted that wide-ranging effects can occur without conscious efforts by judges to give (inappropriately) broad rulings.[165] Instead, rather than being aimed at by the judiciary, these sweeping effects are mediated by the emerging systemic connections between EU governance regimes themselves.

165 For the 'one case at a time' debate between Sunstein and Dworkin, and its repercussions for experimentalist governance, see Simon, 2006, p 51.

4.6 Conclusion

The jury is out on the future of both the EU 2020 Strategy and the European Semester.[166] In the meantime, a look into the recent past might be helpful in formulating some preliminary conclusions. When the Commission introduced EU 2020, the OMC as an instrument was expressly mentioned only in the context of the fight against poverty – and even then the Commission pledged to:

> . . . *transform* the open method of coordination on social exclusion and social protection into a platform for cooperation, peer-review and exchange of good practice, and into an instrument to foster commitment by public and private players to reduce social exclusion, and take concrete action . . . [167]

The explicit wish of the Commission to create a strong governance framework for EU 2020 in itself revealed what went awry with the OMC. Admittedly, its alleged 'failure' is closely connected to the failure of the European Union to achieve the Lisbon objectives, making it very difficult to ascertain which one of the many failures surrounding the Lisbon Strategy actually occurred first. However, from the point of view of the Commission, the OMC did not do what it promised, and the focus of the new EU 2020 was on implementation and its monitoring.[168]

Yet with all of the new, it is good to keep in mind the continuum between yesterday's and tomorrow's OMCs: the EU 2020 Strategy reaffirmed that we will see commonly agreed aims, national reform programmes and peer review – elements that we have come to associate with the OMC approach – in the future as well. If anything, the slight reorientation of EU 2020, with stronger emphasis on use of recommendations, firmly roots the policy co-ordination approach in the EU soft law tradition. One consequence of such entrenchment is that we can consider the relationship between adjudication and policy co-ordination processes in the larger context of judicially reviewable soft law. As yet, the EU courts have handed down no rulings on the legality of country-specific recommendations, but, as argued, their soft law form does not in itself prevent the EU courts from reviewing recommendations. The susceptibility of recommendations to judicial review will ultimately depend on whether the EU courts think that these have legal effects. Whether or not the EU courts arrive at this conclusion depends on the success of the Commission in stepping up the implementation process. If the Commission manages to be convincing in its argument that recommendations have binding (legal) effects, the delivery gap may be bridged. Alongside pragmatic success, the risk of the CJEU finding legal effects and accepting the argument

166 For stocktaking of the European Semester, see European Commission, March 2014, COM(2014) 130 final. In May 2014, the Commission opened a public consultation on the Europe 2020 Strategy.

167 European Commission, March 2010, COM(2010) 2020 final, p 19 (emphasis added). See also de la Porte and Pochet, 2012, p 338.

168 European Council, 2010.

according to which 'a non-binding veneer serves to conceal a binding act'[169] tends to increase too.

Recommendations have also been studied from the perspective of making Member States more accountable for their policy progress. Post-Lisbon recommendations (those adopted in the context bolstered by the new European Semester) may provide stakeholders and the general public with more and accessible information to push for reform in domestic settings. Moreover, I have argued that these recommendations, as well as other relevant policy documents, may become handy in (admittedly exceptional) cases that run the risk of creating a 'second *Mangold*'. If the CJEU gives explicit regard to reasoning and debates from the policy co-ordination process, and permits these to influence its judicial interpretation, its findings might not take the wider EU audience by surprise and therefore challenge the legitimacy of the CJEU. Whilst this recommendation may be instinctively attractive, the practical shortcomings in the organisation of policy co-ordination deliberations, as exemplified here by the European Semester, may render the recommendation nothing more than yet another brand of deliberative elitism. Much more is needed in terms of institutional improvements and modifications (some of which I have identified) to make sure that the recommendation rests on democratically justifiable grounds – that is, that it is matched by factual increases in the conditions of iterated deliberation in the European Semester.

169 Scott, 2011, p 344. It should be noted that pragmatic success may, paradoxically, serve to exclude recommendations from judicial review: if Member States treat recommendations as authoritative guidance, the Court may conclude that they have mainly factual effects and debar them from judicial review.

Chapter 5

The European Chemicals Agency

5.1 Introduction

The number of EU agencies has proliferated in the last decade and a half. One of the most recently created agencies is the European Chemicals Agency (ECHA). Its main task is the management and administration of European chemicals policy, and in this capacity it provides scientific and technical expertise on chemicals to Member States and EU institutions, and acts as an administrator in the centralised system known as 'REACH' – an acronym formed from the 'registration, evaluation, authorisation and restriction of chemical substances'.[1] The ECHA has been operational since summer 2007.

The ECHA provides an intriguing opportunity for case study. Admittedly, analysis of the ECHA institutional and administrative framework will not yield findings that could be called truly ground-breaking. Its institutional design – its organisation, tasks and the nature of its decision-making powers – is a medley of solutions tried and tested in EU agency governance. The novelty lies not so much in the ECHA itself as in its role in the overall framework of the REACH Regulation. First, information takes pride of place in REACH and the ECHA is the guardian of that information. REACH seeks to reverse developments whereby 'the totality of information . . . is dispersed over a wide range of producers and users of substances' by convening them to share their information.[2] The pre-REACH regime was generally perceived to be inefficient in ensuring that chemicals were manufactured and imported within safe limits, and in encouraging the search for safer alternatives. The key dilemma was that it placed unreasonable demands on public authorities to demonstrate the risks of chemicals to human health or to the environment before more stringent standards could be imposed, creating no incentive for manufacturers or importers to begin thinking about alternatives.

1 Regulation (EC) No 1907/2006 concerning the Registration, Evaluation, Authorisation and Restriction of Chemicals (REACH) and establishing a European Chemicals Agency. REACH is accompanied by Regulation (EC) No 1272/2008 on classification, labelling and packaging of substances and mixtures, and by Regulation (EU) No 528/2012 concerning the making available on the market and use of biocidal products.

2 Fleurke and Somsen, 2011, p 361.

In 2001, when the European Commission first proposed REACH, reversal of the burden of proof suited the optimistic tone of the Lisbon Strategy, taking EU chemicals regulation in the direction of the 'dynamic knowledge-based economy' and 'sustainable economic growth'.[3]

Second, REACH, although a Regulation, 'essentially is a framework' that leaves 'important questions to the discretion of a range of public and private authors within the regime', and the ECHA wields 'real power and influence' that is not visible until norm application.[4] Decision-making structures under REACH are highly complex, but the bottom line is that Member States, the Commission and the ECHA share powers. No one of them is capable of taking definitive action on its own; actors are duty-bound (often by express provision of REACH) to submit their views to other actors for consideration and to take the opinions of those other actors into account. Final decisions emerge as a result of these joint, multi-actor inter-relationships and dependencies. Despite some deplorable deficiencies, non-governmental actors and other stakeholders are also given opportunities to express their views and to contribute to decision making.

In keeping with the general theme of the case studies, my aim in this chapter is to analyse aspects of the judicial review of EU agencies. Gaps in legal or administrative control over agency decision making, and growing concerns for transparency and accountability, have worried observers, whilst difficulties with establishing review of agencies' tasks by the judiciary are well laboured in the literature.[5] Whilst providing an overview of these discussions, I shall, however, focus attention on the ECHA. With its dynamic and demanding decision-making procedures, the ECHA provides an unparalleled opportunity to reconsider the potential of judicial review in a context characterised by increased information and the experimentalist values and conditions of EU governance.

5.2 The European Chemicals Agency

5.2.1 Institutional design

The ECHA was agreed upon in 2006 under the REACH Regulation adopted by a legislative act of the Council and the European Parliament. The agency serves the EU institutions, Member States, firms and stakeholders on issues related to EU chemicals policy. It is located in Helsinki, with some 500 employees, which makes it one of the largest EU agencies. Its institutional design is typical of an EU agency: as with other agencies, the ECHA is also governed by a management board responsible for overseeing that the agency performs the tasks set out in its basic act, with an executive director appointed to discharge the agency's

3 Ibid, p 358. See also European Commission, February 2001, COM(2001) 88 final.

4 Fleurke and Somsen, 2011, pp 363 and 365.

5 These include, but are not limited to: Busuioc, 2009; Busuioc, 2013; Chiti, 2009; Curtin, 2007; Korkea-aho, 2013; Vos, 2000; Yataganas, 2001.

daily operations.[6] The management board nominates the executive director and has authority over the ECHA work programme, budget and annual report. The management board has one representative from each Member State and a maximum of six representatives appointed by the Commission, involving three individuals from interested parties without the right to vote. In addition, the European Parliament has the right to appoint two independent members.

The ECHA currently hosts four committees. The Committee for Risk Assessment (RAC) and the Committee for Socio-Economic Analysis (SEAC) are scientific bodies, with a central role in preparing the opinion of the ECHA on applications for authorisations and proposals for restrictions, the RAC addressing risks to human health or the environment and the SEAC considering the socio-economic impact of activities.[7] A recently established Biocidal Products Committee manages the activities needed to ensure compliance with a new Biocidal Products Regulation, while the fourth committee is the Member State Committee (MSC), established to serve as a broker between Member States in instances of REACH decision making. Each Member State nominates one member to the MSC committee, whereas the members of the two REACH scientific committees are appointed by the management board from among candidates nominated by the Member States on the basis of their expertise.[8] Moreover, the Forum for Exchange of Information on Enforcement (simply, 'the Forum' or 'Enforcement Forum') provides a platform for collaboration between national competent authorities on whom the enforcement of REACH falls.[9] The Board of Appeal, a place to appeal against decisions taken by the ECHA.[10]

Finally, a statutory requirement cuts across REACH to develop contacts with stakeholders and interested parties.[11] As Scott (2009a) points out, the term 'interested party' is not determined anywhere in the Regulation, so that it is 'sufficiently open-ended' to include a wide variety of actors.[12] In addition to having three observer seats on the management board, stakeholders can also attend meetings of all committees and the Forum by invitation.[13] Furthermore, interested parties are, as will be seen, given several opportunities to voice their views and submit comments in actual decision-making situations. The next sections explain how decision making occurs and how different actors exercise their powers, the focus being on the ECHA.

6 The Secretariat works under the executive director, providing technical and administrative support.
7 Article 76.
8 The ECHA website contains a list of members of four committees with CVs and declarations of interest. Most members seem to be employed by national research institutes, universities or relevant administrations.
9 Article 86.
10 Article 85 and Regulation (EC) No 771/2008 laying down the rules of organisation and procedure of the Board of Appeal of the ECHA. See also Bronckers and van Gerven, 2009, pp 1844–9.
11 Article 108.
12 Scott, 2009a, p 929.
13 Articles 85(4) and 86(1).

5.2.2 'R' for registration

Substances that are manufactured or imported into the European Union have to be registered with the ECHA. Only registered substances can be marketed. If no data are submitted, then marketing is prohibited. This key principle, which lays the responsibility on private actors to prove that their chemical is safe, is known as the 'no data, no market' rule.[14] REACH includes circumstantial rules for determining what kinds of substances require registration, and ECHA discretion is accordingly limited. The main principle is that the registration requirement covers substances on their own or in preparation in quantities totalling over 1 tonne per producer or importer yearly.[15] In addition, in some cases, substances in articles must also be registered. In this last respect, the ECHA has some discretion, and it can take decisions requiring producers or importers of articles to register a substance if it has grounds for suspecting that the substance is released and presents a risk to human health or the environment.[16] The ECHA decision cannot be appealed before the Board of Appeal, but it can be challenged before the General Court.

The registration process kicks off with a registrant submitting a technical dossier, which involves all physico-chemical, toxicological and ecotoxicological information that is relevant and available to the registrant.[17] It is widely agreed that producers have a negative incentive to underestimate risk in order to avoid agency intervention,[18] and REACH attempts to combat this tendency by laying down detailed rules on the minimum information to be contained in the dossier. Despite these more elaborate requirements set out in Annexes to REACH, the ECHA does exercise considerable discretion in evaluating registration documents because information requirements are laid down 'in open-ended, standard-based, terms; adequacy, reliability, and scientific validity for example'.[19] It is hardly a surprise that, out of a total of 20 decisions that the Board of Appeal has given thus far, nearly half have concerned registration and compliance requirements.[20] Yet, in light of the numbers of registration dossiers in total, the Board of Appeal figures are insignificant. To illustrate, the first registration deadline in 2010 totalled 24,675 dossiers, covering 4,300 substances. Even before this deadline, the ECHA had

14 Article 5. See also Heyvaert, 2007.

15 Article 6(1). Note that the general registration requirement applies to chemicals manufactured in the European Union, but subsequently exported. See Scott, 2009a, p 921, fn 134.

16 Article 7(1) and (5).

17 Article 12(1). In addition, the registrant remains obliged to provide any *new* information in respect of the health and environmental risks of the substance. Some observers doubt how often this actually happens given that a fee is payable in these cases. See Fleurke and Somsen, 2011, p 374.

18 Hey, Jacob and Volkery, 2007, p 1865. They suggest this to be 'a key governance problem of REACH'. According to the registration audit undertaken by ClientEarth and EEB in 2012, the majority of dossiers demonstrated 'serious compliance deficiencies': ClientEarth and EEB, 2012, p 6.

19 Scott, 2009b, p 62.

20 Accessed 30 June 2014, http://echa.europa.eu/about-us/who-we-are/board-of-appeal/decisions.

received more than 143,000 pre-registrations, because REACH, unlike earlier legislation, also covers substances already being manufactured or marketed in Europe (called 'phase-in substances'). On condition that their substances were pre-registered before 2009, companies with phase-in substances to register could benefit from an eight-year transition period before formal registration.

Numbers are massive and most registrations are only summarily checked.[21] The ECHA undertakes the 'completeness check' for each registration. This takes place in an automated way: it does not involve analysis of the adequacy or relevance of the information submitted by the applicant, and for this reason the ECHA is required to perform random, more intrusive 'compliance checks' for at least 5 per cent of registrations in each tonnage category.[22] By the end of 2013, the ECHA had published its results of first compliance checks, covering some 1,130 registration dossiers. It concluded that 69 per cent of all dossiers under evaluation were non-compliant on two main accounts: incomplete information regarding identification and composition of the substance; and insufficient justification for not submitting the required studies or missing information.[23] The ECHA has no powers to remove a substance from the market in cases of non-compliance, and where the ECHA decides that registration does not meet the information requirements, it can only prepare a draft decision requiring the registrant to improve its original dossier.[24] The procedure required for adoption of a final decision is a good example of a decision-making process spreading power to several actors. The ECHA has power to take the final decision unless a Member State proposes an amendment to the draft proposal. Should this happen, the ECHA is entitled to decide only if it enjoys unanimous support from the MSC. If the Committee does not back up the ECHA, the Commission will decide in the form of an examination procedure.[25]

5.2.3 'E' for evaluation

Where the majority of substances require merely formal registration, substances produced or manufactured in quantities of 100 tonnes or more yearly require additional, but mandatory, information. In these cases, the ECHA carries out a 'dossier evaluation'. This involves the abovementioned compliance check, as well as examination of the testing proposals included in the technical dossier.[26] Further

21 The ECHA's 2013 General Report notes that around 7,500 substances have been registered: ECHA, December 2013, p 11.

22 Articles 20, 23 and 28.

23 Animated by the poor quality of registrations, NGOs renewed their call for the introduction of 'naming and shaming of bad registrations', pointing out that it is common currency in some EU agencies (eg the European Medicines Agency, or EMA). See ClientEarth and EEB, 2012, pp 12 and 45.

24 Article 41(3).

25 Article 51 of REACH; Art 5 of the Comitology Regulation No 182/2011.

26 Article 40.

to this dossier evaluation, which is technically part of registration, the onus of the evaluation stage is on those situations in which the data submitted reveal that the substance constitutes a risk to human health or the environment. Subsequently, and irrespective of the volume, a 'substance evaluation' is undertaken. Substance evaluation involves two separate stages: first is identification of substances; second, actual evaluation. In respect of the first stage, the ECHA assumes the position of a co-ordinator.[27] Its main task is to draft a list of priority substances that require substance evaluation, using risk-based criteria developed in collaboration with Member States. This list, which determines which chemicals are to be evaluated, is known as the 'Community Rolling Action Plan' (CoRAP) and is valid for three years.[28] A given substance must be included on the list if grounds exist for suspecting that it constitutes a risk to human health or the environment. A Member State may notify the ECHA of a substance that is not on the CoRAP whenever it has information that might indicate that a chemical is a priority substance for evaluation. The ECHA decides whether or not to add the proposed substance to the CoRAP after having received an opinion from the MSC.[29] The ECHA decision is not susceptible to appeal before the Board of Appeal, yet it has been suggested that the ECHA should explain why it has not included a substance that a Member State has proposed. The wording of Art 44(2) of the Regulation – substances 'shall' be included – indicates that refusal to include a substance could be subject to judicial review.[30]

In the second stage, Member States take on a leading role. The CoRAP assigns substances to national regulatory authorities, which carry out the actual evaluation of the substance. The assigned Member State authority adopts a draft decision and submits it, together with any comments by the registrant or downstream user,[31] to the ECHA and to other Member States. Although no legal obligation exists to include third parties, the practice has emerged allowing third parties to submit information on substances under evaluation.[32] Member States can propose amendments to the draft decision to the ECHA. If the ECHA does not receive any amendment proposals, it takes the decision as proposed by the evaluating Member State. In practice, before taking a decision, the ECHA has screened draft decisions for coherence and, if necessary, requested further information.[33] If the ECHA receives a proposal for amendment, it may modify the draft decision. The ECHA

27 Nothing in the text of REACH prevents the ECHA from assuming a more active role than that of a co-ordinator, and NGOs have accused it of adopting an unnecessarily 'self-limiting interpretation of REACH'. See ClientEarth and EEB, 2012, p 36.

28 The first CoRAP for 2012–13 included 90 substances; the second CoRAP for 2013–14, 115 substances. The second plan contains only 62 *new* substances, since 53 substances were already part of the first CoRAP.

29 Articles 44(2) and 45(5).

30 Scott, 2009b, p 69.

31 For a 'downstream user', see Art 3(13).

32 ClientEarth and EEB, 2012, p 33.

33 ECHA, December 2013, p 23.

then has to refer the draft decision, together with proposed amendments, to the MSC.[34] Should the Committee reach unanimous agreement on the draft decision, the ECHA decides accordingly. Failing this, the European Commission takes the final decision.[35] The first substance evaluations were prepared and partially published in early 2014. Altogether, 47 substances were evaluated by Member States, resulting in 37 draft decisions requesting more information to ground risk assessment.

5.2.4 'A' for authorisation

REACH requires that 'substances of very high concern' (SVHCs) must be authorised, regardless of volumes of production and import. Without authorisation, they cannot be marketed.[36] Authorisation applies automatically to certain categories of substances generally viewed as potentially dangerous, for example carcinogenic, mutagenic or reprotoxic substances, and persistent, bioaccumulative and toxic, and very persistent and very bioaccumulative substances. Furthermore, the authorisation requirement may be extended to include additional substances. This is intended to target substances for which scientific evidence suggests probable serious effects on human health or the environment, which gives rise to a level of concern equivalent to that for other substances listed.[37]

Again, two distinct stages are involved: first, identification of substances that require authorisation (Annex XIV, which lists substances requiring authorisation, was blank when REACH was adopted); and second, the actual grant of authorisation. A decision to add a certain substance to Annex XIV is taken under a decision-making procedure involving intricate negotiations, and rounds of comments and opinions. The Commission and Member States can initiate the process by submitting a technical dossier for the inclusion of a substance. Only Member States and the Commission enjoy this right.[38] Now, while the ECHA cannot act independently, the Commission decision to start the process is factually taken by the ECHA, since it prepares a dossier for the Commission on request. The influence of the ECHA is also augmented by its function as a filter for civil society contribution. It publishes the dossier on its website and invites all interested parties to comment within three months of the date of publication. After this period, the ECHA has to update its dossier, taking into account comments received, thus rendering it the actual decision maker in balancing public and private

34 Registrants or downstream users may express their views afresh if Member States propose amendments to the draft decision. The MSC must take into account any comments received. See Art 51(5).

35 Articles 51 and 52.

36 Article 56.

37 Article 57(a)–(f).

38 Article 59(2)–(3). Furthermore, the ECHA recommends to the Commission certain substances from the candidate list to be included in the final list: Art 58(3).

interests. The dossier must then be circulated for comments to other Member States and interested parties. If there are no comments, the substance that the Member State or the Commission has proposed is included on the preliminary list, known as the 'candidate list'. In the event of comments, the matter is forwarded to the MSC, which takes a decision that must be unanimous. If the MSC cannot reach agreement, the Commission steps in.[39] The Commission also takes a decision, upon the recommendation of the ECHA, on the final list (that is, Annex XIV).[40]

The authorisation process has provoked the expected reaction from the industry. Chemicals companies have challenged several ECHA decisions to include substances on the candidate list, giving rise to the question of whether a decision to include a substance on the candidate list is an admissible act. In a representative ruling, rejecting the ECHA interpretation according to which the decision is preliminary and hence not susceptible to review, the General Court, and subsequently the Court of Justice, perceived the decision as admissible, but dismissed the challenge on substantive grounds, upholding ECHA discretion and scientific judgement.[41] This ruling also touched upon the role of the ECHA in the inclusion of substances in Annex XIV. Specifically, the applicant challenged inclusion of the substance in light of the principle of equal treatment. In the applicant's view, it was not fair that its substance was picked and not some other, marketed by its rivals. The General Court highlighted the multi-actor approach of the evaluation, where the Commission and Member States have the initiative, not the ECHA, and hence the latter cannot be held accountable for a decision emanating from a process that it did not itself set in motion.[42] From the point of view of the REACH text, the conclusion is sound: the ECHA itself cannot initiate the procedure, yet in practice the decision-making powers of the ECHA and the Commission are intricately enmeshed.

The second stage concerns grant of authorisation. The ECHA is the receiving authority for all applications for authorisation, managing practical issues of authorisation. The duty to submit necessary information lies with the industry, as in registration.[43] The decision-making process is once again multi-level. In the

39 Article 59(9). So far, the candidate list includes 155 and Annex XIV, ie the final list, 22 substances.

40 Article 58(1). Is inclusion of a substance on the candidate list necessary for its inclusion on the final list? The question is not only theoretically important: the European Parliament exercises greater influence over adoption of the final list than the candidate list. Scott, 2009b, p 71, argues that although a positive answer to the question could be implied by the provisions of REACH, it 'seems unlikely' that the final list must be exclusively based on the candidate list.

41 Case T-93/10 *Bilbaína de Alquitranes, AS and others v ECHA*, 7 March 2013, NYR; appealed as Case C-287/13 P *Bilbaína de Alquitranes, AS and others v ECHA*, 22 May 2014, NYR. In Case T-1/10 *PPG and SNF v ECHA* [2011] ECR II-6576, appealed as Case C-626/11 P *PPG & SNF v ECHA*, 26 September 2013, NYR; T-1/10 RENV, pending at time of writing, the Court of Justice clarified that the decision to include a substance on the candidate list can be challenged before publication of the list on the website.

42 Case T-93/10 *Bilbaína de Alquitranes, AS and others v ECHA*, 7 March 2013, NYR, [72].

43 For the information requirement, see Art 62 and Scott, 2009b, pp 66–8.

first step, the information is analysed and assessed by an ECHA expert committee. Information on applications for authorisation must also be made available on the ECHA website in order to allow interested parties to submit information on alternative substances or technologies. The SEAC will take these comments into account.[44] When the draft decisions by SEAC and RAC are prepared, the applicant is invited to submit comments, in which case both committees will reconsider their opinions. REACH does not specify whether third parties can comment upon draft opinions, but neither is this expressly ruled out. Much depends on the ECHA's discretion in deciding whether and to what extent draft opinions and any attachments are made publicly available.[45] Upon conclusion of consultation, the ECHA must submit both draft opinions to the Commission, the Member States and the applicant. The Commission acts as a final decision maker. It is not bound by the text of REACH to take committee opinions into account or to offer a detailed explanation for reasons in case of departure. However, despite the absence of an explicit provision, the case law of the Court of Justice of the European Union (CJEU) would (arguably) suggest that the Commission is obliged to take into account scientific expertise offered by the committees and to provide reasons in order to justify its departure from those opinions.[46]

The Commission has to grant authorisation if the risks are shown to be adequately controlled. Authorisations are granted on a use-specific basis and conditionally, with requirements pertaining to monitoring and review processes. If the risks are impossible to keep fully under control, authorisation may still be granted if it is shown that the socio-economic benefits outweigh the risk to human health or to the environment, and if no suitable alternative substances or technologies are available. The authorisation holder will, in both cases, be obligated to reduce exposure to as low a level as possible.[47] The importance of information is pronounced in this latter case, where authorisation is granted against 'better' judgement, socio-economic benefits tilting the balance in favour of authorisation. Scott (2009b) suggests that allocation of the burden of proof is unclear in these cases and that authorisation may be granted on the grounds of information not submitted by the applicant.[48] Yet the main principle remains that the applicant must submit information and necessary evidence for authorisation. Whether the information submitted by the applicant qualifies as sufficient to grant authorisation is again determined by open-ended standards. These standards leave discretion to the ECHA committees, which are, moreover, obliged to take into account information from interested parties.

44 Article 64(1), (2) and (4)(b).
45 Article 64(6).
46 Scott, 2009b, p 77.
47 Article 60(10).
48 Scott, 2009b, p 67. See also Fleurke and Somsen, 2011, p 386.

Instead of authorisation, particular uses of a substance can be restricted if they present 'an unacceptable risk to human health or the environment'.[49] The difference between authorisation and restriction is that, with respect to the former, 'all uses of listed chemicals are banned unless applicants can defend a specific use', whereas 'in the context of the restriction procedure it is the authorities that must provide justifications for banning specific uses (or in some cases production)'.[50] Restrictions are listed in Annex XVII. This may be amended at any time if an unacceptable risk emerges that is not adequately controlled by existing measures. A Member State or the Commission can ask the ECHA to prepare a dossier for a restriction on the manufacture, marketing or use of dangerous substances. Interestingly, the ECHA examines the Commission's request to initiate the restriction procedure and submits a dossier only if it agrees with the Commission. Information on restriction dossiers is publicly available on the ECHA website, and interested parties can submit comments and/or socio-economic analysis.[51] The committees prepare draft opinions, taking into account the contributions submitted, post them on the website and, in case of comments, modify their opinions.[52] Should the Commission's final decision differ from what was proposed by the Member State or the ECHA, the Commission must state reasons for its decision.

5.2.5 *Preaching REACH: Information and implementation*

As with other EU agencies and institutions, the ECHA is under an obligation to adhere to the general EU law framework on access to information and on transparency of decision making.[53] Based on the information available on its website, the ECHA intends not only to meet, but also to go beyond, these legal requirements. To this end, it has adopted codes of conduct and several policy documents that establish channels of communication and operationalise a regular dialogue with its stakeholders.[54] These commitments are not simply an exercise in public relations, but are potentially important, because the ECHA holds significant amounts of (legally relevant) information. According to recent estimates, it has

49 Article 68.

50 Fleurke and Somsen, 2011, p 370. Since entry into force, REACH has restricted seven substances, total numbers (including restrictions decided before REACH) amounting to 63.

51 Article 69(1), (2) and (6).

52 Article 71. The applicant does not have the right to be heard. See Scott, 2009b, p 77.

53 See also Arts 11–13 of Regulation (EC) No 1367/2006 on application of the provisions of the Aarhus Convention on Access to Information, Public Participation in Decision Making and Access to Justice in Environmental Matters to Community Institutions and Bodies. These strengthen the publicity requirements of REACH Regulation, yet the simultaneous coexistence of general transparency rules, the REACH rules and the Aarhus rules may give rise to problems. See Bronckers and van Gerven, 2009, pp 1839–43; Heyvaert, 2008, p 16.

54 Accessed 30 June 2014, http://echa.europa.eu/about/documents_en.asp.

made information on more than 10,000 substances from more than 40,000 dossiers available online.[55] Information produced within REACH is normally publicly available through the ECHA website, except where disclosure of information would undermine commercial interests. It is up to the ECHA to decide when this is the case. On the one hand, the ECHA may, in certain cases, permit disclosure of commercially sensitive information; on the other, it can also prevent submission of information that is normally available if submission would harm commercial interests and if it accepts as valid the justification presented for withholding the information by the company.[56] The extent to which the information is publicly available has already caused several fallings-out between the ECHA and civil society. At least one case has been brought before the courts by two environmental non-governmental organisations (NGOs), challenging the decision of the ECHA to withhold documents containing information on the registration stage.[57]

Another point of great importance to understanding the system of REACH is its implementation. Despite the fact that REACH is a regulation, it leaves, as noted, many important questions open. In some accounts, REACH is described as 'a framework regulation that leaves many political questions to the discretion of the bodies created for implementation'.[58] This latitude is, however, considerably circumscribed by the production of ECHA guidance documents in the context of REACH Implementation Projects (RIPs).[59] In the main text of REACH, neither RIPs nor guidance documents are explicitly mentioned, but guidance documents have an important role to play in REACH for the Commission is reluctant (owing to fresh memories from a nightmarishly complex legislative process leading up to REACH) to suggest revisions to the legislative text. Therefore the pressure to keep up with technical progress is discharged through lower-level guidance-writing. The main objective of guidance documents is to facilitate the implementation of REACH by explaining and describing good practice on how to satisfy legal obligations, and to provide additional information to the text of REACH. At the time of writing, there are in total 21 guidance documents, some already revisited once, taking up approximately 2,000 pages.[60] The documents encompass all of the technical aspects of REACH, but at least some of them may have a normative significance too. They are non-binding, and the cover page of each ECHA guidance document reads 'the information in this document does not constitute legal advice'. It seems realistic to argue that they are nonetheless

55 ECHA, December 2013, pp 15 and 33.
56 Articles 118(1) and 119(2).
57 Case T-245/11 *ClientEarth and International Chemical Secretariat v ECHA*, pending at time of writing.
58 Hey, Jacob and Volkery, 2007, p 1865.
59 Recital 24.
60 Accessed 30 June 2014, http://guidance.echa.europa.eu/. The ECHA also adopts guidance documents in respect of the Biocidal Products Regulation and of Regulation (EU) No 649/2012 concerning the export and import of hazardous chemicals.

highly influential in practice, not least because the ECHA endorses them in its operations.[61]

5.2.6 Delegation and control: 'Independent and unelected civil servants ... in the beautiful but rather remote Helsinki'?[62]

The CJEU articulated the legal parameters of agency decision making as early as 1958. According to the principle enshrined in the so-called '*Meroni* doctrine', delegation of powers is acceptable only when powers are clearly defined and can be subjected to review; under no circumstances could 'a discretionary power implying a wide margin of discretion' be delegated to bodies other than EU institutions.[63] Although the EU Court specifically spoke of a 'wide' margin of discretion, constitutional scholarship has interpreted the judgment as forbidding any delegation of discretionary powers – that is, political powers – to EU agencies. In the 2008 Communication, the Commission confirmed and paraphrased this anti-delegation principle in the agency context. A key principle is that EU agencies cannot be entrusted with powers to adopt general regulatory measures; instead, they are 'limited to taking individual decisions in specific areas where defined technical expertise is required, under clearly and precisely defined conditions and without genuine discretionary power'.[64] Moreover, the Commission emphasised the importance of institutional balance, arguing that EU agencies cannot be given powers that may have an effect on obligations explicitly bestowed upon the Commission by the Treaty (by way of example, the Commission mentions here its role as the guardian of Union law).

The anti-delegation principle coincides with the functional separation in risk regulation between risk assessment and risk management. Here, the idea is to establish a solid boundary between assessment, which falls within the remit of independent and objective experts (also understood as agents), and management, which belongs to politically accountable decision makers (conceived of as principals). Only politically answerable decision-making bodies should take political decisions. There are, however, views that this kind of frontier between assessment and management is virtually impossible to determine, let alone to police in practice. Most importantly, this is because the precise meaning of 'political decision making', underpinning the separation between risk assessment and risk management, is complex and unclear, as well as highly contingent on the

61 The guidance-writing process is a complex, multi-actor exercise. The ECHA has published a guidance document laying down detailed rules on how the final decision on guidance is to be taken. See ECHA, December 2013. For more detailed elaboration of ECHA guidance-drafting, see Korkea-aho, 2013.

62 Heyvaert, 2008, p 14.

63 Case 9/56 *Meroni & Co., Industrie Metallurgiche SpA v ECSC High Authority* [1957–58] ECR 133.

64 European Commission, March 2008, COM(2008) 135 final, p 5.

context.[65] For instance, the European Food Safety Agency (EFSA), the agency responsible for risk management in the area of safety of food and feed, is characterised as a 'normative agency'.[66] Although it does not have direct regulatory authority or final decision-making powers, the terms of the basic act indirectly confer important legal effects on the decisions of the EFSA simply because of the underlying legislative obligation to base the regulation of food and feed upon risk assessment. Furthermore, doubts exist as to what to make of the role of the Commission as principal, for it is the view of the Commission acting as a principal to subordinate agents that underpins both the anti-delegation principle and the functional separation between risk assessment and risk management. The Commission is usually represented in agency scientific committees and is responsible for administrative supervision of agency activities, but it does not have the competence to review decisions of EU agencies, nor those of their boards of appeal.

Whilst strengthening control of agencies by the Commission may initially seem to be a good idea, it furnishes the Commission with an opportunity to persuade and direct agency decision making behind the scenes, 'without appearing to do so'.[67] Interestingly enough, the Commission itself is openly reluctant to take on the role of principal. Its main argument is that, although it usually has a representative(s) on the management board, the Commission is always in a minority, and sometimes its representatives are not entitled to vote. Accordingly, the Commission poses the question whether, and if so, to what extent, it can be perceived to be accountable for decisions taken by an EU agency.[68]

The *Meroni* principle has garnered ample attention and much scathing criticism. For many, it has severely aggravated the problems of agency decision making by permitting technocrats and experts to 'get away' with their decisions rather than rendering them accountable. The anti-delegation doctrine, in the view of critics, has managed to create a situation in which the reality of EU agency decision making does not correspond to the requirements of the 'formal constitution'.[69] Some go so far as to suggest that the principle in itself is not a problem, but rather the way in which it has been interpreted for political convenience. Chiti (2009) argues that the 'essential *ratio*' of the *Meroni* doctrine is the principle of institutional balance – something that the CJEU has been willing to reinterpret quite dynamically over the years, whereas the Commission has adopted a conservative approach in order to preserve its own prerogatives.[70] In essence, then, the conventional principal–agent framework of analysis makes little sense and has just

65 Shapiro, 2005, p 347.

66 Chalmers, 2003, p 538. Similarly about the European Aviation Safety Agency, see Chiti, 2009, p 1405.

67 Busuioc, 2009, p 614.

68 European Commission, March 2008, COM(2008) 135 final, p 5.

69 Lenaerts and Verhoeven, 2002, p 48. See also Dehousse, 2002, p 17.

70 Chiti, 2009, pp 1423–4.

as little value in providing tangible answers to problems arising in the context of EU agency governance.[71]

Now, only a handful of agencies have been granted independent – although, in most cases, non-discretionary – powers: the Office for Harmonisation in the Internal Market (OHIM); the Community Plant Variety Office (CPVO); the European Aviation Safety Agency (EASA); the ECHA; and, most recently, three European supervisory authorities. The establishment of these specific EU agencies has not been seen as contradicting the doctrinal position set by *Meroni* or as ruffling the feathers of Member States.[72] Their emergence, however, while within the bounds of *Meroni* jurisprudence, seems to provide evidence of 'attempts to create a more independent and autonomous structure in the form of European Regulatory Agencies that would be delegated with certain specific (discretionary) regulatory functions'.[73] Yet, in my view, the ECHA is the first EU agency to seriously test the boundaries of the *Meroni* principle. A detailed scrutiny of decision-making procedures under REACH demonstrates that the ECHA has been entrusted with discretionary powers that may not be deemed entirely appropriate in light of the classic anti-delegation principle and, in particular, of how it has traditionally been understood by EU institutions. Recent subsequent developments in respect of new supervisory authorities have continued to batter the doctrine.[74]

Should we then, accepting the inevitability of shortcomings and the correctness of criticism levelled at the *Meroni* doctrine, conclude that the agents (EU agencies) are out of bounds? The answer is 'no' – at least if we limit analysis to the ECHA. REACH marks the first attempt to marry theory and practice: the departure from established doctrinal positions occurs not only in practice (as arguably happens quite often in the current system), but also is visible from the legal provisions of REACH itself. The REACH Regulation does not build on the traditional principal–agent relationship, and the legislative text makes it clear that, in some cases, the ECHA has actual discretionary decision-making powers. Admittedly, instances exist in which the ECHA needs a request from the Commission to begin the process, or cases in which the Commission is the final decision maker (although this usually happens only if Member States and the ECHA cannot work out a decision between themselves); nevertheless, REACH is genuinely exceptional in being straightforward about real responsibilities, how these are divided and who is in charge of what action or task. To this extent, it is regrettable that some new judgments depict a timid ECHA, an agency that has not come to terms with its

71 Curtin, 2007; Senden and van den Brink, 2012, p 23.

72 See Chiti, 2009, p 1421, and the literature that he cites. See also Case C-217/04 *United Kingdom v European Parliament and Council* [2006] ECR I-3771, in which the UK disputed not the establishment of the European Security and Information Agency (ENISA) per se, but the choice of legal basis: ex Art 95 EC instead of ex Art 308 EC.

73 Curtin, 2007, p 528.

74 Curtin, Hofmann and Mendes, 2013, p 17. See also Case C-270/12 *United Kingdom v Parliament and Council*, 22 January 2014, NYR.

own powers, trying instead to hide behind the Commission – a practice that (as the General Court has on one occasion pointed out) finds 'no support' in the Treaties.[75]

The conclusion is not, then, that the ECHA is irresponsibly let loose to exercise discretionary powers; rather, it may reasonably be argued that its activities are controlled in a manner very distinctive to the overall design of REACH.[76] The whole point of REACH is to interlink different actors to work together, so that no one is capable of taking a decision on its own without having to give regard to what others have to say. For this reason, REACH has great potential to mitigate the concerns usually associated with agency decision making. Laying out the steps to be taken by the Commission and the ECHA, REACH manages to meet – and then go beyond – the objectives pursued by the anti-delegation principle. For instance, REACH grants the ECHA a measure of autonomy as regards the CoRAP. However, this 'devolution' is accompanied by a concomitant effort to make the ECHA collaborate with others, and to render the powers exercised by the ECHA as manifest and transparent as possible, in order to permit others to monitor and provide feedback. Clear signposting helps to make the ECHA more meaningfully accountable to both the administration and the citizens of the European Union.

That being concluded, it is time to analyse the role of courts in review of EU agency governance in three specific contexts.

5.3 EU agencies and judicial action

As if to celebrate the approaching 50th anniversary of *Meroni*, the CJEU re-endorsed its judgment in 2005 in *Alliance for Natural Health*.[77] Whilst not offering much that is new, one thing that the judgment made plainly obvious should be noted here: the *Meroni* doctrine plays a stronger role in the establishment of an EU agency than it does in thinking about its subsequent control. Put differently, there seems to be no common understanding between the EU institutions over the form of control put forward in *Meroni*: what the purpose and role of such 'strict' review is, or what those 'objective' criteria could be. The situation is perhaps slightly different after the *ESMA* judgment, handed down in 2014.[78] When adjudicating the establishment of the European Securities and Markets Authority (ESMA), the

75 Case T-93/10 *Bilbaína de Alquitranes, AS and others v ECHA*, 7 March 2013, NYR, [59]. The issue was about interpretation of Art 263 TFEU on which the ECHA attempted to rely when contending that only the Commission has the regulatory power to adopt acts susceptible to review.

76 See also Bronckers and van Gerven, 2009, p 1827. Although, in their view, delegation of powers to the ECHA is too limited and ambiguous in many cases, reflecting negatively on the effectiveness of legal remedies available: ibid, 1853–4.

77 Joined Cases C-154/04 and C-155/04 *The Queen, on the application of Alliance of Natural Health and others v Secretary of State for Health and National Assembly for Wales* [2005] ECR I-6451, [90]. See also Case C-301/02 P *Carmine Salvator Tralli v European Central Bank* [2005] ECR I-4071.

78 C-270/12 *United Kingdom v Parliament and Council*, 22 January 2014, NYR.

CJEU based its approving judgment on two elements in particular: that the powers of ESMA were clearly delineated and that they were open to *judicial* review.[79] However, the implications of this new case, as well as more broadly of *Meroni* cases, for the function of judicial review are not clearly established,[80] and it is interesting that the Communication on the future of EU agencies, with the bold title 'The Way Forward', does not include a single reference to the courts.[81]

In some ways, the Commission's approach to and vision of the way ahead is excusable, and can even be justified. A number of legal and practical excuses exist for judges not to engage in judicial review of decisions by EU agencies. Yet when agency activities are on the increase and have become 'harder', these excuses need to be re-evaluated. The conclusion most commonly arrived at on the basis of this re-evaluation is that the growing agency powers need to be counterbalanced by strong(er) procedural rights.[82] My argument, which I develop in the rest of this chapter, is that this rights-based approach is not entirely convincing or adequate. In the next sections, I consider three particular issues that, in my view, stand in the way of a more rights-based approach to EU agency governance: first, I discuss the judicial treatment of EU agency decisions and (scientific) opinions; second, how the EU courts should review consensus-seeking risk regulation; and finally, whether Art 263(4) TFEU needs to be reinterpreted in relation to agency decision making. The picture that emerges is not quite what we might expect. The rights-based approach is generally suboptimal in meeting the demands of an accountable chemicals policy in the absence of a governance regime that makes decisions, the rationales behind them and decision-making practices open and accessible to permit scrutiny and monitoring.

5.3.1 Agency scientific opinions and decisions in the EU courts: Judicial risk management?

Scientific and technical expertise is immensely important to EU law-making and governance-making. This is especially so in the case of EU environmental

79 See ibid, [53]. Furthermore, the CJEU paid particular attention to two things: that the Agency's discretion is circumscribed by a consultation requirement, and that the measures it takes are intended as preliminary. See ibid, [50].

80 Arguably, though, the autonomous interpretative authority of the EU courts is an important element of the *Meroni* doctrine. Consider the following: the Administrative Commission on Migrant Workers adopts decisions and recommendations; the CJEU has, in several cases, applied the *Meroni* criteria and denied the binding interpretation given by the Administrative Commission on account of not wanting to disturb institutional balance – that is, not wanting to give up its interpretative authority. See, eg, Case 98/80 *Romano v Institut National d'Assurance Maladie-Invalidité* [1981] ECR 1241, [20]; Case C-21/87 *Borowitz v Bundesversicherungsanstalt für Angestellte* [1988] ECR 3715, [19]; Case C-102/91 *Knoch v Bundesanstalt für Arbeit* [1992] ECR I-4341, [52]. See von Bogdandy, Arndt and Bast, 2004, p 132.

81 European Commission, March 2008, COM(2008) 135 final.

82 Among others, Chiti, 2009, p 1406. See also Case C-269/90 *Technische Universität München v Hauptzollampt München-Mitte* [1991] ECR I-5469, [14].

policymaking, where the European Union is to attain a 'high level of protection' and, to this end, has to 'take account of available scientific and technical data'.[83] One among many implications here is that the European courts are increasingly called upon to review measures based on scientific evidence.

Ex Art 230 EC did not include decisions of EU agencies in the list of reviewable acts. However, the basic acts of agencies often included provisions making judicial review possible, in particular where EU agencies had final decision-making powers. With the entry into force of the Lisbon Treaty, Art 263(1) TFEU now explicitly mentions acts of 'bodies', 'offices' or 'agencies' of the Union intended to produce legal effects in relation to third parties as being susceptible to judicial review. In addition to this general reviewability clause, REACH also includes specific provision on challengeable acts: decisions of the ECHA (those that cannot be challenged internally before the Board of Appeal) or decisions of the Board of Appeal can be brought before the EU courts. REACH does not specify what those decisions are, implying that if the right of appeal is not expressly prohibited, it is permitted.[84] In addition, Commission decisions within the REACH framework can be judicially challenged. In both cases, the conditions identified in Art 263 TFEU apply.

When analysing susceptibility to judicial review of measures taken in an agency context, an important distinction should be observed: decisions that alter the legal situation of an individual can be challenged, although based on scientific expertise. I return to these later. Another matter, which I discuss now, concerns the susceptibility to judicial review of a scientific opinion, delivered (for example) by a scientific committee. In these situations, 'procedural and judicial protection is more rudimentary, on the assumption that the activity carried out by the relevant European agencies, being instrumental, cannot directly affect an individual position and therefore does not require any particular protection of private parties'.[85] Usually, scientific opinions adopted by EU agencies cannot be directly challenged before the EU courts. They are understood to be preparatory – that is, non-binding acts prepared for the Commission to deploy in its final decision making. The General Court has been very clear that scientific opinions (in this

83 Article 191 TFEU.

84 Article 94(1). REACH instead limits the scope of appeal before the Board of Appeal: appeals can be brought against decisions taken under Arts 9, 20, 27(6), 30(2) and (3), and 51. See Art 91(1). Article 92 determines who can bring an action to the Board of Appeal. It provides a formula that in essence is the rule borrowed from ex Art 230(4) EC: 'Any natural or legal person may appeal against a decision addressed to that person, or against a decision which, although addressed to another person, is of direct and individual concern to the former.' Because Art 94(1) concerning challengeable judicial acts contains a direct reference to ex Art 230 EC (Art 263 TFEU), this means that, after entry into force of the Lisbon Treaty, the scope of the right to appeal is wider before the EU courts than it is before the Board of Appeal. However, this does not seem logical and it could be argued that the scope of Art 92(1) of REACH should be reinterpreted to be in line with Art 263 TFEU.

85 Chiti, 2009, p 1407.

case, those of the EFSA) may not be judicially reviewed 'as such': '[T]he applicants have not prima facie put forward evidence to establish that the Court has jurisdiction to hear and determine actions for annulment challenging EFSA's acts *as such*.'[86]

The key to the courts' reasoning seems to lie in the apparently neutral expression 'as such'. Namely, in the earlier *Artegodan* judgments,[87] scientific opinions submitted by the then European Medicines Evaluation Agency (EMEA) – now the European Medicines Agency (EMA) – Committee for Proprietary Medicinal Products (CPMP) were found to be 'none the less extremely important so that any unlawfulness of that opinion must be regarded as a breach of essential procedural requirements rendering the Commission's decision unlawful'. In other words, the EU courts permit private parties to challenge scientific opinions alongside the Commission decision 'within the context of an appeal against the ultimate decision taken by the Commission'.[88] In its *Artegodan* ruling, the General Court also elaborated the scope of such review. Short of powers to 'substitute its own assessment for that of the scientific committee', the General Court declared its competence to review whether the committee functions adequately, whether its opinions are internally consistent and whether reasons are fully stated.[89] Concerning this final aspect, the Court explained that it may interrogate whether the scientific opinion contains a statement of reasons from which it is possible to ascertain the considerations upon which the opinion is based, and whether it establishes a 'comprehensible link between the medical and/or scientific findings and its conclusions'.[90]

Although the General Court used the word 'only' when describing its scope of review, in practice its procedural review is potentially quite detailed and demanding. In requiring a scientific committee to establish 'a comprehensible link' between the scientific findings and its conclusions, the EU courts impose an unambiguous obligation upon an EU agency to refer to key reports and scientific expert opinions on which it bases its own opinion, and to explain, in the event of a significant departure from them, the reasons why it has done so. In my view, though, the innovative multi-level decision-making design of REACH takes care of the obligation formulated in the *Artegodan* case.

86 Joined Cases T-311/06 R I, T-311/06 R II, T-312/06 R and T-313/06 R, *FMC Chemical SPRL, Arysta Lifesciences SAS, Otsuka Chemical Co. Ltd v European Food Safety Authority (EFSA)* [2007] ECR II-21, [56] (emphasis added). See also Case T-397/06 *Dow AgroSciences Ltd v EFSA* [2008] ECR II-90, especially [59].

87 Joined Cases T-74/00, T-76/00, T-83/00, T-84/00, T-85/00, T-132/00, T-137/00 and T-141/00 *Artegodan GmbH and others v Commission* [2002] ECR II-4945, [197]. See also Chiti, 2009, p 1420, fn 72.

88 Bronckers and van Gerven, 2009, p 1870.

89 Joined Cases T-74/00, T-76/00, T-83/00, T-84/00, T-85/00, T-132/00, T-137/00 and T-141/00 *Artegodan GmbH and others v Commission* [2002] ECR II-4945, [200].

90 Ibid.

Let me explain what I mean. By requiring the CPMP to state its reasons, the General Court attempted to ensure that the pharmaceutical substance in question 'has undergone a detailed and objective scientific assessment, based on a comparison of the most representative scientific opinions with the scientific arguments advanced by the pharmaceutical laboratories concerned'.[91] In contrast, within REACH, when a scientific opinion reaches the courts, it has already undergone rounds of deliberation by ECHA committees, national authorities, the Commission and/or interested parties. Not only does this increase the scientific validity and the popular authority of the scientific opinion, but it also returns the benefits of the *Artegodan* case back to the courts: it gives the EU courts a better and more legitimate standing to defer to expertise that has been subjected to rounds of consultation. Here, the EU governance arrangement both creates information and scrutinises it, providing a good example of a situation in which 'traditional' adjudication and new governance may work surprisingly well together to strengthen the legitimacy of both.

However, unlike many other EU agencies, the ECHA enjoys some independent decision-making authority, and the decisions that it takes in this role can be challenged before the courts because they bring about a change in the legal situation of an individual. This is the other category of situations referred to earlier. The ECHA can, for example, take decisions requiring producers or importers of articles to register a substance under certain conditions.[92] Its decision may have significant consequences for small and medium-sized enterprises (SMEs), for which the costs incurred by registration requirements can be high. The decision cannot be appealed before the Board of Appeal, but is reviewable by the General Court. The problem that now emerges is the scope of review. One could argue that, in these cases, standard (procedural) formulas of 'manifest error', 'misuse of powers' or 'clearly exceeded bounds of discretion' render the ECHA decision 'unlawful'.[93] The problem, however, is that this judicial formula of broad discretion was originally developed for cases in which it was the Commission, not the EU agency, which enjoyed a wide measure of discretion: the CJEU has expressly stated that where the Commission enjoys a wide measure of discretion, judicial review is accordingly limited.[94] Moreover, it is arguable whether the EU courts are satisfied with simply reviewing the formal (procedural) aspects of the EU agency decision.

91 Ibid.

92 Article 7(5).

93 Case C-120/97 *Upjohn Ltd v The Licensing Authority established by the Medicines Act 1968* [1999] ECR I-223, [34]. See a recent decision by the European Ombudsman upholding an ECHA interpretation on the basis that nothing suggests its being 'manifestly wrong': *Decision of the European Ombudsman closing the inquiry into complaint 2469/2011/VL against the European Chemicals Agency*, 12 March 2014, [31].

94 Case C-15/10 *Etimine v Secretary of State for Work and Pensions* [2011] ECR I-6681, [60].

The *Pfizer* judgment was an early sign of the willingness of the EU courts to play a potentially new role in terms of the substantive reasonableness of a decision, albeit of a Commission decision.[95] The ruling concerned a regulation aimed at withdrawing authorisation for certain antibiotic substances in animal farming. Whereas an EU-level expert committee did not find any risks in the use of virginiamycin, the Commission and Council decided to disregard the experts' opinion. The General Court, whilst accepting the decision of the EU institutions, established some explicit requirements of the quality of scientific evidence: such evidence must be 'sufficiently reliable and cogent'.[96] Moreover, it undertook a detailed analysis of the scientific opinions in order to determine whether the institutions could reasonably take the view that they did. The approach adopted in the *Pfizer* case alludes to the fact that the EU courts might not be as reluctant to review the substantive reasonableness of a decision as conventional wisdom has it: the scope of review has widened as the substantive correctness and reasonableness of both Commission and EU agency decisions has increasingly been included as an important factor affecting their legality. In respect of the decisions adopted by EU agencies, the widening of the scope of aspects for judicial review may, in fact, be introduced as a strategic judicial countermove to the increased powers of EU agencies.

The courts seem to be building their review of substantive aspects of decision making on the idea of 'judicial risk management': that a richer information base prompts alternative interpretations, allowing the courts to ask whether an actor could have done otherwise and on what grounds.[97] When evaluating the ECHA's decision making regarding the inclusion of harmful substances on the candidate list for authorisation, the CJEU deferred to the ECHA decision, but in return engaged in a more intensive review.[98] In this particular judgment, the General Court more or less deconstructed the ECHA reasoning to demonstrate that the agency had not abused its discretion. One of the problems is that, upon assuming this role of judicial risk manager and facing a mountain of impenetrable scientific minutiae, the judges may be inclined to focus on those things that they understand.[99] Of course, this presents a fundamental trait of human psychology, which cannot be entirely eliminated. In addition, judicial intervention always involves interpretative elements, with judges reshaping the factual questions presented to

95 For early CJEU case law and how it has slowly come to adopt a more comprehensive review, see Vos, 2014.

96 Case T-13/99 *Pfizer Animal Health v Council* [2002] ECR II-3305, [162].

97 See also Vos, 2014, p 228.

98 Case T-93/10 *Bilbaína de Alquitranes, AS and others v ECHA*, 7 March 2013, NYR, [76]–[77]. The Court of Justice upheld the General Court ruling on appeal: see Case C-287/13 P *Bilbaína de Alquitranes, AS and others v ECHA*, 22 May 2014, NYR.

99 Miller and Curry, 2013, p 68, compared expert and non-expert judges in reviewing US agency decision making, and their conclusion is thought-provoking: '[T]he fact that expert judges are considerably less deferential to the agency than their nonexpert counterparts suggests that there is some reason to suspect that too much deference is regularly granted to agencies.'

them. However, in circumstances of deep scientific complexity, the risks of 'judicial risk management' are bound to be greater, and harm, more substantial. The way in which REACH was dealt with in national parliaments is telling. When interviewed about the course of national debates on REACH, a Dutch parliamentarian commented, in rather disillusioned tones, about the popularity of animal testing: 'People thought, "Look, that's an interesting subject." This showed that politicians focus automatically on what they can understand.'[100]Admittedly, politicians are more inclined than judges to focus on comprehensible things simply because they think that those issues will also make sense to their voters. Animal testing is an instructive example of a political issue that has a near-universal appeal for a broad range of potential voters. However, observation of the dynamics also reveals the potential risks involved in 'judicial risk management'.

In the first preliminary reference under REACH, UK chemical companies sought clarification over Art 6(3) concerning allowable levels of monomers in polymers. In the main, these companies claimed that REACH was ambiguous: in particular, they argued that there was a lack of clarity and a lack of scientific basis in the relevant Article. The English High Court referred the question to the Court of Justice. According to the referral, the claimants maintained that 'Article 6(3) has no proper scientific basis', whereas Justice Jackson paraphrased the question concerning the 'validity of Article 6(3)'.[101] In the Court of Justice ruling, lack of scientific basis was no longer referred to.[102]

5.3.2 'My science is better than yours'? A consensus-enhancing approach to risk regulation

Cases involving complex scientific opinions and technical expertise are demanding not only in terms of their content, but also in terms of their potential to juxtapose national expertise and EU expertise.[103] Member States in particular are tempted to refer to 'non-science-based factors' in regulating risk,[104] and whenever the EU courts review such cases, they have to tread very carefully: they wish to be seen neither to be hampering internal market integration nor undermining the sovereign concerns of a Member State's constitutional order. In order to tackle problems before they escalate, the basic acts of EU agencies usually include provisions intended to identify potential divergences between Member States and the EU institutions.[105]

100 Neuhold and de Ruiter, 2010, p 66.
101 *R (on the application of SPCM SA and others) v Secretary of State for Environment, Food & Rural Affairs* [2007] EWHC 2610 (Admin), [5] and [7].
102 Case C-558/07 *SPCM SA and others v Secretary of State for the Environment, Food and Rural Affairs* [2009] ECR I-5783.
103 For example, Case C-1/00 *Commission v France* [2001] ECR I-9989.
104 Alemanno, 2007, p 8.
105 Disagreements can, of course, occur between two EU agencies, to which end bilateral memoranda of understanding have been signed between several EU agencies.

In food safety regulation, for example, the EFSA has to exercise vigilance in order to identify at the earliest possible stage any potential source of conflict between its scientific opinions and opinions issued by national food authorities or other bodies carrying out similar tasks. When a situation emerges involving actors with conflicting views and opinions, incompatible values and choices, the EFSA must co-operate with the aim of resolving differences of opinion. In cases in which co-operation does not bring parties any closer to each other and failure occurs in finding common ground, the EFSA must prepare a common document that is made publicly available, identifying uncertainties and sources of irresolution.[106] Scientific consensus is also attempted through Art 36, which mandates the EFSA to promote networking among authorities and organisations that operate in the same field. However, the EFSA is not in a decisive role in which it can simply establish and dictate its opinion; the most that it can do, formally speaking, is to inform the Commission of irresolvable tensions. Informally, the situation is otherwise. The EFSA possesses not only a voice, but also prestige and weight. In most cases, the parties are motivated to reach harmonious agreement before their disagreement goes deeper and, perhaps most importantly, public, and where this is the case it is likely that the EFSA is overpowering.

What about REACH? The ECHA is under no general statutory obligation to facilitate consensus on scientific opinions; what instead seems to serve as a general statutory obligation is acknowledgement and teasing out of disagreements. Paradoxically, consensus is sought by giving participants with different opinions opportunities to express their views and to share their concerns at many levels of decision making. Indeed, one of the key principles of REACH seems to be encouraging contestations. As Scott (2009b) explains:

> Member States (and the Commission) are empowered, on the basis of clearly defined procedures, to seek to use their local knowledge to persuade the European Union as a whole, of the need to revise applicable norms, in order to ensure effective fulfilment of the Regulation's framework goals.[107]

Such aspirations embedded in REACH might effectively prevent deadlock from developing between the national and European levels, and reduce the need to involve the courts. What is important to observe is that consensus is not expected to flow inexorably from honest and bona fide aspirations to co-operate; rather, consensual ambitions are accompanied with a clear template for decision making and clearly articulated procedural norms. For instance, the modus operandi of ECHA scientific committees is consensual, but when this fails, REACH prescribes that reasoning and justifications presented in favour of both minority and majority

106 Article 30 of Regulation (EC) No 178/2002.

107 Scott, 2009b, p 58. In keeping with the spirit, annual ECHA general reports highlight issues that have given rise to controversies among REACH stakeholders. See, eg, ECHA, December 2013, p 51.

opinions must be made publicly available.[108] Moreover, in terms of high-profile supranational–national conflicts, the MSC is charged with finding a solution in cases stipulated in REACH.[109]

Conflicts can emerge or escalate at the implementation stage too. The ECHA guidance-writing process, which seeks to set out more detailed rules within the framework of REACH, will undoubtedly bring out differences of opinion; indeed, it has already done so. Rarely, though, do disagreements endure. In one such instance, disagreement arose over the definition of 'an article' in the Guidance on Requirements for Substances in Articles, with six Member States leaving dissenting opinions on the ECHA website.[110] Even with revision of the guidance document, this group of Member States could not be persuaded to revise their opinions, and the Commission invited them to demonstrate – the somewhat odd choice of word by the Commission was 'quantify' – possible risks involved in the current (Commission) interpretation of the provision in question.[111] This disagreement over the interpretation of 'article' has recently been brought to the EU courts in a preliminary ruling from France.[112] In section 5.4, 'Iterated deliberation: Opportunities and limitations', I consider the role of the courts as a party to the conflict and show how clearly defined procedures, and the information generated through them, can be advantageous to the review function of courts.

5.3.3 An inclusive chemicals policy: Within REACH?

After the adoption of REACH, EU chemicals policy is now more inclusive than it has ever been. This can be ascertained simply by comparing the statutory opportunities for stakeholders to have their views heard and taken into account both before REACH and then after REACH.[113] This constitutes a clear improvement over the previous regime and REACH scores reasonably well in comparison to other contexts of risk regulation, although it is hardly perfect. Heyvaert (2008), for instance, draws attention to the importance of scientific expertise for EU chemicals policy and raises the important question of whether the input of NGOs is bound to remain insignificant despite all opportunities offered to them, because NGOs may not possess the relevant scientific expertise to ensure effective input.[114] Whilst environmental NGOs themselves have been content with opportunities to participate in REACH decision making, they have

108 Article 85(8).
109 Article 76(1) e.
110 For the controversy, see Korkea-aho, 2013.
111 European Commission, February 2013, COM(2013) 49 final, p 5.
112 Case C-106/14 *FCD & FMB*, pending at time of writing.
113 Stakeholders were also included in the legislative process leading up to REACH: see Hey, Jacob and Volkery, 2007, p 1869. For a more sceptical view of 'inclusive governance' with respect to European agencies, see, eg, Chiti, 2009, p 1402.
114 Heyvaert, 2008, p 2.

expressed concern about the slow pace at which REACH has been implemented. In so doing, however, they demonstrate possession of the relevant scientific or other knowledge to participate, and their activities more broadly dispel some worries over whether or not NGOs are sufficiently qualified to influence scientific decision making.[115]

In this subsection, I take up the question of whether more generous participation rights, guaranteed through legally binding EU rules, affect EU courts' reasoning in terms of standing, and whether they should do so in cases in which non-privileged applicants initiate legal proceedings in the context of agency decision making. I begin by discussing a ruling that demonstrates how the EU courts have approached and understood participation rights in the context of Art 263(4) TFEU.

5.3.3.1 Participation rights and the question of standing

The *FECOAV* case concerned the grant of a plant variety right by the CPVO.[116] The claimant *Federación de Cooperativas Agrarias de la Comunidad Valenciana* (FECOAV), a Spanish federation of unions of farming co-operatives, challenged a decision before the CPVO Board of Appeal, claiming that assignment of a particular mandarin variety negatively affected their trade, and was therefore of direct and individual concern to them. The Board of Appeal dismissed the challenge, arguing that the plaintiff did not have standing, as required by Art 68 of the Basic Regulation.[117] Turned down by the Board of Appeal, FECOAV then appealed to the General Court.[118] The Court began its analysis by drawing attention to the 'outside lane' offered by the Basic Regulation: Art 59 provides that 'any person may lodge with the Office a written objection to the grant of a Community plant variety right'. This 'objector' will be a party to the proceedings together with the applicant, which means, among other things, that the objector is entitled to appeal against the decision to the Board of Appeal,[119] and then again to the EU courts. Now, FECOAV had not objected to the application for the plant variety right and was not qualified as an objector. This being the case, FECOAV had to submit evidence that it was directly and individually concerned by the decision, as laid down in Art 68 of the Basic Regulation. Since FECOAV did not meet the threshold, it was accordingly denied standing.

115 See, eg, ClientEarth and EEB, 2012, or the activities of the International Chemical Secretariat (ChemSEC), a Swedish-based NGO, which published its own list of SVHCs in order to urge the European Union to follow in its footsteps.

116 Case T-95/06 *Federación de Cooperativas Agrarias de la Comunidad Valenciana v Community Plant Variety Office* [2008] ECR II-31. The CPVO administers a system of intellectual property rights that are granted to plant varieties in Member States.

117 Council Regulation (EC) No 2100/94 on Community plant variety rights (the Basic Regulation).

118 The applicant had three pleas in law, but I focus only on standing.

119 Article 67(1) of the Basic Regulation.

Perhaps somewhat surprisingly, although dismissing the claim, the Court responded at some length to the claimant's plea about lack of effective judicial protection. Scope of judicial protection was interestingly linked to the role played by an objector: in the Court's view, the claimant had an (obviously missed) opportunity to take part in the proceedings before the CPVO. If it had done so, it would have gained the status of an objector, and would thus also have submitted adequate evidence of being individually and directly concerned.[120] On these grounds, the Court concluded that it was incorrect to say that there was no effective judicial protection. The stance that the Court took in this case is clearly vulnerable to criticism. Theoretically, the greatest problem is that it unhelpfully conflates participation in decision making and access to justice, which, as argued shortly, is problematic because they serve different purposes. From a pragmatic point of view, the question is: how likely is it that the potential objector will happen to become aware of a public notice of an application for the right to object in the Official Gazette of the CPVO and lodge an objection?[121] In terms of theoretical assumptions and practical opinions, the answer is very much open.

5.5.3.2 Evaluation and the implications for REACH actors

Could FECOAV have expected a different outcome after the Lisbon Treaty? The strictness of the pre-Lisbon doctrine of 'direct' and 'individual' concern was crystallised in the *Plaumann* judgment. [122] In essence, it required that persons other than those to whom a decision was addressed might claim to be individually concerned only if that decision affected them 'by reason of certain attributes peculiar to them, or by reason of circumstances which differentiate them from all other persons and distinguishes them individually'.[123] However, the Lisbon Treaty brought about some important changes: non-privileged applicants may not only challenge an act that is addressed to them, or that is of direct and individual concern to them (retaining the *Plaumann* judgment), but also 'a regulatory act which is of direct concern to them and does not entail implementing measures'.[124] In other words, the requirement of 'individual concern' does not apply to regulatory acts, and non-privileged applicants need not demonstrate that they are differentiated from all others affected by the measure.

120 Case T-95/06 *Federación de Cooperativas Agrarias de la Comunidad Valenciana v Community Plant Variety Office* [2008] ECR II-31, [107], [109] and [115]–[117].

121 At the time of the ruling, the Gazette was an internal magazine, issued every two months and delivered only on request. Since October 2010, it has been available online.

122 Case 25/62 *Plaumann & Co. v Commission of the EEC* [1963] ECR 95.

123 Ibid, [107]. The restrictive interpretation was reconfirmed in Case C-50/00 P *Unión de Pequeños Agricultores v Council* [2002] ECR I-6677, despite the more expansive opinion of AG Jacobs. In Case T-177/01 *Jégo-Quéré & Cie SA v Commission* [2002] ECR II-2365, the General Court was willing to relax the restrictions, but its ruling was overruled on appeal: C-263/02 *Commission v Jégo-Quéré & Cie SA* [2004] ECR I-3425.

124 Article 263(4) TFEU.

The term 'regulatory act' is not defined in the Lisbon Treaty. In the recent case law of the CJEU, Art 263(4) is, in this respect, now interpreted to include only *non-legislative* measures: acts of general application.[125] What about the two other requirements included in the new paragraph? It should be observed that since the majority of cases about the scope of ex Art 234 EC were dismissed because of lack of individual concern, no need arose to establish the existence of a 'direct concern', and the relevant case law is infinitely more limited than that of individual concern. An EU measure is of 'direct concern' if it directly affects the legal situation of the individual and no discretion is left to the addressees of that measure who are responsible for its implementation, implementation being purely automatic and resulting from EU rules alone without application of other intermediate rules.[126]

If *FECOAV* were adjudicated now, the claimant would have to demonstrate that the measure it wishes to challenge is a regulatory act and that it is directly affected by that act. The first hurdle seems cleared, but the second one presents more of a problem. As far as *FECOAV* goes, and where the context of the decision is in authorisation, demonstrating direct concern should not be too difficult. In particular, this is because a positive authorisation decision can directly affect the legal situation of another manufacturer or importer.[127] Would the situation look different in the context in which the claimant is a NGO or an academic who claims to be affected by virtue of the role formalised in legislation? Here, I return to REACH and have in mind stakeholders such as environmental NGOs that are neither manufacturers nor importers, but which have actively used the participation rights afforded to them by REACH to bring forward legally relevant information.[128] Recall the REACH authorisation system: once an application for authorisation reaches the ECHA, it is forwarded to the scientific committees for consideration. The ECHA must make information on the application for authorisation available on its website. The committees are required to give regard to information on alternative substances or technologies submitted by interested parties, and the draft opinion of the SEAC must involve an analysis of these contributions. In addition, the SEAC can ask both the applicant and third parties to submit additional information on alternative substances or technologies. In comparison: both for the CPVO and the ECHA, third parties are a source of additional information and knowledge. Where an objector submits information to the CPVO

125 Case T-18/10 *Inuit Tapiriit Kanatami and others v European Parliament and Council* [2011] ECR II-5599, [56]; appealed as C-583/11 P *Inuit Tapiriit Kanatami and others v Parliament & Council*, 8 November 2011, NYR. See also Case T-262/10 *Microban v Commission* [2011] ECR II-7697, [21] and [23]. For the argument that a regulatory act should be extended also to cover soft acts that generate 'a certain legal effect', see Senden and van den Brink, 2012, p 79.

126 T-127/05 *Lootus Teine Osaühing v Council* [2007] ECR II-1, [39]; Case T-223/01 *Japan Tobacco Inc. and JT International SA v European Parliament and Council* [2002] ECR II-3259, [45] and [46]. See also Herman, 2010, pp 392 and 405, and Ward, 2004, p 213.

127 See also Bronckers and van Gerven, 2009, p 1869.

128 Lee, 2008, p 136.

in order to attempt to prevent the grant of a plant variety right, under REACH interested parties (other manufacturers, NGOs, academics) are also allowed to object to the authorisation application by producing information on alternative substances or technologies. If this succeeds, authorisation will not be granted, or if granted, it will be so only upon more stringent conditions. The importance of third-party information is highlighted by the fact that, in some cases, authorisation will also be granted if no suitable alternative substance or technology is available and the socio-economic benefits outweigh the risks.[129] In other words: information submitted by third parties on alternative substances and technologies mediates the discretion of the Commission, which is the final decision maker.

Problems are likely to arise with respect to those stakeholders who are not manufacturers or importers, but who have actively participated in the authorisation process and who would now like to challenge the outcome. Despite their influential role, the EU courts are likely to interpret the 'direct concern' criterion strictly to exclude a challenge by those who have used their 'objector' rights in REACH in the capacity of an actor other than manufacturer or importer.[130] However, if environmental NGOs have been involved in submitting comments, for example, they have, in my view, gained a distinct position in the authorisation procedure and should be allowed to challenge the final decision. Relaxation of the standing can be supported on at least two grounds. First, the strict reading of direct concern does not take into account the fact that important procedural rights have been afforded to interested parties in legislation and that the authorisation decision can be decisively influenced by information submitted by interested parties on alternatives. Second, requiring the applicant to demonstrate direct effects on its legal situation is a problem especially for NGOs and does not make sense in the context of the role played by environmental NGOs. It is suitable when envisaging an individual with market-based rights, but not to an environmental NGO acting in the interests of the environment, protecting public, rather than private, interests.[131] For these reasons, it is suggested here that when participation rights are afforded to interested parties *by legislation* and when interested parties have *actually shaped* decision making at the agency level – for example by means of their

129 Article 60(4).

130 Participation in the preparation of legislation does not ensure standing in subsequent proceedings. See Case T-16/04 *SA Arcelor v European Parliament and the Council* [2010] ECR II-211, [87] and [119]–[121]. See also Case C-258/02 P *Bactria Industriehygiene-Service Verwaltungs GmbH v Commission* [2003] ECR I-15105. This case law, however, dates from before Art 263 TFEU.

131 Case C-115/09 *Bund für Umwelt und Naturschutz Deutschland, Landesverband Nordrhein-Westfalen eV v Bezirksregierung Arnsberg* [2011] ECR I-3673. In her opinion, AG Sharpston described the application for judicial review as seeking 'to challenge the contested administrative decision in so far as it authorises activities which, it is alleged, will have an adverse effect on the environment as such. *In that sense, it may be said that the environmental NGO is seeking to act on behalf of the environment itself*': ibid, [1], emphasis added. See also the ruling, in which the Court of Justice ruled in favour of the NGOs, which are to be allowed to rely on impairment of rules that embody the public interest without having to prove an individual right: ibid, [46].

knowledge about alternative substances and technologies – it would appear legitimate to give interested parties standing to ensure that their input has been adequately taken into account. Substituting dangerous substances with less harmful alternatives is a central aim of REACH and recognising the role played here by NGOs would encourage them to produce information on alternatives.[132]

This recommendation requires that the direct concern criterion be considered fulfilled when the applicant produces evidence of active involvement in the process leading up to the authorisation decision. The ECHA acts as a natural 'watchdog' to ensure that this 'new' access to justice is not abused (that is, that interested parties do not submit frivolous opinions in order to be able to argue for standing). By linking standing to active and genuine involvement by parties interested in the decision-making process in this way, the move would be controlled.

5.3.3.3 Afterword: Procedural provisions vs judicial review

The foregoing comprises a recommendation according to which participation in the decision-making process should be accompanied by standing. Now, one could argue that the logic does indeed limp: whilst I criticised the CJEU in the *FECOAV* case for linking participation in the decision-making process with standing, so that participation ends up compensating for deficits in access to justice, I do not seem to be in a position to defend my own recommendation, which equally relates participation and standing. In both situations, participation in the decision-making process is determinative for recognition of standing: in *FECOAV*, to deny standing; and in REACH, to grant standing. The limping logic seems only to worsen given recent judicial developments. In a preliminary reference that came to the Court of Justice a few years after the General Court's ruling in *FECOAV*, the former ruled that, however wide participation rights in the decision-making procedure might be, they do not entitle a Member State (here, Sweden) to limit NGO access to a review procedure.[133]

It is generally held that participation in decision making and access to justice serve different purposes, and they should be decided independently of each other.[134] Although, broadly speaking, I agree with this view, I believe that the picture that unfolds is subtler than at first assumed and that the implications of procedural provisions for judicial protection should be subjected to a rigorous context-based analysis. Let me explain what contextualises my recommendation. I do not recommend that the EU courts should draw some straightforward consequences from *actual* participation in cases in which they decide to *deny* standing (because it is, in any case, haphazard whether someone actually participates, and accumulating negative consequences can be quite significant for

132 Fleurke and Somsen, 2011, p 390.

133 Case C-263/08 *Djurgården-Lilla Värtans Miljöskyddsförening v Stockholms kommun genom dess marknämnd* [2009] ECR I-9967. I will discuss the case in more detail in Chapter 6.

134 See, eg, Mendes, 2011, p 150, and Senden, 2013, p 72.

an individual applicant). Participation in decision making may be trivialised if it has unfavourable implications for standing. Perversely, it might even make sense not to participate so as to be able to claim standing in order to appeal the decision. Instead, the positive evaluation of standing on the basis of actual participation (actual participation is a plus factor when claimed for standing) does not involve the risk of accumulating negative consequences and actually motivates participation when the decision is being made.

5.4 Iterated deliberation: Opportunities and limitations

The focus of this chapter has been on the ECHA and, more broadly, those EU agencies with important roles in risk regulation. As elaborated earlier, EU agency governance is traditionally seen to be based on the functional separation of risk assessment and risk management – a separation that seems to be failing the goals set for it. What functional separation fails to capture (or at least does not realise) is that agencies not only prepare or make decisions, but also demonstrate that those decisions are justified on technical and scientific grounds. The EU courts have increasingly highlighted this in their rulings – but, in a way, it is already too late by the time a dispute is referred to the courts.

REACH is departing from this functional separation (policy vs science) in an unprecedented way. By interlocking different actors to work together, the governance framework sets out an itinerary for deliberation that attempts to make visible, to all those involved, the grounds on which the decision is taken, and to put to the test the justifications in light of comments and suggestions. This marks a change in emphasis – a new message in line with iterated deliberation. The authorisation procedure seizes (at least some of) the main features of iterated deliberation. But similarities can be found in other contexts of REACH decision making too, such as in the restrictions process. Because I have discussed the authorisation procedure already, I shall here demonstrate how iterated deliberation works by way of the restrictions process. Restrictions are imposed when an unacceptable risk to human health or the environment arises from the manufacture, use or marketing of substances. Both the Commission and a Member State can initiate a process, submitting a dossier *explaining* the need for EU-level action. The ECHA publishes the dossiers on the internet and *invites* all interested parties to submit comments on the proposed restrictions.[135] Next, the RAC and SEAC prepare draft opinions, *taking into account* the views of the interested parties. Reflecting the importance of these draft opinions to the public, the ECHA is required to publish them on its website, thus *inviting* interested parties to give their comments on their content. Then the SEAC *revises* its opinion, *incorporating* subsequent

135 Article 69(1) and (6).

comments.[136] Next, the opinions are referred to the Commission and published on the internet. If the conditions for imposing restrictions are satisfied (that is, if there is an unacceptable risk to human health or to the environment), the Commission adopts a draft amendment to Annex XVII. When its opinion diverges from the original proposal by the Member State or the ECHA, or if it does not take into account the opinions of the ECHA committees, the Commission is required to *give a detailed explanation* for differences in opinion.[137]

In short, all three elements of iterated deliberation can be found in this particular process of REACH decision making. First, iterated deliberation encourages reasoned discussion, and creates a situation in which the Commission, Member States and the ECHA are required to take into account each other's views and those of interested parties. Whilst encouraging the inclusion of arguments, REACH does not subject them to scientific peer review only, but it also manages to encompass more 'societal' peer review, viewing the concerns of interested parties as an integral part of decision making. The second feature of iterated deliberation relates to its openness and receptiveness to opposition and criticism. REACH decision making is constructed with a view to inviting diverse, even conflicting, views and to elaborating the differences between them prior to making a decision. Finally, the third element is there too: REACH deliberations include several 'points of entry' for parties, as highlighted in this chapter. This form of decision making encourages the scientific committees to give serious regard to information from third parties, knowing that they are invited to re-comment upon draft opinions. In this way, public participation is not a mere administrative necessity with little output, but an essential element of risk deliberation geared to finding legitimate and effective measures.

Perhaps more importantly still, iterated deliberation seems to have the potential to positively affect the form and substance of judicial review. I next briefly revisit the three problems discussed in section 5.3 and suggest how those concerns might be mitigated by taking iterated deliberation into consideration.

5.4.1 Revisiting the judicial review of acts and opinions by agencies

In recent years, the EU courts have shown more interest in reviewing science-based decision making, in terms not only of formal correctness, but also of substantive acceptability. One of the problems, I have argued, is the chance that judges might 'over-focus' on things that they can comprehend and understand. A larger question that arises here is whether the courts are trying to become what they are not – that is, judicial risk managers or scientific experts themselves.[138] Can

136 Articles 70 and 71(1)–(2).
137 Articles 72(2) and 73.
138 Vos, 2014.

the framework of iterated deliberation redirect any such tendency? On the one hand, the repeated process of testing arguments and opinions increases the amount of information available to reviewing courts, eliciting a stronger judicial response. For instance, when looking at the existence of legal remedies in REACH, some observers have commented that the ECHA and its committees 'must address these comments [comments from interested parties] in the statement of reasons of their decisions and opinions, making *ex post* judicial control more effective'.[139] On the other hand, repetition of arguments also gives the judges more (deliberatively) legitimate standing to defer to the evidence of peer review emerging from iterated deliberation because scientific evidence is assessed among peers (those who can reasonably be expected to understand the argument and assess its merits).

The idea of peer review, especially in its latter form, is not new in the judicial context. Alemanno (2007) has suggested that the courts can tap into the mechanisms and results of scientific peer review in two ways: the judges can either request experts to analyse the scientific evidence submitted by the parties to a dispute, or they can exercise a less intense review if the scientific evidence in the case has been peer reviewed.[140] An example that he offers concerns a ruling by the North American Free Trade Agreement (NAFTA) Tribunal on an investment dispute between the Canadian Methanex Corporation and the United States.[141] The company produces methanol, which was forbidden by California in 2002 on the basis of harm to the environment and to human health. Methanex maintained that the ban was not a bona fide environmental action, but instead a measure intended to restrict trade. The Tribunal did not accept this claim and approved the scientific evidence submitted for the ban. It highlighted that the scientific evidence 'was subject at the time to public hearings, testimony and peer-review', concluding that 'its emergence as a serious scientific work from such an *open and informed debate* is the best evidence that it was not the product of a political shame engineered by California'.[142]

REACH does, in fact, involve elements of this kind of scientific peer review. When a company applies for registration, the ECHA undertakes a completeness check and, in some cases, a compliance check. As for the latter, which is a more substantial and intrusive form of review, the ECHA ensures that registration is consistent with the information requirements laid down in REACH. Each technical dossier submitted alongside registration must specify, in relation to certain categories of information, whether the information it contains has been reviewed before submission. REACH does not explicitly require a reviewer to be independent, but only to have appropriate experience. However, it is clearly in the interests of the chemicals industry and any individual applicant to demonstrate

139 Bronckers and van Gerven, 2009, pp 1852–3 (emphasis original).

140 Alemanno, 2007, p 25. See also Alemanno, 2010, pp 362–7.

141 *Methanex Corp. vs. United States of America*, Final Award of the Tribunal on Jurisdiction and Merits, 3 August 2005.

142 Alemanno, 2007, pp 25–6 (emphasis original).

how independent and appropriate the review has been: with this satisfied, there is less need for detailed examination of the dossier at the registration stage.[143] Now, whilst Alemanno is primarily concerned with expert (scientific) peer review, for me iterated deliberation results in the emergence of a peer review that entails a commitment both to scientifically robust decision making and to virtues of public participation.

What is the significance for the EU courts? Certainly, even successfully undertaken iterated deliberation does not remove the need for the courts to engage in reviewing science-based measures, and deliberation – increasing the information available to the courts – can occasionally result in more intense judicial action. Nonetheless, iterated deliberation has two distinct merits. First, information discussed and reviewed along the lines of iterated deliberation tempers the danger of judges focusing only on issues that seem comprehensible to them. The broader dynamic here is the same as in the suggestion made by Bronckers and van Gerven (2009). In their view, expanding the scope of decisions that fall within review by the Board of Appeal should be preferred because internal review increases and prepares ('digests') information for the EU courts.[144]

Second, iterated deliberation offers us a new perspective from which to assess the courts' deference and the intensity of their review. The benchmarks of iterated deliberation single out those decisions that have not been preceded by wide-ranging discussions and consultation. Judges should not so easily defer to a decision when:

1 it has been reached whilst keeping the interested parties and/or the European Parliament out of the decision-making process;
2 there is sustained opposition or, conversely, there is no sign of conflicting opinions or ambiguity (indicating that no, or limited, attention has been paid to inputs and contributions); or
3 reasons are not justified with respect to the legislative text or its objectives, or linked to anything that has been previously raised in discussions.[145]

To take an example, in contrast to the restrictions process, the authorisation process limits both parliamentary involvement and public participation. When reviewing scientific evidence in the context of the authorisation procedure, the EU courts are advised to impose a stricter and more 'intense' review of decisions taken in the authorisation process than, for example, in the restrictions procedure, during which scientific evidence has been more thoroughly discussed and can thus more

143 Scott, 2009b, p 64. According to NGOs, this has not worked as well as expected and, eg, toxicity studies submitted by applicants are best described as what they call 'grey literature': see ClientEarth and EEB, 2012, p 6.

144 Bronckers and van Gerven, 2009, p 1858.

145 For similar benchmarks, see Eskridge and Ferejohn, 2010, p 265, and Chapter 7, section 7.3.2, 'Courts utilising new governance instruments'.

legitimately be deferred to. In two authorisation cases currently pending before the EU courts,[146] the applicants claim that the ECHA did not take into account all information available or provided by the industry during the commenting period, hence offering an opportunity to test the benchmarks in practice.

Another way in which to increase the information base to make judicial scrutiny relevant and meaningful is to consult guidance documents, such as ECHA guidance documents. They could be relied upon by the courts in matters of substance, as well as in matters concerning the manner in which risk assessment ought to be undertaken. Because this will involve rethinking the soft law status of such guidance, I consider the issue in Chapter 6, along with similar Common Implementation Strategy (CIS) guidance.

5.4.2 Revisiting consensus

Cases involving disputes between 'national' science and 'European' science have led to adoption of norms written to lay presumption on consensus as the aim of decision making. These provisions now form a pivotal element of modern EU risk regulation. Does consensual decision making require judicial reorientation? As such, consensual aspects of decision making do not call for intense review of the decision-making process. I have, however, pointed out in Chapter 3 that consensual decision making runs the risk of making competing and differing opinions more difficult to represent. Therefore, I suggested reconceptualising consensus as the absence of sustained opposition. For the courts to be able to ascertain this, the process leading to a decision must contain the views and justifications of those in the minority. Consensual forms of decision making might then indicate a need for context-based review, which can be thought of as a demanding task, given the distance of courts from actual decision making. However, in the context of REACH, information is plentiful: the courts reviewing a Commission decision have access to information that reveals, for example, whose proposal it was originally, how much support exists for expert opinions, how unanimous the experts are, whether the actors have changed their minds in the course of decision making, how widely the interested parties have been consulted and whether there is sustained opposition in the MSC. In this respect – and especially where the disagreement has arisen during guidance-writing, as in the example referred to earlier concerning definition of an 'article' – ECHA guidance documents can also be helpful, including opposing views, which are, in addition, publicly available on the internet. Moreover, the EU courts may ask to hear 'witnesses', including civil servants and, if appropriate, the directors of EU agencies.[147]

146 Case T-134/13 *Polynt and Sitre v ECHA* and Case T-135/13 *Hitachi Chemical Europe and others v ECHA*, both pending at time of writing.

147 For the courts' right to do so, see Curtin, 2007, p 535.

The strength of this model can be made more evident by comparing it to solutions adopted in other areas of risk regulation. For instance, risk regulation in one potentially explosive area – decision making in relation to genetically modified organisms (GMOs) – is supported by 'several out-of-court mechanisms for participating actors at all levels to resolve conflicts between them (before GMO approval is granted or rejected)'.[148] Nevertheless, persistent political struggles have come to mean that, in practice, decisions are taken 'by the comitology committees composed of Member States representatives, or by the Commission in the absence of a qualified majority either in committees or in the Council'.[149] Whilst the regime may be effective, it is not generally considered legitimate.[150] Without engaging in deeper analysis of the problems of EU decision making on GMOs, one thing should be noted about the role of judicial review: more active oversight by the EU courts in GMO decision making is viewed as likely to produce more legitimate outcomes. The EU courts, however, have little, if any, evidence of how different opinions and views have been included and addressed, and what kind of role various actors play in decision making over GMOs (for example what kind of role the EFSA or other 'out of court mechanisms' have had in risk assessment) giving rise to judicial review, which is potentially seen as random and vulnerable to accusations of bias or prejudice.[151]

What could explain this difference between governance regimes? A cursory comparison between the conditions of judicial review in REACH and GMO regimes appears to return us to the same argument: in complex regulatory environments, one of the aims of, and justifications for, deliberative decision making is elaboration and publication of differences. For this to happen, a framework is needed, which again corroborates the insight by scholars of experimentalism that 'best' deliberative decision-making arrangements are highly formalised and structured. By now, it is no doubt clear to readers that REACH is distinguished for the complexities of its procedures. The more structured the decision making, the easier it is for participants to contest and oppose,[152] and for the courts to review and monitor: this is precisely the difference between the REACH and GMO regimes.

148 Dąbrowska, 2010, p 187.

149 Ibid, p 181.

150 See ibid, p 195.

151 Note, though, that the EFSA is duty-bound to publish a variety of documents pertaining to the work carried out by its scientific committees, including information on minority views: see Art 38 of Regulation EC No 178/2002.

152 Simon, 2006, p 48, explains the importance of formalisation to revisability as follows: a norm cannot be disputed or contradicted if it is known only to some chosen individuals who do not want or do not know how to articulate it to others.

5.4.3 Revisiting inclusiveness

The goal of inclusive risk regulation is to incorporate consumers, businesses and NGOs to provide input into decision making, and to allow them to make more informed judgements about risks themselves. The adequacy of inclusive governance has been subject to intensified scrutiny, and subsequently the focus has increased on developing a general EU law framework on transparency and access to information as preconditions for public participation. Despite this unprecedented interest in participation, the discussion has suffered from unrealistic expectations and wishful thinking. I have already discussed at length the issue of public participation from a deliberative democratic theory perspective. Here, I wish only to reaffirm the main point: that more attention should be given to the institutional design by distinguishing more clearly between the different degrees, functions and aims of participation. Public participation is a complex institutional exercise, which needs to be carefully structured if it is hoped to deliver results. In particular, this is so in risk regulation, where the role of the wider public continues to generate controversy. A consistent claim has been that public participation jeopardises the quality of decision making, and results in inefficiency and inconsistencies – the conundrum being how to include the general public in a way that does not unreasonably slow down decision making.

The framework for iterated deliberation highlights the importance of response and consideration. EU policy on participation should increasingly focus on the quality of public participation, making decision-making bodies accountable to input from public participation. I am not assuming that authorities would commit themselves to anything more than considering the views of the public in their subsequent deliberations, but the authorities' efforts to give regard to dialogue with a wider public should be encouraged and, if needed, also demanded on a more regular basis in the course of judicial review. Again, REACH may be leading the way. First, REACH stands out among risk regulation frameworks by giving to interested parties an influential role in decision making. There are multiple provisions through which interested parties can enter the decision-making stage. Whilst I shall not recap them here and whilst appraisal of their actual effectiveness remains to be offered by future research, which might observe their actual workings, it could be argued that early involvement of stakeholders (input by interested parties is usually taken into account by the ECHA scientific committees at an early stage of the decision-making process[153]) ensures that they can exercise a decisive impact on the outcome. The role of interested parties is less important in rule-making. The guidance-writing procedure, which lays down important specifications for the REACH framework, channels civil society contributions through ad hoc expert groups, yet the importance of these contributions is clearly recognised.

153 This is beneficial also because it decreases the role of the Commission in designing and managing consultation and participation rights. For criticism of the existing system, which relies on 'the grace and favour of the Commission', see Craig, 2012, p 303.

5.5 Conclusion

This discussion of the judicial role in the context of REACH may, quite rightly, prompt the view that REACH has been (too much of) an 'easy case' for a discussion of the review function of the EU courts. In many ways, REACH is unprecedented in its willingness to co-operate and incorporate, and, as a result, many of the dilemmas associated with EU agency governance are less likely to occur within REACH. However, it is not free from problems, some of which have been discussed in this chapter. Beyond them, REACH has been a spot-on choice for the argument that I wished to make.

The highly technical character of REACH not only puts national parliaments or the public at a disadvantage, but also makes amply clear that the EU courts have very limited means to control the activities of risk-regulating agencies. From a democratic theoretical point of view, this might be as good as it gets. Political institutions should not rely on the courts to correct faults and systemic failures in existing institutional design. If it is true that the current way of handling risk does not appear 'to ensure that the reasons underlying the decisions clearly indicate the policy choices adopted (judgments, uncertainties and biases in scientific assessment), thus setting them apart from the scientific results on which they rely, so that every citizen (and the courts) can identify them',[154] then the problem to be tackled lies in institutional manifestations of risk analysis, not in the role of the courts. No amount of rights-based judicial review can (or, for that matter, should) make up for systemic and chronic failures in existing institutional design. A more realistic and promising prospect is often a reform of the institutional design itself, which moreover lends itself to be enforced by the courts, if real-life applications of the design fail to impress.

Early observers cannot but be struck by REACH's structural design, which is no doubt its greatest deliberative success hitherto witnessed. For scholars of governance, it comes as no surprise to be reminded that both the White Paper on European governance[155] and the White Paper on the strategy for a new chemical control system,[156] preparing the ground for REACH, were drafted and published in the same year: 2001. But there is no reason for complacency, and room exists for improvement. The first thing is that deliberation constitutes a process of coming up with new alternatives,[157] not simply commenting on a shortlist of policy options. For this reason, deliberative democratic theory should take seriously opportunities to suggest new alternatives. Bohman (2006) has argued that the 'capacity to begin', rather than being subject to consultation or being given opportunities to contest, is truly a threshold for a democratic minimum. Such a capacity can be institutionalised in two ways: first, the power of citizens to change

154 Alemanno, 2007, p 11.
155 European Commission, July 2001, COM(2001) 428 final.
156 European Commission, February 2001, COM(2001) 88 final.
157 Elster, 1998, p 11.

the basic normative framework; and second, their capacity to 'set an item on an open agenda' and to begin a public discussion.[158] In REACH, however, '[n]either industry actors or NGO voices, nor academics or other experts, are given formal recognition as catalysts for revision in the light of new information or better understanding'.[159] But non-institutionalised actors are not the only ones whose opportunities for deliberation require constant monitoring; deliberation by institutionalised actors could also be at risk of being frustrated. The strong, if not dominant, role that the Commission plays in ECHA guidance-drafting is problematic from the perspective that it destroys the level playing field (or at least, in principle, 'egalitarian' peer culture) among network participants. I have shown elsewhere how those Member States that oppose the Commission are identified as troublemakers that needed to be proselytised. The strategy that is deployed in these cases brings out the dark side of iterated deliberation. In the particular instance of disagreement over the definition of an 'article', the Commission did not trigger the update of an ECHA guidance document because the need arose to take into account new scientific or technical developments; instead, the Commission wanted to publish the guidance without dissenting opinions and exerted considerable pressure on Member States to follow its lead.[160]

The second issue up for consideration and reform relates to standing. Although well-functioning practices of consideration and response might be important, they cannot sufficiently capture the importance of one particular group of stakeholders to decision making on chemicals. As described, interested parties may wield a considerable influence over decision making on authorisation by submitting information on alternatives to chemical substances, yet their efforts are given no formal recognition in subsequent judicial proceedings. The significance of such information is highlighted by the fact that authorisation can be rejected if enough information on suitable alternative substances or technologies can be amassed. On the basis of examination of EU agency legislation and practice, as well as case law, I have argued that these qualified third parties should be allowed to challenge decisions taken under REACH before the EU courts. This approach seems to require the EU courts to adopt a broader interpretation of direct concern, but it would also more closely reflect the value of iteration, and operationalise the fact that deliberations should be considered and taken into account by decision-making bodies.

The third issue, which needs to be monitored in the years to come, concerns the issue of industry capture, which has already surfaced in battles between the ECHA and NGOs. Problems have cropped up over the information that the former holds – in particular, what constitutes information that has to be publicly available on the

158 Bohman, 2006, p 221.
159 Scott, 2009b, p 75.
160 Korkea-aho, 2013, p 373.

basis of REACH.[161] The Commission has (although mildly) chastised the ECHA 'at cruising speed' for gaps in communication and transparency.[162] These might be more than initial hiccups: beneath the battles lurks a larger issue of the relationship between the regulator and regulatees, and how these roles are (re)interpreted in REACH. It nevertheless seems clear that it is not REACH as an institutional framework standing in the way of accessible and accountable agency governance, but rather the ECHA, which could be well advised to interpret REACH provisions less timidly.

161 ClientEarth and EEB, 2012, pp 25–6. The European Ombudsman has given decisions on a handful of complaints concerning disagreements as to the scope of publicly disseminated information, all of them from Emily O'Reilly and all decided in favour of the ECHA: accessed 30 June 2014, http://www.ombudsman.europa.eu/cases/advancedsearch.faces. In *Decision of the European Ombudsman closing his own-initiative inquiry OI/12/2012/EIS concerning the European Chemicals Agency (ECHA)*, 27 May 2013, O'Reilly's predecessor, P. Nikiforos Diamandouros, recommended that the ECHA publish its annual report on handling requests for public access to documents.

162 European Commission, February 2013, COM(2013) 49 final, p 11.

Chapter 6

The Common Implementation Strategy for the Water Framework Directive

6.1 Introduction

The third and final case study is concerned with implementation of the Water Framework Directive (WFD).[1] The Directive was adopted in 2000 after long and tumultuous negotiations. Indeed, political disagreements played some role in shaping the final text of the Directive: openness was a result of negotiators considering what was in fact possible in the squeeze of multiple policy imperatives, in meeting the demands of both economic growth and environmental quality. Open-ended Articles, requiring specification from those who implement and apply them, were a conscious choice too, however, based on the fact – visible in its name – that the WFD is a *framework directive*. Although not formally defined in the Treaties, framework directives set out the main objectives and applicable principles, and establish binding procedures (such as reporting, permitting), whilst formulation of concrete substantive measures occurs after legislation has been passed.[2] In other words, many critical issues have been left unresolved and must be addressed in the course of implementation, by means of 'daughter' directives, comitology, or implementation by Member States themselves.[3]

Nonetheless, the WFD is not a typical example of decentralised implementation whereby Member States transpose directives into national legislation in a somewhat isolated manner, whilst the Commission is tasked with monitoring and scrutinising national measures in the context of Arts 258 and 260 TFEU. Implementation is organised through the Common Implementation Strategy (CIS), which entails a network of actors seeking a common understanding of the intricacies of the Directive and formulating non-binding guidance to assist in implementing it. The CIS comprises representatives from the Commission and national administrations, as well as experts and stakeholders, and is led by meetings of the Water Directors,

1 Directive 2000/60/EC of the European Parliament and Council of 23 October 2000 establishing a framework for Community action in the field of water policy, *OJ L* 327/1, 22 December 2000. For the legislative history of WFD, see Kaika and Page, 2003.

2 von Homeyer, 2009, pp 17–18. See also Korkea-aho, 2014.

3 Scott and Holder, 2006, p 225.

who are normally the heads of the water division in national environmental ministries.[4] The CIS has emerged as such a forum without any legislative initiative, or even a reference in the WFD, and is 'neither constituted nor regulated by any recognisably *legal* act'.[5]

In some respects, the WFD CIS is characterised by the presence of features also found in EU policy co-ordination instruments, discussed in Chapter 4, and the Registration, Evaluation, Authorisation and Restriction of Chemicals (REACH) Regulation, discussed in Chapter 5. The EU 2020 Strategy and the WFD both articulate broad, general objectives for Member States to interpret and accomplish in diverse national settings. To this end, they provide a forum for co-operation and exchange of best practices and experiences. Both REACH and the WFD are procedurally quite specific, yet substantive outcomes are left to be determined in implementation. In particular, REACH Implementation Projects (RIPs) and the CIS share many important features in their design and outcomes. Finally, all three governance instances attempt to foster commitment to public participation. From the lawyer's point of view, however, it is the WFD CIS that poses the hardest questions for law and judicial accountability. First, the implementation network CIS is not mentioned in the legislative text of the WFD, unlike altogether similar implementation projects in REACH. Second, the WFD uses a broad, integrative approach to reach its environmental objectives. Its vague and ambiguous provisions are partly the result of a wish to cater for national variations and policy preferences in the form of framework regulation, but also to an unprecedented commitment to ecologically far-reaching aims that do not readily yield to exact rule-making. Third, the CIS generates vast amounts of information within the parameters of a legally enforceable directive, which has potentially quite radical and profound implications for the review function of the EU courts. Before explicating the courts' role, a short introduction to the WFD CIS is given.

6.2 The Common Implementation Strategy for the Water Framework Directive

6.2.1 The WFD: Long-term sustainable water management

The main objective of the WFD is to enable Member States to achieve good surface water and groundwater status by the end of 2015. This long-term objective is defined in Art 4, the core provision of the WFD.[6] In addition to this positive objective, the WFD also introduces a potentially quite demanding negative obligation to prevent further deterioration of the status of surface water and

4 von Homeyer, 2009, p 20.
5 Scott and Holder, 2006, p 236 (emphasis original).
6 For the complexity of Art 4, see van Kempen, 2012, p 520.

groundwater.[7] Applying to all surface and groundwater bodies, both the positive and negative obligation ambitiously cover a wide range of water resources, including rivers, lakes, groundwater, estuaries and coastal waters. Other important aims that informed the EU legislature when it designed the Directive were to integrate emission limit values with environmental quality standards, to ensure that water prices create incentives to use water resources efficiently, and to involve stakeholders and citizens in water regulation.[8]

Numerous exceptions and extensions affect these basic obligations, permitting Member States to take into account national conditions in applying a common European water regime. One of the most important of these concerns artificial and heavily modified bodies of water. Member States can designate a body of surface water as artificial or heavily modified when changes to the hydromorphological characteristics of that water resource, which would be necessary to achieve good ecological status, would have significant adverse effects on the infrastructure.[9] In addition to a range of exceptions built in, openness and flexibility mark many provisions of the WFD more generally. Many of the key terms in the Directive, ranging from assessing good water status to identifying what disproportionate costs mean in relation to artificial or heavily modified water bodies, involve several simultaneously applicable elements that are subject to the judgement of those who implement the WFD, thus enhancing domestic discretion.[10] As already noted, this open-endedness, together with corresponding discretion in implementation, can be explained by reference to the long and legally complex negotiations that preceded adoption of the WFD. For instance, since EU environmental measures affecting quantitative management of water resources, and town and country planning, as well as land use, require unanimity in decision making (now Art 175 TEU), the WFD was formulated quite broadly to avoid application of the unanimity rule.[11]

Perhaps most importantly, though, open-textured norms and the emergence of complex governance techniques beyond legislation reflect the Directive's ambitious goals and 'its progressive and holistic overall approach to the water environment', which cannot be reached with clear-cut and assertive provisions or 'one size fits all' rules.[12] The holistic approach attempted by the WFD is conspicuous by virtue of two things in particular. First, the WFD replaced a number of classic top-down directives that dealt separately with issues of water management – bathing water, groundwater, surface water and drinking water – bringing water-related issues

7 The quality of surface water is judged by reference to chemical status and ecological status, whereas groundwater is evaluated according to quantitative status and chemical status.
8 European Commission, March 2007, COM(2007) 128 final, p 3.
9 Article 4(1)(a)(iii).
10 Lee, 2009, p 35.
11 von Homeyer, 2010, p 142.
12 Lee, 2009, p 35.

under a common regulatory roof.[13] Second, the WFD adopts a comprehensive focus on river basins, not on specific pollutants or sources of pollution. The central concept, a 'river basin', is an ecological rather than an administrative unit, thus increasingly acknowledging the importance of ecosystems in the legal and administrative regulation of water.[14] In other words, ecosystems are not being adapted to the requirements of legislation, but rather legislation is being drafted differently so that it can accommodate and better respond to the unique complexity of ecosystems.

What shape does river-basin-derived regulation take in legislation? The basic procedural skeleton in the WFD consists of the following steps. First is the cataloguing and characterisation of river basin districts. Member States must identify each river basin lying within their national territories; international river basins covering more than one country require cross-border action. This first step also involves identifying competent authorities and compiling registers of protected areas. Once river basins have been identified, and after they have been grouped into river basin districts, Member States are required to draw up a river basin management plan for each river basin district. Annex VII includes detailed provisions as to what this kind of a plan must include.[15] The most important part of plans is the programme of measures, which sets out – for several years at a time – national actions necessary for achieving the environmental objectives of the WFD. The first of these programmes have been fully operational as of 2012.

The framework nature of the WFD comes through most visibly when looking at its provisions. Whilst the WFD is substantively open, its procedural provisions are precise and detailed. According to one observer, 'monitoring requirements are set out as comprehensively and thoroughly as could be hoped'.[16] In specifying procedural obligations, Annexes are especially important. For instance, in relation to monitoring groundwater status, Annex V includes elaborate provisions on interpretation and presentation of monitoring results – to the extent that a highly prescribed classification of colour-coded dots must be used to present the data on a map![17] Yet not all procedural norms are precise and easy to apply. To give an example: the WFD seeks to ensure that the public plays a role in the development of a common water regime. Article 14 states that 'Member States shall encourage the active involvement of all interested parties in the implementation of this Directive . . . for each river basin district, they publish and make available for comments to the public'. The Article then enumerates a set of documents that fall under this category. Yet neither 'active involvement' nor the 'public' are defined in the WFD or its Annexes, and the whole Article reads like a strategic planning

13 For a more comprehensive review of European legislation on water prior to the WFD, see Page and Kaika, 2003.

14 Lee, 2009, p 29.

15 Article 13(1)–(4).

16 Howarth, 2007, p 185.

17 Annex V, paras 2.2, 2.4 and 2.5.

document, leaving much to the discretion of national authorities, as will be seen shortly. It should, furthermore, be noted that the distinction between substance and procedure is not always simple to draw. For instance, the requirement to achieve 'good status' seems substantive, but as Howarth (2009) argues: '[A]ctual achievement of good status is not a substantive requirement. Putting in place measures is what is legally required and this is largely a procedural matter.'[18]

By way of conclusion, the WFD marks a change in emphasis for EU water policies, moving from fragmented water regulation to a sustainability paradigm, refocusing on persistent environmental problems. It aims to fully integrate environmental concerns into sectoral policies, with the conceptualisation of water as both an economic and environmental resource.[19] Finally, it wishes not to prescribe the content of regulation, but to provide a common framework for action by laying down an interesting mix of substantively open-ended, but procedurally precise, provisions.[20] As explained by commentators: 'Far from being a single piece of legislation as that term is normally understood, the WFD is better seen as the initiation of a comprehensive program designed to guide further action by the EU and the Member States.'[21] One thing that the WFD has – albeit informally – initiated is the CIS, which is discussed next.

6.2.2 The CIS: Institutional design

Implementation of the WFD is both a lengthy and complex process. The timetable includes nine preparatory years alone, and the whole implementation process is staggered over many decades. The time span covered under the WFD continues to 2027, when the last deadline extensions run out.[22] Short-term action is managed by a cyclical process, repeated on a six-year basis. The first management cycle is now under way, with the deadline in 2015. Time is not the only challenge. Although one of the aims for the WFD was to simplify existing water legislation, complexity has continued to exist to date. The final legal text is vague owing to a genuine paucity of technical and scientific information on the basis of which to legislate in detail. Additionally, the diverse circumstances of Member States stipulated freedom of national action. Nonetheless, some sort of common understanding seemed necessary at the time of adoption of the WFD to avoid implementation failure resulting from incompatible implementation practices among Member

18 Howarth, 2009, p 412. Another aspect, which diminishes the substantive bite of the 'good status' requirement, is the amount of exceptions and derogations that can be invoked in relation to its realisation.

19 von Homeyer, 2010, p 142; Lee, 2009, p 29; Morgera, 2012, p 266.

20 The WFD bears a resemblance to what are called 'superstatutes' in US legal scholarship. They 'are aimed at big problems and must last a long time', which is why their distinguishing feature is that 'they set forth broad definitions of key terms such as "navigable waters" ', which are open to judgment: Eskridge and Ferejohn, 2010, p 267.

21 Trubek and Trubek, 2007, pp 15–16. See also Uitenboogaart et al, 2009, p 2.

22 von Homeyer, 2010, p 143.

States. Thus the Common Implementation Strategy (CIS) was established in order to support implementation, and to encourage a diversity of new and innovative solutions to scientific, technical and practical questions in an evolving EU water regime.[23]

The CIS is not referred to in the text of the WFD, reflecting in part the well-established principle of EU law that implementation falls within the remit of Member States and that directives bind them only to the result to be achieved (Art 291 TFEU).[24] A sharp-eyed reader, however, takes note of Recital 14 to the WFD, which reads: 'The success of this Directive relies on close cooperation and coherent action at Community, Member State and local level.' The emphasis lies on the informal nature of this co-operation, which is married to high-level political action. Member State Water Directors, the Norwegian Water Director and Commission officials convened in Paris in 2000. They reached an agreement, which was formally adopted as the first Working Programme in 2001, only five months after entry into force of the WFD. In Paris, the Water Directors set out a number of aims for the project that they were about to launch. The most fundamental goal envisaged for the CIS was to reach a common understanding of the technical and scientific implications of the WFD. More specifically, the aim was to develop supporting guidance documents in order to help Member States in practical implementation of the WFD. Another equally important aim was to establish a smooth flow of information between the Commission and Member States. Additional aims mentioned in the Working Programme involved capacity-building in Member States, the involvement of stakeholders, coherence between water policy and other sectoral policies, as well as between water directives and other environmental directives, and early initiation of candidate countries.[25]

Diverse tasks require a diversity of actors and administrative resources, and the CIS is built upon a multi-actor organisational frame. The CIS involves representatives from the Directorate-General for the Environment (DG Environment) and from Member States, as well as experts and stakeholders. These actors have their own place in a three-level institutional structure: the Water Directors' Joint Group, the Strategic Co-ordination Group (SCG) and Working Groups. The joint group of EU and Member State Water Directors plays a key role in the CIS. They steer the whole process by providing strategic guidance on future trends of WFD implementation and by validating the results of the working groups. They

23 Water Directors of EU Member States, 2 May 2001, p 1. See also von Homeyer, 2009, p 22; Page and Kaika, 2003, p 338; Trubek and Trubek, 2007, p 17.

24 Craig, 2010, p 273.

25 Water Directors of EU Member States, 2 May 2001, pp 2–3. Since 2001, the CIS has now subsumed the co-ordination of several related directives: the Floods Directive (2007/60/EC), the Environmental Quality Standards Directive (2008/105/EC) and the Groundwater Directive (2006/118/EC). See European Commission, November 2012, COM(2012) 673 final, p 13. Co-ordination also takes place between the CIS and the implementation of the Marine Strategy Directive (2008/56/EC).

meet twice a year under the co-chairmanship of the Commission and the Member State holding the presidency of the Council of the European Union. The Working Programme, however, underlines the informal character of the Water Directors' Group: it intends to function 'without attaining the character of a board with formal competence'.[26] A similar two-chair combination of the Commission and the Member State assumes responsibility over the SCG, which co-ordinates and oversees activities in working groups, evaluates their outcomes, prepares documents and provides input for Water Directors' meetings. Moreover, this middle-level group is responsible for the further development of the Working Programmes. All Member States are represented in the SCG. Non-governmental organisations (NGOs) and stakeholders may also be invited as observers and/or be consulted.[27] Actual work on WFD specifications takes place in working groups. Under the watchful eye of the SCG, these prepare technical guidance documents, which are the main output of the CIS. Working groups are created on an ad hoc basis for different activities and projects, and none of them is intended as permanent. The number of working groups has varied according to the applicable Working Programme and the overall progress of the implementation process. At the time of writing, the number is nine.[28] They are chaired by the Commission or either one lead country or two, which tend to be larger and more affluent Member States.[29] Most working group members are national officials and experts from those Member States that wish to take part in working group activities.[30]

The CIS is an expert-driven process. More than 1,000 experts have taken part in joint implementation activities over the years.[31] Yet already the first Working Programme acknowledged the importance of the active involvement of stakeholders, NGOs and civil society more generally. Its starting point was that the implementation process should be based on the principles of openness and transparency, and that 'creative' participation of interested parties should be encouraged and facilitated. Stakeholders can be involved in two principal ways: as observers in the work of the SCG, or as participants in working groups. The Water Directors level is excluded from participation by stakeholders. The involvement of stakeholders is ad hoc: it depends upon considerations of the Commission and Member States, which are to identify what kind of involvement is 'needed for each situation of the implementation process'.[32] In other words, the role of stakeholders is determined on a case-by-case basis, depending on the scope and subject matter of the relevant process, or on the specific mandate of a working group. The

26 Water Directors of EU Member States, 2 May 2001, p 12.
27 Ibid.
28 Water Directors of EU Member States, 2013, p 6.
29 von Homeyer, 2010, p 145.
30 Water Directors of EU Member States, 17 June 2003, p 20. The average size of a working group is 30–40 members.
31 Water Directors of EU Member States, 30 November–1 December 2006, p 2.
32 Water Directors of EU Member States, 2 May 2001, pp 13–14.

guiding principle is that participants from stakeholder groups and NGOs 'should be invited when they can contribute to the work with a specific expertise'.[33] Such an approach should 'ensure both the effective participation of and contribution from the interested parties and to enhance their understanding of the different elements related to the process'.[34] Both the European Environmental Bureau (EEB) and the Worldwide Fund for Nature (WWF) have participated in the activities of working groups, and are affiliated to the SCG as observers.[35]

The most visible input of the CIS is the development of guidance documents intended to assist in practical implementation of the WFD.[36] At the time of writing, the body of CIS guidance consists of 29 guidance documents on matters ranging from analysis of pressures and impacts on water, to monitoring and public participation. Embodying an impressive number of specifications, clarifications and interpretations on a variety of issues pertinent to implementation of the WFD, guidance documents provide advice on the general methodological approach, but also attempt to take into account specific circumstances and existing practices in each Member State.[37] Guidance documents are prepared and, if no opposition emerges, decided upon in working groups. In case of disagreements, draft guidance is discussed by the SCG. If the SCG cannot resolve the problem, it issues an opinion to the Water Directors, who take a final decision. Reflecting their institutional origin in the administrative network, guidance documents have an informal and legally non-binding character, and are 'placed at the disposal of Member States who wish to use them on a voluntary basis'.[38] However, their non-binding nature poorly reflects their political, practical and also legal importance, and it is expected that Member States will at least feel obliged to comment on why they have not complied with this informal guidance.[39]

Guidance documents and other results of the CIS can be formalised by the Commission under comitology, in which case they represent legally binding standards for Member States. The intercalibration exercise, for example, was formalised by a Commission decision.[40] The exercise is a key element in identifying

33 Ibid.

34 Ibid.

35 WWF and EEB, 2004, p 10.

36 These can be found on the Commission intranet site, CIRCABC: accessed 30 June 2014, https://circabc.europa.eu/faces/jsp/extension/wai/navigation/container.jsp.

37 Draft guidance was tested in 15 selected pilot river basins across Europe. Testing is a response to 'heavy criticism of outdated and unscientific regulation of water in the past, as well as a more general recognition of the importance of learning in environmental regulation': Lee, 2009, pp 47–8.

38 Water Directors of EU Member States, 2 May 2001, p 2.

39 Lee, 2009, p 53.

40 Commission Decision of 20 September 2013 establishing, pursuant to Directive 2000/60/EC of the European Parliament and of the Council, the values of the Member State monitoring system classifications as a result of the intercalibration exercise and repealing Decision 2008/915/EC, *OJ L* 266/1, 8 October 2013.

common indicators for defining ecological status in a harmonised way. In other words, its goal is to articulate a common understanding of what 'good ecological status' means, so that 'good status' in Finland is comparable to 'good status' in Portugal, and to guarantee that this understanding is compatible with the Directive's provisions. Not only does the CIS harmonise understanding of key elements of the WFD or fill in the gaps left by the WFD, but it also offers a platform to prepare related legislation. For instance, in the WFD, provision is made for adoption of more specific legislation: daughter directives on groundwater (Art 17)[41] and priority substances (Art 16)[42] were adopted in 2006 and 2008, respectively. These daughter directives were factually prepared by CIS expert groups, which have since continued as CIS working groups to pave the way for the directives' smooth implementation.

Whilst the CIS has been widely illustrated and its operation elucidated by legal governance researchers, we nevertheless know significantly less about its implications for, and the forms it takes in, adjudication, to which I turn next.

6.3 The judicial role and the WFD CIS: Tension between uncertainty and information

Analysis of the role of the courts in relation to the WFD might well be begun by noting that the WFD is binding legislation and that nothing in the WFD CIS appears to be interfering with 'normal' ways of doing things. Thus, whilst the soft law of CIS guidance documents clarifies minor and prominently technical gaps that have been deliberately left by legislation, emphasis remains on the legislative text of the WFD and the ultimate interpretative authority stays with the EU courts. This account, however, relies on assumptions that are misguided and lack a sound basis in reality. Whilst the official emphasis may formally be on the legislative framework, the gaps that occur throughout the WFD challenge this formal view. As a whole, the legislative framework is best described as vague and amorphous. Studying what the legislative text says amounts to a 'half serving', because the CIS gives a more specific meaning to a number of legislative provisions. How does this affect the courts, the task of which it is to adjudicate the WFD?

The basic tension relevant to analysis of the judicial role in the WFD CIS emerges from this dual dynamic between uncertainty and information. On the one hand, the ambiguity of underlying legislative provisions signifies ample discretion in implementation, and the critical question is whether the authorities take on the responsibility that the WFD places upon them, how they handle uncertainties arising in connection with application of the Directive and how they can be

41 Directive 2006/118/EC of the European Parliament and Council of 12 December 2006 on the protection of groundwater against pollution and deterioration, *OJ L* 372/19, 27 December 2006.

42 Directive 2008/105/EC of the European Parliament and Council of 16 December 2008 on environmental quality standards in the field of water policy, . . . *OJ L* 348/84, 24 December 2008.

monitored in this task by the Commission.[43] The question of enforceability of the WFD was frequently raised in the course of law-making. Many feared that the WFD would be 'over ambitious in its objectives, insufficiently stringent in its legal formulation and too generous in the discretion'.[44] Indeed, nearly 15 years of implementation practice have now shown that the initial worries were not entirely ill-founded and that Member States are often at sea as to what is required of them.[45] On the other hand, it has been argued that 'by providing clearer background standards and information than the legislation itself . . . the Common Implementation Strategy may even make more traditional formal legal action more straightforward'.[46] The idea is that novel implementation practices not only assist Member States when complying with the Directive's requirements, but also ease the tasks of both the Commission and the courts, acting thus on increased, more accurate and more timely information.

Whether, and in what ways, the Commission, as the guardian of EU law, and the EU courts use and could use 'clearer background standards' and 'information' in exercising their respective powers in a legislative framework riddled with gaps and ambiguities is the main question to be asked in the next subsections. First, I focus on enforcement activities against Member States – more specifically, on the infringement procedure (Art 258 TFEU). Although there is research on implementation of EU environmental directives, problems of enforcement action in the specific context of framework directives have not been discussed. Second, I provide an analysis of whether and how the CIS affects the Court of Justice of the European Union (CJEU) when asked to adjudicate on the WFD and, in particular, to interpret the provisions of the underlying legislative framework. An important part of this analysis addresses the unclear legal authority of CIS interpretative guidance before the courts. Finally, I discuss the role of environmental NGOs in ensuring that environmentally ambitious framework laws are not given short shrift by national authorities.

6.3.1 The Commission and the WFD

6.3.1.1 Trends of infringement litigation in the era of framework legislation

Member States are responsible for implementing EU law, and the responsibility falls on Member States to explain and rectify any delays, or other shortcomings and omission, as requested by the Commission. This principle, as it currently stands, applies to framework directives too. If the Commission is not satisfied with Member State compliance, it can take the matter before the Court of Justice,

43 Hedelin and Lindh, 2008, pp 335 and 338–40.

44 Howarth, 2009, p 394.

45 van Kempen, 2012, p 500.

46 Lee, 2009, p 47.

asking it to declare an infringement of EU law by the Member State under Art 258 TFEU. As is well known to students of EU law, the Commission has virtually unchecked discretion to decide whether and when to issue a reasoned opinion, and whether or not to take a matter before the Court. This discretion with respect to Art 258 TFEU has been widely challenged and criticised. The risk is that the Commission does not use its powers fairly and objectively, but allows political and other factors to affect its decision making.[47] Powers aside, it is notoriously hard for the Commission to ensure timely and adequate implementation of legislation, especially of environmental law. The key problem is that the Commission cannot investigate actual practices in Member States, thus having to rely on information from Member States themselves, or from third parties such as citizens or environmental NGOs. Member States are often, unsurprisingly, reluctant or slow to offer a complete (truthful) picture of the state of affairs and to submit the information that the Commission requests. The Commission also lacks adequate resources to cover all national measures transposing EU legislation, to analyse the data, or – if necessary – to act upon the information that it has received from third parties. Finally, there is the problem of the direction of action: assuming that the Commission acts on information received from third parties, the 'bite' of enforcement action is most acutely (but perhaps also asymmetrically) felt in those Member States in which citizens and environmental NGOs are active in contacting the Commission.[48]

Monitoring implementation of EU environmental framework legislation poses additional difficulties, and the Commission here also enters into a realm of substantive ambiguity, if not procedural vagueness. The framework quality of a legal instrument increases the workload of the Commission because there are no specific legal or other criteria according to which Member State performance might be unequivocally monitored and assessed.[49] As a legal instrument, a directive does not prescribe the form and methods for achieving a particular result, so that Member State freedom of action remains altogether complete. In the case of a framework directive, this feature is more pronounced than in a 'classic' directive. Moreover, the law on Member State discretion as regards directives is 'underdeveloped', and the approach of the Court of Justice inconsistent.[50] In the earlier years of enforcement of environmental legislation, the EU Court tended to evaluate domestic discretion from the vantage point of manifest error (and instructed national courts to do the same): only if a Member State was manifestly in breach of the law would the Court then rein in the Member State. In later years, the Court came to adopt a slightly different approach. Although the Court of

47 Craig and de Búrca, 2011, p 415; Harlow and Rawlings, 2006; Krämer, 2009, p 25; Scott, 2011, pp 344–5. For the Commission's role in enforcement of EU law, see Andersen, 2012.

48 For problems of implementation of environmental law, see European Commission, March 2012, COM(2012) 95 final.

49 See also Uitenboogaart et al, 2009, p 5.

50 Hilson, 2004, p 237.

Justice has continued to insist that the mere fact of a situation not being in conformity with the objectives set out in a directive does not justify the conclusion that a Member State has failed to fulfil its obligation under that directive, nevertheless it has somewhat qualified its insistence. In the landmark *Irish Waste* case,[51] for example, the Court ruled that if the situation 'persists' and 'leads in particular to a significant deterioration in the environment', such a situation may indicate that that Member State has exceeded its margin of choice. However, it is readily apparent that standards like this, which require the Commission to undertake intense and resource-heavy work in order to be able to produce evidence about the existence of 'persistence' and 'significant deterioration', render exercise by the Commission of its enforcement powers slow and cumbersome. Based on examination of recent environmental case law, Prete and Smulders (2010) suggest that the Court of Justice arrives more often than it used to at the conclusion that the Commission lacks evidence to support its claims, and in their view this connects to the overly technical nature of the directives.[52]

Now, in order to establish that a Member State has not fulfilled its obligations under the framework directive, the Commission needs to be in a position (a) to identify and articulate Member State obligations in an unambiguous and unqualified way, and (b) to demonstrate, by way of scientifically reliable information, that environmental objectives laid down by the directive have not been achieved. As a result, successful infringement litigation as regards framework legislation needs be backed up by information that the Commission finds not only rather difficult and time-consuming, but also legally problematic to put together. As discussed in detail in the subsection entitled 'Article 258 TFEU litigation in the WFD', *Commission v Germany*[53] perfectly epitomises the Commission's ongoing sufferings with the framework nature of legislation.

In light of what has been argued thus far, the fact that the European Union is involved to an increasing extent in the process of implementing its own policies is then like a missing piece of a puzzle being returned,[54] when EU involvement is driven just as much by a benevolent offer to help Member States as by a motivated search for self-serving information. Particularly in the recent past, Commission involvement in implementation was seen as a way in which to maintain the efficiency of the EU executive in monitoring fulfilment of Member State obligations under the Treaties. Contemporary scholarship instead has interpreted Art 258 TFEU as involving a *proactive* responsibility, falling on the Commission, to guide and facilitate implementation.[55] From the point of view of the Commission, the CIS has the potential to proactively prevent problems and to make the Commission's monitoring task somewhat more straightforward. By co-operating

51 Case C-494/01 *Commission v Ireland* [2005] ECR 1-3331, [169].

52 See Prete and Smulders, 2010, pp 38–9.

53 Case C-525/12 *Commission v Germany*, pending at time of writing.

54 Armstrong, 2011; Curtin and Egeberg, 2008, p 649; Schwarze, 2012, p 291.

55 Chiti, 2012; Senden, 2013, p 63.

with Member States through the CIS, the Commission receives first-hand information on national circumstances, and on issues in relation to which Member States may have problems and need to be monitored more closely.[56] This aspect was highlighted in the latest CIS Working Programme, in which the information flow was seen as allowing the Commission to helpfully 'obtain an up to date picture' on WFD activities on the ground.[57] The Commission will not only receive information on individual Member States, but will also be in a position to contrast country-specific information with comparable information concerning other Member States. De Búrca (2010) detects similar developments in the area of the EU anti-discrimination regime, commenting that the Commission 'appears to view the design of the new anti-discrimination regime mainly as a way of gaining more accurate information on what is happening regionally and locally with a view to more effective enforcement of the centrally agreed rules'.[58] Yet because the anti-discrimination regime has given rise to an insubstantial amount of litigation, the impact of 'more accurate' information on the judicialised stage of the infringement procedure has not been tested – and it is to this that I turn now, in the context of WFD. I begin by illuminating how the CIS generates more specific standards and criteria according to which national implementation can be monitored.

6.3.1.2 How the CIS affects Commission discretion

One of the main aims of the WFD is to increase the amount of reliable and up-to-date information on European waters. During preparation of the WFD, this specific objective was sought by inserting various reporting and monitoring requirements into the legislative text. The first of many WFD-related analyses concerned an environmental assessment of all of the impacts from human activities, and an economic analysis of water uses and cost-recovery levels (the so-called 'Article 5 analysis', the deadline for which was 2004). This, however, was but a modest beginning. With the first management cycle drawing to an end in 2015, the reporting requirements are now going to bite fully. For instance, in 2011, the Commission received 128 river basin management plans, which it had to analyse in detail. The interesting question that now arises is how the Commission undertakes assessment of various reports. In 2004, the Commission evaluated national Article 5 analyses quite synoptically, primarily checking that the national report was submitted in time, and that it was clear and complete. Yet it is clear that the more WFD implementation progresses, the more intense the assessment expected of the Commission.

Assessment is an important, but so far critically understudied, aspect of increased reliance on reporting and other information-enhancing mechanisms as a means

56 Interview with Commission officials, 3 June 2014, on file with author.

57 Water Directors of EU Member States, 2013, p 5.

58 de Búrca, 2010, p 232.

of legal regulation. Apart from obvious technical and practical problems involved here,[59] legal problems are also many. How to articulate fair and legitimate evaluation criteria? In particular, how can the Commission reconcile fairness of comparison and diversity of conditions across the European Union, especially when the underlying legal standards are ambiguous and in need of clarification and specification?[60] And how to evaluate the evaluator – that is, how to assess Commission discretion in enforcement? The CIS regime seems to provide one possible answer to a specific problem that has emerged as a result of the use of reporting as a promising mechanism of legal regulation. It has been anticipated by scholars that, after the initial period of 'running in' the WFD, the Commission will come to review information submitted more critically and to measure Member State performance according to benchmarks originally developed in the CIS.[61] Interestingly, when reviewing national Article 5 analyses, the Commission consulted and sought endorsement from benchmarks developed within the CIS.[62] The importance of CIS norms may also grow in the assessment phase if, as suggested by the Commission, use of peer reviews is introduced to evaluation of national reports.[63]

The CIS, as a means of harmonising evaluation criteria, may not go down too well with the courts. The CJEU has recently assessed the criteria according to which the Commission reviews national reports.[64] An EU-wide scheme for greenhouse gas emissions allowance trading was adopted in 2003,[65] and for the first years of operation of the Directive, Member States were required to draw up a five-year national allocation plan (NAP). The plan determined the total quantity of allowances in the Member State and included a proposal for their allocation. This had to be based on objective and transparent criteria, taking into account the terms of the Directive and comments obtained from the public. The plan was published and notification sent to other Member States and the Commission, which had to accept the plan before it became operational. The Commission could refuse to do so, if, in its view, the NAP was not compatible with the Directive's criteria. Poland and Estonia submitted their plans in 2006 for the period 2008–12. Arguing that several criteria specified in Annex III of the Directive had been infringed, the Commission reduced the total annual quantity of emissions allowances in the NAPs. The countries appealed to the General Court, which held

59 For their elaboration, see European Commission, November 2011, SWD(2012) 379 final, p 7.

60 European Commission, April 2009, SEC(2009) 415 final, p 14.

61 Scott and Holder, 2006, p 231.

62 European Commission, March 2007, COM(2007) 128 final, pp 7–8.

63 European Commission, November 2012, COM(2012) 673 final, p 16.

64 Case T-183/07 *Poland v Commission* [2009] ECR II-3395, appealed as Case C-504/09 P *Commission v Poland*, 29 March 2012, NYR; T-263/07 *Estonia v Commission* [2009] ECR II-3463.

65 Directive 2003/87/EC of the European Parliament and Council of 13 October 2003 establishing a scheme for greenhouse gas emission allowance trading within the Community, *OJ L* 275/32, 25 October 2003. Note that allowances are now allocated on an EU-wide basis and that NAPs are no longer in use. For the current system, see Vedder, 2011, p 114.

that, by refusing to accept the NAPs on the basis of doubts as to the reliability of the data used by Estonia and Poland, the Commission had exceeded its powers. On appeal, the Court of Justice concurred. Both courts began analysis by referring to the formal legal nature of the Directive. As a result of freedom of action guaranteed by a directive, the Commission is under an obligation to prove that the instruments chosen by Member States are contrary to EU law. In respect of the Directive in question, only Member States had the power to draw up the NAP and to determine the total quantity of allowances.[66] The powers of the Commission were accordingly limited, it being entitled *only* to verify conformity of the NAP with the criteria of the Directive and its Annexes. If it were to decide to reject a NAP, the Commission would have to give a reasoned decision.[67] The real surprise lies in the view that the Court took with respect to assessment criteria. The Commission has no powers to replace data provided by Member States with its own data obtained from its own assessment method or to fix the maximum level for the total quantity of allowances. Furthermore, the Commission cannot apply a single method of assessing NAPs. The General Court explained:

> [T]o allow the Commission to use a single method of assessing NAPs for all the Member States would amount to acknowledging it as having not only a veritable power of uniformisation in the context of implementing the allowance trading system, but also a central role in the drawing up of NAPs. Neither such a power of uniformisation nor such a central role were conferred on the Commission by the legislature in the Directive, in the context of its power of reviewing NAPs.[68]

The key principle to be inferred from this judgment seems to be that the Commission should monitor Member State performance in a manner that is at once thorough, non-discriminating and yet sensitive to national circumstances – that is, highly individualised. The question that remains open after the ruling is: how to do so? Would the CIS be of help here? Can the Commission actually use CIS-derived standards? In view of the last question, it should be noted that the role of non-official Commission working documents in infringement litigation was recently brought before the courts. The Commission claimed that, having not included in national legislation the criteria laid out in a Commission working document, Austria had failed to fulfil its obligations. Dismissing the Commission's claim, the Court of Justice pointed out that the document has no binding legal value, drew attention to the fact that the document was published many years after expiry of the deadline for transposition and noted that the criteria

66 Case T-183/07 *Poland v Commission* [2009] ECR II-3395, [85].

67 Ibid, [89].

68 Ibid, [106]. The Court of Justice stressed equality of assessment: in its view, equal treatment between Member States is ensured by 'examining the plan submitted by each of them with the same degree of diligence': Case C-504/09 P *Commission v Poland*, 29 March 2012, NYR, [67].

included in the working document did not appear to stem from the underlying legislation.[69]

What are the implications of these two rulings for Commission use of the CIS? Given the central role of the Commission in adopting CIS guidance, it is only natural to expect Commission discretion to be influenced by CIS standards and it to monitor Member States in light of those standards.[70] The Commission has also explicitly confirmed the relationship between the CIS and evaluation. It recently asked the CIS to identify the concept of 'ecological flow', which the Commission needs if it is to monitor Member State progress in achieving good groundwater status.[71] The Commission has not expressly referred to guidance in its pleadings (those that are publicly available),[72] which seems a wise choice in light of the case against Austria. However, and in so far as this particular case seemed to hinge on the fact that the working document did not stem from underlying legislative provisions, it does not answer the specific question of whether the CIS can be used to clarify the content of WFD obligations. In this respect, it is interesting to note that CIS strategic documents have emphasised that activities undertaken within the CIS stem 'from specific formal obligations in the WFD', and that CIS standards and benchmarks can be traced back to the provisions (however ambiguous and vague) of the WFD, thereby technically deriving their possible legal effects from the underlying legislation.[73] That being so, although the *Austria* judgment clarifies that Member States do not have to include additional non-binding rules in their *transposing* legislation, it leaves open the question of whether or not the use of CIS standards as *clarifying* the scope of Member State obligations is permitted.

What about the Commission's increased role? The stance that the CJEU took in the allowances trading case was influenced by its apparent reluctance to hand over the power of uniformisation to the Commission. However, when returning to the CIS, it does not seem conceivable to argue that recourse to criteria and benchmarks developed by the CIS amounts to strengthening the role of the Commission. This should become clear when looking at what the alternatives are. The other option (besides deployment of CIS standards) is that the Commission reviews national reports in light of the WFD and its Annexes. This nonetheless means (owing to the substantive vagueness of many WFD provisions) that the Commission will review reports in light of its autonomous interpretation of legislative provisions. This outcome does not seem warranted, especially keeping in mind the CJEU's obvious reluctance to increase the powers of the Commission, along with the origin of CIS standards in a decentralised and deliberative regime

69 Case C-555/10 *Commission v Austria*, 28 February 2013, NYR, [58].

70 See also Heyvaert, 2009, p 649, for the argument that informal good practice codes are used 'as a benchmark for compliance with a "hard law" prescription' in international law.

71 European Commission, November 2012, COM(2012) 673 final, p 6.

72 Yet Commission officials confirmed that they have referred to CIS guidance in infringement litigation documents: interview with Commission officials, 3 June 2014, on file with author.

73 See, eg, Water Directors of EU Member States, 30 November 2009, p 1.

comprising several hundred experts, national representatives and environmental NGOs. Admittedly, the Commission is in a better position to monitor national progress by means of new implementation regimes such as the CIS and, in this respect, one could say that the Commission's role has been reinforced. In my view, however, the emerging connection between the CIS regime and Commission discretion in enforcement actually tames the latter's influence and makes it more transparent. The CIS offers a new way in which to make the manner and means by which the Commission exercises its discretion in respect of Art 258 TFEU visible and subject to scrutiny. The impact of the CIS on Commission discretion is an instructive example of the usefulness of new governance: it 'officialises and subjects to public discipline this process of resolution of ambiguity, rather than, as traditional judicial practice tends to do, treating it as an insider's secret'.[74]

6.3.1.3 Article 258 TFEU litigation in the WFD

The overview of enforcement, covering the first decade of the WFD, shows that the Commission has focused on enforcement of deadlines and conformity of transposition. According to the Commission, few of the then 15 Member States transposed the WFD into their national legislation by the deadline (22 December 2003). Therefore, as early as 2004, the Commission had launched 11 infringement cases, out of which a total of five cases ended before the Court of Justice.[75] Overall, the Commission reported that it was not satisfied with the quality of transposition, and, in particular, that there were severe shortcomings in relation to several Articles concerning environmental objectives, recovery of costs for water services and public participation.[76] After transposition was taken care of, the Commission shifted its attention to conformity checks. Between 2007 and 2012, a total of 22 non-conformity cases were initiated, with over half of the cases negotiated and closed between the Commission and the Member State. In its third WFD report from 2012, involving the latest information on enforcement numbers, the Commission emphasises the living nature of conformity checking and iterates that it will 'stay alert' to potential cases of non-conformity in so far as they affect achievement of the WFD objectives.[77] Finally, the Commission has closely followed the application of national provisions, and, in 2011, it began proceedings against five Member States for failures

74 Sabel and Simon, 2006, p 399.

75 In five cases, the Court of Justice ruled against Member States: Case C-33/05 *Commission v Belgium*, 15 December 2005, NYR; Case C-32/05 *Commission v Luxembourg* [2006] ECR I-11323; Case C-67/05 *Commission v Germany*, 15 December 2005, NYR; Case C-85/05 *Commission v Italy* [2006] ECR I-9 (summary publication); and Case C-118/05 *Commission v Portugal* [2006] ECR I-11 (summary publication).

76 European Commission, March 2007, SEC(2007) 362 final.

77 European Commission, November 2011, SWD(2012) 379 final, p 12.

in adopting and communicating river basin management plans, with four rulings given in 2012.[78]

Reflecting the technical nature of cases, the majority of infringement rulings by the Court of Justice have been straightforward and required little legal scrutiny from the Court.[79] In the only case of some significance, the Commission argued that Luxembourg is required to adopt national framework legislation in order to comply with the WFD requirements. The Court contested that interpretation, pointing out that the provisions of the WFD cannot be understood as obliging Member States to adopt national framework legislation or to support the view that such a measure would, at any rate, be necessary to ensure the aims that the WFD hopes to achieve.[80] The second part of the ruling concerned transposition of some of the provisions of the WFD. According to the Commission, the definitions set out in Art 2 (terms such as 'river basin' and 'good chemical status') had not been transposed into national law. Here, the Court agreed with the Commission, concluding that national transposition was inadequate. The Court acknowledged the importance of key concepts to achieving the environmental objectives of the WFD and explained that Art 2, read together with other provisions, 'imposes on Member States *precise* obligations to be implemented within the prescribed timescales in order to prevent deterioration of the status of all bodies of surface water and groundwater'.[81] Another point of contestation addressed transposition of Art 14, requiring Member States to launch the public participation phase in respect of river basin management plans by 2006. Luxembourg contested the action, arguing that the period for complying with the obligation had not yet expired. This was, strictly speaking, correct, because the legal proceedings were initiated in 2005. The Court, however, pointed out that Art 14 is intended to confer on interested parties a right to be actively involved in implementing the WFD, including river basin management planning in particular. Although the deadline had not expired at the time that legal proceedings began, national transposition measures were nonetheless necessary to make the deadline legally binding on the national authorities and to ensure that individuals can ascertain, well in advance, the full extent of their rights provided for by the WFD.[82]

This particular ruling is important to understanding the nature of framework directives. The general starting point, which the Court of Justice confirmed, is that framework directives do not have to be implemented by way of adopting national framework legislation. Domestic discretion is not, however, unfettered. Framework directives are, as already seen, characterised by (vague) key terms and deadlines

78 Case C-366/11 *Commission v Belgium*, 24 May 2012, NYR; Case C-297/11 *Commission v Greece*, 19 April 2012, NYR; Case C-223/11 *Commission v Portugal*, 21 June 2012, NYR; Case C-403/11 *Commission v Spain*, 4 October 2012, NYR.

79 For the cases, see Korkea-aho, 2014.

80 Case C-32/05 *Commission v Luxembourg* [2006] ECR I-11323, [51].

81 Ibid, [63] (emphasis added).

82 Ibid, [81].

that are staggered over many years, and the Court seemed to have captured the essence of how to promote these features. As for key terms, Member States need to transpose the definitions adopted in the directive into national legislation, with binding force. As such, key terms may have a mere functional role in respect of more specific obligations to which the directive gives rise, yet they frame and shape further action by Member States, for which reason their uniform transposition across the European Union becomes very important. In addition, framework directives build upon deadlines that gradually expire irrespective of the deadline of formal 'framework' transposition. The relationship between these more specific deadlines and the general legal transposition deadline is unclear, as the case against Luxembourg illustrates.[83] With respect to public participation provisions the Court again appeared to give weight to the objective pursued by the provision(s) in question: because the aim of Art 14 WFD is to encourage the active involvement of interested parties, Member States are required to adopt national measures well in advance (that is, by the deadline of formal 'framework' transposition), so that individuals can make use of their rights in plenty of time.

Commission v Germany, pending at the time of writing, will be a second important ruling in the WFD context.[84] Once decided, it will significantly affect the Commission's role in, and interpretation of, the whole regulatory framework. Here, I focus only on those aspects of the ruling that have implications for the Commission acting as the guardian of EU law. The substantive focus of the case is the concept of 'water services', which has generated controversy since adoption of the WFD and as regards several Member States.[85] Advocate General (AG) Jääskinen's opinion does not bode well for the enforcement of framework legislation: in his view, the Commission claim should be dismissed, for it is not clear from the application what the Commission actually claims, nor is a clear definition of the scope and nature of Member State failure provided by the Commission.[86] In the AG's view, the Commission application also fails because, if successful, it would amount to harmonisation of national water legislation, which is inappropriate given the wide discretion that the WFD affords to Member States.[87] Both of the AG's arguments address seminal aspects of framework regulation – that is, the nature of framework regulation as a harmonising measure, as well as the question of how judicial action should deal with the further development of framework norms – so that much hinges on the Court of Justice's ruling.

83 See also the first WFD preliminary ruling for problems with the temporal application of Art 4: Case C-43/10 *Nomarchiaki Aftodioikisi Aitoloakarnanias and others v Ypourgos Perivallontos, Chorotaxias kai Dimosion ergon and others*, 11 September 2012, NYR.

84 Case C-525/12 *Commission v Germany*, pending at time of writing.

85 Of two requests for preliminary rulings so far made to the CJEU, Case C-461/13 *Bund für Umwelt und Naturschutz Deutschland*, pending at time of writing, also concerns clarification of the concept 'water services'.

86 Opinion of AG Jääskinen in Case C-525/12 *Commission v Germany*, given on 22 May 2014, [30].

87 Ibid, [88].

In conclusion, the picture of two extremes is clear: the simple cases are very straightforward, while the difficult cases call into question the viability and legitimacy of the whole regime. The relative simplicity of the majority of infringement rulings results from two things, which are, moreover, essential for understanding the Directive. First is the procedural approach adopted in the WFD: Member States are required, by the text of the WFD, to set up various monitoring and surveillance arrangements, and to inform the Commission. If a Member State fails to do so, the Commission does not have to gather additional information on the breach by the Member State or the ecological status of the environment. Outside procedural norms, the Commission is weak, as is well illustrated by the case against Germany. This argument should not be taken to imply that procedural norms are always readily complied with and enforced. The scope and application of procedural norms have become contested too, as different models have been drawn upon in national implementation. In particular, problems have emerged in connection with participation requirements.[88]

The second possible factor explaining the absence of complications in enforcement is the information generated through the CIS, which assists in monitoring and readies the Commission to initiate and argue cases before the Court of Justice. Nevertheless, as the *Germany* case indicates, WFD requirements are not easily translated into judicial language, and it is unclear how the Commission can clearly articulate the scope and nature of Member State failure if Member State obligations are not clearly laid down in the WFD. This indicates that the amount of tricky litigation will only increase in the future. As argued, the CIS offers direction, but as long as it is unclear whether the use of the CIS is permitted, the Commission might be better off in the shadows, persuading Member States outside the courts by using information generated through the CIS.

6.3.2 The Court of Justice of the European Union and the WFD

I have argued in the foregoing how the exercise of Commission enforcement powers is mediated by the CIS. The powers of the Commission under Art 258 TFEU are, however, only one side of the coin: once the Commission decides to begin infringement proceedings, the Court of Justice becomes involved too. Use by the Commission of CIS standards may lead to the establishment of two-tier monitoring if the guiding effect of CIS guidance is not acknowledged by the EU courts. This can hardly be considered desirable progress. Hence an analysis is needed of of whether, and if so, how, the CIS influences court practices. Early observers anticipated that CIS guidance documents would be 'of significant importance in the course of interpreting the WFD by the European Court of

88 In particular, Case C-32/05 *Commission v Luxembourg* [2006] ECR I-11323 and Case C-43/10 *Nomarchiaki Aftodioikisi Aitoloakarnanias*, 11 September 2012, NYR.

Justice in the event of a lawsuit'.[89] The importance of the CIS for the EU courts would seem to cover both Art 258 TFEU and Art 267 TFEU actions.

The critical issue, on which this highly optimistic observation is conditional, is whether the CJEU is actually able or willing to use CIS guidance when adjudicating on the WFD. Put differently, the unclear legal authority of guidance appears to prevent the EU courts from giving explicit regard to interpretative soft law guidance. The CJEU's reluctance to use CIS guidance in the *interpretation* of underlying framework legislation is based on similar reservations to those that it holds as regards *review* of soft law guidance more generally. CIS guidance is non-binding – that is, soft law. As is clear from the discussion in Chapter 4 concerning country-specific recommendations, the main thrust of established case law is that the EU courts review measures that have been (a) adopted by EU institutions, and which, regardless of their nature or form, (b) are intended to generate legal effects. Since review of CIS guidance by the EU courts involves a set of specific problems that do not arise in connection with country-specific recommendations, it is necessary to consider the implications of the EU courts' case law on soft law for CIS guidance. What I will say about CIS guidance will apply to the guidance documents issued by the European Chemicals Agency (ECHA) too, unless noted otherwise.

6.3.2.1 The review of CIS guidance by the EU courts

According to the authorship rule (i), measures adopted by an EU institution can be reviewed.[90] Being adopted by the Agency, ECHA guidance overcomes the authorship requirement.[91] Networks such as the CIS have no formal status as a Union body, and their outputs seem to be excluded from the scope of review on that basis alone.[92] However, CIS guidance does not explicitly address the question of who is considered to be its author. The first strategic document begins describing 'constructive and productive cooperation' between Member States and the Commission in adoption of the WFD, which 'should be continued for that purpose and taken to even greater heights'.[93] A similarly co-operative tone can be found in

89 Newig, Pahl-Wostl and Sigel, 2005, p 337, fn 4.

90 The challengeability of acts of EU agencies is now confirmed in Art 263 TFEU. Prior to the new Article, it was unclear whether the EU agencies qualified as 'authors' under ex Art 230 EC, although the EU Court gave a positive answer to the question in Case T-411/06 *Sogelma–Societá generale lavori manutenzioni appalti Srl v European Agency for Reconstruction (EAR)* [2008] ECR II-2771, [37].

91 Note, though, that the Second Consultation Guidance is not unequivocal about the final decision maker. It observes that, when consensus is not possible, majority and minority views will be recorded and made public, then concludes that a 'final version of the guidance document will be prepared by the ECHA Secretariat', implying that the ECHA is to be regarded as the author: ECHA, December 2013, pp 8–9.

92 Senden and van den Brink, 2012, p 69.

93 Water Directors of EU Member States, 2 May 2001, pp 2.

the guidance documents. The reader is introduced to the document with a description of the process leading up to adoption of the guidance as 'a collaborative programme' and of the outcome as 'an informal consensus position on best practice agreed by all partners'. CIS guidance is said to embody a 'coherent and harmonious' understanding, which has been arrived at through the joint activities of both Member States and the Commission.[94] A strong presumption is thus laid on joint authorship. The force of this presumption is considerably watered down by frequent references in the strategic document to the fact that responsibility for implementation of the WFD 'resides fully within the competence of the individual Member State', and that the CIS 'neither could nor should challenge this fundamental principle'.[95] There is also a disclaimer, which states that the opinions expressed in the document are informal and, in particular, that 'the views expressed in the document do not necessarily represent the views of the European Commission'.[96] However, the case law of the EU courts demonstrates that they do not accept disclaimers and expressions at face value. They have held that 'it is not enough that an act should be described as a "decision of the Member States" for it to be excluded from review'.[97] The EU courts evaluate the content of a measure and the process leading up to its adoption before they decide whether it is a Member State or an EU institution that has authored the measure in question.[98] Now, the role of the Commission is important to the operation of the CIS. The Commission is one of the Water Directors, in addition to which it is tasked with co-chairing the SCG. Moreover, the Commission, together with a Member State or two, co-chairs most working groups. Despite its intense and multi-level involvement in the CIS, it is unlikely that the role the Commission plays would be enough to persuade the EU courts of its authorship. The EU courts are likely to perceive CIS guidance documents as interpretative acts produced by the joint action of Member States for Member States themselves.

The discussion on CIS guidance ably demonstrates how futile and 'artificial' it is to attempt to find a sole author for EU guidance.[99] A largely formalistic desire to find only one author is increasingly difficult in the area of environmental guidance, in which joint working methods have been promoted and used for years. The whole organisation of the CIS and the resulting acts, CIS guidance documents, are built on the basis of a 'new partnership working method'.[100] Scott (2011) argues – albeit in the context of guidance adopted in large hydro projects – that the whole 'point of a partnership working method' is that guidance documents 'are drafted

94 European Commission, January 2004, CIS Guidance Document No 2.
95 Water Directors of EU Member States, 2 May 2001, p 1.
96 See, eg, European Commission, January 2004, CIS Guidance Document No 1.
97 See Joined Cases C-181/91 and C-248/91 *European Parliament v Council and Commission* [1993] ECR I-3685, [14].
98 Ibid, [15].
99 Scott, 2011, p 338.
100 Water Directors of EU Member States, 2 May 2001, p 2.

and endorsed by both the Commission and the Member States'.[101] I share her opinion that guidance documents are 'hybrid' instruments and therefore should be treated as such in authorship analysis by the EU courts.

Second, and although the Commission might be regarded as the author of CIS guidance, guidance documents appear not to create legal effects, as required under Art 263 TFEU. This understanding is explicitly rejected on the first page of both CIS and REACH guidance documents. Moreover, the nature of CIS guidance, as well as the context in which documents are prepared, speaks out against intentional legal effects. The majority of CIS guidance documents consist of technical and scientific documents produced by experts in an expert organisation. But, as we saw in Chapter 4, substance prevails over form, and non-binding guidance might be deemed to have legal effects in three situations. First, guidance can have legal effects if it introduces new obligations, or adds to primary or secondary legislation. In order for the CJEU to arrive at this conclusion, the imperative wording of guidance is immensely significant. Guidance has no legal effects if it is 'fleshing out' existing obligations,[102] or rendering obligations 'more explicit'.[103] Second, guidance can also have legal effects if it aims at giving more information on the ways in which an EU institution exercises its discretionary powers. In addition, the EU courts have required that these rules of conduct be published. Third, certain soft law measures can generate legal effects in non-binding form. These are exceptional cases and a legal basis is usually either provided for in legislation or implied.[104]

Applying these three categories, first, to ECHA guidance, a situation referred to in the second point may well actualise. The CJEU is likely to find legal effects in a situation in which an EU agency's guidance document containing rules of conduct is based on a wrong interpretation of EU law. Moreover, if an EU agency has based its decision on this erroneous guidance, the CJEU might then engage in review of the legality of that guidance document. In that case, the guidance can be reviewed alongside the contested decision.[105] What about the WFD CIS? The second and third categories are unlikely, for which reason I focus on the first. As already noted, legally binding obligations are laid down in framework legislation,

101 Scott, 2011, p 339. She discusses AG Jacobs' opinion, delivered on 16 December 1992, in Joined Cases C-181/91 and C-248/91 *European Parliament v Council and Commission*. In these cases, the Parliament sought annulment of a decision adopted at a meeting of the Council to provide special aid to Bangladesh (Case C-181/91) and of the measures taken by the Commission to implement that decision (Case C-248/91). The problem was whether a decision presented as a decision of the Member States meeting in Council can be challenged under ex Art 173 EC. AG Jacobs argued that 'decisions of the Member States meeting in Council do not form part of the Community legal order in the strict sense, but are nevertheless part of the *acquis communautaire*; as their very title suggests, they have a *hybrid* character': Opinion, [18] (emphasis added).

102 Case C-325/91 *France v Commission* [1993] ECR I-3283, [14].

103 Case C-366/88 *France v Commission* [1990] ECR I-3571, [23].

104 For all three categories, see Scott, 2011, pp 337–43.

105 Case T-123/00 *Dr Karl Thomae GmbH v Commission* [2002] ECR II-5193, [97].

and Member States are invited to further specify and develop these commonly agreed norms and principles. The CJEU expressly recognised this in *Commission v Luxembourg*.[106] It alluded to the CIS when it held (self-consciously keeping to sole authorship) that 'the common principles and overall framework for action which it [WFD] lays down are to be *developed subsequently by the Member States*'.[107] Now, this 'subsequent development' is published in the form of CIS guidance, with caveats for the information involved: it has only 'an informal and non-legally binding character'.[108] CIS guidance carefully avoids imperative words and expressions. But even if guidance were written in an imperative fashion, it would be hard to judge whether the guidance document introduces new obligations or not. The reason for this is that existing legal obligations against which new legal obligations are measured are articulated in framework legislation, when it becomes nearly impossible to say where the existing obligation ends and a new obligation begins.[109] Framework legislation, such as the WFD, is premised on further development of legally binding obligations, and for this reason additional guidance can always be described as imposing 'new' obligations. This renders the above categorisation, and more generally the concept of soft law, a conceptually irrelevant tool with which to determine what kind of guidance can be reviewed. Either it renders *all* guidance reviewable and annullable (guidance can always be described as going 'beyond' existing obligations), or *none* at all (because it is impossible to say where the existing obligation ends and a new one begins). The consequences are in neither case particularly commendable. But problems should not be read as preventing judicial review of guidance; rather, they require us to pay closer attention to the rationale of such a review.

Four specific reasons could be given for the argument that the EU courts should review CIS guidance and, by analogy, use the guidance themselves when interpreting the Directive (for the latter argument, see the next subsection). First, Member States frequently adhere to soft law guidance and treat it, in most cases, as authoritative and influential material. Scott (2011) points out that soft law guidance serves to reassure actors that their activities will be deemed to be in accordance with legislation.[110] But the Member States are not the only actors who will find such material influential. If and when a Member State acts in accordance with guidance, 'it seems improbable that the Commission will perceive the existence of a breach of European law'.[111] In other words, guidance will determine the ways in which the Commission uses its discretion, as already discussed in more detail earlier in this chapter. Thus the second reason to argue for judicial review of CIS guidance lies in its potential to subject the discretionary powers of the

106 Case C-32/05 *Commission v Luxembourg* [2006] ECR I-11323.
107 Ibid, [41] (emphasis added).
108 Water Directors of EU Member States, 2 May 2001, p 2.
109 Scott, 2011, p 342.
110 Ibid, 344.
111 Ibid.

Commission to scrutiny by the courts.[112] Third, judicial review of guidance would act as a safety mechanism in those situations in which guidance clearly 'underperforms'.[113] By 'underperformance', Scott refers in her case study to circumstances in which guidance clearly falls short of the substantive requirements laid out elsewhere in legislation, or those in which the process leading up to adoption of guidance is in procedural terms far from satisfactory. Fourth, perhaps the case against judicial review of guidance was formerly stronger because there was no material on which the EU courts could have based their evaluation of the procedural and substantive quality of guidance documents – but as REACH and WFD have shown, more of the necessary material and information is now available for the courts to make sure that guidance documents are both procedurally and substantially acceptable, thus clearing at least one obstacle out of the way.[114] For instance, each WFD guidance document is accompanied by an annex, which includes the details of all those who assisted in drafting the document and whom to contact for further information.

But if the concept of soft law is as incomprehensible as it is argued to be in the case of guidance, are we effectively saying that *all* non-legislative guidance should be reviewed? I am willing to adopt this alternative because the case law of the EU courts (which limits its review of soft law to cases in which it adds to legislation) is based upon a series of categorisations and characterisations that no longer make sense in the current evolutionary phase of EU (environmental) legislation. Of course, it is *sometimes* possible to determine where and when guidance adds to, or detracts from, the underlying legislation. This is especially so when the underlying framework legislation is precise, for example in laying down procedural requirements. Sometimes too, as in Scott's case study, an international soft law agreement has been codified into EU law by the Commission and the Member States; hence the CJEU would have normative material to support its review of EU guidance and to explicitly identify where EU guidance has 'underperformed' – that is, detracted from underlying obligations. But it is normally unusual to have precise legislative terms or soft law instruments on which such an analysis could be based, and it is more common that the EU courts have only open-ended legislation against which to mirror non-legislative guidance, in which case the concept of soft law becomes irrelevant for determining the scope of judicial review.

This argument for opening judicial review to cover all non-legislative guidance will, if accepted, lead to adjustments to the case law. However, these adjustments

112 Remember that the discretionary decision of the Commission about whether or not to open proceedings against a Member State cannot be challenged before the EU courts.

113 Scott, 2011, p 345. This sort of evaluation is not new to the CJEU, which has reviewed national guidance in the context of infringement proceedings and concluded that Member States are in breach of their obligations on the basis that they have adopted guidance that *limits* the scope of a directive, ie underperforms in view of the directive. For these cases, see Hilson, 2004, p 231.

114 See Scott, 2011, p 355.

are necessary to take into account that the nature of guidance is simply no longer grasped by the traditional judicial distinction between 'soft law' and 'hard law'. It is plainly difficult not only to make this distinction in practice, but also to adopt the view of guidance documents as a form of soft law. In my view, there are good reasons to argue that CIS guidance is special and specific,[115] and should be seen as an integral and evolving part of the whole legislative framework, rather than as a complementary body of soft law.

The special nature of soft law guidance and the fact that the underlying legislation is vague should be reflected not merely in the scope of judicial review, but in its depth too. The EU courts should restrict their review to checking that guidance complies with the parameters of the 'formal EU transparency regime' and that guidance is not adopted with a view to keeping certain actors out of the process or steering clear of basic procedural requirements.[116] Similarly, whilst the EU courts may be advised to engage in a more intense scrutiny of CIS guidance in order to find out whether it has detracted from the WFD (where the legislative text of the WFD allows it), they should lessen the intensity in those cases in which it appears that the guidance is not clearly falling short of the requirements laid down in legislation and therefore avoid finding that CIS guidance goes beyond (adds to) the underlying legislation.

Finally, it is useful to note that this recommendation for review of all non-legislative guidance will not mean that the EU courts are to be swamped with cases. Potential applicants for judicial review are environmental NGOs and the European Parliament, and as far as the former are concerned, the requirements laid down in Art 263(4) TFEU would effectively serve to regulate access to the courts.[117]

6.3.2.2 The use of CIS guidance as part of legal reasoning by the CJEU

Neither the CIS nor its guidance documents have been explicitly referred to in the judgments of the EU courts thus far.[118] Should the EU courts themselves give regard to CIS guidance when interpreting the Directive? The issue that this question entails relates to the indirect legal effects of soft law. The Court has accepted the existence of such indirect effects, imposing a duty on a multiplicity of actors to take soft law into account. These duty-bound actors involve Member States,[119] national courts[120] and the

115 For the argument that implementation of the old Integrated Pollution Prevention and Control (IPPC) Directive (now the Industrial Emissions Directive) gives rise to a new type of law, see Lange, 2008, p 270.

116 Scott, 2011, pp 350–1.

117 For the question of standing, see also ibid, p 349. For the role of the European Ombudsman in review of guidance documents, see Ehnert, 2014.

118 For PEACH guidance documents, see Korkea-aho 2013.

119 Case C-288/96 *Germany v Commission* [2000] ECR I-8237.

120 Case C-322/88 *Salvatore Grimaldi v Fonds des maladies professionnelles* [1989] ECR I-4407.

Commission.[121] The precise scope of the obligation varies depending on the actor in question. Instead, the CJEU has remained ambivalent about the effects of soft law on itself, and the growing use of framework legislation has not prompted it to reconsider or clarify its position. The EU courts appear far more interested in providing guidance for other actors on how to take soft law instruments into account than in venturing to do so themselves.

We could, of course, say that the EU courts have the ultimate and autonomous authority to interpret the underlying framework legislation (however open-ended and ambiguous), and to take a final and binding decision on the interpretation of norms. Nonetheless, and in the absence of a CJEU ruling,[122] my argument is that this notion of autonomous judicial authority is extremely – and increasingly – problematic in the context of framework legislation for four reasons. First, it overlooks the nature of framework legislation that needs to be interpreted, determined and specified, a task recognised by the CJEU itself in *Commission v Luxembourg*.[123] Consequently, the EU courts are faced with a dilemma: if they decide to ignore the informal reality in which Member States operate whilst implementing the WFD, their rulings, although formally impeccable, risk being empty and misleading if they fail to take into account the real content and the context of implementation. They contribute to creating and sustaining a gap between the formal and real authority of law. Such a gap has long been argued to exist in EU constitutional law, yet to my mind the gap developing here is more critical. In the end, it concerns the understanding of what the applicable law is.[124] The first WFD preliminary ruling from Greece illustrates some of the dangers emanating from disregard of norm development in implementation.[125] At the heart of the case was the question of whether or not diversion between two river basins is acceptable. Usually, neither EU nor national courts possess the relevant knowledge to determine whether and to what extent ecological facts fit obligations laid out in framework legislation. Although, from a strictly formal point of view, the ruling does not leave much room for criticism, the ruling of the Court of Justice, in disregarding CIS guidance, offered no clear direction for national courts. Advocate General Kokott urged national courts to ensure an adequate informational basis for decision making and reminded them of the 'results of the

121 For example, Joined Cases C-223/99 and C-260/99 *Agorá Srl v Ente Autonomo Fiera Internazionale di Milano; Excelsior Snc di Pedrotti Runa & C v Ente Autonomo Fiera Internazionale di Milano* [2001] ECR I-3605, [41], or Case C-310/99 *Italy v Commission* [2002] ECR I-2289, [52]. For all three categories, see Senden and van den Brink, 2012, pp 62–3.

122 Advocate General Jääskinen discussed the interpretation of the WFD in his opinion in Case C-525/12 *Commission v Germany*, but, since the ruling has not been handed down at the time of writing, I will not discuss it here. Suffice it to say that the AG preferred a literal interpretation: Opinion, [56].

123 Case C-32/05 *Commission v Luxembourg* [2006] ECR I-11323.

124 On this point, see also Dawson, 2013, p 229.

125 Case C-43/10 *Nomarchiaki Aftodioikisi Aitoloakarnanias*, 11 September 2012, NYR.

transposition of the WFD'.[126] Whether or not she meant the CIS is open to interpretation.

Second, judicial disregard of guidance creates, and in some cases worsens, the asymmetrical situation in which perceptions of standards of judicial enforcement by the main actors differ. Put simply, we have the Commission, which deploys benchmarks from the CIS to monitor and evaluate Member States (which also observe CIS guidance), as well as to initiate legal proceedings for breach of EU law, and then we have the EU courts, which refuse to give regard to CIS standards. This most certainly militates against meaningful adjudication.

Third, a concern has recently been raised about the fact that imprecise norms are increasingly accompanied with hard enforcement powers.[127] Although the main target of the observation is Economic and Monetary Union (EMU) and ways in which fiscal scrutiny operates in the European Union, this remark has a more general resonance and is insightful in analysing how judicial powers evolve in situations in which the courts adjudicate on binding, but imprecise, legislation. If we are concerned about the growing space that framework legislation leaves for the courts, the recommendation for use of guidance by the courts would go some way towards diminishing that space.

Fourth, and relatedly, there seem to be no superior reasons to think that the EU courts' independent interpretation of framework legislation should be considered 'better' or 'more legitimate' than that of CIS actors in cases of genuine ambiguity. I find the Commission's evolving practice of treating CIS guidance as part of the WFD legislative framework immensely more defensible than any measure of judicial restraint in this respect. Non-legislative guidance is an important tool to make EU (environmental) legislation susceptible to implementation in Member States. For this reason, it seems intellectually and institutionally prejudiced to refuse to understand this and to draw the necessary conclusions. Whilst the Commission's activities make it, in the best-case scenario, more accountable in the exercise of its enforcement powers, whether this is intentional or not is irrelevant here, judicial prejudices in this respect would hamper, rather than contribute to, accountability.

My contention is that the EU courts *should recognise the value of soft law guidance* in the interpretation of underlying framework legislation. My argument is not, of course, that the CJEU should – in all cases and without exception – accept the interpretation chosen by CIS guidance documents; however, I do think that the CJEU should discuss it, and if it decides not to follow it, give reasons for not doing so. If a multiplicity of actors, experts, national competent authorities, NGOs and citizens are expected to take part in time-consuming activities, and to make nuanced judgements about complex outcomes, it is unclear why the EU courts should be exempted from even considering them. In a couple of recent cases on

126 Opinion of AG in Case C-43/10 *Nomarchiaki Aftodioikisi Aitoloakarnanias*, 11 September 2012, NYR, [119].

127 Terpan, 2014.

archetypal questions of interpretation of EU law, the EU courts have shown more openness and flexibility towards interpretative guidance. In one case, the Court of Justice, sharing AG Mengozzi's frustration with the Urban Waste Water Treatment Directive, quipped that the Directive is technical and drafted in an imprecise and general fashion. In its view, the absence of specific points of reference in the Directive would force the Court to go beyond its jurisdiction, for which reason it then endorsed the AG's request to the Commission to adopt guidelines. The Court argued that:

> [S]ince the concept of 'unusually heavy rainfall' is not defined by Directive 91/271, it is legitimate for the Commission, in carrying out its supervision of compliance with European Union law, to adopt guidelines . . . as the Court does not have jurisdiction to define numerically obligations laid down by that directive.[128]

Whilst this is an invitation for the Commission to adopt guidance, a stronger indication of the newly discovered openness towards interpretative guidance, and evidence of actual use of guidance documents, is found in two recent judgments. First, the judgment about Finnish implementation of the Habitats Directive is rather interesting in its unusual reference to the guidance document adopted by the Commission.[129] Authorisation of wolf hunting on a preventive basis formed the substance matter of the case. When evaluating whether killing a limited number of specimens has an adverse effect on the objectives envisaged in the Habitats Directive, the CJEU 'followed' the views contained in the guidance document.[130] In the second case, a German court asked the CJEU whether it could use the Commission guidance when interpreting one particular provision in the Medicinal Products Directive.[131] The CJEU answered that account may be taken of the definition of that term in the guidance document, for the guidance document 'may provide useful information for the interpretation of the relevant provisions'.[132] What is even more noteworthy is that, in the next section of the judgment, the CJEU itself entertained the interpretation provided in the guidance document.

In these two cases, explicit references to the guidance documents are highly interesting and special because they recognise the capability of guidance to generate legal effects outside the three traditional categories identified earlier – perhaps even indicating that the CJEU is gradually relaxing its policies in relation

128 Case C-301/10 *Commission v United Kingdom (Urban Waste)*, 18 October 2012, NYR, [61].

129 Case C-342/05 *Commission v Finland* [2007] ECR I-4713.

130 Ibid, [29].

131 Case C-308/11 *Chemische Fabrik Kreussler & Co. GmbH v Sunstar Deutschland GmbH, formerly John O. Butler GmbH*, 6 September 2012, NYR.

132 Ibid, [25]. For another preliminary reference in which guidance documents were discussed, see Case C-473/07 *Association nationale pour la protection des eaux et rivières-TOS and Association OABA v Ministère de l'Ecologie, du Développement et de l'Aménagement durables* [2009] ECR I-319.

to guidance involving traditional scientific expertise offered by the Commission. It seems to be enough for the CJEU that the Commission has *formal* authorship; in the German case, for instance, it was clear from the ruling that the Commission guidance document was factually prepared by a group of experts from the national authorities, the Commission and professional industry associations.[133] What poses more of a problem is network-based guidance, in view of which these cases offered no evidence of relaxation of standards. Such guidance is a hybrid product, not complying with traditional categories of authorship.

6.3.3 Stakeholders and the WFD

6.3.3.1 Two settings for participation

The WFD encompasses two different, although interrelated, settings for participation. The primary setting for public participation is the national implementation process. Article 14 requires that Member States encourage active involvement by all interested parties in implementation of the Directive. Member States are left to their own devices to decide the details of the arrangements that are necessary here, with the exception of public information and consultation, in regard to which the WFD is more prescriptive in requiring Member States to ensure public information and consultation in the production, review and updating of river basin management plans.[134] Such a plan is a key instrument for increasing the transparency and openness of national water regulation. As Lee (2009) explains, when a water resource does not meet, or is at risk of failing to meet, good water status, 'an explanation has to be provided, both of the failure and of the extra monitoring and remedial obligations that kick in'.[135] The obligation to explain and give reasons contributes to overall accountability, at least if explanations and justifications are allowed out into the open. In so far as Member States and the Commission are concerned, this seems to be the case, since national plans are sent to other Member States and to the Commission, allowing mutual peer review. But, then again, how well the report enhances accountability in relation to *members* of the national public depends on the extent to which they are included in each Member State.

The CIS offers another infrastructure for participation. The first Working Programme acknowledged that effective participation of, and contribution from, interested parties is essential to implementation of the WFD, and that the principles of openness and transparency should guide the process. As already explained, stakeholders are allowed to participate as observers in the SCG and as participants

133 Ibid, [25].

134 Annex VII lays down, among other things, that river basin management plans must include 'a summary of the public information and consultation measures taken, their results and the changes to the plan made as a consequence': Annex VII, A 9.

135 Lee, 2009, p 37.

in working groups. More detailed arrangements are worked out on an ad hoc basis. To guide discretion here, CIS actors adopted a guidance document on public participation in the WFD.[136] There is an interesting twist to its adoption: CIS guidance on public participation, laying out why and how national authorities should include stakeholders and/or the general public in national implementation, was not anticipated in the initial CIS Work Programme, but was included at the request of environmental NGOs.

Civil society has expressed its satisfaction with both the level of involvement in preparation of the document and the quality of the final outcome. In the view of the NGOs involved in CIS activities, the guidance document is 'of a considerably high standard. The text is clear and unambiguous and easily accessible to stakeholders and members of the public.'[137] Problems, unsurprisingly, largely emerge in the application of that guidance document in Member States, as will be seen shortly. Moreover, actual participation practices in the CIS have been viewed rather positively: the EEB and the WWF use words such as 'positive', 'very informative' and 'fruitful' to describe their participation in the CIS process.[138] Both NGOs have been closely engaged in implementation of the WFD and have published several 'snapshot' reports on specific issues of implementation.[139] The fact that environmental NGOs focus their efforts and criticisms on improving the quality of substantive *outcomes*, rather than the quality of procedural *arrangements* of participation, is, in my view, emblematic of the promises that the CIS has been able to reclaim.

This is an important testimony to the CIS and, perhaps more importantly, to the capacity and resilience of ad hoc and legally non-binding procedures to result in meaningful forms of public participation. Its success can be said to be slightly obscured by two facts. First, only two environmental NGOs (the EEB and WWF) have been actively participating. The scientific nature of the CIS community has perhaps acted as a filter to more extensive involvement, although the limited resources and niche expertise of environmental NGOs certainly have a role to play here too. Second, it should be recalled that neither the European Parliament nor national parliaments have a formal place in the CIS. The role of elected officials tends to be insignificant in processes like the CIS because the work takes place over a lengthy period, which calls for long-term thinking – that is, thinking that extends beyond electoral terms.[140]

136 Water Directors of EU Member States, November 2002.
137 WWF and EEB, 2004, p 29.
138 Ibid, pp 24 and 64. This is clearly reflected in the Working Programme adopted later that year, which introduces the CIS as an example of good governance at the EU level: see Water Directors of EU Member States, 2–3 December 2004, p 11.
139 Accessed 30 June 2014, http://www.eeb.org/index.cfm/activities/biodiversity-nature/water/.
140 Baber and Bartlett, 2009, p 98. For the role of elected politicians in networks more generally, see Klijn, 2008, p 27.

Whilst the CIS has scored well in allowing stakeholders into its activities and in strengthening their impact on the process, the active involvement of interested parties in national implementation has not shaped up quite as encouragingly.[141] Early reports on transposition indicated that Member States were not committed to encouraging and facilitating the active involvement of interested parties. The Finnish Act, for example, provides only for minimum conditions in terms of the availability of documents and opportunities to submit opinions; it does not answer the seminal question of how its provisions *encourage* the involvement of interested parties.[142] It comes as no surprise, then, that absence of civil society was one of the main findings of empirical research undertaken in Ireland too. The authors believe that national NGOs are too small and unorganised to offer a sustained and critical contribution to the national implementation process.[143] Similar news has been reported from the UK, where the implementation process has taken on a technical turn, with the result of 'excluding broader public discussion'.[144]

By way of conclusion, it seems correct to say that participatory practices within the WFD are polarised, or, as Lee (2009) has put it, 'two-tiered': an opportunity exists for active involvement by a small group of interested parties, whilst the general public needs to be satisfied with a much more limited opportunity for consultation.[145] Certainly, these two layers, or tiers, are not entirely exclusive, but complementary and mutually reinforcing. For instance, it was thanks to this small group of interested parties (that is, influential environmental NGOs) that the guidance document on public participation saw daylight. In addition, more connections are emerging between the activities of these two groups. In more recent updates of the CIS Work Programme, CIS actors have committed themselves to facilitating dissemination of its activities and products to the general public, for example developing more accessible summaries of guidance documents.[146]

6.3.3.2 Environmental civil society taking participation to court

Since the right to participate in river basin management plans is a right legally guaranteed in the WFD, much possible litigation focuses here. Yet with the details of participatory systems being left for Member States to work out, national variation inevitably occurs. This is not simple to assess judicially because the WFD does not offer yardsticks for the EU courts to use when reviewing national implementation. The first WFD preliminary ruling well demonstrated these

141 See, eg, Behagel and Turnhout, 2011; Howarth, 2009.

142 Act on Water Resources Management, which came into force on the 31 December 2004 (*Laki vesienhoidon ja merenhoidon järjestämisestä* 30.12.2004/1299). See also Allan, 2011.

143 Flynn and Kröger, 2003, p 157.

144 Howarth, 2009, p 415. See also Howarth, 2007, p 180, fn 155.

145 Lee, 2009, p 45.

146 Water Directors of EU Member States, 30 November 2009, p 2.

problems of review.[147] One of the questions that the referring court asked concerned limitations in participation, because the Greek management plan was adopted as an ad hoc law, hence entirely bypassing the consultation requirements of the WFD. Advocate General Kokott began her analysis by considering whether or not a procedural gap exists. In her view, the WFD does not permit derogation from participation requirements, for which reason the situation presented in the preliminary reference 'does not constitute a legal lacuna'; instead, to her mind, 'the Union legislature must be assumed to have *consciously* refrained from providing for a comparable exception for legislative process'.[148] National plans, whatever their form, cannot be prepared without adequate involvement of the public. The Court of Justice, however, accepted the exclusion of the general public on the basis that the national plan did not fall within the meaning of the Directive. This ruling demonstrates how procedural provisions, although generally perceived to be easily enforceable because of their exact nature, can be fairly difficult to enforce against Member States without encroaching upon legitimate domestic discretion.

Could the case law on the Aarhus Convention on access to information, public participation in decision making and access to justice in environmental matters be thought to provide some general guidance?[149] The first case to be analysed here concerns the Irish transposition of Art 3(1) of the Aarhus Directive 2003/35.[150] The Commission alleged that domestic legislation included a narrower interpretation of the concepts of 'the public' and 'the public concerned' than required by the Directive. Once again, the Court began by recalling that transposition of a directive does not necessarily require the provisions to be reproduced verbatim in the national context. It is the objective of the Article that matters, not the form it takes. Whether domestic legislation transposed the Article adequately is a question that could be assessed 'only with regard to all of the rights, which that directive accords to "the public concerned", since those two aspects are indissociable'.[151] As the Commission had not established to what extent the public

147 Case C-43/10 *Nomarchiaki Aftodioikisi Aitoloakarnanias*, 11 September 2012, NYR.

148 Opinion of AG Kokott in Case C-43/10 *Nomarchiaki Aftodioikisi Aitoloakarnanias*, 11 September 2012, NYR, [127] (emphasis original).

149 Upon ratification of the Aarhus Convention, the European Union adopted two directives: Directive 2003/4/EC of the European Parliament and of the Council of 28 January 2003 on public access to environmental information . . ., *OJ L* 41/26, 14 February 2003; and Directive 2003/35/EC of the European Parliament and of the Council of 26 May 2003 on public participation in respect of the drawing up of certain plans and programmes relating to the environment, *OJ L* 156/17, 25 June 2003. In addition, there is Regulation (EC) No 1367/2006 of the European Parliament and of the Council of 6 September 2006 on the application of the provisions of the Aarhus Convention on Access to Information, Public Participation in Decision-making and Access to Justice in Environmental Matters to Community institutions and bodies, *OJ L* 264/13, 25 September 2006. Note, though, that Art 2(5) of Directive 35/2003 expressly excludes the WFD from its scope, the idea being that the WFD contains the provisions necessary to meet the requirements of the Aarhus Directive. See Howarth, 2007, p 179.

150 Case C-427/07 *Commission v Ireland* [2009] ECR I-6277.

151 Ibid, [57].

concerned did not have the rights that rightfully belonged to it, the complaint was unfounded.

Djurgården-Lilla is another of the early interpretations given by the Court of Justice of the EU Aarhus legislation.[152] The matter came to the EU court as a preliminary reference from Sweden. The municipality of Stockholm had concluded a contract with an electricity company for construction of a tunnel to house electric cables to replace overground high-tension cables. The environmental NGO Miljöskyddsförening appealed against the decision to grant development consent, but that appeal was held to be inadmissible on the ground that the Miljöskyddsförening had not fulfilled the condition laid down in national legislation that it must have at least 2,000 members to be entitled to an appeal. The Court of Justice was asked whether such a provision complied with the requirements of the Aarhus Directive. The Directive, as the Court again acknowledged, leaves to national legislatures the task of determining the conditions under which an NGO is entitled to appeal. However, national discretion is circumscribed by the requirement that national rules must, first, ensure 'wide access to justice', and second, render effective the provisions of the Directive.[153] The Court held that national law can determine the number of members that an NGO must have in order to have certain privileges, but that the number of members cannot be fixed by national law at such a level that it runs counter to the objectives of the Directive. Because only two NGOs in Sweden fulfilled the requirement introduced in national legislation, the Court held – taking into account the problems that this created for *local associations* – that national legislation was not in conformity with the Aarhus Directive. Finally, the Court emphasised that although the national rules offer opportunities to participate at an early stage of decision making, those opportunities (however extensive and inclusive) cannot be understood to remedy the situation in which judicial remedies against a decision adopted at the end of the decision-making procedure are available only under very restrictive conditions.[154]

Are any general observations to be inferred from these cases, particularly in respect of interpretation of public participation in the WFD? A starting point is

152 Case C-263/08 *Djurgården-Lilla Värtans Miljöskyddsförening v Stockholms kommun genom dess marknämnd* [2009] ECR I-9967.

153 Ibid, [45]. In a similar preliminary reference case from Germany, the Court of Justice also ruled in favour of NGOs. It held that Art 10a in the Environmental Impact Assessment Directive precludes national legislation that requires that an action challenging an administrative measure is admissible only if the measure affects the claimant's individual public law rights: Case C-115/09 *Bund für Umwelt und Naturschutz Deutschland, Landesverband Nordrhein-Westfalen eV v Bezirksregierung Arnsberg* [2011] ECR I-3673.

154 Case C-263/08 *Djurgården-Lilla Värtans Miljöskyddsförening v Stockholms kommun genom dess marknämnd* [2009] ECR I-9967, [48]–[49]. Although I very much agree with the stance adopted in this case here, it should be noted that the Court managed to overlook this crucial difference between participation in decision making and access to justice in Case T-95/06 *Federación de Cooperativas Agrarias de la Comunidad Valenciana (FECOAV) v Community Plant Variety Office* [2008] ECR II-31, discussed in Chapter 5.

that national provisions must be binding, precise and clear, because they confer rights on individuals.[155] A verbatim transposition is not necessary, and a Member State is deemed to have adequately taken care of its obligations when the rights enshrined in the Directive are formally guaranteed in national legislation. It is for the Commission to provide evidence that the public does not enjoy these rights in practice. Instead, the Member State will have to tread very carefully when determining the conditions upon which the public can exercise its legal rights. National discretion is very much restricted. The *Djurgården-Lilla* case shows that the EU courts interpret provisions on access to justice very broadly, thus practically pre-empting freedom of action to adopt restrictive national provisions.[156]

Now, Art 14 of the WFD requires national legislation to ensure that Member States publish and make available environmentally relevant information, and to guarantee public consultation. Judging from the above cases, the window of discretion to introduce additional conditions for use of these rights in the national context seems very narrow, in particular should such legislation end up adversely affecting local associations. What about the positive dimension? Article 14 of the WFD is written in such a way as to inculcate proactive attitudes among Member States: it requires them to encourage the active involvement of all interested parties. The meaning of this is not altogether clear. The CIS guidance document on participation argues that it indicates 'a higher level of participation than consultation. Active involvement implies that stakeholders are invited to contribute actively to the planning process by discussing issues and contributing to their solution.'[157] Generally speaking, Art 14 appears to lay down a more far-reaching obligation on Member States than, for example, the obligation introduced by Art 1 of the Aarhus Directive to 'provide for the public participation', and to 'improve the public participation'. It is for national legislatures to decide what the active involvement of all interested parties means in a national setting.

To conclude, while the CJEU reviews the formal terms of national transposing legislation fairly stringently to ensure that Member States do not shy away from their responsibilities, it takes a back seat in review of actual application of the provisions. Admittedly, there is no one right or best way in which to encourage the involvement of interested parties, which makes it difficult to bring Member States to account on application of the Article. This was well demonstrated in the Greek preliminary ruling discussed earlier. The reason is that an obligation such as the one to encourage public involvement does not have 'the rights core' that could be enforced along the lines identified in *Commission v Ireland*. However, and as the guidance document on participation rightly points out, the obligation to encourage involvement by interested parties is binding upon Member States, and the objective is not met by simply fulfilling more prescriptive requirements concerning information and consultation. Therefore, the guidance document recommends

155 In this respect, see Case C-427/07 *Commission v Ireland* [2009] ECR I-6277, [55].
156 For the same view, see Ryall, 2010, pp 1519–21.
157 Water Directors of EU Member States, December 2002, p 18.

that national authorities should draw up a strategy or national plan, indicating action to be taken in different contexts of implementation of the WFD.[158] It is debatable whether Art 14 gives the necessary legal basis for the courts to require such information. Even though it may be unenforceable, such a national plan would be beneficial. It would keep Member States accountable to the letter and the spirit of Art 14, requiring positive action without prescribing what that action should be and thus unnecessarily pre-empting the possibility to tailor participation processes to the specific context of the Member State.

6.4 Iterated deliberation in the WFD

The first CIS management cycle will not be completed until 2015, but because the WFD builds upon gradually expiring deadlines, some valuable information is already available on whether the CIS process has managed to deliver the expected results and fulfil its objectives. Here, my focus is on finding out how the WFD CIS meets the iterated deliberation ideals of reason-giving, problem-solving orientation and participation (see Chapter 3).

Starting with *reason-giving*, clear evidence is available of policy learning stemming from the further development of arguments and considerations in a discursive process of implementation. That opinion is more generally shared among those analysing implementation of the WFD. The CIS has facilitated pooling of best practices, and data from a multiplicity of sources have been collated, analysed and shared. EU-wide data sharing has given rise to experimentation and exchange of views between Member States, with the additional benefit of saving finite resources and costs in implementing environmental regulation.[159] National policy learning has been confirmed by means of empirical research too.[160] Learning in the WFD is triggered and sustained by the CIS. Whilst the framework is firmly enshrined in legislation,[161] the CIS is continuously being developed, revised and improved, in terms of both substantive focus and procedural arrangements. Revision is an ongoing process. The first update of the overall Strategy and Work Programme was agreed in 2003 (for the years 2003 and 2004), and again in 2004 (for the years 2005 and 2006). From 2006, the revision has been undertaken every third year: the latest took place in 2012, covering the period 2013–15. Altogether, since its inception in 2001, the CIS has been revised five times. It is interesting to note how CIS actors themselves understand the provisional nature of their co-operation: the 2003 review opens by saying that 'this follow-up strategy does not replace or

158 Ibid, p 32.

159 von Homeyer, 2010; Lee, 2009, p 47; Sabel and Zeitlin, 2007; Scott and Holder, 2006; Trubek and Trubek, 2007.

160 See Allan, 2011; Behagel and Turnhout, 2011; Flynn and Kröger, 2003; Hedelin and Lindh, 2008; Howarth, 2009; Tippett et al, 2005.

161 Revision of the legislative framework is anticipated to take place in 2019. See European Commission, November 2012, COM(2012) 673 final, p 20.

re-negotiate these agreed principles [agreed in the first Work Programme in Paris] but rather strengthen the commitment of all involved parties towards these agreements'.[162] The CIS actors give, as it were, new reasons for the common project, and renew and reaffirm their willingness and sincere commitment to continue. Additionally, guidance documents are updated frequently to ensure that their *raison d'être* holds up.

Second, there is the *problem-solving orientation*. As discussed earlier, consensus-based decision making might operate to silence dissenting opinions, and to stifle free inquiry and discussion, but the CIS seems to have avoided most pitfalls in this respect. The CIS actors listen and pay attention to both inside and outside criticism. The 2004 CIS review, for instance, acknowledged that several environmental NGOs had identified some 'gaps', 'deficiencies' or 'shortcomings', and that these critical comments and observations should create 'motivation to avoid becoming complacent and to increase efforts to tackle these challenges'.[163]

Finally comes *participation*. The CIS has created an impressive network of more than 1,000 experts from more than 30 countries, and from 25 stakeholder and other organisations.[164] As noted in this chapter, as a platform the CIS has worked to accommodate stakeholders, and seems largely responsive to their needs and suggestions for improvement, allowing itself to develop in an organic fashion that may not always be envisaged in the Work Programme. The use of so-called 'drafting groups' within working groups is a good example.[165] These small units prepare and develop documents for meetings; they also ensure that written comments by working group members are accounted for 'in a balanced way', which makes them very interesting from the point of view of responsive participation in iterated deliberation.

Although the CIS, as an institutional structure, has garnered largely positive reviews, it is important not to be blind to gaps and uncertainties that may yet remain. The good performance of the CIS has been slightly tarnished because the WFD implementation results have not been entirely convincing. A review undertaken by an environmental NGO of the first published national river basin management plans deplored the plans for being poorly prepared, half-finished or missing altogether. It did not address the CIS as such, but, of course, substandard plans indicate that the CIS has not been as effective on the ground as one might have hoped.[166] Moreover, according to recent estimates, the aim of good ecological status by 2015 is likely to be met only in 53 per cent of the surface water bodies in the European Union.[167] These less-than-great results might explain why the Commission formalised its position as permanent co-chair of all working groups

162 Water Directors of EU Member States, 17 June 2003, p 8.
163 Water Directors of EU Member States, 2–3 December 2004, p 2.
164 European Commission, March 2007, SEC(2007) 362 final, p 44.
165 For additional information, see Water Directors of EU Member States, 17 June 2003, pp 19–20.
166 See EEB, 2010. See also Behagel and Turnhout, 2011; Howarth, 2009.
167 European Commission, November 2012, COM(2012) 673 final, p 3.

in 2012, having previously acted as such only in some important working groups. It remains to be seen how the stronger position of the Commission influences the self-reflexive spirit in which CIS actors have operated for nearly 15 years.

For present purposes, however, it is interesting to note that the CIS authorities, including the Commission, are calling for inclusion of more deliberative elements in the CIS in order to step up the progress of implementation. The learning dimension stands to be further strengthened, for instance by the introduction of peer review between river basins.[168] This voluntary and tailored exercise – the Commission proposes to handpick Member States – would especially target draft river basin management plans by subjecting them to review by other national district authorities. The Commission explicitly wishes this experiment to result in better compliance with WFD requirements. It remains the task of future research to assess the effectiveness of peer evaluations in securing compliance. Experiences from economic policy co-ordination have highlighted that: '[D]eclarations of breach of obligation depend on the behaviour of peers for their effectiveness. If peers are unconcerned about breach, then the sanction is rendered useless.'[169]

6.4.1 A template for enforcement of EU (environmental) legislation?

As seen, both the academic and practising, hands-on, communities have been cautiously positive with progress so far, although some serious work remains to be done in implementation. In particular, the Commission has expressed its contentment with the CIS, observing that it has contributed to the emergence of a 'common understanding' on many major issues.[170] The Commission is therefore 'convinced that this approach has already delivered better results than a more formalistic approach to implementation'.[171]

CIS collaboration is a good example of how 'fundamentally domestic implementation processes are subject to varying degrees of European influence'.[172] The self-evident aim of this 'European influence' is to improve the overall EU implementation record. Could the CIS serve as a future template for enforcement of EU legislation? Judging the future on the basis of recent Commission proposals, some alignment is already present. The 2012 Communication introduced a few ideas on how to improve compliance in Member States. One of these new ideas is the 'Structured Implementation and Information Framework' (SIIF). These new frameworks would be 'designed to clarify the main provisions of a directive as well as identify the types of information needed to demonstrate how EU law is being

168 Water Directors of EU Member States, 2013, pp 3 and 5. See also European Commission, November 2012, COM(2012) 673 final, p 16.

169 See Hodson and Maher, 2004, p 807.

170 European Commission, March 2007, COM(2007) 128 final, p 10.

171 Ibid.

172 Armstrong, 2011, p 18.

implemented on the ground'.[173] A SIIF would be built around a specific piece of EU legislation – that is, a directive or a regulation. It is not yet clear which particular forms it would take, but focus is likely to be on managing information flow. SIIFs are linked to 'partnership implementation agreements' (PIAs), another new idea introduced by the Commission in its quest to improve compliance. These are ad hoc agreements between the Commission and Member States, intended either to contribute to implementation of a specific legal text or to remedy a problematic domestic situation (such as an illegal landfill) after the event.[174] When signing a PIA, the Commission enters into an informal understanding with the Member State that it will not initiate formal proceedings during the term of the agreement. Both initiatives, being currently in the pipeline in the European Union, are hugely interesting, not least because they involve features tried and tested with the CIS. Both introduce a bespoke approach to judicial enforcement, giving rise to broader questions of the suitability of such tailored approaches to the highly formalised exercise of judicial powers. The Commission is likely to introduce both initiatives as a natural extension of its powers under Art 258 TFEU, but much of what has been argued in this chapter in relation to a similar CIS suggests that these new initiatives involve more than simply publishing more data online, so that any experimentation with either of the proposed instruments should be subjected to scrutiny, drawing upon experiences from the CIS.

One of my arguments in this chapter has been that norms agreed by the CIS shape the perceptions and evaluations on which compliance decisions by the Commission and the Court are based. I will conclude by analysing what this kind of development looks like from the point of view of civil society – an important, but often neglected, actor in Art 258 TFEU actions.

6.4.2 Civil society: 'Mad about the courts'?

Environmental NGOs that have been happy with the CIS are against the use of CIS norms in compliance monitoring, insisting upon judicial review, which takes its one and only standard from the WFD, not from the CIS. They fear that the consensual approach to implementation results in lower ambitions and that guidance documents reflect the lowest common denominator.[175] This distrust was first publicly discussed by CIS actors themselves in 2003 in the course of finalising the first batch of guidance documents. The next year, the environmental NGOs returned to the matter in their published resource document *'Tips and Tricks'*,[176] which appeared only a few months before the final update of the 2004 Working Programme. The Water Directors were clearly familiar with the critique that the environmental NGOs had levelled against them and commented that:

173 European Commission, March 2012, COM(2012) 95 final, p 5.

174 Ibid, p 10.

175 WWF and EEB, 2004, p 11.

176 Ibid.

> [T]he general 'consensus-based' decision-making is the appropriate model for a process such as the Common Implementation Strategy. This has not led to a compromise in terms of the quality and the ambition of the results during the last two years. However, despite the improvements, it will be necessary to critically monitor the performance of the chosen decision-making process in order to avoid a lowering of standards . . .[177]

It is not easy to reject or prove the link between consensus-based decision making and the compromised quality of the content of guidance. However – and given that the WFD is an open-ended legislative text, at least as far as substantive norms go – the argument, which favours judicial review drawing its yardsticks solely from the WFD, serves only to leave the job of plugging the gaps to the courts. But this is precisely what EU civil society appears to be longing for: EU civil society activists more generally expect the courts to step in where legislation has 'failed' to be specific enough, and they also look to the courts as a source of clarity and precision. On the basis of interviews conducted amongst EU anti-discrimination actors of civil society, de Búrca (2010) writes that most of the actors:

> . . . are critical of the open-ended nature of the legislation, of the failure to 'clarify' or 'define' many of the key terms such as indirect discrimination, reasonable accommodation, or even to specify more precisely what the new specialized equality bodies are intended to be and do. They remain very much focused on the Court as the appropriate actor to provide clear and uniform answers on the meaning of the legal provisions, and on the idea of litigation as the route to clarification of norms and thereby strengthening the anti-discrimination regime.[178]

Focusing again on the CIS, the problem that environmental NGOs have with the CIS regime relates to the quality of its outcomes. One might, however, argue that the CIS includes a mechanism, endogenous to its institutional design, with which to control the quality of outcomes. In preparing *'Tips and Tricks'*, environmental NGOs systematically analysed each CIS guidance document and focused particularly on open issues on which the working groups could not agree. As might be recalled, if agreement cannot be reached at the working group level, the issues are first submitted to the SCG, and finally to the Water Directors. Each time, the upper level is informed of problems and differences in opinion at the lower level. The resource document reveals something of interest: in the majority of cases in which it criticises the working groups for not keeping up with the 'best practices approach' (the meaning of which is not clarified in the document), the Water Directors resolved the issue by adopting final guidance, the content of

177 Water Directors of EU Member States, 2–3 December 2004, p 6.
178 de Búrca, 2010, p 227 (footnote omitted).

which then followed the 'best practices approach' favoured by the environmental NGOs.[179] Admittedly, the evidence is incidental and plainly too small to support definitive conclusions, but even as it is, this seems to be suggesting that possible quality problems with consensus-based decision making can be remedied by ensuring that deliberation is iterated at many levels.

Certainly, one noteworthy reason why the upper level has tended to adopt more stringent standards than the lower level is that the Commission enjoys more influence over the SCG and in the Water Directors than over the working groups. For this reason, it can endorse and push for more ambitious interpretations of the WFD. Likewise, it has been argued that the Water Directors want their influence to manifest itself and are consequently keen to adopt rigorous standards.[180] However, it is also possible to think that iterated deliberation, which proceeds from one level to another, each time accompanied by more information about arguments and opinions (dissenting and otherwise), can positively affect the quality of final outcomes. One might even say that the practice of deliberation 'is capable of inculcating environmental values which may encourage an ongoing sense of environmental responsibility for those involved in decision making'.[181]

6.5 Conclusion

Nearly 15 years' experience with the WFD has demonstrated that the initial feelings shared by many were indeed correct: the WFD is a milestone of EU environmental governance. It is not a milestone simply because it is an ecologically ambitious piece of legislation, nor is it a milestone because its implementation has taken novel shape in the form of the CIS. Clearly, the latter is a long-awaited and much needed strategic response to the problems of EU environmental law and governance, which has, perhaps as a surprise to many, worked very well, to the extent that its institutional ideas are now being replicated in ongoing experiments in implementation of EU environmental law. To top it all, its general structure and specific outcomes have been commended by environmental NGOs.

What, however, defines the milestone achievement for present purposes is that the CIS is clearly a deliberative regime. The 'injection' of deliberative values has not only contributed to better implementation practices, but may also have brought these reoriented practices to bear on the enforcement functions of both the Commission and the Court. I have analysed these new implementation practices and argued that it is especially in the interests of the Commission to sponsor and participate in the CIS. The Commission appears to understand that, through the

179 See WWF and EEB, 2004, pp 25–6, 32–3, 41, 43, 46, 48, 50–1. In some cases, it was agreed that more work was needed. On the whole, however, there appear to have been only two cases in which environmental NGOs felt that the final outcome was quite unsatisfactory: ibid, pp 43 and 55.

180 See von Homeyer, 2009, p 21.

181 Scott and Holder, 2006, p 218.

CIS, it receives more trustworthy information on the progress made by Member States when implementing the underlying legislation; it can then use this information in pursuing more effective enforcement strategies. Whilst this might seem to be expanding the powers assigned to the Commission from those that existed before, the link that emerges between the exercise of Commission discretion and CIS guidance cuts the powers right back by making the Commission's enforcement powers more visible and thus permitting their scrutiny.

Neither the CIS nor its guidance documents have been mentioned in judgments thus far, for reasons of their non-binding nature. But, as if anticipating problems, environmental NGOs have insisted upon review, which takes its one and only standard from the WFD, not from the CIS. The reason is not the soft law format of CIS guidance, but fear that the consensual approach adopted in the CIS results in lower ambitions and that guidance documents therefore tend to the lowest common denominator. However, the argument in this chapter is that both arguments are theoretically flawed. First, the soft law argument – according to which the courts should not take non-binding acts into account when they interpret framework legislation – poorly reflects the fundamental characteristics of framework directives and categorically frustrates the idea of framework legislation. Second, as to criticism based on fear of consensus, no democratic or pragmatic guarantee exists that the EU courts are generally more ambitious than CIS actors themselves would be, even though, in individual situations, this may turn out to be the case.

Chapter 7

Adjudicating new governance

Five pictures

7.1 Introduction

We are, by this stage, familiar with the empirical evidence of the case studies, and what kinds of problems and challenges new governance instruments entail for the courts. We have also described and evaluated the ways in which the EU courts could be expected to respond to the problems, dilemmas and concerns engendered by these new developments. This final chapter now proceeds to discuss these insights in a more systematic and integrated manner, focusing on accountability-related findings. The main question to be asked in this chapter is whether the relationship between new governance and adjudication involves an unexplored point of synergy in exercising judicial accountability.

The three preceding case studies have painted a diverse and complex picture of the real life of EU governance. The conditions of, and detailed arrangements for, decision-making processes vary, but what they all have in common is that the virtues of co-operation and deliberation are prevalent and increasingly important. In contexts such as EU environmental law and policymaking, which has suffered for decades from implementation deficit, the benefits of the approach are difficult to ignore or overlook. The empirical understanding of new governance systems in the European Union not only offers encouraging results and experiences (as well as those not so reassuring and inspirational), but also valuable and surprising insights into the theory and practice of deliberation. These insights can be summarised in a nutshell: iterated deliberations that are detectable, more or less visibly, in the case studies give rise to norms and rules that shape normative behaviour. What is characteristic of these new types of norm created and applied in and by new governance bodies is that they instigate and uphold mechanisms intended to hold actors accountable.[1] This body, or collection, of norms and rules forms a system of *peer review accountability*. Precisely what form it takes in each governance system and under what circumstances it can be successful depends on a range of factors typical of the governance context, as has been demonstrated.

1 I would like to thank Charles Sabel for suggesting this to me.

The question now to be taken up here is whether, and if so, how peer review accountability emerging in new governance contexts shapes the review function of the courts. Interactions between adjudication and new governance have become frequent, and the ways in which they interact with each other, manifold. Much of what has gone on seems to corroborate observations about the relationship between EU governance and the courts as 'dynamic' and 'reciprocal'.[2] This account of repeated interchanges means not only that the EU courts will provide criteria and apply them in order to 'catalyse' innovations, but also that the EU courts' own practices and methods of working will be transformed as a result of new governance processes. The case study evidence collected in this book not only gives new material to support the thesis of mutual interrelationships between adjudication and new governance, but also suggests that the interactions are more common than expected and that new interrelationships are discoverable.

When adjudicating new governance instruments, the courts can be pictured as:

1 shaping governance arrangements;
2 utilising forms of governance in their review;
3 catalysing regulatory innovations;
4 acting as a regulatory penalty default; and
5 adapting and changing.

Drawing on the three governance case studies, the analysis in this chapter fleshes out these five dimensions and substantiates their special value in different governance environments. Although the account is given from the perspective of the courts, the proposed typology tries to demonstrate how the relationship between new governance and the courts is mutual, with the courts shaping new governance and new governance shaping the courts and their relationship to, and impact on, governance instruments.

In the next section, I first articulate peer review accountability, after which I briefly reiterate the conditions of this mode of accountability in the three case study examples. In the next step, I connect this accountability perspective to the role of the courts by means of a five-dimensional analysis. Finally, I conclude.

7.2 The accountability perspective on deliberation: Peer review accountability

The potential of deliberation and discussion to hold actors accountable to actions and omissions is certainly not a hitherto undiscovered idea. The deliberative qualities of the Court of Justice of the European Union (CJEU), the European Parliament, the European Ombudsman, or even civil society have been extensively

2 Scott and Sturm, 2007. See also Hervey, 2010.

elaborated and studied in the literature.[3] The courts, in particular, have been depicted as 'public accountability forums' providing a wide range of actors with the opportunity for 'getting facts out into the open and subjecting them to public debate and deliberation'.[4] For Curtin (2007), deliberations in, and also perhaps by, the courts provide a remedial answer to the most persistent problem of EU governance: the 'chronic lack of transparency of the overall system'.[5] Similarly, Harlow and Rawlings (2007) discuss and document large 'accountability networks', such as the European Network of Ombudsmen, which brings together officials united by a shared professional ethos and common purpose to hold national and supranational authorities to account. In these contributions, as in many others, accountability through deliberation is associated with, and realised by, particular institutions, actors or authorities that make the underworld of EU governance more understandable and transparent by requesting facts or justifications underpinning decisions, or reviewing and disclosing information otherwise not easily accessible or altogether concealed. In other words, accountability is constructed in (authoritative) institutions that are intended to facilitate and foster discussion and reflection over a decision, usually after it has been taken.

The idea of 'peer review accountability' instead envisions a new kind of accountability design, which is not tied to the existence and operation of some institutionalised forums. It is particularly suited to the EU governance context, which places less emphasis upon institutions such as the Parliament and the EU courts, and which relies on deliberation and dialogue to rope the parties in to work together. It is deliberation itself that constitutes accountability and sustains it, not any particular institution or fixed forum.

Perceiving deliberation as a condition for peer review accountability is a pragmatic approach to deliberation. Deliberation is not predicated on any imaginary or assumed consensus by all those affected, or on some correct procedures that will help us to find the truth. Consider the Common Implementation Strategy (CIS): iterated deliberations in the CIS do not result in a consensus among all those drinking water (in other words, all those affected) on what 'good water' is, nor can one assume that the truth about 'good' or 'bad' water can be found through procedurally impeccable CIS practices; instead CIS actors come to a practical understanding of what 'good' water means for now, whilst also agreeing on the arrangements that allow them to enter into discussions again in the future. As a result, the normative material that emerges from these deliberations is provisional, incomplete and often merely diagnostic. The same can be said of all examples of new governance included in this book. In all of them, an act of deliberation does not – primarily, at least – lend itself to changing preferences through discussion and reflection, but to facilitating the emergence and evolution

3 See Curtin, 2007, pp 534–8; Curtin, 2009; van Hoecke, 2001; Vos, 2000, p 1125.
4 Curtin, 2007, p 541.
5 Ibid, p 540.

of norms and arrangements that hold actors to account on the quality of water, on chemicals policy, or on the progress of sustainable development.

Deliberation contributes to accountability by instituting and sustaining mutual monitoring by those who are in, and belong to, the same group or network of actors. A network is an important construction for those interested in peer activities, for networks provide a concrete environment in which to render participants accountable to their peers, or what Lange (2010) calls, 'fellow professionals'.[6] For instance, one definition of peer accountability emphasises 'mutual monitoring of one another's performance *within a network* of groups, public and private, sharing common concerns'.[7] Monitoring by network peers is vital not only because they know what they are doing – that is, because they have the relevant expertise or common interests – but also because they are in a position to learn from the mistakes of the past and to implement the necessary changes. In this respect, peer review accountability comes close to the 'dynamic accountability' of Sabel and Zeitlin (2010). Sabel and Zeitlin begin by documenting a range of problems displaying the classic principal–agent accountability. This has increasingly proven to be inadequate and limited as the principles of command-and-control regulation on which principal–agent accountability depends have been subjected to criticism and replaced with alternatives. These shifts are especially pronounced in the European Union. Dynamic accountability, instead, works well in the Union, because it is a type of accountability that is not built on, and hence does not presume, the existence of a central, delegating authority of a principal, but accepts multiple, fluid and overlapping decision makers. It is a type of accountability that is exercised in 'the full repertoire of processes by which EU decision makers learn from and correct each other even as they set goals and performance standards for the Union'.[8]

Peer accountability is, however, considered as affording a rather weak form of legitimacy, to the extent that it is legitimate at all. This is often discussed as the legitimacy problem of peer activities. But if such a problem exists, from where does it derive? It follows from a lack of credible control: since networks of peers are often informal and their operation is usually based on horizontal, rather than vertical, collaboration, the only sanctioning method is soft 'naming and shaming'. Its force is based on the adverse effects on future co-operation that it entails,[9] not capable of removing concerns about congenial inside 'dealings'. Put differently, however effective the processes of accountability may become within networks, network peers do not seem to be in a position to provide the externally legitimate view of accountability that is required. The question that remains is how to ensure that those outside have a sufficiently informed understanding of what is going on inside. Papadopoulos (2010) sums up the situation well: '[C]ontrol *in* the network does not

6 Lange, 2010, pp 59–60.
7 Goodin, 2003, p 378 (emphasis added).
8 Ibid.
9 Harlow and Rawlings, 2007, p 545; Colin Scott, 2009, p 180.

substitute control *of* the network.'[10] The missing link between internal and external concerns Lange (2010) too, for, according to her, networks enjoy a special type of legitimacy, best described as 'credibility'.[11] In her view, credibility needs be accompanied by accountability exercised by actors, not at the same level, but higher in the institutional structure. To summarise: the same reason that explains the appeal of peer forms of accountability best explains the distrust felt about them. The attractiveness of dynamic and other new forms of accountability rests on the fact that they take seriously the distance of contemporary instruments from the command-and-control regulation and refuse to maintain the facade of an unbroken chain of authority. Out with the bathwater has also gone the proverbial baby, for new forms of accountability have, inadvertently or not, also distanced themselves from command-and-control institutions such as the courts, which have traditionally been responsible for delivering an external accountability check.

The form of peer review accountability that I advance here is strongly influenced by Sabel and his collaborators' idea of dynamic accountability, but peer review accountability is more clearly connected to actual processes of deliberation in new governance instruments. This is intended to draw attention to the potential of these deliberations to form the 'missing link', and to affect judicial accountability structures and enforcement strategies. The shared efforts of all those participating in governance mechanisms not only strengthen internal accountability processes, but also support those outside charged with monitoring. While 'peer accountability' and 'peer review accountability' have been used interchangeably to this point, the latter term is preferred in what follows. The notion of 'review' encompasses those documented aspects of peer activities that are particularly important for the courts because they need written documentation to exercise their review function.

Peer review accountability is not only a theoretical concept. Both new legislative developments in the European Union and the case studies in this book provide examples of practical applications of the peer review approach to accountability.[12] As for the former, the founding regulations of three new EU banking authorities include provisions about peer review: for instance, Art 30 of the Basic Regulation establishing the European Banking Authority (EBA)[13] imposes upon the EBA the task of periodically organising and conducting peer reviews with a view to strengthening consistency between the competent authorities in supervisory outcomes. Before moving on to the courts, I discuss peer review accountability in the latter respect, in the contexts of the three case studies.

10 Papadopoulos, 2010, p 1040 (emphasis original).

11 Lange, 2010, p 60.

12 Senden and van den Brink, 2012, p 68. See also Korkea-aho 2013 where I have tested this argument in the context of an actual dispute in REACH decision-making.

13 Regulation (EU) No 1093/2010 of the European Parliament and of the Council of 24 November 2010 establishing a European Supervisory Authority (European Banking Authority), . . ., *OJ L* 331/12, 15 December 2010.

7.2.1 The European Semester

As argued in Chapter 4, the primary function of the European Semester as a policymaking instrument is to facilitate a common understanding amongst the Member States, EU institutions and stakeholders on policy challenges, to initiate elaboration and analysis of the means by which to achieve identified objectives, and to subject the ways in and strategies with which Member States have chosen to the mutual scrutiny of peers. If we analyse the European Semester and the deliberations undertaken within its framework, as we did earlier, we will easily recognise that it conforms least to the pattern of iterated deliberation, therefore quickly discounting any hopes of exercising accountability through such deliberation. The European Semester is prepared in a multi-actor format, but as such it does not provide a platform for iteration of arguments and thus for genuine learning. The mere fact that examples of peer review are hard to come by is consistent with this gloomy view. In addition, non-governmental organisation (NGO) representatives, and members of the European Parliament and national parliaments, have only limited access to the deliberations, spurring accusations that EU-wide policy co-ordination processes are an empty exercise between the European Union and national administrations with no tangible outcomes.

Recent scholarly literature has attempted to rethink operation of policy co-ordination instruments by shifting attention to their effects on the accountability of national political structures. De Ruiter (2010), for one, has suggested that instead of focusing solely on aspects of involvement and inclusiveness (of civil society), we should examine the use of information as an accountability mechanism. He argues that EU-level policymaking strategies 'increase the accountability of a political structure by adding to the possibilities open to parliamentarians to monitor and evaluate executive behaviour and put pressure to modify that behaviour in accordance with their preferences'.[14] However, the problem, which de Ruiter does not neglect, relates to the random nature of use of information in furthering accountable governing. Most importantly, national parliamentarians depend on their governments to disclose information on policies; alternatively, if this is not working, they are required to engage in resource-intensive work by themselves to locate the information and to monitor the progress of a particular policymaking package.[15]

A further step down the road to ensuring that deliberations result in norms that hold actors to account is the growing use of recommendations in the context of EU policy co-ordination instruments. Recommendations could be expected to create more information and to provide a concrete framework for collective stakeholder activities. For example, country-specific recommendations pin down in an easily accessible format what kinds of actions are needed in each Member State and provide national stakeholders with a road map for policy implementation,

14 de Ruiter, 2010, p 877.
15 See also Benz, 2007, p 516.

on the basis of which they can hold their respective Member States to account. This view is shared by Harlow and Rawlings (2007), who write that 'recommendations for improvement issued by the Commission' can be perceived 'as a form of accountability'.[16] When seeking to influence political actors both at the EU and the national levels, recommendations would provide NGOs and other interested parties with a helpful identification of areas in need of improvement and concrete suggestions for measures that should be taken.

Research on policy co-ordination processes has moved in the direction of introducing and highlighting its information-enhancing characteristics as a way in which to increase overall accountability. But there are fewer and institutionally weaker ways in which to put this information to good use, the absence of the courts being but one of them. As is clear from the case study focusing on environmental policymaking through the European Semester, realising the potential of iterated deliberation and ensuring peer review accountability as part of the institutional architecture of EU policy co-ordination processes needs some substantial changes in order to function even sub-optimally. But as it now stands, the European Semester cannot really be said to add significantly to accountability either at the national or EU level.

7.2.2 The European Chemicals Agency

The European Chemicals Agency (ECHA) is a new player in EU chemicals policy. Despite its 'newcomer' status, it is part of a more established group of EU agencies that have a role to play in preparing or making decisions in EU risk regulation. One of the long-term aims of EU risk regulation has been to give these decisions a strong and credible basis. What functional separation (which, as is clear from Chapter 5, attempted to limit the discretion ascribed to subordinate agents) failed to capture is that the EU agencies do not simply prepare or make decisions; in doing so, they also demonstrate that decisions are justified on technical and scientific grounds and, with an increasing degree of societal involvement, are also socio-economically acceptable. The EU courts have increasingly highlighted the scientific credibility of decisions in their rulings, but, in a way, it is too late by the time a scientific dispute is referred to the courts. The governance framework of the Registration, Evaluation, Authorisation and Restriction of Chemicals (REACH) Regulation seeks to correct this 'slack' by setting out an itinerary for deliberation. One of its main purposes, when interlocking different actors to work together, is to make visible the justificatory basis on which the decision is taken and to reiterate these justifications in light of a range of comments and suggestions received. Pooling of expertise from multiple sources makes particular sense in the context of technically complex regulation, confronted with likelihoods,

16 Harlow and Rawlings, 2007, p 546. For strengthening the accountability dimension of EU policy co-ordination, see also Armstrong, 2010, pp 48–52, and Dawson, 2011, p 151.

uncertainties and fearful 'what if?'s. This kind of deliberation does not necessarily purport to change the parties' fundamental preferences, but to make reflection of issues in need of both scientific expertise and socio-economic considerations more transparent, open and accounted for.

How do these deliberations contribute to keeping actors to account? Two things are to be highlighted about peer review accountability in the activities of the ECHA. The first remark follows from the agency's openness to dealing with multiple parties at different stages of the decision-making process. The iterated deliberation of REACH includes several points of entry for interested parties and creates situations in which institutional peer actors – that is, the Commission, the Member States and the ECHA – are required to take into account each other's views and those of interested parties, not once, but repeatedly, for new information and insights. This openness, combined with repeated interactions of hearings and invitations to comment, extends an aspect of accountability into risk regulation to areas normally left unaccounted for.

The second thing to be recalled is that REACH is based upon the (correct) assumption that the discretion of agents is impossible to limit, so as to still render control humanly possible. Experience tells us that prescribing agencies to some predetermined results is bound to fail too. As a result, the whole infrastructure of accountability needs to be rethought. A truly accountable chemicals policy is possible only when actors can justify their actions to those peers who are equipped with the expertise that bears on resolution of the matter. This kind of peer review accountability may still be complementary to other more established forms of exercising legal accountability within the framework of REACH. However, it does, as demonstrated later in this chapter, assist the EU courts in exercising scrutiny over EU chemicals law and policy.

7.2.3 The Water Framework Directive Common Implementation Strategy (WFD CIS)

The *raison d'être* of the CIS is to facilitate and monitor national implementation of the Water Framework Directive (WFD). This particular task is delegated to over a thousand experts, authorities and stakeholders, whose collaborative activities in the pursuit of effective water policies form the nucleus of the CIS. CIS deliberations create a pyramid-shaped network, with the aim of introducing peer-to-peer discussions. A great deal of the work of interpreting and specifying WFD standards is accomplished in working groups that are open to (national) experts and stakeholders. These experts and stakeholders are assigned to individual working groups on the basis of their knowledge and interests, and the overall strategy in this respect is to pool the expertise and interests of participants, ensuring that they have comparable expertise and equal interests to their peers. The next level is constituted by the Strategic Co-ordination Group (SCG), in which a different group of peer interests comes into play. Under the chairmanship of the Commission and one Member State, Member State representatives co-ordinate and guide activities in the working groups, evaluate their outcomes, prepare documents and provide input for the Water Directors' meetings. Finally, the most exclusive peer interests are debated and defended at the pinnacle, in the Water Directors Group, which national Water Directors (normally the heads of the water departments in national environmental ministries) attend. Their task is to steer the overall process by providing strategic guidance on current trends in and future challenges to WFD implementation, and to edit the results of the working groups.

Operation of the CIS provides perhaps the most striking example of peer review accountability that ensues from deliberations. CIS actors deliberate and debate concerns and issues relevant to implementation of the WFD, with a view to arriving at a more harmonious understanding of the complexities and intricacies of the Directive. The fruits of this collaborative engagement are encapsulated in CIS guidance documents. But how do these or any other technical documents produced in the CIS amount to keeping CIS actors to account? In the working groups, experts and stakeholders contradict and challenge information presented by other experts and stakeholders with well-matched expertise. Working the way upward, in the SCG and the Water Directors' meetings, the Member States are questioned on their policy choices and on implementation problems by the Commission and other Member States. Finally, guidance documents make public the common understanding that has been reached by CIS actors and subject it to public scrutiny by other interested parties outside the CIS. For instance, (insider) environmental NGOs have used information enshrined in the guidance documents to shed more light on the progress of WFD implementation, publicly criticising reluctant or obstructive Member States and commending more ambitious ones. Also, the WFD itself includes provisions that seek to facilitate the peer review dimension in implementation. Under Art 18 of the WFD, the Commission prepares reports on the progress of implementation, drawing on summary reports from Member States. The Commission sees reporting as a way in which to inform not only EU institutions, but also the public, on WFD implementation. Moreover, reporting provisions enshrined in the WFD enhance the peer review element, providing 'a feedback to the Member States on their current performance'.[17]

Whilst being aware of different preoccupations and challenges in each case study, my view is that these three examples of EU new governance demonstrate that a definite potential exists for iterated deliberation to hold a larger share of (perhaps previously unaccountable) decision-making bodies to account. More significantly still, the unparalleled benefit of peer review accountability, which arises from iterated deliberation, is that it 'is no longer forced on every occasion to respond to a mythical (especially in the EU) ideal of straightforward lines of accountability in legislation'.[18]

17 European Commission, March 2007, SEC(2007) 362 final, p 4.
18 Lee, 2009, p 54, commenting on the governance debate in the European Union more generally.

7.3 Adjudicating new governance: Five pictures

The practices of iterated deliberation contribute to the development of norms and normative functions that embody a new culture of peer review accountability. That being said, these practices of iterated deliberation do not result in law as we normally (want to) understand the term. The results and end products in the three governance examples are called, among others, 'ECHA guidance document', 'CIS guidance document', 'country-specific recommendation', 'Commission communication', or 'strategic document'. This normative material most closely resembles what we have come to know as 'soft law' – that is, non-binding law. It is soft law since it does not usually generate legal effects.

It should be recalled at the outset that although legislation is not simply hard law and new governance, soft law, the tendency (for obvious reasons of simplicity) is to introduce new governance as an alternative to policymaking that results in binding (hard law) outcomes, thus labelling new governance as non-binding, soft-law-like. But being 'soft' or 'soft-law-like' should not be confused with being uncoercive or uninfluential. Quite the opposite: soft law is sometimes harder and more influential than traditional, legally binding hard law. Often, in new governance mechanisms, soft and hard elements are also combined in such a way as to produce complex systems of 'soft' hard law and 'hard' soft law.[19] These and other similar observations ultimately challenge the notion of law and the premises upon which the very idea of normativity rests.[20] Why not, then, stop classifying different types of norm if very little is to be gained from the binary logic of hard law versus soft law? The one major reason for sticking to old mores seems to be the importance of the positive determination of normativity in adjudication. In the view of Thürer (1990), the distinction between laws and non-laws is necessary since the Court of Justice is constrained only by the law, being duty-bound to ensure that, in interpreting and applying the Treaties, the law is duly observed.[21] Despite important legal (indeed law-like) and practical effects, soft law cannot generally be judicially enforced, which, in the final analysis, underlies the binary system of hard law and soft law.[22] This argument is a familiar one from international law: Abbott and Snidal (2000) argue that most international law is soft, linking softness with the absence of an independent judiciary supported by compulsory enforcement powers.[23] Finally, soft law is also determined by reference to adjudication by those

19 See, eg, Heyvaert, 2009, p 647.

20 The concept of law has been intensely debated in global administrative law (GAL). See, among others, contributions by Kingsbury, 2009, and Somek, 2010b. Somek accuses GAL of usurping too much within its theoretical and empirical umbrella, and observes that, along the way, law is lost. Adjudication, enforcement and the judges (which he calls 'the chieftains of the critical attitude': Somek, 2010b, p 991) have a prominent role in his critique levelled against GAL, and it appears to be the absence of an (enforceable) legal right that most bothers him.

21 Thürer, 1990, p 135.

22 Senden, 2004, p 112; Terpan, 2014; Trubek, Cottrell and Nance, 2006, p 68.

23 Abbott and Snidal, 2000, p 422. For problems with 'redundant' and 'undesirable' soft law in international law, see Klabbers, 1996, and Klabbers, 1998.

interested in accountability: '[S]oft law is a device that is used to have an effect but it by-passes normal systems of accountability',[24] one of those normal systems being the role of the courts with powers to enforce regulations.

It is here that this book suggests a change of perspective and seeks to make its most distinctive contribution to the existing research. As indicated by this academic commentary, soft law is conceptualised as an instrument to circumvent accustomed systems of accountability, but what I propose is that soft law can factually be seen as strengthening those systems. Even though, as forcefully asserted by Papadopoulos (2010), control in the network does not substitute control of the network, my argument is that it is control in the network that increasingly *makes* control of the network *possible*. Peer review accountability, despite largely taking soft law form, influences and shapes the parameters of adjudication in an unprecedented way, becoming a useful, if not necessary, condition for enforcement of hard law.[25] Without ongoing accountability in governance regimes, judicial control of new governance is difficult – in some cases, impossible. Shared efforts of all those taking part in governance mechanisms make the exercise of the courts' review function more targeted and effective, as well as ultimately contributing to the realisation and sense of accountable governance.

Several reasons explain why the connection between adjudication and new governance has rarely been addressed from this specific perspective. Armstrong, as long ago as 1998, noted that the law is all too often 'construed in instrumental terms, particularly as the medium by which the Court of Justice has pursued a pro-integrationist agenda'.[26] His argument is that the idea of law as a medium, with the corresponding image of the Court of Justice deploying law as a hammer to pound in the nails of EU integration, must be reconciled with the idea of law as an institution. One concrete consequence of this reconciliation, in his view, is an increased ability to appreciate the ways in which law itself shapes the actions of the EU Court. Furthermore, whilst EU governance may be moving quickly, changes in institutions, such as in the judiciary, often occur slowly – or at least their observation requires time, which has not been there (because of the relative 'newness' of the phenomenon of new governance in the European Union) in the first place. Moreover, it has not been until recent years that EU governance research, in particular its legal dimension, has seen more bottom-up studies. In turn, this has permitted the birth and development of a more nuanced picture of the key legal institutions, including the EU courts.

Even those who have seen the connection have struggled to find evidence for it. As suggested by Hervey (2010), the relationship between adjudication and EU governance can be conceptualised along a continuum ranging from 'gap', through 'hybrid recognition', to 'mutual transformation'. These forms of interaction, as is

24 Trubek, Cottrell and Nance, 2006, p 66.

25 For the argument that the notion of enforcement will change 'by its suffusion with new governance', see Sabel and Simon, 2006, p 404.

26 See Armstrong, 1998, p 156.

readily seen, are the same as those used in describing the relationship between law and new governance. While the first rejects any reciprocal influence, the second and third types recognise some form of interaction, to the extent that, in the third type, 'a mutually transformative relationship' between adjudication and EU governance instruments is advantageous, connecting 'the best features from each process in a symbiotic interaction'.[27] Focusing on the EU social policy sector, Hervey found evidence for the 'gap' and 'hybrid recognition', but struggled to find support for the emergence of 'mutual transformation', partially because new governance mechanisms are a relatively new phenomenon in the particular area of study. Nevertheless, similar results of little or no interaction in the second and third categories have been observed more broadly. Smismans (2010) conducted a study on the effects of the Lisbon Strategy on European law, concluding that while the strategy has influenced policymaking at the level of ideas and beliefs, it could not be said to have had a discernible effect on case law.[28]

In light of the empirical evidence from the case study chapters, this three-dimensional account seems, however, to miss important factors and elements of the relationship that should be explained and accounted for in conceptualisations of the relationship between adjudication and new governance. It is upon this wish to better contextualise the typology of this relationship in actual governance instruments that I now suggest a new *five*-dimensional account of the relationship between adjudication and new governance.[29]

When adjudicating new governance instruments, the courts can be pictured as:

1 shaping governance arrangements;
2 utilising forms of governance in review;
3 catalysing regulatory innovation;
4 acting as a regulatory penalty default; and
5 adapting and changing.

As immediately becomes clear, this proposed typology expands on earlier conceptualisations of the relationship between the courts and new governance, but adds new categories and important contextual elements to account for the increasing complexity of that relationship. I now discuss each of the five dimensions in turn.

7.3.1 Courts shaping governance mechanisms

The role of courts in shaping governance mechanisms is the baseline case in a series of interactions taking place between the courts and governance. The judiciary is seen as an umpire, constituting the final authority in ensuring the

27 Ibid, p 152.
28 Smismans, 2010, p 504. See also Stefan, 2014.
29 This typology has evolved out of discussions with Joanne Scott.

(procedural) acceptability of governance instruments, with analysis often grounded in the context of two large discussions: proceduralisation, and constitutionalisation. As for the former, *proceduralisation* captures the development by which law declines to offer detailed normative standards for action, but instead provides guidance by laying down a procedural framework for actors to work within.[30] In the specific context of the courts shaping new governance, proceduralisation is then understood to refer to situations in which the courts approach governance instruments from a procedural point of view, in which the courts are involved to make sure that diverse governance instruments comply with a host of procedural rights. These include, but are not limited to, the right to be heard and consulted, transparency, the rights to access to information and access to justice. The content of these rights does not give rise to much of a disagreement because the majority of procedural rights are enshrined in the general principles of EU law or formalised in legislation, with the EU Charter of Fundamental Rights and its principles of good administration being particularly important in this respect. Hence their enforcement by the courts has gone, and will continue to go, uncontested. Rather, the argument often raised in this respect is a different one: more is expected (and needed) from the courts. In the case of new governance, however, the soft law form prevents the courts from exercising its shaping function. But does it really?

The preceding case study chapters have analysed, for example, the right to access to REACH information, the legal protection of WFD stakeholders and the level of judicial review provided regarding country-specific recommendations or CIS guidance documents. In the majority of these situations, the effectiveness of a right does not vary according to the form of the legal act.[31] Consider, for example, the right to access to documents, in respect of which both legislation and case law are in place to safeguard realisation of the right. Despite these legislative and juridical safeguards, the effectiveness of this right arguably leaves too much to be desired. What is important for present purposes is that 'this [ineffectiveness] seems not to concern soft law acts more than hard law acts'.[32] Similar indiscriminate logic can be observed as regards the right to access to justice. Standing restrictions in Art 263(4) TFEU have effectively prevented most private litigants from seeking legal remedies before the EU courts. However, this problem is not specific to new governance and its soft law instruments, although it may be exacerbated in new governance as a result of the claim for more participatory and inclusive governance,

30 de Búrca and Scott, 2006, p 10.

31 The Open Method of Coordination (OMC) seems to be a special case, not least because a fundamental disagreement has emerged about whether it is, or gives rise to, law at all. As argued in Chapter 4, my view is that the OMC and its successor, the European Semester, creates soft law, but the problem for the courts seems to reside in the absence of a legal act, the dilemma familiar from the old *An Taisce* case: Case T-461/93 *An Taisce & WWF UK v Commission* [1994] ECR II-733; appealed as Case C-325/94 P *An Taisce and WWF UK v Commission* [1996] ECR I-3727.

32 Senden and van den Brink, 2012, p 27. Of course, the fact that the right is weak in relation to both soft law and hard law acts does not justify the conclusion that a strong right is strong in relation to soft law and hard law acts. Space, however, precludes further development of this line of argument.

but it does affect EU law in its hard and soft versions. Of course, the Lisbon Treaty's inclusion of a 'regulatory act' and its interpretation by the CJEU could be argued to have everything to do with the soft law/hard law distinction. Yet the relevant distinction, which the CJEU here observes, is not between soft law and hard law, but between general rules (legislation) and individualised rules.[33] To offer a final example, the preventive effect of the soft law form is further reduced as a result of the courts being open to making exceptions for the form of rule-making, for instance by reviewing a soft law document for its legal effects or giving regard to a soft law document. As we will recall from Chapter 6, the EU courts have taken soft law guidance into account *in so far as* authorship remains with the Commission. In other words, the courts have been prevented not by the absence of legal effects, but by the lack of Union authorship.[34]

These and many other possible examples, in my view, suggest that soft law is not nearly as huge a hindrance to ensuring an adequate level of judicial review and protection as is conventionally believed. This is an important aspect to emphasise, because the discussion on adjudication and new governance is often unhelpfully clouded by soft law concerns, preventing us from targeting the right cause. Often, the soft law discussion masks problems of judicial review that lie deeper down and require targeted action elsewhere. In respect of most procedural rights, for instance, the question to be addressed is not about the form of rule-making, but about the person who is allowed to initiate procedures. Senden and van den Brink (2012) propose giving the European Parliament a stronger role in bringing a case before the EU courts in situations in which procedural rights are infringed and, in doing so, target the right cause. As a privileged applicant, the Parliament does not need to prove its interest in bringing a case.[35] Another suggestion worth looking into is conferral of formal status on implementing measures and mechanisms in framework legislation itself (such as reference to the CIS in the WFD) in order to address the problem that arises for adjudication in cases in which a multiplicity of actors share the authorship of soft law guidance documents.

In conclusion: I am not recommending letting go altogether of the distinction between soft and hard law, but rather paying much less attention to it, or approaching it with a more discernible eye, asking what it factually hides from sight, be it then problems with the authorship requirement or something else entirely. For instance, the case law on soft law, which prima facie emphasises the enforceability of rules and norms, is perhaps more accurately described as an attempt on the part of the EU courts to protect the institutional balance in the

33 Case T-18/10 *Inuit Tapiriit Kanatami and others v Parliament & Council* [2011] ECR II-5599.

34 Here, soft law is understood to refer to the absence of legal effects of a legal act. From the point of view of the courts, the notion of reviewable soft law is wider: the existence of legal effects and authorship. See Chapter 6, section 6.3.2, 'The Court of Justice of the European Union and the WFD'.

35 Senden and van den Brink, 2012, p 81.

European Union by ensuring that the Commission does not hide binding legal obligations under a veneer of non-bindingness.[36]

Involvement of the courts can also be analysed through the lenses of *constitutionalisation*. Just as with proceduralisation, in constitutionalisation the courts' involvement can be interpreted as a means to ensure that rule-making outside the formal constitution is subject to a set of values – that is, constitutional values.[37] What are those constitutional values that are implicated here? It is necessary to note at the outset that proceduralisation and constitutionalisation are often addressed together, because the content and scope of procedural rights are predicated upon a number of constitutional distinctions. Shaw (1999) connects both in the notion of a 'procedural approach to constitution-building', which phrase she uses to describe the role of the courts in civic republicanism, but the examples that she gives well describe the issues that constitutionalisation involves for the courts more generally:

> The courts can be employed in the context of a procedural approach to constitution-building to deal with issues as diverse as accession and secession, conflicts between individual and group rights whenever participation within the intercultural dialogue becomes contested, and perhaps most controversially to manage the structure of flexibility and differentiation which are probably both an inevitable and even desirable feature of a large and diverse EU.[38]

A strictly procedural approach to constitution-building appears beneficial, because it is capable of navigating the troubled waters of controversial issues, such as those mentioned in Shaw's example. In a more limited view of governance, a procedural approach to constitution-building seems nevertheless to be aimed at more high-flying contexts, thus providing little concrete guidance for the courts as shaping actual governance arrangements. Consider participation, which is a good example of a procedural right that is predicated upon constitutional judgements about the value of representation within public engagement. The withering of classical forms of democracy in the European Union, and the rise of alternative forms of democratic justification, has meant that universal (constitutional) criteria for participation no longer exist and, as the case study chapters demonstrated, each governance regime has a fresh take on whom it accepts as a participant. Although new articles of the Lisbon Treaty, such as Art 11 TEU on participation, have undoubtedly stressed the constitutional importance of concepts such as participation, they provide little direction on how to operationalise those concepts. The case-by-case determination that is required to give effect to participation as a constitutional value and right may be difficult to undertake in adjudication. This,

36 See Scott, 2011, p 344.
37 See, eg, Curtin, Hofmann and Mendes, 2013.
38 Shaw, 1999, p 596.

then, is why the courts' role in shaping governance frameworks in accordance with participation rights is likely never to be crucial, even in the unlikely case of relaxation of standing restrictions providing a larger group with access to the courts, which would be desirable in other respects.

7.3.2 Courts utilising new governance instruments

The use and impact of governance instruments on the courts has occupied a central role in this book. In particular, Chapter 6 on the WFD offers plenty of insights into the relationship that has emerged between the CIS and the Commission in the context of Art 258 TFEU litigation. This and other examples to be introduced next demonstrate that the courts are increasingly acknowledging the information-enhancing function of new governance, while the examples highlight the significance of increased or more accurate information for effective judicial activities. In the following subsections, I briefly discuss three contexts in which forms of new governance may be seen to be assisting the courts when exercising their review function.

7.3.2.1 Implementation networks

When looking for instances of use of new governance information in adjudication, interpretative guidance of implementation networks is the most natural place to start. Network-based guidance is, however, a hybrid product, and the EU courts have utilised information in the form of interpretative guidance only when the sole author is an EU body, thus excluding guidance prepared in implementation networks unless the Commission has assumed formal authorship. This applies more widely: use by the courts of information produced in the CIS implementation network does not take place directly, but the impact is mediated through the Commission, as elaborated next.

Owing to the complex framework nature of the WFD, it very early became clear to the Commission that it is strongly advisable to deal with problems as early as possible and in good-spirited dialogue with Member States.[39] The impact of the CIS on infringement litigation is difficult to ascertain straightforwardly, because we do not have comparable numbers from the situation in which the CIS does not exist. However, and given the continued interest of the Commission in operating through the CIS, it seems settled that the CIS has been effective in putting together information and creating a platform to enforce the WFD 'beyond' Art 258 TFEU. Certainly, the CIS operates in the helpful shadow of formal proceedings, for the Commission has, from time to time, reminded the Member States that its formal powers under the Treaties will be available if the CIS fails to impress. A suspicion arises, though, whether the complex nature of the WFD will, in fact, lend itself

39 European Commission, March 2007, SEC(2007) 362 final, pp 4 and 13.

easily to formal enforcement, so that the Commission is likely to put in more effort within the CIS rather than outside it. It may now be intuitively convincing to think that the work the Commission undertakes within the CIS reduces the volume of infringement litigation. However, the causal connection between the CIS and infringement litigation seems to defy straightforward interpretations: I have shown elsewhere how the number of infringement judgments in the WFD has been high and has outnumbered those relating to other environmental framework directives.[40]

Two factors in particular seem to explain the results. First, the CIS and other forms of bilateral collaboration that give the Commission an opportunity to settle things informally also endow the Commission with valuable information that it can then use to start formal enforcement proceedings, should it seem necessary. Second, the high volume of WFD infringement litigation can also be explained by reference to the procedural nature of the underlying framework legislation. The WFD regulates by laying down procedural steps to be taken, and the deadlines by which they need to be completed and reported to the Commission. This form of regulation shapes subsequent litigation strategies: in cases of non-communication, the Commission is immediately ready to initiate enforcement action without the need to engage in extensive and time-consuming preparations in order to gather evidence against the Member State concerned.

To date, no examples can be given of conscious utilisation of the CIS by the courts, and better examples of the mutual interrelationship between the CIS and adjudication are given later in this chapter.

7.3.2.2 EU agencies

Just like implementation networks, EU agencies can also 'form the eyes and ears of the Commission', and the data put together by agencies such as the European Railway Agency (ERA) can end up being decisive in relation to Commission discretion over whether or not to start an infringement procedure.[41] With this being an extension of the argument made above, however, I now look at the other issue of great importance. In this book, the role that information plays in technically demanding adjudication has been given a great deal of attention. My argument, which I have elaborated in the context of the ECHA in Chapter 5, is that governance instruments create more and better reference points for the courts to address, and take into consideration what takes place in different systems of governance, and what are the arguments and aspects that are justified or otherwise with respect to the particular aims of the institution in question. A wider information basis then either allows the courts to engage in more intense and targeted review, or enables judges to withdraw entirely from assessing substantive

40 Korkea-aho, 2014.
41 Versluis and Tarr, 2013, p 320.

aspects of decision making.[42] Irrespective of the intensity of review in a particular context, it is clear that more information naturally reflects upon the conduct of the review function:

> [E]xplicit reason-giving eases the work of other decision-making units and of outside monitors: it provides a record that other decision-makers can consult (and perhaps learn from) in deciding how to solve problems and which monitors (legislators and courts) can refer to in judging whether solutions adopted in particular locations are appropriate, and how they might be improved in the light of experience elsewhere.[43]

An illustrative example is the recommendation that I have made as regards review of decisions made in REACH. The idea is to help the EU courts to focus their legality review on situations in which the decision and the scientific evidence accompanying it have not gone through peer review in the form of iterated deliberation. To take a simple example, in contrast to the restrictions procedure, the authorisation procedure under REACH limits both parliamentary involvement and public participation. Now, reviewing decisions taken in the context of the authorisation procedure, the EU courts are advised to impose a stricter review of decisions taken here than in the restrictions procedure. This is an example of what I have called in this book the 'intensity of judicial review', and what was in fact recently implemented in the decision of the European Ombudsman.[44] Evaluating the appropriateness of the ECHA's interpretation of Art 119 of REACH relating to publicity of information under the Regulation, the Ombudsman noted that the ECHA 'took into account a number of considerations . . . and involved in the process a large group of stakeholders'. That the ECHA had genuinely 'attempted to strike a fair balance between what were at times distinctly competing interests' then favourably reflected on her conclusion that the interpretation was acceptable.[45]

An essentially similar argument has been made with respect to agency interpretation in the United States. In their book, Eskridge and Ferejohn (2010) advise the US Supreme Court to 'openly announce deliberation as a plus factor in judicial review' and to defer to the agency interpretation when it is 'accompanied by an open process of public input and agency response'.[46] In a more detailed prescription, they advise the courts to defer to deliberations that (a) are open and public, (b) take into account multiple contributions and give reasons that are linked to statute, and finally (c) give regard to wider public norms. It is interesting that

42 For the argument that the EU courts use the duty to give reasons as 'a substitute for substantive review', see Türk, 2013, p 134.

43 Cohen and Sabel, 1997, p 329.

44 *Decision of the European Ombudsman closing the inquiry into complaint 1826/2010/VL against the European Chemicals Agency*, 18 December 2013.

45 Ibid, [46].

46 Eskridge and Ferejohn, 2010, p 265.

they develop this argument in the chapter that discusses agency dynamism with respect to environmental 'superstatutes', which are similar to EU framework directives in that they are, at the same time, both 'detailed' and 'relatively general, abstract, and theoretical'.[47] The authors do appreciate the fact that some kind of agency dynamism or norm evolution is necessary and inescapable if a statute has wide-ranging societal effects, and if the agency is to do its job properly in pursuing the aims of the statute. But their central message is that judges can, and should, respect the interpretations of the agency if the deliberations that accompany the decision are publicly justified and debated.

7.3.2.3 Civil society

The helpful role of civil society for adjudication is not a new thing. EU environmental law scholarship has long been aware of the information that diverse interest groups disclose to the Commission in the context of Article 258 litigation.[48] Citizens and environmental NGOs have usually approached the Commission through the informal mechanism of an environmental complaint, which was given standard form in 1999, available electronically. Recent developments indicate that the Commission is running down the operation of the mechanism of environmental complaint, and is more strongly relying on bilateral discussions between itself and the Member State concerned to handle complaints from citizens and local associations.[49] In addition, as is clear from Chapter 6, the Commission is moving towards tailored and bilateral forms of compliance promotion that highlight peer review among Member States and the Commission to ensure respect for the WFD, but as yet no information is available on what kind of role civil society will have in these tailored agreements. Some indication is given by the establishment of the EU Aarhus Centre, opened in Brussels in 2011. Operating under the auspices of a large EU-wide environmental organisation, ClientEarth, the Centre has taken its name from the Aarhus Convention on access to information, to justice and the right to public participation, and it aims to improve implementation of Convention rights. According to its website, it is 'using the law as a tool for change',

47 Ibid, p 267.

48 Weale et al, 2000, p 298. The role of the complainant is generally considered untenable. Even though the Commission acts on the information thus obtained, the 'informants' have no role in subsequent proceedings, they cannot challenge the Commission decision whether or not to open legal proceedings, and they do not enjoy a privileged position in terms of transparency and openness of decision making by the Commission. See Craig and de Búrca, 2011, p 410; Harlow and Rawlings, 2006, p 465.

49 Krämer, 2009, p 29. For the operation of the 'EU Pilot' as it is called, see online, accessed 30 June, 2014, http://ec.europa.eu/internal_market/scoreboard/performance_by_governance_tool/eu_pilot/index_en.htm. The European Ombudsman conducted an own-initiative report on the EU Pilot system: see *Decision of the European Ombudsman closing own-initiative inquiry OI/2/2011/OV to the European Commission*, 10 April 2014.

which suggests a build-up of frustration with formal channels of complaints procedure.[50]

What about the impact of civil society knowledge in adjudication? Nearly 15 years ago, in its White Paper on European governance, the Commission urged that the European Union must increase its efforts to include civil society as it 'plays an important role in giving voice to the concerns of citizens and delivering services that meet people's needs'.[51] Thus far, the EU courts have seemed unmoved by the rapid rise of civil society discourse, but some recent judgments, including the *Djurgården-Lilla*[52] and *Bund für Umwelt*[53] cases, suggest that they are at last willing to respond judicially to the rise of civil society towards the upper echelons of the European Union, and to take into account the information and knowledge of civil society. The opinion of AG Sharpston in *Djurgården-Lilla*, discussed in Chapter 6, includes an insightful description of the 'special supervisory role' that environmental NGOs play in the governance of environmental compliance.[54] With particular regard to the courts' review function, she draws attention to two things: first, citizens should be encouraged to turn to NGOs to voice their concerns, so that the courts will not end up being overloaded with individual cases; and second, the knowledge and skills that the NGOs possess help the courts to decide cases brought before them.[55] For these reasons, she argued for wide access to justice for local NGOs – an opinion that the CJEU later endorsed in its ruling. Sharpston does not elaborate upon how the 'technical expertise' that NGOs have could help the courts.[56] It is clear that NGOs can channel several separate claims into one manageable one, but this does not require any particular technical skills, and the question remains whether Sharpston perhaps entertained the idea of using NGO expertise in enhancing the information basis of adjudication – an idea that has thus far not been taken up by the courts.

50 Accessed 30 June 2014, http://www.clientearth.org/aarhus-centre/what-we-do/.

51 European Commission, July 2001, COM(2001) 428 final, p 14.

52 Case C-263/08 *Djurgården-Lilla Värtans Miljöskyddsförening v Stockholms kommun genom dess marknämnd* [2009] ECR I-9967.

53 Case C-115/09 *Bund für Umwelt und Naturschutz Deutschland, Landesverband Nordrhein-Westfalen eV v Bezirksregierung Arnsberg* [2011] ECR I-3673.

54 Opinion of AG Sharpston in Case C-263/08 *Djurgården-Lilla Värtans Miljöskyddsförening v Stockholms kommun genom dess marknämnd* [2009] ECR I-9967, [50].

55 Ibid, [62]. For the weak role of citizens in Commission consultations and how they are better off 'joining forces' through environmental NGOs than sending individual contributions, see Marxsen, 2014.

56 In her opinion in Case C-115/09 *Bund für Umwelt* [2011] ECR I-3673, [51], AG Kokott argues that an 'environmental NGO gives expression to the collective interest and may possess a level of technical expertise that an individual may not enjoy. To the extent that a single action brought by an environmental NGO may replace a plethora of equivalent actions that would otherwise be brought by individuals, the effect may be to streamline litigation, reduce the number of claims pending before the courts and improve the efficiency with which limited judicial resources are used to dispense justice and protect rights.'

Yet many open issues remain that should be addressed. Should we instruct and steer individuals to act through NGOs, and accordingly strengthen the role of NGOs as potential litigants? What should we think of, and how ought we to respond to, the evidence cited in Chapter 6 that NGOs long for the courts to provide the answers and view it as a 'failure' if legislation is general? How much can we actually expect from environmental NGOs in terms of 'delivering services that meet people's needs'? They have limited resources, and with all that is currently going on in the EU environmental sector, environmental NGOs need to be seriously picky.

7.3.3 Courts catalysing regulatory innovation

The idea of the courts as catalysing innovation is suggested by Scott and Sturm (2007) to capture a new distinct role for judicial review in oversight of governance instruments. In their view, the courts contribute to, and build, the capacity and legitimacy of various committees, agencies and institutions to create and implement policies, by enunciating norms and normative arrangements that motivate them to respect procedural rights. Their vision resembles what Sabel and Simon (2004) have described as 'destabilization': the judiciary intervenes in the workings of governance with the sole aim of shaking up the status quo, and encouraging the participants themselves to critically review their own working assumptions and beliefs.

It should be observed at the outset that an important distinction exists in relation to shaping by the courts. When *shaping* governance institutions, judges intervene in order to restore the basic procedural conditions, whereas in the *catalysing* role, the courts are engaged in innovating practices that have previously not found a home in judicial practice and which go above the basic process threshold. Concrete examples of the EU courts occupying this role are not easy to come by. Judicial treatment of expertise could, however, be argued to contain seeds of a more catalytic approach to review.[57] The CJEU has clearly taken a more uncompromising approach to reviewing the use of technical expertise in EU-level decision making, demanding that decision makers openly articulate their reasoning, and that the decision is both procedurally and substantively reasonable. However, in cases with complexity or expert parties, the uncompromising approach needs to be delivered even-handedly, so that the judges themselves do not deliver the improvements that they should be catalysing.

Some of the recommendations made in the book involve the catalyst role. Consider, for instance, the recommendation that I made in Chapter 6 concerning enforceability of the public participation provision in the WFD. Provisions, such as that encouraging public involvement in water-related decision making, do not have 'a rights core' that could be enforced against a Member State. A further

57 See also Vos, 2014, p 228.

complication, as pointed out in Chapter 2, is that when each governance regime creates its participants, general rules about participation are difficult to devise, and the scope and nature of participation require ad hoc problem-solving. For the judiciary, this means that no one right or best (enforceable) way exists in which to encourage the involvement of interested parties. Taking a cue from the CIS guidance document on participation,[58] I then recommended that national competent authorities draw up a national strategy, indicating action to be taken in different contexts of WFD implementation. It is debatable whether the WFD gives the necessary legal basis for the courts to catalyse production of such information. Yet such a strategy would be beneficial in requiring positive action, without prescribing what that action should be and thus unnecessarily pre-empting the possibility to tailor participation processes to the specific context of the Member State. Similarly, to give a further example, if the courts were to decide to use CIS guidance documents, as recommended in Chapter 6, they would be in a position to catalyse improvements in respect of procedural rights, because deployment of guidance documents can be expressly conditioned on compliance with basic procedural requirements. To demand that the guidance-drafting process comply with certain minimum standards would respect the freedom of action of Member States to implement a framework directive and would enhance the quality of guidance drafting if it were known that outputs (CIS guidance documents) would be debarred from litigation should procedural requirements not be met.

7.3.4 Adjudication as a regulatory penalty default

The relationship between new governance mechanisms and adjudication involves moments when the courts could be seen acting as a regulatory deterrent. Another fitting term is the notion of 'regulatory penalty default'. In particular, this latter concept refers to situations in which regulatory reform occurs out of fear of the legislator stepping in with a more burdensome, costly and bureaucratic option should things not change voluntarily. Implicit here is the presumption that a default (legislative) option is a form of punishment if nothing is done. For instance, one of the earlier forms of new governance in the European Union, standardisation, was provoked through penalty default: 'It is not so much the credible threat of harmonization that induced standardization but rather the "penalty default" of undesirable legislative harmonization instigated a search for a more efficient regulatory institutional design.'[59] The concept of penalty default is less often invoked in relation to adjudication. It is, however, sometimes argued that the whole governance paradigm emerged in the Union from a wish to escape activist courts: replacing legislation with governance instruments gives those with litigation

58 Water Directors of the EU Member States, November 2002.
59 Armstrong, 2011, p 24. See also Sabel and Zeitlin, 2012.

prospects an attractive option to throw out the courts.[60] These arguments are especially strong in the aftermath of cases such as *Mangold*,[61] as well as *Laval*[62] and *Viking*,[63] in which the CJEU is drawn into making value choices and replacing those of Member States. What about a judicial penalty default in new governance environments? Is adjudication felt to be a highly undesirable alternative among potential litigants and are they happy to be left to their own devices when problems emerge?

From one perspective, a judicial penalty default comes close to what could be described as 'shaping in the shadows'. It is about imposing a credible threat that if, for instance, procedural principles are not followed, the courts will intervene, and the outcome from the point of view of a transgressor will then be worse than it would have been had the principles been followed in the first place. From another perspective, judicial penalty default resembles 'reverse catalysing' – that is, that the courts either create or strengthen the existence of factor(s), which *discourages* governance actors from seeking judicial relief, but to seek self-relief instead. One rather obvious example is the EU courts' case law concerning judicial review of governance. Despite some improvements brought about by the Lisbon Treaty, the level of judicial review and protection concerning governance instruments is low: the scope of conditions on which a non-privileged applicant can initiate proceedings is very limited, to mention but one example.[64] Has this judicial penalty default then given rise to improvements in and by governance instruments themselves? The question is relevant because the connection exists between procedural guarantees and judicial review: the lower the level of protection guaranteed by the courts, the more the pressure to ensure that basic procedural provisions are in place and complied with.[65] Hence the reluctance of the courts to guarantee a satisfactory level of judicial protection (penalty default) could trigger changes in the rule-making process itself; indeed, recent contributions have highlighted the incremental proceduralisation of soft law rule-making. Yet it is difficult to attribute this improvement to the courts' role as wielding a penalty default stick. Given their long-standing negative approach to the relaxation of conditions of judicial review, which is furthermore unlikely to change any time soon, the trigger effect remains absent. In order to work, the judicial penalty default needs to involve a credible threat of involvement, not passive resistance.

A more promising example of judicial penalty default can be given in light of the courts' role in filling gaps in incomplete legislation. From this perspective, the

60 Armstrong, 2011, p 27: '[L]itigation may draw courts into the sorts of value-balancing that litigants might rather avoid: hard legalism may be the penalty default that drives potential litigants to seek alternative governance arrangements.'

61 Case C-144/04 *Werner Mangold v Rüdiger Helm* [2005] ECR I-9981.

62 Case C-341/05 *Laval v Svenska Byggnadsarbetareförbundet* [2007] ECR I-11767.

63 Case C-438/05 *International Transport Workers' Federation and Finnish Seamen's Union v Viking Line* [2007] ECR I-10779.

64 Senden and van den Brink, 2012, pp 68–70.

65 Senden, 2013, p 72.

CIS is perceived as an instrument with which to create rules in order to displace potential default rules imposed subsequently in adjudication.[66] Although the CJEU has not, as yet, explicitly referred to CIS guidance when filling in the gaps of the WFD, thus weakening the claim for a judicial penalty default, the low numbers of WFD cases involving interpretation of concepts – a fact to which I return next – suggests that incipient judicial penalty default is in place. Through detailed guidance production, CIS actors have managed to offer a credible alternative to the courts and retain factual, if not formal, interpretative authority over the interpretation of framework legislation.

7.3.5 Courts adapting and changing

In this subsection, I offer some evidence suggesting that, as a result of new governance, the courts change and adapt. This is by no means an original observation, but the authors referred to at the beginning of this chapter have so far found little concrete evidence for transformations in the judicial role. Primary focus is on the WFD CIS, which at the moment offers the strongest support for the argument that I wish to make, but two other case studies ought to be discussed to the extent that they can provide us with additional information and further insights.

The CJEU has given several judgments on the WFD, yet the majority of cases have been, as the Commission remarks, 'straightforward'.[67] This near-total absence of 'concept litigation', by which I mean a strand of litigation concerned with interpretation and clarification of certain key concepts, stands in stark contrast to other (environmental) litigation. For instance, the entire corpus of waste litigation consists of judgments clarifying the concept of 'waste'.[68] What could explain the low numbers of WFD interpretation cases? The Commission did not touch upon the reasons behind the statistics. My account focuses on the CIS: concept litigation may well be diminishing because the need is not as great as before for the courts to clarify the meaning of norms; instead of the courts, the soft law regime has positioned itself to provide answers to questions of interpretation.[69] Of course, the WFD is, in many ways, an unprecedented directive, and the full picture will not be fully seen and appreciated until after more years in implementation. Yet it is already possible to comment that, while reserving the option for the courts to address severe and persistent irregularities in WFD implementation, the

66 For the original concept of the penalty default rule, see Ayres and Gertner, 1989.

67 European Commission, November 2012, SWD(2012) 379 final, p 16.

68 Lack of a harmonised understanding of the main elements of the Waste Framework Directive (the revised Directive 2008/98/ EC replaced the old Directive in 2008) was widely believed to add to the number of infringement cases. See Milieu Ltd, AmbienDura and FFact for the European Commission, 2009, p 1. For problems relating to implementation of concepts in the area of EU environmental law, see Weale et al, 2000, p 324.

69 For a fuller argument, see Korkea-aho, 2014.

Commission is using the CIS to solve minor interpretative disagreements. The difficulties of the Commission in enforcing the WFD, as illustrated in the pending case *Commission v Germany*,[70] further strengthen the importance of the CIS to enforcement of the WFD.

(Hard) law's authority may become dependent upon soft law in another way, too. Again using the WFD as an illustrative example, I have shown that framework directives lay down general principles and leave national administrators, civil society 'bureaucrats' and scientific experts to develop them subsequently. If the CJEU operates at the level of legislative frameworks, not paying attention to ways in which the framework is further developed in implementation, it contributes to creating and sustaining a gap between the formal and real authority of law. The opening of such a gap is visible from two WFD preliminary rulings.[71] These both revolve around the same question: whether and to what extent WFD provisions are enforceable. Do framework norms enjoy legal authority or are its provisions, as was asked by the referring court in *Bund für Umwelt*, 'merely a statement of an objective for management planning'? A gap between formal and real has long been argued to exist in EU constitutional law, yet to my mind the gap developing here is more critical. In the end, it concerns the understanding of what is the applicable law.[72] With the contours of the judicial approach to framework norms being barely visible to scholarly observation, it is too early to speak about where the courts are going with framework directives. Yet the CJEU should be aware of the gap developing, and the way in which it reflects on its judicial role and responsibilities, in particular in respect of the preliminary ruling procedure. The positive answer given to the national courts concerning use of Commission guidance is a step that should be followed by other similar ones.[73]

As for REACH, at least two ways can be imagined in which the REACH regime might structure the actions of the EU courts. First, the ECHA plays, as do other EU agencies, an important role in mediating consensus over key scientific issues. Moreover, using the inbuilt channels of REACH, Member States, the Commission and, in some cases, third parties can tap into the mechanisms provided for under REACH to negotiate their disagreements. It seems reasonable to expect these procedures to deal effectively with points of contestation before they escalate to the point of litigation. Second, REACH actors produce their own ECHA guidance documents. These, being similar to CIS guidance documents, may make recourse to the courts unwarranted by providing the necessary answers. The ECHA has not been operational for very long and many REACH provisions are not yet fully on

70 Case C-525/12 *Commission v Germany*, pending at time of writing.

71 See Case C-43/10 *Nomarchiaki Aftodioikisi Aitoloakarnanias and others v Ypourgos Perivallontos, Chorotaxias kai Dimosion ergon and others*, 11 September 2012, NYR; Case C-461/13 *Bund für Umwelt und Naturschutz Deutschland*, pending at time of writing.

72 On this point, see also Dawson, 2013, p 29, and van Kempen, 2012, p 500.

73 Case C-308/11 *Chemische Fabrik Kreussler & Co. GmbH v Sunstar Deutschland GmbH, formerly John O. Butler GmbH*, 6 September 2012, NYR.

the go; a credible analysis of courts statistics seems feasible only after a substantially longer period of full implementation. Some indication that the iterated deliberations of REACH might reduce litigation may, however, be found in the fact that the Board of Appeal, where disagreements and disputes resulting from simplified procedures will accumulate more swiftly, have been dealing with very modest numbers of cases. The ECHA has thus far received 45 cases and ECHA general reports have consistently documented that the number of appeals has been lower than anticipated.[74] An environmental NGO, the European Environmental Bureau (EEB), also reported that the cases of the Board of Appeal have been fewer and less significant than it had assumed. It does not see the institutional design of REACH as playing any positive role here, but points a finger at the ECHA, arguing that the 'low number of appeals – in a situation in which it is clear that the quality of the data is low – suggests that ECHA is being too soft and accommodating with industry'.[75]

Much depends on the Board of Appeal's own role. If it evolves into a judicial organ in its own right, actively reviewing and substituting ECHA decisions with its own, it may replace the role to be taken by the CJEU on appeal. Of course, its active intervention may result in increased numbers of appeals to the CJEU by those on the losing side. In the abstract, though, an active Board of Appeal is desirable for REACH stakeholders. Comments on behalf of business representatives express preference for the role of an activist Board of Appeal over that of the EU courts, for the Board of Appeal has 'the technical and scientific expertise that a regular court lacks'.[76]

7.4 Conclusion

The central argument of this book, bolstered by insights from case studies, is that EU law is a framework, and that various governance techniques are deployed to offer specification and precision of general rules. For instance, the European Semester, if not constituting a legally binding framework, shapes discussions and deliberations, providing a normative EU-wide justification for lower-level policies and activities. The REACH Regulation is also complemented by a multiplicity of 'entrepreneurial' activities designed to realise the objectives of EU chemicals policy and which largely centre on a new actor, the ECHA. In water regulation, the WFD CIS solves the issue of incomplete legislation by providing a structure for interpretation and precision of framework norms. Where EU new governance continues to develop in this way, it will evoke controversy and 'tension' between

74 Accessed 30 June 2014, http://echa.europa.eu/about-us/who-we-are/board-of-appeal/decisions. See also Bronckers and van Gerven, 2009, p 1846.

75 ClientEarth and EEB, 2012, p 34.

76 See, accessed 30 June 2014, http://chemicalwatch.com/20063/echa-board-of-appeal-approach-inconsistent-lawyers-say. For a case concerning a decision taken by the ECHA Board of Appeal, see Case T-673/13 *European Coalition to End Animal Experiments v ECHA*, pending at time of writing.

general legal rules and more detailed local norms, therefore necessitating a re-evaluation and possible restructuring of judicial control.[77]

Before throwing up our hands before the rise and spread of new governance, it should be observed that help may come from an unexpected source: in this case, from governance mechanisms themselves. The case studies substantiate observation that forms of deliberative decision-making mechanisms have emerged, some more fully fledged and operational than others, but despite dysfunctions and sub-optimal solutions the findings are convincing. Decisions are taken in a deliberative manner to an extent that clearly exceeds happenstance. What is more important still is that these deliberations give rise to norms and normative arrangements that can hold actors to account for their activities. I have studied these new norms and arrangements under the notion of 'peer review accountability', emphasising the importance of the act of explaining to peers because they – not the courts or other higher-level actors – have the relevant knowledge to assess an explanation and its validity. Peer forms of accountability have then been identified as 'part of a more general trend whereby principles of informal control are becoming more important than formal accountability'.[78]

The underlying idea throughout the book has been to appreciate and promote the interdependence of informal and formal control, not to set one against the other. One manifestation of these increasing synergies concerns the usefulness of EU new governance for adjudication. Although deliberations in governance mechanisms provide little by way of hard, binding law, nevertheless the 'soft' law of the deliberative governance architecture influences and conditions judicial decision making in two ways. First, deliberations result in increased information, which helps the Commission to keep track of what is going on in Member States (a precondition for enforcement), and assists the EU courts in exercising and optimising the level of scrutiny. In this latter respect, forms of EU new governance that require participants to deliberate and exchange reasons in order to produce collective decisions, jointly agreed standards, legislation, peer-reviewed guidance, frameworks of evaluation or other such material make it easier for the courts to decide on the basis of this information whether the need arises to go digging deeper. Sometimes they have to. To give the EU courts some guidance here, I have developed benchmarks of iterated deliberation, all of which are intended to steer judicial review towards matters that appear not to have been satisfactorily deliberated. The benchmarks of iterated deliberation guide the judiciary to place emphasis upon the openness and responsiveness of decision making (participation), opportunities for contestation and conflict (problem-solving), and inclusion and treatment of reasoned justifications (reason-giving). This checklist assists the judiciary in optimising the intensity of review: judges are advised to become more demanding

77 Armstrong, 1998, p 158.
78 Senden and van den Brink, 2012, p 68.

and inquisitorial if it appears that problems exist with performance of any of these standards.

Second, whilst deliberation may enable and empower the Commission and the EU courts, it also simultaneously acts as a restraint upon their activities. For instance, the CIS can be thought of as providing information that comes, primarily through the Commission, to bear on enforcement, whilst the same information also places new limits on the actors of enforcement. CIS guidance, when used by the Commission in its monitoring, has the potential to expose its discretion in enforcement to public scrutiny. As far as the EU courts are concerned, deliberations may end up side-lining the EU courts by providing answers that have usually been obtained from them. Governance regimes such as the CIS provide a platform from which to arrive at harmonised interpretation and understanding of key concepts in legislation, with the result that demand for judicial guidance and direction will be correspondingly lower in the long term. Another new limit for the EU courts emerges from my recommendation that they should acknowledge the legal effects of interpretative soft law guidance when adjudicating framework legislation.

On the whole, then, the lesson that EU legal governance research might take away from this analysis is that adjudication is increasingly made more straightforward – even possible – by new governance frameworks and soft law documents prepared by participants in those frameworks. As a result, soft law comes to be seen as less of a problem for judicial review of new governance than has been thought. Certainly, though, I do not wish to trivialise the problems and concerns associated with the role of the courts in EU new governance. The operation of judicial review in EU governance environments is far from uncomplicated and routine, and there are some variations in the role of the judiciary depending on the particularities of each governance instrument. Yet my aim has been to counter those views that hold new governance and political experimentation more generally to have necessarily sapped the ability of the EU judiciary to monitor and review these experiments. At least, this is not the picture of the EU courts painted by this book. Indeed, as it turns out, the opposite seems to be true.

This book nevertheless takes seriously concerns and expectations arising in relation to the role of the courts in new governance, and to this end it contains several recommendations for fine-tuning institutional design. Now, a different kind of concern emerges. New governance appears to require judges to pay more attention to questions of institutional design, which has been the strong point of American-style (executive) judicial review. Is EU judicial review going to move in the direction of US-style judicial review? Shapiro (2004) does see remarkable similarities between US and EU administrative laws, and notes that 'like causes have like effects'.[79] REACH and WFD CIS bear some resemblance to the US practice of rule-making record, and especially to what is called the 'hard-look

79 Shapiro, 2004, p 260.

doctrine'. The term has a long history that dates back to the New Deal. Initially, the US federal courts deferred to technocratic decision making, but subsequently became more demanding, in particular with respect to transparency and public participation. These developments have frequently been criticised, particularly the proliferation of 'strategic behaviour' or litigation, which has increased in the United States after the courts allowed stakeholders to dispute administrative rule-making on the grounds that their input had not been sufficiently taken into account by the regulatory agency.[80] This has worried many.

Ought the European Union to worry about the spread of strategic litigation too? Whatever similarities exist between similar institutional innovations, they are, however, likely to be leading to very different outcomes in the European Union and the United States. Legal institutions and innovations are always embedded in their social and cultural contexts, and thus 'like causes' may in fact have very different effects and patterns in practice. Moreover, changes have come about via different routes: in the United States, changes were demanded by the judiciary when there was not perhaps a necessary adjustment and understanding of the possibilities and limits of such action in practice; in the European Union, most of the changes have been initiated by legislation, which has possibly allowed – and would do so in the future – things to be rolled out in a more organic fashion and in their intended context. Legislation, especially if it is framework, also offers a more fine-tuned way of doing things than judgments: the rulings of the EU courts, which either affirm or reject a certain outcome, are blunt and thus often ill-suited tools to deploy in review of EU new governance.[81] Moreover, it should be realised that the role that I advocate for the courts is actually quite modest. Whilst I may recommend some changes, for instance to the interpretation of Art 263(4) TFEU in order to allow more actors to access the courts, in many other respects I argue for a more limited role for the courts by requiring them, among other things, to give regard to soft law guidance in the interpretation of framework legislation.

On the whole, this study should be read as neither an apology, nor any form of justification for adjudication. The primary responsibility for defining and guaranteeing suitable conditions for deliberation rests with the institutions themselves; accordingly, the role of judiciaries is limited. The reason to prefer reform of institutional design is that inventive and innovative institutional design will influence more than one dimension of the political process and, in principle, will therefore affect the incentives of institutional actors more broadly. For instance, one issue to address in the future is 'paralysis by analysis':[82] all case studies show an immense growth in the amount of analyses and reports to be submitted, running the risk of legal regulation going 'topsy-turvy' – that is, of reporting mechanisms becoming more important than the underlying substantive provisions. No matter

80 Ibid.
81 Scott and Sturm, 2007, p 593.
82 ClientEarth and EEB, 2012, p 48.

how concerned we are about this, it is a question of institutional design, not one for the courts to organise. Nonetheless, improvement of institutional design need not occur by way of choosing between the courts or some 'other means', and the courts can, in fact, be perceived as part of the institutional design. Certainly, ways other than the judiciary exist to improve the legitimacy and efficacy of EU new governance, but only an institutional design which is antithetical to its own inventive nature would overlook the fact that those 'other means' can be initiated and facilitated by the courts too.

Knowledge, expertise and information have played a large role in this book, and it is fitting to conclude by observing what challenges we might expect to arise here for future research and adjudication. It seems that the three major challenges that arise from the informal and challenging technical nature of EU governance need tackling. First, one has to secure the material. The question of information and knowledge is no longer so much the absence of it, but more one of the identifying, locating and understanding of it. Discussion has recently opened over problems of doing research in the EU governance context, particularly in terms of data gathering and management.[83] The more informal and ad hoc the governance instrument, the greater the risk that knowledge and information will be lost as a result of insufficiently kept records, bad archiving habits, or use of short-term interns and employees who take information with them when they go. This has wider implications for access to information rights: the right to access to information is tantamount to no right at all if information is not gathered and adequately stored in the first place.

Second, once secured, material needs to be reviewed and analysed. The nature of this legal material may be different from that to which lawyers have become accustomed. Legal research and adjudication will increasingly be about sieving through apparently meaningless technical and obscure documents and materials, but which, if overlooked and ignored, insulate legal research and the courts from the real world of EU law and governance.

Finally, legal governance research needs to pay closer attention to the clarity and transparency of underlying assumptions and theoretical premises, whilst simultaneously welcoming criticism, improvement and revision.

It is this trio of tasks that not only academics in the European Union, but also judges, need to puzzle out.

83 Marxsen, 2014; Scott, 2011, p 348.

Bibliography

Literature

Abbott, K W, and Snidal, D, 'Hard and soft law in international governance' (2000) 54 *International Organization* 421–56.

Alemanno, A, 'Science and EU risk regulation: The role of experts in decision-making and judicial review', Paper presented at First Young Researchers Workshop on Science and Law, 31 May–1 June 2007, Istituto Superiore Universitario di Formazione Interdisciplinare (ISUFI), Lecce, Italy, accessed 12 October 2014, http://papers.ssrn.com/sol3/papers.cfm?abstract_id=1007401.

Alemanno, A, 'The dialogue between judges and experts in the EU and WTO', in Fontanelli, F, Martinico, G, and Carrozza, P (eds) *Shaping Rule of Law through Dialogue: International and Supranational Experiences*, 2010, Groningen: Europa Law Publishing, pp 347–76.

Allan, A, 'Implementing the Water Framework and Groundwater Directives in Finland: Lessons from the Genesis Project' (2011) 22 *The Journal of Water Law* 185–96.

Allott, P, 'European governance and the re-branding of democracy' (2002) 27 *European Law Review* 60–71.

Andersen, S, *The Enforcement of EU Law: The Role of the European Commission*, 2012, Oxford: Oxford University Press.

Armstrong, K A, 'Legal integration: Theorizing the legal dimension of European integration' (1998) 36 *Journal of Common Market Studies* 155–74.

Armstrong, K A, 'Inclusive governance? Civil society and the Open Method of Coordination', in Smismans, S (ed) *Civil Society and Legitimate European Governance*, 2006, Cheltenham: Edward Elgar, pp 42–67.

Armstrong, K A, 'Governance and constitutionalism after Lisbon' (2008) 46 *Journal of Common Market Studies* 413–26.

Armstrong, K A, *Governing Social Inclusion: Europeanization through Policy Coordination*, 2010, Oxford: Oxford University Press.

Armstrong, K A, 'The character of EU law and governance: From "Community Method" to new modes of governance' (2011) 64 *Current Legal Problems* 179–214.

Armstrong, K A, and Kilpatrick, C, 'Law, governance, or new governance? The changing Open Method of Coordination' (2007) 13 *Columbia Journal of European Law* 649–77.

Ayres, I, and Gertner, R, 'Filling gaps in incomplete contracts: An economic theory of default rules' (1989) 99 *Yale Law Journal* 87–130.

Azoulay, L, 'The Court of Justice and the administrative governance' (2001) 7 *European Law Journal* 425–41.

Baber, W F, and Bartlett, R V, *Global Democracy and Sustainable Jurisprudence: Deliberative Environmental Law*, 2009, Cambridge, MA: MIT Press.

Barber, B, *Strong Democracy: Participatory Politics for a New Age*, 1984, Oakland, CA: University of California Press.

Barnett, A, 'The creation of democracy?', in Hirst, P, and Khilnani, S (eds) *Reinventing Democracy*, 1996, Oxford: Blackwell Publishers, pp 157–75.

Baxter, R, 'International law in her infinite variety' (1980) 29 *International and Comparative Law Quarterly* 549–66.

Begg, I, 'Is there a convincing rationale for the Lisbon Strategy?' (2008) 46 *Journal of Common Market Studies* 427–35.

Behagel, J, and Turnhout, E, 'Democratic legitimacy in the implementation of the Water Framework Directive in the Netherlands: Towards participatory and deliberative norms?' (2011) 13 *Journal of Environmental Policy & Planning* 297–316.

Bellamy, R, *Liberalism and Pluralism: Towards a Politics of Compromise*, 1999, London: Routledge.

Bellamy, R, and Attucci, C, 'Normative theory and the EU: Between contract and community', in Wiener, A, and Diez, T (eds) *European Integration Theory*, 2nd edn, 2009, Oxford: Oxford University Press, pp 198–220.

Bellamy, R, and Castiglione, D, 'The uses of democracy: Reflections on the European democratic deficit', in Eriksen, E O, and Fossum, J E (eds) *Democracy in the European Union: Integration through Deliberation?*, 2000, London: Routledge, pp 65–84.

Benhabib, S, 'Toward a deliberative model of democratic legitimacy', in Benhabib, S (ed) *Democracy and Difference: Contesting the Boundaries of the Political*, 1996, Princeton, NJ: Princeton University Press, pp 67–94.

Benz, A, 'Accountable multilevel governance by the Open Method of Coordination?' (2007) 13 *European Law Journal* 505–22.

Berger, G, and Steurer, R, 'The EU SDS process in the Member States: SDS Coordinators, National Progress Reports and the Open Method of Coordination', *ESDN Quarterly Report*, March 2007, accessed 12 October 2014, http://www.sd-network.eu/?k=quarterly%20reports&report_id=4.

Berger, G, and Zwirner, W, 'The interfaces between the EU SDS and the Lisbon Strategy: Objectives, governance provisions, coordination and future developments', *ESDN Quarterly Report*, December 2008, accessed 12 October 2014, http://www.sd-network.eu/?k=quarterly%20reports&report_id=11.

Bernard, N, 'A "new governance" approach to economic, social and cultural rights in the EU', in Hervey, T, and Kenner, J (eds) *Economic and Social Rights under the EU Charter of Fundamental Rights: A Legal Perspective*, 2003, Oxford: Hart Publishing, pp 247–68.

Bessette, J, 'Deliberative democracy: The majority principle in Republican government', in Goldwin, R, and Schambra, W A (eds) *How Democratic is the Constitution?*, 1980, Washington, DC: American Enterprise Institute, pp 102–16.

Besson, S, and Martí, J L, 'Introduction', in Besson, S, and Martí, J L (eds) *Deliberative Democracy and its Discontent*, 2006, Farnham: Ashgate, pp xii–xxxi.

Betten, L, 'The democratic deficit of participatory democracy in Community social policy' (1998) 23 *European Law Review* 20–36.

Bignami, F, 'Three generations of participation rights before the European Commission' (2004) 68 *Law and Contemporary Problems* 61–83.

Bignami, F, 'Rethinking interest representation in the European Union: Review of law, legitimacy and European governance – Functional participation in social regulation by Stijn Smismans' (2006) 26 *Oxford Journal of Legal Studies* 439–47.

Bogdandy, A von, Arndt, F, and Bast, J, 'Legal instruments in European Union law and their reform: A systematic approach on an empirical basis' (2004) 23 *Yearbook of European Law* 91–136.

Bohman, J, *Public Deliberation: Pluralism, Complexity, and Democracy*, 1996, Cambridge, MA: MIT Press.

Bohman, J, 'Survey article: The coming of age of deliberative democracy' (1998) 6 *The Journal of Political Philosophy* 400–25.

Bohman, J, 'Expanding dialogue: The internet, the public sphere, and prospects for transnational democracy' (2004) 52 *Sociological Review* 131–55.

Bohman, J, 'Institutional reform and democratic legitimacy: Deliberative democracy and transnational constitutionalism', in Besson, S, and Martí, J L (eds) *Deliberative Democracy and its Discontents*, 2006, Farnham: Ashgate, pp 215–31.

Bohman, J, and Rehg, W, 'Introduction', in Bohman, J, and Rehg, W (eds) *Deliberative Democracy: Essays on Reason and Politics*, 1997, Cambridge, MA: MIT Press, pp ix–xxx.

Borrás, S, and Jacobsson, K, 'The Open Method of Coordination and new governance patterns in the EU' (2004) 11 *Journal of European Public Policy* 185–208.

Bredt, S, 'Prospects and limits of democratic governance in the EU' (2011) 17 *European Law Journal* 35–65.

Bronckers, M, and van Gerven, Y, 'Legal remedies under the EC's new chemicals legislation REACH: Testing a new model of European governance' (2009) 46 *Common Market Law Review* 1823–71.

Búrca, G de, 'Reappraising subsidiarity's significance after Amsterdam', 1999, Harvard Jean Monnet Working Paper 7/99, accessed 12 October 2014, http://www.jeanmonnetprogram.org/archive/papers/99/990701.html.

Búrca, G de, 'The constitutional challenge of new governance in the European Union' (2003) 28 *European Law Review* 814–39.

Búrca, G de, 'New modes of governance and the protection of human rights', in Alston, P, and Schutter, O de (eds) *Monitoring Fundamental Rights in the EU*, 2005, Oxford: Hart Publishing, pp 25–36.

Búrca, G de, 'EU race discrimination law: A hybrid model?', in Búrca, G de, and Scott, J (eds) *Law and New Governance in the EU and the US*, 2006, Oxford: Hart Publishing, pp 97–120.

Búrca, G de, 'Developing democracy beyond the state' (2008) 46 *Columbia Journal of Transnational Law* 221–78.

Búrca, G de, 'Stumbling into experimentalism: The EU anti-discrimination regime', in Sabel, C F, and Zeitlin, J (eds) *Experimentalist Governance in the European Union: Towards a New Architecture*, 2010, Oxford: Oxford University Press, pp 215–35.

Búrca, G de, and Scott, J, 'Introduction: New governance, law and constitutionalism', in Búrca, G de, and Scott, J (eds) *Law and New Governance in the EU and the US*, 2006, Oxford: Hart Publishing, pp 1–12.

Búrca, G de, and Walker, N, 'Law and transnational civil society: Upsetting the agenda?' (2003) 9 *European Law Journal* 387–400.

Busuioc, M, 'Accountability, control and independence: The case of European agencies' (2009) 15 *European Law Journal* 599–615.

Busuioc, M, *European Agencies: Law and Practices of Accountability*, 2013, Oxford: Oxford University Press.

Cane, P, 'Understanding judicial review and its impact', in Hertogh, M, and Halliday, S (eds) *Judicial Review and Bureaucratic Impact: International and Interdisciplinary Perspectives*, 2004, Cambridge: Cambridge University Press, pp 15–42.

Chalmers, D, ' "Food for thought": Reconciling European risks and traditional ways of life' (2003) 66 *Modern Law Review* 532–62.

Cheneval, F, 'The people in deliberative democracy', in Besson, S, and Martí, J L (eds) *Deliberative Democracy and its Discontents*, 2006, Farnham: Ashgate, pp 159–79.

Chiti, E, 'An important part of the EU's institutional machinery: Features, problems and perspectives of European agencies' (2009) 46 *Common Market Law Review* 1395–442.

Chiti, E, 'Governance of compliance', in Cremona, M (ed) *Compliance and the Enforcement of EU Law*, 2012, Oxford: Oxford University Press.

Christodoulidis, E, and Dukes, R, 'On the unity of European labour law', in Prechal, S, and van Roermund, B (eds) *The Coherence of EU Law: The Search for Unity in Divergent Concepts*, 2008, Oxford: Oxford University Press, pp 397–422.

Cohen, J, 'Deliberation and democratic legitimacy', in Bohman, J, and Rehg, W (eds) *Deliberative Democracy. Essays on Reason and Politics*, 1997a, Cambridge, MA: MIT Press, pp 67–91.

Cohen, J, 'Procedure and substance in deliberative democracy', in Bohman, J, and Rehg, W (eds) *Deliberative Democracy: Essays on Reason and Politics*, 1997b, Cambridge, MA: MIT Press, pp 407–37.

Cohen, J, 'Democracy and liberty', in Elster, J (ed) *Deliberative Democracy*, 1998, Cambridge: Cambridge University Press, pp 185–231.

Cohen, J, and Fung, A, 'Radical democracy' (2004) 10 *Swiss Journal of Political Science* 23–34.

Cohen, J, and Sabel, C, 'Directly deliberative polyarchy' (1997) 3 *European Law Journal* 313–42.

Cooney, R, and Lang, A T F, 'Taking uncertainty seriously: Adaptive governance and international trade' (2007) 18 *The European Journal of International Law* 523–51.

Craig, P, *The Lisbon Treaty. Law, Politics, and Treaty Reform*, 2010, Oxford: Oxford University Press.

Craig, P, 'Integration, democracy, and legitimacy', in Craig, P, and Búrca, G de (eds) *The Evolution of the EU Law*, 2nd edn, 2011a, Oxford: Oxford University Press, pp 13–40.

Craig, P, 'Institutions, power, and institutional balance', in Craig, P, and Búrca, G de (eds) *The Evolution of the EU Law*, 2nd edn, 2011b, Oxford: Oxford University Press, pp 41–82.

Craig, P, *EU Administrative Law*, 2nd edn, 2012, Oxford: Oxford University Press.

Craig, P, and Búrca, G de, *EU Law: Text, Cases, and Materials*, 5th edn, 2011, Oxford: Oxford University Press.

Curtin, D, 'Civil society and the European Union: Opening space for deliberative democracy?', in Academy of European Law (ed) *Collected Courses of the Academy of European Law*, 1999, Alphen aan den Rijn: Kluwer Law International, pp 185–280.

Curtin, D, 'Delegation to EU non-majoritarian agencies and emerging practices of public accountability', in Geradin, D, Munoz, R, and Petit, N (eds) *Regulation through Agencies in the EU: A New Paradigm of European Governance*, 2005, Cheltenham: Edward Elgar, pp 88–119.

Curtin, D, 'Framing public deliberation and democratic legitimacy in the European Union', in Besson, S, and Martí, J L (eds) *Deliberative Democracy and its Discontents*, 2006, Farnham: Ashgate, pp 133–56.

Curtin, D, 'Holding (quasi-) autonomous EU administrative actors to public account' (2007) 13 *European Law Journal* 523–41.

Curtin, D, *Executive Power of the European Union: Law, Practices and the Living Constitution*, 2009, Oxford: Oxford University Press.

Curtin, D, and Egeberg, M, 'Tradition and innovation: Europe's accumulated executive order' (2008) 31 *West European Politics* 639–61.

Curtin, D, Hofmann, H, and Mendes, J, 'Constitutionalising EU executive rule-making procedures: A research agenda' (2013) 19 *European Law Journal* 1–21.

Dąbrowska, P, 'EU governance of GMOs: Political struggles and experimentalist solutions?', in Sabel, C F, and Zeitlin, J (eds) *Experimentalist Governance in the European Union: Towards a New Architecture*, 2010, Oxford: Oxford University Press, pp 177–214.

Dawson, M, 'The ambiguity of social Europe in the Open Method of Coordination' (2009) 34 *European Law Review* 55–79.

Dawson, M, *New Governance and the Transformation of European Law: Coordinating EU Social Law and Policy*, 2011, Cambridge: Cambridge University Press.

Dawson, M, 'Soft law and the rule of law in the European Union: Revision or redundancy?', in Vauchez, A, and Witte, B de (eds) *Lawyering Europe: European Law as a Transnational Social Field*, 2013, Oxford: Hart Publishing, pp 221–41.

Dehousse, R, 'Regulation by networks in the European Community: The role of European agencies' (1997) 4 *Journal of European Public Policy* 246–61.

Dehousse, R, 'Misfits: EU law and the transformation of European governance', 2002, Jean Monnet Working Paper 2/02, accessed 12 October 2014, http://www.jeanmonnetprogram.org/archive/papers/02/020201.html.

Dehousse, R, 'The "Community Method" at sixty', in Dehousse, R (ed) *The 'Community Method': Obstinate or Obsolete?*, 2011, Basingstoke: Palgrave MacMillan, pp 3–15.

Derruine, O, and Tiedemann, A, 'The first European Semester and its contribution to the EU 2020', October 2011, accessed 12 October 2014, http://www.greens-efa.eu/fileadmin/dam/Documents/Studies/EUROPEAN%20SEMESTER%20STUDY%20oct2010.pdf.

Devaux, C, 'The role of experts in the elaboration of the Cape Town Convention: Between authority and legitimacy' (2013) 19 *European Law Journal* 843–63.

Dowding, K, Goodin, R E, and Pateman, C, 'Introduction: Between justice and democracy', in Dowding, K, Goodin, R E, and Pateman, C (eds) *Justice and Democracy: Essays for Brian Barry*, 2004, Cambridge: Cambridge University Press, pp 1–24.

Dryzek, J S, *Deliberative Democracy and Beyond: Liberals, Critics, Contestations*, 2000, Oxford: Oxford University Press.

Dryzek, J S, and List, C, 'Social choice theory and deliberative democracy: A reconciliation' (2003) 33 *British Journal of Political Science* 1–28.

Ehnert, T, 'The legitimacy of new risk governance: A critical view in light of the EU's approach to nanotechnologies in food' (2014) *European Law Journal*, forthcoming.

Elster, J, 'Introduction', in Elster, J (ed) *Deliberative Democracy*, 1998, Cambridge: Cambridge University Press, pp 1–18.

Eriksen, E O, 'Deliberative supranationalism in the EU', in Eriksen, E O, and Fossum, J E (eds) *Democracy in the European Union: Integration through Deliberation?*, 2000, London: Routledge, pp 42–64.

Eriksen, E O, 'Deliberation and the problem of democratic legitimacy in the EU: Are working agreements the most that can be expected?' 2006, Center for European Studies, University of Oslo, Working Paper No. 08, accessed 12 October 2014, http://econpapers.repec.org/paper/erparenax/p0219.htm.

Eriksen, E O, and Fossum, J E, 'Post-national integration', in Eriksen, E O, and Fossum, J E (eds) *Democracy in the European Union: Integration through Deliberation?*, 2000, London: Routledge, pp 1–28.

Eskridge Jr, W N, and Ferejohn, J, *A Republic of Statutes: The New American Constitution*, 2010, New Haven, CT: Yale University Press.

Everson, M, and Eisner, J, *The Making of a European Constitution: Judges and Law beyond Constitutive Power*, 2007, London: Routledge.

Fisher, E, 'Unpacking the toolbox – or why the public/private divide is important in EC environmental law', 2001, Florida State University College of Law Public Law and Legal Theory Working Paper No. 35, accessed 12 October 2014, http://papers.ssrn.com/sol3/papers.cfm?abstract_id=283295.

Fisher, E, 'The "perfect storm" of REACH: Charting regulatory controversy in the age of information, sustainable development, and globalization' (2008) 11 *Journal of Risk Research* 541–63.

Fleurke, F, and Somsen, H, 'Precautionary regulation of chemical risk: How REACH confronts the regulatory challenges of scale, uncertainty, complexity and innovation' (2011) 48 *Common Market Law Review* 357–93.

Flynn, B, and Kröger, L, 'Can policy learning really improve implementation? Evidence from Irish responses to the Water Framework Directive' (2003) 13 *European Environment* 150–63.

Flyvbjerg, B, 'Habermas and Foucault: Thinkers for civil society?' (1998) 49 *British Journal of Sociology* 210–33.

Føllesdal, A, 'Normative political theory and the European Union', in Jørgensen, K E, Pollack, M A, and Rosamond, B (eds) *Handbook of European Union Politics*, 2007, London: Sage Publications, pp 317–34.

Fossum, J E, and Menéndez, A J, 'The Constitution's gift? A deliberative democratic analysis of constitution making in the European Union' (2005) 11 *European Law Journal* 380–440.

Frykman, H, and Mörth, U, 'Soft law and three notions of democracy: The case of the EU', in Mörth, U (ed) *Soft Law in Governance and Regulation: An Interdisciplinary Analysis*, 2004, Cheltenham: Edward Elgar, pp 155–70.

Galligan, D, 'Citizens' rights and participation in the regulation of biotechnology', in Francioni, F (ed) *Biotechnologies and International Human Rights*, 2007, Oxford: Hart Publishing, pp 335–59.

Gambetta, D, ' "Claro!" An essay on discursive machismo', in Elster, J (ed) *Deliberative Democracy*, 1998, Cambridge: Cambridge University Press, pp 19–43.

García-Salmones, M, 'Taking uncertainty seriously: Adaptive governance and international trade – A reply to Rosie Cooney and Andrew Lang' (2009) 20 *European Journal of International Law* 167–86.

Gerstenberg, O, 'Expanding the Constitution beyond the Court: The case of Euro-constitutionalism' (2002) 8 *European Law Journal* 172–92.

Gerstenberg, O, and Sabel, C F, 'Directly deliberative polyarchy: An institutional ideal for Europe?', in Joerges, C, and Dehousse, R (eds) *Good Governance in Europe's Integrated Market*, 2002, Oxford: Oxford University Press, pp 289–341.

Goodin, R E, 'Democratic accountability: The distinctiveness of the third sector' (2003) 44 *European Journal of Sociology* 359–93.

Gutmann, A, and Thompson, D, *Why Deliberative Democracy?*, 2004, Princeton, NJ: Princeton University Press.

Harlow, C, 'Civil society organisations and participatory administration: A challenge to EU administrative law?', in Smismans, S (ed) *Civil Society and Legitimate European Governance*, 2006, Cheltenham: Edward Elgar, pp 115–40.

Harlow, C, and Rawlings, R, 'Accountability and law enforcement: The centralized EU infringement procedure' (2006) 31 *European Law Review* 447–75.

Harlow, C, and Rawlings, R, 'Promoting accountability in multilevel governance: A network approach' (2007) 13 *European Law Journal* 542–62.
Hatzopoulos, V, 'Why Open Method of Coordination is bad for you: A letter to the EU' (2007) 13 *European Law Journal* 309–42.
Hedelin, B, and Lindh, M, 'Implementing the EU Water Framework Directive and prospects for sustainable water planning in Sweden' (2008) 18 *European Environment* 327–44.
Held, D, 'Law of states, law of peoples: Three models of sovereignty' (2002) 8 *Legal Theory* 1–44.
Héritier, A, 'New modes of governance in Europe: Policy-making without legislating?', in Héritier, A (ed) *Common Goods: Reinventing European and International Governance*, 2002, Lanham, MD: Rowman & Littlefield Publishers, pp 185–206.
Herman, C, 'Lisbon and access to justice for environmental NGOs: A watershed? A case study using the setting of the total allowable catches under the Common Fisheries Policy' (2010) 7 *Journal for European Environmental and Planning Law* 391–410.
Hervey, T, 'The European Union and the governance of health care', in Búrca, G de, and Scott, J (eds) *Law and New Governance in the EU and the US*, 2006, Oxford: Hart Publishing, pp 179–210.
Hervey, T, 'Adjudicating in the shadow of informal settlement? The Court of Justice of the European Union, "new governance" and social welfare' (2010) 63 *Current Legal Problems* 92–152.
Hey, C, Jacob, J, and Volkery, A, 'Better regulation by new governance hybrids? Governance models and the reform of European chemicals policy' (2007) 15 *Journal of Cleaner Production* 1859–74.
Heyvaert, V, 'No data, no market: The future of EU chemicals control under the REACH Regulation' (2007) 9 *Environmental Law Review* 201–6.
Heyvaert, V, 'The EU chemicals policy: Towards inclusive governance?', 2008, LSE Law, Society and Economy Working Paper No. 07-2008, accessed 12 October 2014, http://eprints.lse.ac.uk/23562/1/WPS2008-07_Heyvaert.pdf.
Heyvaert, V, 'Levelling down, levelling up, and governing across: Three responses to hybridization in international law' (2009) 20 *European Journal of International Law* 647–74.
Hilson, C, 'Legality review of Member State discretion under directives', in Tridimas, T, and Nebbia, P (eds) *European Law for the Twenty-First Century, Vol 1*, 2004, Oxford: Hart Publishing, pp 223–38.
Hirst, P, *Associative Democracy: New Forms of Economic and Social Governance*, 1994, Cambridge: Polity Press.
Hodson, D, and Maher, I, 'Soft law and sanctions: Economic policy coordination and reform of the Stability and Growth Pact' (2004) 11 *Journal of European Public Policy* 798–813.
Hoecke, M van, 'Judicial review and deliberative democracy: A circular model of law creation and legitimation' (2001) 14 *Ratio Juris* 415–23.
Hofmann, H, and Türk, A, 'Conclusions: Europe's integrated administration', in Hofmann, H, and Türk, A (eds) *EU Administrative Governance*, 2006, Cheltenham: Edward Elgar, pp 573–96.
Hofmann, H, Rowe, G, and Türk, A, *Administrative Law and Policy of the European Union*, 2011, Oxford: Oxford University Press.
Holzinger, K, Knill, C, and Schäfer, A, 'Rhetoric or reality? "New governance" in EU environmental policy' (2006) 12 *European Law Journal* 403–20.

Homeyer, I von, 'Participatory governance in the European Union', in Giorgi, L, Homeyer, I von, and Parsons, W (eds) *Democracy in the European Union: Towards the Emergence of a Public Sphere*, 2006, London: Routledge, pp 43–78.

Homeyer, I von, 'The evolution of EU environmental governance', in Scott, J (ed) *Environmental Protection: European Law and Governance*, 2009, Oxford: Oxford University Press, pp 1–26.

Homeyer, I von, 'Emerging experimentalism in EU environmental governance', in Sabel, C F, and Zeitlin, J (eds) *Experimentalist Governance in the European Union: Towards a New Architecture*, 2010, Oxford: Oxford University Press, pp 121–50.

Howarth, W, 'Substance and procedure under the Strategic Environmental Assessment Directive and the Water Framework Directive', in Holder, J, and Gillivray, D (eds) *Taking Stock of Environmental Assessment. Law, Policy and Practice*, 2007, London: Routledge, pp 149–90.

Howarth, W, 'Aspirations and realities under the Water Framework Directive: Proceduralisation, participation and practicalities' (2009) 21 *Journal of Environmental Law* 391–417.

Jacobsson, K, 'Between deliberation and discipline: Soft governance in EU employment policy', in Mörth, U (ed) *Soft Law in Governance and Regulation: An Interdisciplinary Analysis*, 2004, Cheltenham: Edward Elgar, pp 81–101.

João Rodrigues, M, 'The Open Method of Coordination as a new governance tool', 2001, accessed 12 October 2014, http://eucenter.wisc.edu/OMC/Papers/rodrigues.pdf.

Joerges, C, 'Deliberative political processes revisited: What have we learnt about the legitimacy of supranational decision-making?' (2006) 44 *Journal of Common Market Studies* 779–802.

Joerges, C, 'Integration through de-legalisation? An irritated heckler', 2007, European Governance Papers No. N-07-03, accessed 12 October 2014, http://www.connex-network.org/eurogov/pdf/egp-newgov-N-07-03.pdf.

Joerges, C, and Neyer, J, 'From intergovernmental bargaining to deliberative political processes: The constitutionalisation of comitology' (1997) 3 *European Law Journal* 273–99.

Jordan, A J, Schout, A, and Unfried, M, 'The European Union', in Jordan, A J, and Lenschow, A (eds) *Innovation in Environmental Policy? Integrating the Environment for Sustainability*, 2008, Cheltenham: Edward Elgar, pp 159–79.

Kaika, M, and Page, B, 'The EU Water Framework Directive, Part 1: European policy-making and the changing topography of lobbying' (2003) 13 *European Environment* 314–27.

Karkkainen, B C, 'Information-forcing regulation and environmental governance', in de Búrca, G. and Scott, J (eds) *Law and New Governance in the EU and the US*, 2006, Oxford: Hart Publishing, pp 293–321.

Karolewski, I P, 'Pathologies of deliberation in the EU' (2011) 17 *European Law Journal* 66–79.

Kavanagh, A, 'Participation and judicial review: A reply to Jeremy Waldron' (2003) 22 *Law and Philosophy* 451–86.

Kelemen, R D, *Eurolegalism: The Transformation of Law and Regulation in the European Union*, 2012, Cambridge, MA: Harvard University Press.

Kempen, J J H van, 'Countering the obscurity of obligations in European environmental law: An analysis of Article 4 of the European Water Framework Directive' (2012) 24 *Journal of Environmental Law* 499–533.

Kilpatrick, C, 'New EU employment governance and constitutionalism', in Búrca, G de, and Scott, J (eds) *Law and Governance in the EU and the US*, 2006, Oxford: Hart Publishing, pp 121–51.

Kingsbury, B, 'The concept of "law" in global administrative law' (2009) 20 *European Journal of International Law* 23–57.

Kingsbury, B, Krisch, N, and Stewart, R, 'The emergence of global administrative law' (2005) 68 *Law and Contemporary Problems* 15–61.

Klabbers, J, 'The redundancy of soft law' (1996) 65 *Nordic Journal of International Law* 167–82.

Klabbers, J, 'The undesirability of soft law' (1998) 67 *Nordic Journal of International Law* 381–91.

Klijn, E-H, *'It's the Management, Stupid': On the Importance of Management in Complex Policy Issues*, 2008, The Hague: Lemma.

Kohler-Koch, B, and Rittberger, B, 'Review article: The "governance turn" in EU studies' (2006) 44 *Journal of Common Market Studies* 27–49.

Korkea-aho, E, 'Laws in progress? Reconceptualizing accountability strategies in the era of framework norms' (2013) 2 *Transnational Environmental Law* 363–85.

Korkea-aho, E, 'Watering down the Court of Justice? The dynamics between network implementation and Article 258 TFEU litigation' (2014) 20 *European Law Journal* 649–66.

Kraemer, R A, Klasing, A, and Homeyer, I von, 'The EU Open Method of Coordination: Risks and chances for environmental policy', Paper presented at the Conference on Sustainable Development in an Enlarged Union: Linking National Strategies and Strengthening European Coherence, 27–29 April 2003, Vienna, Austria, accessed 12 October 2014, http://ecologic.eu/download/projekte/1800-1849/1821/1821_paper_omc.pdf.

Krämer, L, 'The environmental complaint in EU law' (2009) 6 *Journal for European Environmental and Planning Law* 13–35.

Laffan, B, and Shaw, C, 'Classifying and mapping OMC in different policy areas', 2005, New Modes of Governance Project Paper No. 02/D09, accessed 12 October 2014, http://www.eu-newgov.org/database/DELIV/D02D09_Classifying_and_Mapping_OMC.pdf.

Lafont, C, 'Is the ideal of a deliberative democracy coherent?', in Besson, S, and Martí, J L, (eds) *Deliberative Democracy and its Discontents*, 2006, Farnham: Ashgate, pp 3–25.

Lang, A, and Cooney, R, 'Taking uncertainty seriously: Adaptive governance and international trade – A rejoinder to Mónica García-Salmones' (2009) 20 *European Journal of International Law* 187–92.

Lange, B, *Implementing EU Pollution Control: Law and Integration*, 2008, Cambridge: Cambridge University Press.

Lange, B, 'Thinking about procedure: Understanding legitimacy in EU environmental governance networks', in Dilling, O, Herberg, M, and Winter, G (eds) *Transnational Administrative Rule-Making: Performance, Legal Effects, and Legitimacy*, 2010, Oxford: Hart Publishing, pp 41–76.

Lee, M, *EU Environmental Law: Challenges, Change and Decision-Making*, 2005, Oxford: Hart Publishing.

Lee, M, 'Sustainable development in the EU: The renewed Sustainable Development Strategy 2006' (2007) 9 *Environmental Law Review* 41–5.

Lee, M, 'The environmental implications of the Lisbon Treaty' (2008) 10 *Environmental Law Review* 131–8.

Lee, M, 'Law and governance of Water Protection Policy', in Scott, J (ed) *Environmental Protection: European Law and Governance*, 2009, Cambridge: Cambridge University Press, pp 27–55.

Lenaerts, K, and Verhoeven, A, 'Balance as a guarantee for democracy in EU governance', in Joerges, C, and Dehousse, R (eds) *Good Governance in Europe's Integrated Market*, 2002, Oxford: Oxford University Press, pp 35–88.

Lenschow, A, 'New regulatory approaches in "greening" EU policies' (2002) 8 *European Law Journal* 19–37.

Lenschow, A, 'Europeanisation of public policy', in Richardson, J (ed) *European Union: Power and Policy-making*, 3rd edn, 2006, London: Routledge, pp 55–71.

Lenschow, A, 'Environmental policy in the European Union: Bridging policy, politics and polity dimensions', in Jørgensen, K E, Pollack, M A, and Rosamond, B (eds) *Handbook of European Union Politics*, 2007, London: Sage Publications, pp 413–31.

Lenschow, A, and Sprungk, C, 'The myth of a green Europe' (2010) 48 *Journal of Common Market Studies* 133–54.

Lever, A, 'Democracy and judicial review: Are they really incompatible?' (2009) 7 *Perspectives on Politics* 805–22.

Lobel, O, 'The renew deal: The fall of regulation and the rise of governance in contemporary legal thought' (2004) 89 *Minnesota Law Review* 262–390.

Lombardo, E, 'The participation of civil society', in Castiglione, D, Aziz, M, Lombardo, E, and Longman, C (eds) *Constitutional Politics in the EU: The Convention Moment and its Aftermath*, 2007, Basingstoke: Palgrave Macmillan, pp 153–69.

López-Santana, M, 'The domestic implications of European soft law: Framing and transmitting change in employment policy' (2006) 13 *Journal of European Public Policy* 481–99.

Lord, C, 'Assessing democracy in a contested polity' (2001) 39 *Journal of Common Market Studies* 641–61.

Lowe, P, and Wilkinson, K, 'How do environmental actors make governance systems more sustainable? The role of politics and ideas in policy change', in Adger, N, and Jordan, A (eds) *Governing Sustainability*, 2009, Cambridge: Cambridge University Press, pp 76–98.

Maduro, M, 'Interpreting European law: Judicial adjudication in a context of constitutional pluralism' (2007) 1 *European Journal of Legal Studies* 1–21.

Magnette, P, 'Democracy in the European Union: Why and how to combine representation and participation?', in Smismans, S (ed) *Civil Society and Legitimate European Governance*, 2006, Cheltenham: Edward Elgar, pp 23–41.

Magnette, P, 'A comment on Heinelt and Greven', in Kohler-Koch, B, and Rittberger, B (eds) *Debating the Democratic Legitimacy of the European Union*, 2007, Lanham, MD: Rowman & Littlefields Publishers, pp 249–53.

Mair, P, 'Popular democracy and the European Union polity', 2005, European Governance Papers No. C-05-03, accessed 12 October 2014, http://www.ihs.ac.at/publications/lib/ep3.pdf.

Mansbridge, J, *Beyond Adversarial Democracy*, 1983, Chicago, IL: Chicago University Press.

Martí, J L, 'The epistemic conception of deliberative democracy defended', in Besson, S, and Martí, J L (eds) *Deliberative Democracy and its Discontents*, 2006, Farnham: Ashgate, pp 27–56.

Marxsen, C, 'Open stakeholder consultations at the European level: Voice of the citizens' (2014) *European Law Journal*, forthcoming.

Maurer, A, 'Less bargaining, more deliberation: The Convention Method for enhancing EU democracy' (2003) 1 *Internationale Politik und Gesellschaft* 167–90.

Mendes, C H, 'Is it all about the last word? Deliberative separation of powers' (2009) 3 *Legisprudence* 69–110.

Mendes, J, *Participation in EU Rule-Making: A Rights-Based Approach*, 2011, Oxford: Oxford University Press.

Menéndez, A J, 'The European democratic challenge', 2008, Center for European Studies, University of Oslo, Working Paper No. 04/2008, accessed 12 October 2014, http://www.sv.uio.no/arena/english/research/publications/arena-publications/workingpapers/working-papers2008/wp08_04.pdf.

Miller, B, and Curry, B, 'Experts judging experts: The role of expertise in reviewing agency decision making' (2013) 38 *Law & Social Inquiry* 55–71.

Möllers, C, 'European governance: Meaning and value of a concept' (2006) 43 *Common Market Law Review* 313–36.

Mörth, U, 'Conclusions', in Mörth, U (ed) *Soft Law in Governance and Regulation: An Interdisciplinary Analysis*, 2004, Cheltenham: Edward Elgar, pp 191–200.

Morgera, E, 'Water management and protection in the EU', in Alberton, M, and Palermo, F (eds) *Environmental Protection in Multi-Layered Systems: Comparative Lessons from the Water Sector*, 2012, Leiden: Brill, pp 265–87.

Mutz, D, *Hearing the Other Side*, 2006, Cambridge: Cambridge University Press.

Mutz, D, 'Is deliberative democracy a falsifiable theory?' (2008) 11 *Annual Review of Political Science* 521–38.

Nanz, P, and Steffek, J, 'Global governance, participation and the public sphere' (2004) 39 *Government and Opposition* 314–35.

Neuhold, C, and Ruiter, R de, 'Out of REACH? Parliamentary control of EU affairs in the Netherlands and in the UK' (2010) 16 *Journal of Legislative Studies* 57–72.

Newig, J, Pahl-Wostl, C, and Sigel, K, 'The role of public participation in managing uncertainty in the implementation of the Water Framework Directive' (2005) 15 *European Environment* 333–43.

Neyer, J, 'The deliberative turn in integration theory' (2006) 13 *Journal of European Public Policy* 779–91.

Neyer, J, 'Justice, not democracy: Legitimacy in the European Union' (2010) 48 *Journal of Common Market Studies* 903–21.

Nickel, R, 'Participatory governance and European administrative law: New legal benchmarks for the new European public order', 2006, EUI LAW Working Papers No. 2006/26, accessed 12 October 2014, http://cadmus.eui.eu/handle/1814/6310.

Nino, C S, *The Constitution of Deliberative Democracy*, 1996, New Haven, CT: Yale University Press.

Noonan, K G, Sabel, C F, and Simon, W H, 'Legal accountability in the service-based welfare state: Lessons from child welfare reform' (2009) 34 *Law & Social Inquiry* 523–68.

Österdahl, I, 'The ECJ and soft law: Who's afraid of the EU Fundamental Rights Charter?', in Mörth, U (ed) *Soft Law in Governance and Regulation: An Interdisciplinary Analysis*, 2004, Cheltenham: Edward Elgar, pp 37–60.

Page, B, and Kaika, M, 'The EU Water Framework Directive, Part 2: Policy innovation and the shifting choreography of governance' (2003) 13 *European Environment* 328–43.

Papadopoulos, Y, 'Accountability and multi-level governance: More accountability, less democracy?' (2010) 33 *West European Politics* 1030–49.

Pateman, C, *Participation and Democratic Theory*, 1970, Cambridge: Cambridge University Press.

Peers, S, and Costa, M, 'Accountability for delegated and implementing acts after the Treaty of Lisbon' (2012) 18 *European Law Journal* 427–60.

Peters, A, 'European democracy after the 2003 Convention' (2004) 41 *Common Market Law Review* 37–85.

Peters, B G, and Pierre, J, 'Governance approaches', in Wiener, A, and Diez, T (eds) *European Integration Theory*, 2nd edn, 2009, Oxford: Oxford University Press, pp 91–104.

Pettit, P, 'Reworking Sandel's republicanism' (1998) 95 *Journal of Philosophy* 73–96.

Pierre, J, 'Introduction: Understanding governance', in Pierre, J (ed) *Debating Governance: Authority, Steering, and Democracy*, 2000, Oxford: Oxford University Press, pp 1–10.

Pollack, M A, 'Theorizing EU policy-making', in Wallace, H, Wallace, W, and Pollack, M A (eds) *Policy-Making in the European Union*, 5th edn, 2005, Oxford: Oxford University Press, pp 13–48.

Porte, C de la, and Nanz, P, 'OMC: A deliberative-democratic mode of governance? The cases of employment and pensions' (2004) 11 *Journal of European Public Policy* 267–88.

Porte, C de la, and Pochet, P, 'Why and how (still) study the Open Method of Coordination (OMC)?' (2012) 22 *Journal of European Social Policy* 336–49.

Posner, E, 'The Lamfalussy Process: Polyarchic origins of networked financial rule-making in the EU', in Sabel, C F, and Zeitlin, J (eds) *Experimentalist Governance in the European Union: Towards a New Architecture*, 2010, Oxford: Oxford University Press, pp 43–60.

Prete, L, and Smulders, B, 'The coming of age of infringement proceedings' (2010) 47 *Common Market Law Review* 9–61.

Puetter, U, 'The latest attempt at institutional engineering: The Treaty of Lisbon and deliberative intergovernmentalism in EU Foreign and Security Policy coordination', in Cardwell, P J (ed) *EU External Relations Law and Policy in the Post-Lisbon Era*, 2012, The Hague: TMC Asser Press, pp 17–34.

Raunio, T, 'National parliaments and European integration: What we know and agenda for future research' (2009) 15 *Journal of Legislative Studies* 317–34.

Renn, O, 'Precaution and the governance of risk', in Adger, N, and Jordan, A (eds) *Governing Sustainability*, 2009, Cambridge: Cambridge University Press, pp 226–58.

Rhodes, R A W, 'What is new about governance and why does it matter?', in Hayward, J, and Menon, A (eds) *Governing Europe*, 2003, Oxford: Oxford University Press, pp 61–73.

Romsloe, B, 'Finland and the case of a northern dimension for the EU: Inclusion by bargaining or arguing?', 2005, ARENA Center for European Studies, University of Oslo, Working Paper No. 31, accessed 12 October 2014, http://www.sv.uio.no/arena/english/research/publications/arena-publications/workingpapers/working-papers2005/wp05_31.pdf.

Rosenberg, S W, 'An introduction: Theoretical perspectives and empirical research on deliberative democracy', in Rosenberg, S W (ed) *Deliberation, Participation and Democracy. Can the People Govern?*, 2007, Basingstoke: Palgrave Macmillan, pp 1–22.

Ruiter, R de, 'EU soft law and the functioning of representative democracy: The use of methods of open coordination by Dutch and British parliamentarians' (2010) 17 *Journal of European Public Policy* 874–90.

Ruiter, R de, 'Full disclosure? The Open Method of Coordination, parliamentary debates and media coverage' (2013) 14 *European Union Politics* 95–114.

Ryall, A, 'Annotation of Case C-263/08, *Djurgården-Lilla Värtans Miljöskyddsförening v. Stockholms kommun genom dess marknämnd*, Judgment of the Court (Second Chamber) of 15 October 2009, nyr' (2010) 47 *Common Market Law Review* 1511–21.

Sabel, C F, and Simon, W H, 'Destabilization rights: How public law litigation succeeds' (2004) 117 *Harvard Law Review* 1015–101.

Sabel, C F, and Simon, W H, 'Epilogue: Accountability without sovereignty', in Búrca, G de, and Scott, J (eds) *Law and New Governance in the EU and the US*, 2006, Oxford: Hart Publishing, pp 395–411.

Sabel, C F, and Zeitlin, J, 'Learning from difference: The new architecture of experimentalist governance in the European Union', 2007, European Governance Working Paper No. C-07-02, accessed 12 October 2014, http://edoc.vifapol.de/opus/volltexte/2011/2466/pdf/egp_connex_C_07_02.pdf.

Sabel, C F, and Zeitlin, J, 'Learning from difference: The new architecture of experimentalist governance in the EU', in Sabel, C F, and Zeitlin, J (eds) *Experimentalist Governance in the European Union: Towards a New Architecture*, 2010, Oxford: Oxford University Press, pp 1–28.

Sabel, C F, and Zeitlin, J, 'Experimentalist governance', in Levi-Faur, D (ed) *The Oxford Handbook of Governance*, 2012, Oxford: Oxford University Press, pp 169–83.

Sbragia, A, 'The European Union as coxswain: Governance by steering', in Pierre, J (ed) *Debating Governance: Authority, Steering, and Democracy*, 2000, Oxford: Oxford University Press, pp 219–40.

Schäfer, A, 'A new form of governance? Comparing the Open Method of Coordination to multilateral surveillance by the IMF and the OECD' (2006) 13 *Journal of European Public Policy* 70–88.

Scharpf, F, *Governing in Europe: Effective and Democratic?*, 1999, Oxford: Oxford University Press.

Schmalz-Bruns, R, 'The Euro-polity in perspective: Some normative lessons from deliberative democracy', in Kohler-Koch, B, and Rittberger, B (eds) *Debating the Democratic Legitimacy of the European Union*, 2007, Lanham, MD: Rowman & Littlefields Publishers, pp 281–303.

Schmidt, M, 'The principle of non-discrimination in respect of age: Dimensions of the ECJ's *Mangold* judgment' (2006) 7 *German Law Journal* 505–24.

Scholte, A, ' "In the foothills": Relations between the IMF and civil society', in Higgott, R, Underhill, G, and Bieler, A (eds) *Non-State Actors and Authority in the Global System*, 2000, London: Routledge, pp 256–73.

Schutter, O de, 'The implementation of the EU Charter of Fundamental Rights through the Open Method of Coordination', 2004, Jean Monnet Working Paper No. 07/04, accessed 12 October 2014, http://eucenter.wisc.edu/OMC/Papers/Rights/deSchutter.pdf.

Schütze, R, ' "Delegated" legislation in the (new) European Union: A constitutional analysis' (2011) 74 *Modern Law Review* 661–93.

Schwarze, J, 'European administrative law in the light of the Treaty of Lisbon' (2012) 18 *European Public Law* 285–304.

Scott, C, 'Governing without law or governing without government? New-ish governance and the legitimacy of the EU' (2009) 15 *European Law Journal* 160–73.

Scott, J, 'Law, legitimacy and EC governance: Prospects for "partnership" ' (1998) 36 *Journal of Common Market Studies* 175–94.

Scott, J, 'From Brussels with love: The transatlantic travels of European law and the chemistry of regulatory attraction' (2009a) 57 *The American Journal of Comparative Law* 897–942.

Scott, J, 'REACH: Combining harmonization and dynamism in the regulation of chemicals', in Scott, J (ed) *Environmental Protection: European Law and Governance*, 2009b, Oxford: Oxford University Press, pp 56–91.

Scott, J, 'In legal limbo: Post-legislative guidance as a challenge for European administrative law' (2011) 48 *Common Market Law Review* 329–55.

Scott, J, and Holder, J, 'Law and new environmental governance in the European Union', in Búrca, G de, and Scott, J (eds) *Law and New Governance in the EU and the US*, 2006, Oxford: Hart Publishing, pp 211–42.

Scott, J, and Sturm, S, 'Courts as catalysts: Rethinking the judicial role in new governance' (2007) 13 *Columbia Journal of European Law* 565–94.

Scott, J, and Trubek, D, 'Mind the gap: Law and new approaches to governance in the European Union' (2002) 8 *European Law Journal* 1–18.

Senden, L, *Soft Law in European Community Law*, 2004, Oxford: Hart Publishing.

Senden, L, 'Soft post-legislative rulemaking: A time for more stringent control' (2013) 19 *European Law Journal* 57–75.

Senden, L, and Brink, A van den, 'Checks and balances of soft EU rule-making', 2012, Study for the Directorate-General for Internal Policies, Policy Department Citizens' Rights and Constitutional Affairs, accessed 12 October 2014, http://www.uu.nl/SiteCollectionDocuments/REBO/REBO_RGL/REBO_RGL_EUROPA/Rapport%20EP%20Soft%20Law%20Rule%20making.pdf.

Shaffer, G C, and Pollack, M A, 'Hard vs. soft law: Alternatives, complements, and antagonists in international governance' (2010) 94 *Minnesota Law Review* 706–99.

Shapiro, M, 'Administrative law unbounded: Reflections on government and governance' (2001) 8 *Indiana Journal of Global Legal Studies* 369–77.

Shapiro, M, 'Judicial review and bureaucratic impact: The future of European administrative law', in Hertogh, M, and Halliday, S (eds) *Judicial Review and Bureaucratic Impact: International and Interdisciplinary Perspectives*, 2004, Cambridge: Cambridge University Press, pp 251–68.

Shapiro, M, ' "Deliberative," "independent" technocracy vs democratic politics: Will the globe echo the EU?' (2005) 68 *Law & Contemporary Problems* 341–56.

Shaw, J, 'Postnational constitutionalism in the European Union' (1999) 6 *Journal of European Public Policy* 579–97.

Shaw, J, 'Constitutional settlements and the citizen after the Treaty of Amsterdam', in Neunreither, K, and Wiener, A (eds) *European Integration after Amsterdam: Institutional Dynamics and Prospects for Democracy*, 2000, Oxford: Oxford University Press, pp 290–317.

Simon, W H, '*Toyota* jurisprudence: Legal theory and rolling rule regimes', in Búrca, G de, and Scott, J (eds) *Law and New Governance in the EU and the US*, 2006, Oxford: Hart Publishing, pp 37–64.

Smismans, S, *Law, Legitimacy, and European Governance: Functional Participation in Social Regulation*, 2004, Oxford: Oxford University.

Smismans, S, 'How to be fundamental with soft procedures? The Open Method of Coordination and fundamental social rights', in Búrca, G de, and Witte, B de (eds) *Social Rights in Europe*, 2005, Oxford: Oxford University Press, pp 217–38.

Smismans, S, 'Civil society and European governance: From concepts to research agenda', in Smismans, S (ed) *Civil Society and Legitimate European Governance*, 2006, Cheltenham: Edward Elgar, pp 3–19.

Smismans, S, 'New governance: The solution for active European citizenship, or the end of citizenship?' (2007) 13 *Columbia Journal of European Law* 595–622.

Smismans, S, 'New modes of governance and the participatory myth' (2008) 32 *West European Politics* 874–95.

Smismans, S, 'European constitutionalism and the democratic design of European governance: Rethinking directly deliberative polyarchy and reflexive constitutionalism', in Tuori, K, and Sankari, S (eds) *The Many Constitutions of Europe*, 2010, Farnham: Ashgate, pp 169–93.

Smismans, S, 'From harmonization to co-ordination? EU law in the Lisbon governance architecture' (2011) 18 *Journal of European Public Policy* 504–24.

Snyder, F, 'The effectiveness of European Community law: Institutions, processes, tools and techniques', in Daintith, T (ed) *Implementing EC Law in the United Kingdom: Structures for Indirect Rule*, 1995, Chichester: John Wiley & Sons, pp 49–87.

Somek, A, *Individualism: An Essay on the Authority of the European Union*, 2008, Oxford: Oxford University Press.

Somek, A, 'The argument from transnational effects I: Representing outsiders through freedom of movement' (2010a) 16 *European Law Journal* 315–44.

Somek, A, 'The concept of "law" in global administrative law: A reply to Benedict Kingsbury' (2010b) 20 *European Journal of International Law* 985–95.

Sossin, L, 'The politics of soft law: How judicial decisions influence bureaucratic discretion in Canada', in Hertogh, M, and Halliday, S (eds) *Judicial Review and Bureaucratic Impact: International and Interdisciplinary Perspectives*, 2004, Cambridge: Cambridge University Press, pp 129–60.

Steele, J, 'Participation and deliberation in environmental law: Exploring a problem-solving approach' (2001) 21 *Oxford Journal of Legal Studies* 415–42.

Stefan, O A, 'European competition soft law in European courts: A matter of hard principles?' (2008) 14 *European Law Journal* 753–72.

Stefan, O A, 'Helping loose ends meet? The judicial acknowledgement of soft law as a tool of multi-level governance' (2014) *Maastricht Journal of European and Comparative Law*, forthcoming.

Steurer, R, and Berger, G, 'The Lisbon Strategy and sustainable development strategies across Europe: How different governance arrangements shape the European coherence of policy documents', 2010, Institute of Forest, Environmental, and Natural Resource Policy Discussion Paper No. 1-2010, accessed 12 October 2014 http://papers.ssrn.com/sol3/papers.cfm?abstract_id=2342118.

Sunstein, C R, *The Second Bill of Rights: FDR's Unfinished Revolution and Why We Need It More than Ever*, 2004, New York: Basic Books.

Szyszczak, E, 'Experimental governance: The Open Method of Coordination' (2006) 12 *European Law Journal* 486–502.

Terpan, F, 'Soft law in the European Union: The changing nature of EU law' (2014) *European Law Journal*, forthcoming.

Thompson, D F, 'Deliberative democratic theory and empirical political science' (2008) 11 *Annual Review of Political Science* 497–520.

Thürer, D, 'The role of soft law in the actual process of European integration' (1990) 2 *L'avenir du libre, échange en Europe: Vers un espace economique européen? Collection de Droit Europeen* 131–8.

Tippett, J, Searle, B, Pahl-Wostl, C, and Rees, Y, 'Social learning in public participation in river basin management: Early findings from HarmoniCOP European case studies' (2005) 8 *Environmental Science & Policy* 287–99.

Trubek, D, and Trubek, L, 'New governance and legal regulation: Complementarity, rivalry, and transformation', 2007, University of Wisconsin Law School, Legal Studies Research Paper No. 1047, accessed 12 October 2014, http://papers.ssrn.com/sol3/papers.cfm?abstract_id=908229.

Trubek, D, and Trubek, L, 'The world turned upside down: Reflections on new governance and the transformation of law' [2010] *Wisconsin Law Review* 719–26.

Trubek, D, Cottrell, P, and Nance, M, ' "Soft law", "hard law", and EU integration', in Búrca, G de, and Scott, J (eds) *Law and New Governance in the EU and the US*, 2006, Oxford: Hart Publishing, pp 65–94.

Tully, J, 'The unfreedom of the moderns in comparison to their ideals of constitutional democracy' (2002) 65 *Modern Law Review* 204–28.

Tulmets, E, 'Experimentalist governance in EU external relations: Enlargement and the European Neighbourhood Policy', in Sabel, C F, and Zeitlin, J (eds) *Experimentalist Governance in the European Union: Towards a New Architecture*, 2010, Oxford: Oxford University Press, pp 297–324.

Tuori, K, *Ratio and Voluntas: The Tension between Reason and Will in Law*, 2011, Farnham: Ashgate.

Tuori, K, and Tuori, K, *The Eurozone Crisis: A Constitutional Approach*, 2014, Cambridge: Cambridge University Press.

Türk, A, 'Oversight of administrative rulemaking: judicial review' (2013) 19 *European Law Journal* 126–42.

Uitenboogaart, Y, Kempen, J van, Wiering, M, and Rijswick, H van, *Dealing with Complexity and Policy Discretion: Cross-Country Comparison of the Implementation Process of the EU Water Framework Directive in Five Member States*, 2009, Nijmegen: Nijmegen School of Management, Radboud University Nijmegen.

Usui, Y, 'The democratic quality of soft governance in the EU Sustainable Development Strategy: A deliberative deficit' (2007) 29 *European Integration* 619–33.

Vedder, H, 'Diplomacy by directive? An analysis of the international context of the Emissions Trading Scheme Directive', in Evans, M, and Koutrakos, P (eds) *Beyond the Established Legal Borders*, 2011, Oxford: Hart Publishing, pp 105–22.

Versluis, E, and Tarr, E, 'Improving compliance with European Union law via agencies: The case of the European Railway Agency' (2013) 51 *Journal of Common Market Studies* 316–33.

Vos, E, *Institutional Frameworks of Community Health and Safety Legislation: Committees, Agencies and Private Bodies*, 1999, Oxford: Hart Publishing.

Vos, E, 'Reforming the European Commission: What role to play for EU agencies?' (2000) 37 *Common Market Law Studies* 1113–34.

Vos, E, 'EU risk regulation reviewed by the European courts', in Asselt, M B A van, Everson, M, and Vos, E (eds) *Trade, Health and the Environment: The European Union Put to the Test*, 2014, London: Routledge, pp 213–32.

Waldron, J, *Law and Disagreement*, 1999, Oxford: Oxford University Press.

Walker, N, and Búrca, G de, 'Reconceiving law and new governance' (2007) 13 *Columbia Journal of European Law* 519–37.

Walling, A, 'Guidance for guidances' (2006) 29 *Regulation* 6–7.

Ward, A, 'The draft EU Constitution and judicial review of EU measures', in Tridimas, T, and Nebbia, P (eds) *European Union Law for the Twenty-First Century: Rethinking the New Legal Order, Vol 1*, 2004, Oxford: Hart Publishing, pp 209–21.

Weale, A, 'Contractarian theory, deliberative democracy and general agreement', in Dowding, K, Goodin, R E, and Pateman, C (eds) *Justice and Democracy: Essays for Brian Barry*, 2004, Cambridge: Cambridge University Press, pp 79–96.

Weale, A, Pridham, G, Cini, M, Konstadakopulos, D, Porter, M, and Flynn, B, *Environmental Governance in Europe: An Ever Closer Ecological Union?*, 2000, Oxford: Oxford University Press.

Weiler, J H H, *The Constitution of Europe: 'Do the New Clothes Have an Emperor?' and Other Essays on European Integration*, 1999, Cambridge: Cambridge University Press.

Wilkinson, M, 'Review article: Between constitutionalism and democratic experimentalism? New governance in the EU and the US' (2007) 70 *Modern Law Review* 680–700.

Withana, S, Kretschmer, B, and Farmer, A, 'Environmental policy in the European Semester: Assessing progress to date', 2013, An Institute for European Environmental Policy (IEEP) report for the Greens/EFA Group of the European Parliament, accessed 12 October 2014, http://www.greens-efa.eu/fileadmin/dam/Documents/Publications/GND/ENVIR__POLICY_web.pdf.

Yataganas, X A, 'Delegation of regulatory authority in the European Union: The relevance of the American model of independent agencies', 2001, Jean Monnet Working Papers No. 3/01, accessed 12 October 2014, http://www.jeanmonnetprogram.org/archive/papers/01/010301.html.

Zeitlin, J, 'The Open Method of Coordination and the governance of the Lisbon Strategy' (2008) 46 *Journal of Common Market Studies* 436–46.

Zeitlin, J, 'Is the Open Method of Coordination an alternative to the Community Method?', in Dehousse, R (ed) *The Community Method: Obstinate or Obsolete?*, 2011, Basingstoke: Palgrave Macmillan, 135–47.

Official EU documents

Committee on the Environment, Public Health and Food Safety, *Report on the Environmental Aspects of Sustainable Development*, December 2005, 2005/2051(INI), accessed 12 October 2014, http://www.europarl.europa.eu/sides/getDoc.do?type=REPORT&reference=A6-2005-0383&language=MT ('Ferreira Report').

European Chemicals Agency, *Second Revision to the Consultation Procedure for Guidance*, December 2013, Doc. MB/63/2013 (final), accessed 12 October 2014, http://echa.europa.eu/documents/10162/13608/mb_63_2013_revision_consultation_procedure_guidance_en.pdf.

European Chemicals Agency, *ECHA General Report 2013*, April 2014, ECHA-14-A-05-EN, accessed 12 October 2014, http://echa.europa.eu/documents/10162/13560/mb_04_2014_general_report_2013_en.pdf.

European Commission, *White Paper Laying down a Strategy for a Future Chemicals Policy*, February 2001, COM(2001) 88 final, accessed 12 October 2014, http://eur-lex.europa.eu/legal-content/EN/TXT/PDF/?uri=CELEX:52001DC0088&from=EN.

European Commission, *European Governance: A White Paper*, July 2001, COM(2001) 428 final, accessed 12 October 2014, http://eur-lex.europa.eu/legal-content/EN/TXT/PDF/?uri=CELEX:52001DC0428&from=EN.

European Commission, *Communication from the Commission: Towards a Reinforced Culture of Consultation and Dialogue – General Principles and Minimum Standards for Consultation of Interested Parties by the Commission*, December 2002, COM(2002) 704 final, accessed 12 October 2014, http://ec.europa.eu/governance/docs/comm_standards_en.pdf.

European Commission, *Communication from the Commission: On the Collection and Use of Expertise by the Commission – Principles and Guidelines: Improving the Knowledge Base for Better Policies*, December 2002, COM(2002) 713 final, accessed 12 October 2014, http://ec.europa.eu/governance/docs/comm_expertise_en.pdf.

European Commission, *Economics and the Environment: The Implementation Challenge of the Water Framework Directive*, January 2004, CIS Guidance Document No 1, accessed 12 October 2014, https://circabc.europa.eu/sd/a/cffd57cc-8f19-4e39-a79e-20322bf607e1/Guidance%20No%201%20-%20Economics%20-%20WATECO%20(WG%202.6).pdf.

European Commission, *Identification of Water Bodies*, January 2004, CIS Guidance Document No 2, accessed 12 October 2014, https://circabc.europa.eu/sd/a/655e3e31-3b5d-4053-be19-15bd22b15ba9/Guidance%20No%202%20-%20Identification%20of%20water%20bodies.pdf.

European Commission, *Communication from the Commission to the Council and the European Parliament: On the Review of the Sustainable Development Strategy – A Platform for Action*, December 2005, COM(2005) 658 final, accessed 12 October 2014, http://eur-lex.europa.eu/legal-content/EN/TXT/PDF/?uri=CELEX:52005DC0658&from=EN.

European Commission, *Communication from the Commission: Follow-up to the Green Paper 'European Transparency Initiative'*, March 2007, COM(2007) 127 final, accessed 12 October 2014, http://eur-lex.europa.eu/legal-content/EN/TXT/PDF/?uri=CELEX:52007DC0127&from=EN.

European Commission, *Communication from the Commission to the European Parliament and the Council: Towards Sustainable Water Management in the European Union – First Stage in the Implementation of the Water Framework Directive 2000/60/EC*, March 2007, COM(2007) 128 final, accessed 12 October 2014, http://eur-lex.europa.eu/legal-content/EN/TXT/PDF/?uri=CELEX:52007DC0128&from=EN.

European Commission, *Commission Staff Working Document: Accompanying Document to the Communication from the Commission to the European Parliament and the Council 'Towards Sustainable Water Management in the European Union' – First Stage in the Implementation of the Water Framework Directive 2000/60/EC*, March 2007, SEC(2007) 362 final, accessed 12 October 2014, http://ec.europa.eu/environment/archives/water/implrep2007/pdf/sec_2007_0362_en.pdf.

European Commission, *Communication from the Commission to the Council and the European Parliament: Progress Report on the Sustainable Development Strategy 2007*, October 2007, COM(2007) 642 final, accessed 12 October 2014, http://ec.europa.eu/danmark/documents/alle_emner/institutionelle/071224_comm_pdf_com_2007_0642.pdf.

European Commission, *Communication from the Commission to the European Parliament and the Council: European Agencies – The Way Forward*, March 2008, COM(2008) 135 final, accessed 12 October 2014, http://eur-lex.europa.eu/LexUriServ/LexUriServ.do?uri=COM:2008:0135:FIN:EN:PDF.

European Commission, *Communication from the Commission to the European Parliament, the Council, the European Economic and Social Committee and the Committee of the Regions: A Renewed Commitment to Social Europe – Reinforcing the Open Method of Coordination for Social Protection and Social Inclusion*, July 2008, COM(2008) 418 final, accessed 12 October 2014, http://europa.eu/legislation_summaries/employment_and_social_policy/social_inclusion_fight_against_poverty/em0011_en.htm.

European Commission, *Commission Staff Working Document: Accompanying Report from the Commission to the European Parliament and the Council in Accordance with Article 18.3 of the Water Framework Directive 2000/60/EC on Programmes for Monitoring of Water Status*, April 2009,

SEC(2009) 415 final, accessed 12 October 2014, http://ec.europa.eu/environment/archives/water/implrep2007/pdf/sec_2009_415_en.pdf.

European Commission, *Communication from the Commission to the European Parliament, the Council, the European Economic and Social Committee and the Committee of the Regions: Mainstreaming Sustainable Development into EU policies – 2009 Review of the European Union Strategy for Sustainable Development*, July 2009, COM(2009) 400 final, accessed 12 October 2014, http://eur-lex.europa.eu/legal-content/EN/TXT/PDF/?uri=CELEX:52009DC0400&from=EN.

European Commission, *Commission Staff Working Document: Lisbon Strategy Evaluation Document*, February 2010, SEC(2010) 114 final, accessed 12 October 2014, http://register.consilium.europa.eu/doc/srv?l=EN&f=ST%206037%202010%20INIT.

European Commission, *Proposal for a Regulation of the European Parliament and of the Council Laying down the Rules and General Principles Concerning Mechanisms for Control by Member States of the Commission's Exercise of Implementing Powers*, March 2010, COM(2010) 83 final, accessed 12 October 2014, http://www.europarl.europa.eu/meetdocs/2009_2014/documents/com/com_com(2010)0083_/com_com(2010)0083_en.pdf.

European Commission, *Communication from the Commission: Europe 2020 – A Strategy for Smart, Sustainable and Inclusive Growth*, March 2010, COM(2010) 2020 final, accessed 12 October 2014, http://eur-lex.europa.eu/LexUriServ/LexUriServ.do?uri=COM:2010:2020:FIN:EN:PDF.

European Commission, *Communication from the Commission to the European Parliament, the Council, the European Economic and Social Committee and the Committee of the Regions: Improving the Delivery of Benefits from EU Environment Measures: Building Confidence through Better Knowledge and Responsiveness*, March 2012, COM(2012) 95 final, accessed 12 October 2014, http://cor.europa.eu/en/activities/stakeholders/Documents/com2012-95final.pdf.

European Commission, *Commission Staff Working Document: European Overview (1/2) Accompanying the Document 'Report from the Commission to the European Parliament and the Council on the Implementation of the Water Framework Directive (2000/60/EC): River Basin Management Plans*, November 2012, SWD(2012) 379 final, accessed 12 October 2014, http://ec.europa.eu/environment/water/water-framework/pdf/CWD-2012-379_EN-Vol1.pdf.

European Commission, *Communication from the Commission to the European Parliament, the Council, the European Economic and Social Committee and the Committee of the Regions: A Blueprint to Safeguard Europe's Water Resources*, November 2012, COM(2012) 673 final, accessed 12 October 2014, http://eur-lex.europa.eu/legal-content/EN/TXT/PDF/?uri=CELEX:52012DC0673&from=EN.

European Commission, *Report from the Commission to the European Parliament, the Council, the European Economic and Social Committee and the Committee of the Regions: General Report on REACH*, February 2013, COM(2013) 49 final, accessed 12 October 2014, http://eur-lex.europa.eu/LexUriServ/LexUriServ.do?uri=COM:2013:0049:FIN:EN:PDF.

European Commission, *Communication from the Commission to the European Parliament, the Council, the European Economic and Social Committee and the Committee of the Regions: A Decent Life for All – Ending Poverty and Giving the World a Sustainable Future*, February 2013, COM(2013) 92 final, accessed 12 October 2014, http://ec.europa.eu/europeaid/documents/2013-02-22_communication_a_decent_life_for_all_post_2015_en.pdf.

European Commission, *Communication from the Commission to the European Parliament, the Council, the European Economic and Social Committee and the Committee of the Regions: Strengthening the Social Dimension of the Economic and Monetary Union*, October 2013, COM(2013) 690 final, accessed 12 October 2014, http://eur-lex.europa.eu/LexUriServ/LexUriServ.do?uri=COM:2013:0690:FIN:EN:PDF.

European Commission, *Communication from the Commission: Annual Growth Survey 2014*, November 2013, COM(2013) 800 final, accessed 12 October 2014, http://ec.europa.eu/europe2020/pdf/2014/ags2014_en.pdf.

European Commission, *Communication from the Commission to the European Parliament, the Council, the European Economic and Social Committee and the Committee of the Regions: Taking Stock of the Europe 2020 Strategy for Smart, Sustainable and Inclusive Growth*, March 2014, COM(2014) 130 final, accessed 12 October 2014, http://ec.europa.eu/europe2020/pdf/europe2020stocktaking_en.pdf.

European Commission, *Communication from the Commission to the European Parliament, the Council, the European Economic and Social Committee and the Committee of the Regions: 2014 European Semester – Country-Specific Recommendations: Building Growth*, June 2014, COM(2014) 400 final, accessed 12 October 2014, http://ec.europa.eu/europe2020/pdf/csr2014/eccom2014_en.pdf.

European Council, *Presidency Conclusions*, Lisbon European Council, 23 and 24 March 2000, accessed 12 October 2014, http://www.europarl.europa.eu/summits/lis1_en.htm.

European Council, *Presidency Conclusions*, Göteborg European Council, 15 and 16 June 2001, accessed 12 October 2014, http://ec.europa.eu/smart-regulation/impact/background/docs/goteborg_concl_en.pdf.

European Council, *Review of the EU Sustainable Development Strategy (EU SDS): Renewed Strategy*, 26 June 2006, Doc. No. 10917/06, accessed 12 October 2014, http://register.consilium.europa.eu/doc/srv?l=EN&f=ST%2010917%202006%20INIT.

European Council, *Presidency Conclusions*, Brussels European Council, 14 December 2007, accessed 12 October 2014, http://www.consilium.europa.eu/ueDocs/cms_Data/docs/pressData/en/ec/97669.pdf.

European Council, *Presidency Conclusions*, European Council, 10–11 December 2009, accessed 12 October 2014, https://www.consilium.europa.eu/uedocs/cms_data/docs/pressdata/en/ec/111877.pdf.

European Council, *Presidency Conclusions*, European Council, 17 June 2010, accessed 12 October 2014, http://ec.europa.eu/eu2020/pdf/council_conclusion_17_june_en.pdf.

European Parliament, *The European Semester: Main Steps at EU Level*, December 2013, accessed 12 October 2014, http://www.europarl.europa.eu/document/activities/cont/201401/20140117ATT77764/20140117ATT77764EN.pdf.

European Parliament and Council, *Decision No. 1386/2013/EU of the European Parliament and of the Council of 20 November 2013 on a General Union Environment Action Programme to 2020 'Living Well, within the Limits of Our Planet', 28 December 2013*, OJ L 354/171, accessed 12 October 2014, http://eur-lex.europa.eu/legal-content/EN/TXT/?uri=CELEX:32013D1386 ('Seventh EAP').

Water Directors of EU Member States, *Common Implementation Strategy for the Water Framework Directive (2000/60/EC): Strategic Document*, 2 May 2001, accessed 12 October 2014, http://ec.europa.eu/environment/water/water-framework/objectives/pdf/strategy.pdf.

Water Directors of EU Member States, *Public Participation in Relation to the Water Framework Directive*, Guidance Document No 8, November 2002, accessed 12 October 2014, https://circabc.europa.eu/sd/a/0fc804ff-5fe6-4874-8e0d-de3e47637a63/Guidance%20No%208%20-%20Public%20participation%20(WG%202.9).pdf.

Water Directors of EU Member States, *Common Implementation Strategy for the Water Framework Directive (2000/60/EC): Carrying forward the Common Implementation Strategy for the Water Framework Directive – Progress and Work Programme for 2003 and 2004*, 17 June 2003, accessed

12 October 2014, http://ec.europa.eu/environment/water/water-framework/objectives/pdf/strategy2.pdf.

Water Directors of EU Member States, *Common Implementation Strategy for the Water Framework Directive (2000/60/EC): Moving to the Next Stage in the Common Implementation Strategy for the Water Framework Directive – Progress and Work Programme for 2005 and 2006*, 2–3 December 2004, accessed 12 October 2014, http://ec.europa.eu/environment/water/water-framework/objectives/pdf/strategy3.pdf.

Water Directors of EU Member States, *Common Implementation Strategy for the Water Framework Directive (2000/60/EC): Improving the Comparability and Quality of the Water Framework Directive Implementation – Progress and Work Programme for 2007–2009*, 30 November–1 December 2006, accessed 12 October 2014, http://ec.europa.eu/environment/water/water-framework/objectives/pdf/strategy4.pdf.

Water Directors of EU Member States, *Common Implementation Strategy for the Water Framework Directive (2000/60/EC): Work Programme 2010–2012 – Supporting the Implementation of the First River Basin Management Plans*, 30 November 2009, accessed 12 October 2014, https://circabc.europa.eu/sd/a/13b85784-3596-46bc-8c6b-0edc9328a070/FINAL%20work%20programme%20CIS%202010-2012%20-endorsed%20by%20WD.pdf.

Water Directors of EU Member States, *Common Implementation Strategy for the Water Framework Directive (2000/60/EC) and the Floods Directive (2007/60/EC): Work Programme 2013–2015 – Strengthening the Implementation of EU Water Policy through the Second River Basin Management Plans*, 2013, accessed 12 October 2014, http://ec.europa.eu/environment/water/water-framework/objectives/pdf/Work%20Programme%202013-2015.pdf.

Other documents

ClientEarth and European Environmental Bureau (EEB), *Identifying the Bottlenecks in REACH Implementation: The Role of ECHA in REACH's Failing Implementation*, October 2012, accessed 12 October 2014, http://www.eeb.org/EEB/?LinkServID=53B19853-5056-B741-DB6B33B4D1318340.

European Environmental Bureau (EEB), *10 Years of the Water Framework Directive: A Toothless Tiger? A Snapshot Assessment of EU Environmental Ambitions*, July 2010, accessed 12 October 2014, http://www.eeb.org/?LinkServID=B1E256EB-DBC1-AA1C-DBA46F91C9118E7D&showMeta=0.

Milieu Ltd, AmbienDura and FFact for the European Commission, *Study on the Feasibility of the Establishment of a Waste Enforcement Agency: Revised Final Report*, December 2009, accessed 12 October 2014, http://ec.europa.eu/environment/waste/pdf/report_waste_dec09.pdf (the 'Feasibility Study').

World Commission on Environment and Development (WCED), *Report of the World Commission on Environment and Development: Our Common Future*, 1987, accessed 12 October 2014, http://www.un-documents.net/wced-ocf.htm (the 'Brundtland Report').

World Wide Fund for Nature (WWF) and European Environmental Bureau (EEB), *'Tips and Tricks' for Water Framework Directive Implementation: A Resource Document for Environmental NGOs on the EU Guidance for the Implementation of the Water Framework Directive*, March 2004, accessed 12 October 2014, http://www.rivernet.org/general/docs/200403_EEB_WWF_Tips&Tricks.pdf.

Interviews and personal communication

Personal communication with the Commission, email dated 3 February 2014 (on file with author)
Interview with Commission officials, Brussels, 3 June 2014.

Table of cases

Court of Justice of the European Union

Case 9/56 *Meroni & Co., Industrie Metallurgiche, SpA v ECSC High Authority* [1957–58] ECR 133
Case C-25/62 *Plaumann & Co. v Commission of the EEC* [1963] ECR 95
Case C-22/70 *Commission v Council (ERTA)* [1971] ECR 263
Case C-138/79 *Roquette Frères v Council* [1980] ECR 3333
Case C-98/80 *Romano v Institut National d'Assurance Maladie-Invalidité* [1981] ECR 1241
Case C-21/87 *Borowitz v Bundesversicherungsanstalt für Angestellte* [1988] ECR 3715
Case C-70/88 *European Parliament v Council* [1990] ECR I-2041
Case C-322/88 *Salvatore Grimaldi v Fonds des maladies professionnelles* [1989] ECR I-4407
Case C-366/88 *France v Commission* [1990] ECR I-3571
Case C-269/90 *Technische Universität München v Hauptzollampt München-Mitte* [1991] ECR I-5469
Case C-303/90 *France v Commission* [1991] ECR I-5315
Case C-102/91 *Knoch v Bundesanstalt für Arbeit* [1992] ECR I-4341
Joined Cases C-181/91 and C-248/91 *European Parliament v Council & Commission* [1993] ECR I-3685
Case C-325/91 *France v Commission* [1993] ECR I-3283
Case T-461/93 *An Taisce & WWF UK v Commission* [1994] ECR II-733
Case T-521/93 *Atlanta AG and others v European Community* [1996] ECR II-1707
Case C-253/94 P *Roujansky v Council* [1995] ECR I-7
Case C-311/94 *IJssel-Vliet Combinatie BV v Minister van Economische Zaken* [1996] ECR I-5023
Case C-325/94 P *An Taisce and WWF UK v Commission* [1996] ECR I-3727
Case C-57/95 *France v Commission* [1997] ECR I-1627
Case T-135/96 *UEAPME v Council* [1998] ECR II-2335
Case C-288/96 *Germany v Commission* [2000] ECR I-8237
Case C-120/97 *Upjohn Ltd v The Licensing Authority established by the Medicines Act 1968* [1999] ECR I-223
Case T-13/99 *Pfizer Animal Health v Council* [2002] ECR II-3305
Joined Cases C-223/99 and C-260/99 *Agorá Srl v Ente Autonomo Fiera Internazionale di Milano; Excelsior Snc di Pedrotti Runa & C v Ente Autonomo Fiera Internazionale di Milano* [2001] ECR I-3605
Case C-310/99 *Italy v Commission* [2002] ECR I-2289
Case C-1/00 *Commission v France* [2001] ECR I-9989
Case C-50/00 P, *Unión de Pequeños Agricultores v Council* [2002] ECR I-6677
Joined Cases T-74/00, T-76/00, T-83/00, T-84/00, T-85/00, T-132/00, T-137/00 and T-141/00 *Artegodan GmbH and others v Commission* [2002] ECR II-4945
Case T-123/00 *Dr Karl Thomae GmbH v Commission* [2002] ECR II-5193
Case T-177/01 *Jégo-Quéré & Cie SA v Commission* [2002] ECR II-2365

Case T-223/01 *Japan Tobacco Inc and JT International, SA v European Parliament and Council* [2002] ECR II-3259
Case C-494/01 *Commission v Ireland* [2005] ECR I-3331
Case C-258/02 P *Bactria Industriehygiene-Service Verwaltungs GmbH v Commission* [2003] ECR I-15105
Case C-263/02 *Commission v Jégo-Quéré & Cie SA* [2004] ECR I-3425
Case C-301/02 P *Carmine Salvator Tralli v European Central Bank* [2005] ECR I-4071
Case T-84/03 *Turco v Council* [2004] ECR II-4061
Case C-301/03 *Italy v Commission* [2005] ECR I-10217
Case T-16/04 *Arcelor SA v European Parliament & Council* [2010] ECR II-211
Case C-27/04 *Commission v Council* [2004] ECR I-6649
Case C-144/04 *Werner Mangold v Rüdiger Helm* [2005] ECR I-9981
Joined Cases C-154/04 and C-155/04 *The Queen, on the application of Alliance of Natural Health and others v Secretary of State for Health & National Assembly for Wales* [2005] ECR I-6451
Case C-217/04 *United Kingdom v European Parliament & Council* [2006] ECR I-3771
Case T-374/04 *Germany v Commission* [2007] ECR II-4431
Case C-32/05 *Commission v Luxembourg* [2006] ECR I-11323
Case C-33/05 *Commission v Belgium*, 15 December 2005, NYR
Joined cases C-39/05 P and, C-52/05 P *Sweden & Maurizio Turco v Council of the European Union* [2008] ECR I-4723
Case C-67/05 *Commission v Germany*, 15 December 2005, NYR
Case C-85/05 *Commission v Italy* [2006] ECR I-9 (summary publication)
Case C-118/05 *Commission v Portugal* [2006] ECR I-11 (summary publication)
Case T-127/05 *Lootus Teine Osaühing v Council* [2007] ECR II-1 (summary publication)
Case C-341/05 *Laval v Svenska Byggnadsarbetareförbundet* [2007] ECR I-11767
Case C-342/05 *Commission v Finland* [2007] ECR I-4713
Case C-438/05 *International Transport Workers' Federation & Finnish Seamen's Union v Viking Line* [2007] ECR I-10779
Case T-95/06 *Federación de Cooperativas Agrarias de la Comunidad Valenciana (FECOAV) v Community Plant Variety Office* [2008] ECR II-31
Case C-268/06 *Impact v Minister for Agriculture and Food and others* [2008] ECR I-2483
Joined Cases T-311/06 R I, T-311/06 R II, T-312/06 R and T-313/06 R *FMC Chemical SPRL, Arysta Lifesciences SAS, Otsuka Chemical Co. Ltd v European Food Safety Authority (EFSA)* [2007] ECR II-21
Case T-397/06 *Dow AgroSciences Ltd v EFSA* [2008] ECR II-90 (summary publication)
Case T-411/06 *Sogelma and Societá generale lavori manutenzioni appalti Srl v European Agency for Reconstruction (EAR)* [2008] ECR II-2771
Case T-183/07 *Poland v Commission* [2009] ECR II-3395
Case C-263/07 *Commission v Luxembourg* [2007] ECR I-180 (summary publication)
Case T-263/07 *Estonia v Commission* [2009] ECR II-3463
Case C-427/07 *Commission v Ireland* [2009] ECR I-6277
Case C-473/07 *Association nationale pour la protection des eaux et rivières-TOS and Association OABA v Ministère de l'Ecologie, du Développement et de l'Aménagement durables* [2009] ECR I-319
Case C-558/07 *SPCM SA and others v Secretary of State for the Environment, Food and Rural Affairs* [2009] ECR I-5783
Case C-263/08 *Djurgården-Lilla Värtans Miljöskyddsförening v Stockholms kommun genom dess marknämnd* [2009] ECR I-9967

Case C-115/09 *Bund für Umwelt und Naturschutz Deutschland, Landesverband Nordrhein-Westfalen eV v Bezirksregierung Arnsberg* [2011] ECR I-3673
Case C-504/09 P *Commission v Poland*, 29 March 2012, NYR
Case T-1/10 *PPG & SNF v ECHA* [2011] ECR II-6576, T-1/10 RENV, pending at time of writing
Case C-15/10 *Etimine v Secretary of State for Work and Pensions* [2011] ECR I-6681
Case T-18/10 *Inuit Tapiriit Kanatami and others v Parliament & Council* [2011] ECR II-5599
Case C-43/10 *Nomarchiaki Aftodioikisi Aitoloakarnanias and others v Ypourgos Perivallontos, Chorotaxias kai Dimosion ergon and others*, 11 September 2012, NYR
Case T-93/10 *Bilbaína de Alquitranes, AS and others v ECHA*, 7 March 2013, NYR
Case T-262/10 *Microban v Commission* [2011] ECR II-7697
Case C-301/10 *Commission v United Kingdom (Urban Waste)*, 18 October 2012, NYR
Case C-555/10 *Commission v Austria*, 28 February 2013, NYR
Case C-223/11 *Commission v Portugal*, 21 June 2012, NYR
Case T-245/11 *ClientEarth & International Chemical Secretariat v ECHA*, pending at time of writing
Case C-297/11 *Commission v Greece*, 19 April 2012, NYR
Case C-308/11 *Chemische Fabrik Kreussler & Co. GmbH v Sunstar Deutschland GmbH, formerly John O. Butler GmbH*, 6 September 2012, NYR
Case C-366/11 *Commission v Belgium*, 24 May 2012, NYR
Case C-403/11 *Commission v Spain*, 4 October 2012, NYR
Case C-583/11 P *Inuit Tapiriit Kanatami and others v Parliament & Council*, 8 November 2011, NYR
Case C-626/11 P *PPG & SNF v ECHA*, 26 September 2013, NYR; T-1/10 RENV, pending at time of writing
Case C-270/12 *United Kingdom v Parliament & Council*, 22 January 2014, NYR
Case C-525/12 *Commission v Germany*, pending at time of writing
Case T-134/13 *Polynt & Sitre v ECHA*, pending at time of writing
Case T-135/13 *Hitachi Chemical Europe and others v ECHA*, pending at time of writing
Case C-287/13 P *Bilbaína de Alquitranes, AS and others v ECHA*, 22 May 2014, NYR
Case C-461/13 *Bund für Umwelt und Naturschutz Deutschland*, pending at time of writing
Case T-673/13 *European Coalition to End Animal Experiments v ECHA*, pending at time of writing
Case C-106/14 *FCD & FMB*, pending at time of writing

European Ombudsman

Decision of the European Ombudsman closing his own-initiative inquiry OI/12/2012/EIS concerning the European Chemicals Agency (ECHA), 27 May 2013, accessed 12 October 2014, http://www.ombudsman.europa.eu/de/cases/decision.faces/en/50278/html.bookmark.
Decision of the European Ombudsman closing the inquiry into complaint 1826/2010/VL against the European Chemicals Agency, 18 December 2013, accessed 12 October 2014, http://www.ombudsman.europa.eu/cases/decision.faces/en/52914/html.bookmark.
Decision of the European Ombudsman closing the inquiry into complaint 2469/2011/VL against the European Chemicals Agency, 12 March 2014, accessed 12 October 2014, http://www.ombudsman.europa.eu/cases/decision.faces/en/53796/html.bookmark.

Decision of the European Ombudsman closing own-initiative inquiry OI/2/2011/OV to the European Commission, 10 April 2014, accessed 12 October 2014, http://www.ombudsman.europa.eu/en/cases/decision.faces/en/54039/html.bookmark.

International courts

Methanex Corp. vs. United States of America, Final Award of the Tribunal on Jurisdiction and Merits, 3 August 2005, accessed 12 October 2014, http://www.italaw.com/sites/default/files/case-documents/ita0529.pdf.

UK

R (on the application of SPCM SA and others) v Secretary of State for Environment, Food & Rural Affairs [2007] EWHC 2610 (Admin).

Index

For Product Safety Concerns and Information please contact our EU representative GPSR@taylorandfrancis.com
Taylor & Francis Verlag GmbH, Kaufingerstraße 24, 80331 München, Germany

www.ingramcontent.com/pod-product-compliance
Ingram Content Group UK Ltd.
Pitfield, Milton Keynes, MK11 3LW, UK
UKHW020011200926
475702UK00014B/1826

9781138241510